Sleep and Development

Sleep and Development

Familial and Socio-Cultural Considerations

EDITED BY

MONA EL-SHEIKH

OXFORD
UNIVERSITY PRESS

OXFORD
UNIVERSITY PRESS

Oxford University Press, Inc., publishes works that further
Oxford University's objective of excellence
in research, scholarship, and education.

Oxford   New York
Auckland   Cape Town   Dar es Salaam   Hong Kong   Karachi
Kuala Lumpur   Madrid   Melbourne   Mexico City   Nairobi
New Delhi   Shanghai   Taipei   Toronto

With offices in
Argentina   Austria   Brazil   Chile   Czech   Republic   France   Greece
Guatemala   Hungary   Italy   Japan   Poland   Portugal   Singapore
South Korea   Switzerland   Thailand   Turkey   Ukraine   Vietnam

Library of Congress Cataloging-in-Publication Data
Sleep and development : familial and socio-cultural considerations / edited by Mona El-Sheikh.
    p. cm.
ISBN 978-0-19-539575-4
1. Sleep disorders. 2. Sleep deprivation. 3. Families.   I. El-Sheikh, Mona.
RC547.S5165 2011
616.8'498—dc22   2010020135

1 3 5 7 9 8 6 4 2
Printed in the United States of America
on acid-free paper

Contents

Foreword

Ronald E. Dahl

Sleep is a many-splendored thing. It is as mysterious, multifaceted, and complex as it is a simple (and regular) necessity for an enjoyable and healthy life. These issues are particularly salient from a developmental perspective—where it is becoming increasingly clear that sleep is important from a biological, behavioral, psychological, cognitive, emotional, social, and cultural perspective.

At a biologic level, there is growing evidence that sleep plays a crucial role in plasticity and neural development, contributes to basic aspects of learning and memory, and occupies a key role in basic regulatory and metabolic processes. Moreover, all of these processes are undergoing rapid changes during early development, consistent with the idea that sleep is particularly important to the developing brain and body.

At a behavioral level, sleep–wake patterns represent a central organizing principle. Not only is sleep the singularly most prevalent behavior during the early years (infants and young children spend more hours asleep than in all waking activities combined) but also, more generally, sleep and wakefulness influence (and are influenced by) a wide range of behaviors in many complex ways. This is true not only at the level of individual behavior, but also at the level of social and family interaction. The most dramatic example is that if a young child cannot sleep, it is extremely likely that at least one adult (if not multiple others) will also have their sleep disrupted.

Sleep has become an increasing focus of interest for many psychologists for a variety of reasons. This work ranges from psychological approaches to disorders like insomnia to investigations into links between sleep and psychological processes (such as attention) and disorders (such depression, anxiety, and bipolar disorder).

There has been similar growth in understanding the importance of sleep in relation to cognitive and emotional processes, such as the importance of sleep to memory and learning, and the impact of sleep deprivation on mood and emotion regulation. For example, irritability, increases in negative mood, and decreases in positive mood and motivation represent some of the best documented consequences of inadequate sleep.

However, the effects of sleep deprivation go far beyond psychological, cognitive, and emotional processes. Insufficient sleep has been associated with (and suspected to have some causal links) to several serious health outcomes, including accidents, aggression, appetite/obesity, metabolic syndrome, and cardiovascular health among others.

At the most fundamental level, however, sleep is increasingly being recognized as a complex behavior that is naturally embedded in family, social, and cultural contexts. This is particularly salient in relation to children's sleep—something that has been clearly evident to pediatricians and family practitioners for decades. Sleep problems have long been among the three most prevalent concerns–along with eating and elimination issues–to the parents of young children.

Finally, as described in numerous chapters in this book, there is also growing interest (and serious concerns) about sleep from a public health perspective. Children of all ages, and adolescents in particular, are often getting what appears to be insufficient sleep for optimal functioning and health. The most frequent causes of these decrements in sleep are clearly the consequences of social, family, and cultural influences, rather than biological. The increasing 24/7 pace of life combined with access to technology (e.g., constant access to bright lights, television, music, internet, cell phone, and text messages) is steadily eroding time for bed and sleep. Given the aforementioned importance of sleep for physical, cognitive, emotional health, as well as learning, the evidence that many children and adolescents are getting less sleep during important periods of development is raising many provocative (and important) questions.

As we recognize both the importance and complexity of sleep— particularly from a developmental perspective—a central question to consider is this: How should we best advance understanding of the developmental, clinical, and public health aspects of this many-splendored thing we call sleep?

The answers are unlikely to emerge from research within any one discipline alone. The most important and practical questions about sleep in children and adolescents in contemporary society are not addressable by studies within any single discipline such as neuroscience, developmental psychology, clinical investigations, or epidemiology; rather, it will require an integrated approach that includes a broader understanding of the family, social, and cultural contexts in which sleep occurs, develops, goes awry, and influences and interacts with an immense range of different aspects of life.

Granted, this is a tall order. Luckily, Mona El-Sheikh and her colleagues have taken a huge step toward accomplishing this set of goals. In this volume, *Sleep and Development: Familial and Socio-Cultural Considerations*, they have taken a truly multidisciplinary approach, and have provided an impressive array of perspectives. These range from general frameworks for considering family and social contexts, to specific topics such as attachment, marital conflict, parenting, parental psychopathology, effects of trauma, the impact of child sleep disturbances on parents' sleep and daytime function, impact on children's cognitive and behavioral adjustment, an anthropological perspective in the cultural ecology of sleep, consideration of the impact of postindustrial societies, children's sleep in the context of socioeconomic status, race, and ethnicity, consideration of sleep in relation to economic disadvantage, and children's sleep, cognition, and academic performance in the context of socioeconomic status and ethnicity. The book also considers a broad range of related sleep issues in adolescents, as well as methodological issues including assessment of sleep, family functioning, and family-based interventions for sleep problems in infants and young children.

This kind of breadth of approaches and perspectives is an extremely valuable contribution to the field. This book provides a matrix of understanding the family and socio-cultural contexts that is not only pragmatically helpful and interesting, but also will help to frame future investigations that will lead to a deeper and better integrated understanding of sleep and development across numerous disciplines.

Introduction and Overview
Salient Issues in the Consideration of Sleep in Context

Mona El-Sheikh

Sleep deprivation, poor sleep quality, and erratic sleep schedules in children have unfortunately become common in the United States and many other countries. While common wisdom has always been that children need sufficient sleep, the consequences of poor sleep for children's development have only recently begun to be investigated scientifically. Rapidly accumulating evidence suggests that multiple domains of child development are related to sleep, including cognitive development, emotional and behavioral adjustment, physical growth and health, and the incidence of numerous medical disorders.

Although sleep is a fundamental biological process that affects the health and well-being of persons of all ages, it is also a social phenomenon. Many aspects of sleep are receiving scholarly attention, but studies of how relations between the family environment or the broader socio-cultural milieu and child developmental outcomes may be impacted by sleep have been relatively scarce. Pediatric sleep studies, for example, rarely incorporate current knowledge in child development and family functioning domains. Similarly, the importance of such a fundamental aspect of human development as sleep has yet to be brought to the forefront of research that focuses on individuals' adjustment or on family functioning. Whereas notable exceptions may be found, only recently have research paradigms begun to emerge that explicate linkages between sleep, familial and cultural processes, and child development. Given the multifaceted nature of the questions, the majority of the emerging research paradigms are multidisciplinary. Exciting new discoveries are being made in many labs that document important relations between family processes, the socio-cultural milieu, and multiple facets of children's sleep and adaptation. These novel and recent discoveries are the focus of this book.

The first part of the book (Sleep: Familial Influences) is comprised of chapters that address cutting edges of advancement in theory and empirical evidence in the field. In addition to reviewing pertinent literatures, many of the authors postulate conceptualizations and discuss directions for future research that would accelerate understanding of the interface between family functioning, children's sleep, and their developmental outcomes. Collectively, chapters in this section demonstrate that family processes influence sleep of individuals—especially children, young adolescents, and their parents. Although less attention has been paid to reciprocal effects, how sleep influences family functioning is also addressed. Chapters in the book focus on the development of individuals from infancy through young adolescence, and mostly address typically developing children but pertinent clinical populations are also considered. Conceptual and empirical integration in these areas is likely to enhance understanding of developmental, familial, and sleep processes.

Reflective of the state of the science in this area, the book is not exhaustive in describing the role of sleep in all familial and socio-cultural contexts. Rather, the objective is to present current knowledge, highlight areas in need of research, facilitate the dialogue among family processes, pediatric sleep, and child development researchers, and provide some of the methodological tools (e.g., sleep and family functioning assessments) that will help accelerate the pace and quality of this young yet rapidly developing interdisciplinary field.

In the chapter on parental marital conflict and children's adaptation by Mona El-Sheikh and Ryan Kelly, the authors highlight the significance of the interparental marital relationship for children's sleep, and propose a conceptual framework for understanding the role of sleep as an intervening variable linking exposure to marital aggression and children's development. The overview provided by Stephen Erath and Kelly Tu is organized around a conceptual model which contends that children's sleep is influenced by (and influences) parental sleep-related cognitions and behaviors as well as the general context of the parent-child relationship. Building on the importance of links between family relationships and sleep, Peggy Keller examines the connection between various sleep parameters and attachment security across the life span, with a focus on these relations in infancy and childhood, and considers various plausible conceptual frameworks. Two subsequent chapters in this section, "Parental Psychopathology and Children's Sleep" by Ron Seifer, and "Effects of Trauma on Children's Sleep" by Carol Glod, address children's sleep in the context of nonnormative familial and contextual experiences including parental depression, child abuse, natural disasters, and wars.

While the aforementioned chapters focus on family processes as they influence children's sleep, Lisa Meltzer and Anna Westin provide a comprehensive review of consequences of children's sleep disruptions for the adjustment of parents and families, highlighting the importance of transactional models in this emerging field. In the final chapter in this section, Angela Staples and John Bates review the literature on relations between young children's sleep problems and their cognitive and behavioral adjustment, and discuss the importance of parenting and child temperament when examining links between sleep and adjustment.

In addition to familial influences, the socio-cultural context affects the individual's sleep parameters directly or indirectly through family functioning; this issue is addressed in the second part of this book (Sleep: Socio-Cultural Influences). Consideration of sleep from an anthropological perspective and in a societal and cultural context is imperative for a better understanding of the individual's development and adaptation. For example, knowledge about the developmental cultural ecology of sleep is of paramount importance, and is discussed eloquently by Carol Worthman. Toward explication of children's sleep in a societal and cultural context, Melissa Burnham and Erika Gaylor discuss a variety of normative daytime and nighttime sleeping environments of infants and young children, including sleeping arrangements (e.g., co-sleeping, sleep partners) in "Sleep Environments of Young Children in Post-Industrial Societies."

Furthermore, social and ecological variables that influence sleep, and may in turn affect family functioning and the individual's well-being and health, are pivotal for a better understanding of child development. Based on the literature presented and discussed by Les Gellis, racial-ethnic and socioeconomic factors can have a major impact on children's sleep. Not only are direct associations found between either ethnicity or socioeconomic variables and children's sleep, but sleep parameters can also interact with the broader socio-cultural milieu to influence children's functioning as illustrated and discussed by Joseph Buckhalt and Lori Staton. Amy Wolfson and Melissa Richards expand on this issue in their chapter where they review young adolescents' struggles with insufficient sleep and the myriad of environmental factors that pose significant challenges for sleep at this developmental stage (e.g., school start times, screen use, and caffeine consumption).

The third part of the book (Assessment of Sleep, Family Functioning, and the Ecology of Economic Disadvantage) is comprised of three chapters that address important methodological issues, offer guidance to researchers, and help bridge gaps in research methodology used by disparate scientific groups. In the first chapter of this section, Brian Ackerman and Eleanor Brown describe recent approaches to conceptualizing the ecology of economic disadvantage as well as discuss and evaluate various representations of such disadvantage (e.g., low socioeconomic status, income poverty, and poverty-related stressors). The conceptual and methodological issues that the authors address are of great importance to all researchers studying sleep and well-being in the context of economic adversity.

Toward facilitating incorporation of family functioning measures in pediatric sleep research, Mark Cummings, Kalsea Koss, and Kathleen Bergman provide an overview of best practices for examining family processes including information about choices to be considered in selecting assessments of family functioning when examining children's development. Conversely, in the chapter that follows, Avi Sadeh summarizes state of the science sleep methodology, which is pivotal for researchers interested in incorporating sleep assessments in their child development and family processes research endeavors.

In the fourth and final part of the book (Intervention for Sleep Problems), Courtney Johnson and Jodi Mindell provide vital information in their chapter "Family Based Interventions for Sleep Problems of Infants and Children." Their presentation of normative sleep habits and common sleep problems from infancy through adolescence, and treatments for behaviorally based sleep problems with family considerations, are of great significance for researchers studying sleep and development.

Authors of the chapters have come to the topic of sleep from diverse academic disciplines and areas of inquiry that relate to sleep, culture, and families including anthropology, pediatrics, nursing, human development and family studies, education, developmental psychology, developmental psychopathology, epidemiology, and clinical interventions. Bringing them together to contribute to this volume has been accomplished in the context of my belief that integration of knowledge and approaches across disciplines is fundamental for a vigorous comprehensive science of sleep as it relates to the individual's multifaceted development and adaptation. As E. O. Wilson (1998) has so cogently written:

> Disciplinary boundaries within the natural sciences are
> disappearing, to be replaced by shifting hybrid domains in
> which consilience is implicit. These domains reach across
> many levels of complexity, from chemical physics and physical
> chemistry to molecular genetics, chemical ecology, and
> ecological genetics. None of the new specialties is considered more
> than a focus of research. Each is an industry of fresh
> idea and advancing technology.
>
> (*Consilience: The Unity of Knowledge.*
> New York: Random House, p. 11)

It is my fervent wish that this volume will be the source of many further fresh ideas and advances that emanate from the gathering together of different perspectives and disparate energies of a multitude of sleep scientists.

Contributors

Brian P. Ackerman, PhD
Professor of Psychology
University of Delaware

John E. Bates, PhD
Professor of Psychological and
    Brain Sciences
Indiana University

Kathleen N. Bergman, BA
Graduate Student and Research
    Assistant
Department of Psychology
University of Notre Dame

Eleanor D. Brown, PhD
Assistant Professor of
    Psychology
West Chester University of
    Pennsylvania

Joseph A. Buckhalt, PhD
Wayne T. Smith Distinguished
    Professor
Special Education, Rehabilitation,
    Counseling/School Psychology
Auburn University

Melissa M. Burnham, PhD
Associate Professor
Human Development and Family
    Studies
University of Nevada, Reno

E. Mark Cummings, PhD
Professor and Chair in Psychology
University of Notre Dame

Ronald E. Dahl, MD
Professor of Public Health
Institute of Human Development
University of California, Berkeley

Mona El-Sheikh, PhD
Leonard Peterson & Co., Inc.
    Professor
Human Development and Family
    Studies
Auburn University

Stephen A. Erath, PhD
Assistant Professor
Human Development and Family
    Studies
Auburn University

Erika E. Gaylor, PhD
Early Childhood Researcher
Center for Education and
  Human Services
SRI International

Les A. Gellis, PhD
Visiting Assistant Professor
Department of Psychology
Syracuse University

Carol Glod, PhD, RN, FAAN
Professor of Nursing
Bouve College of Health Sciences
Northeastern University

Courtney Johnson, PhD
Post-doctoral Fellow of
  Psychology
Children's Hospital of
  Philadelphia

Peggy S. Keller, PhD
Assistant Professor of Psychology
University of Kentucky

Ryan J. Kelly, MA
Doctoral Student
Human Development and Family
  Studies
Auburn University

Kalsea J. Koss, BS
Graduate Student and Research
  Assistant
Department of Psychology
University of Notre Dame

Lisa J. Meltzer, PhD
Assistant Professor of Pediatrics
University of Pennsylvania
School of Medicine
Clinical Psychologist
Children's Hospital of Philadelphia

Jodi A. Mindell, PhD
Professor of Psychology
Saint Joseph's University
Associate Director
Sleep Center
Children's Hospital of
  Philadelphia

Melissa Richards, BA
Department of Psychology
College of the Holy Cross

Avi Sadeh, DSc
Professor of Psychology
Tel Aviv University

Ronald Seifer, PhD
Professor of Psychiatry and
  Human Behavior
Brown University

Angela D. Staples, PhD
Psychological and Brain Sciences
Indiana University, Bloomington

Lori E. Staton, MS
Research Associate III
Human Development and Family
  Studies
Auburn University

Kelly M. Tu, MS
Doctoral Student
Human Development and Family
 Studies
Auburn University

Anna M. L. Westin, MS
Doctoral Student of
 Psychology
University of Maryland,
 Baltimore County

Amy R. Wolfson, PhD
Professor and Chair of
 Psychology
College of the Holy Cross

Carol M. Worthman, PhD
Samual Candler Dobbs Professor
 of Anthropology
Emory University

Part I

Sleep: Familial Influences

I

Sleep in Children

Links with Marital Conflict and Child Development

Mona El-Sheikh and Ryan J. Kelly

Introduction

Children's exposure to marital conflict and sleep problems are pivotal risk factors for myriad mental and physical health problems, yet scholars have only recently begun to investigate relations between these important domains of children's lives. In this chapter, we extend the dialogue on family functioning, pediatric sleep, and child development research with the hope of highlighting how concurrent examinations of familial processes and children's sleep can illuminate children's adaptation and maladaptation. Our main objective is to review the small but growing body of literature that establishes a connection between children's exposure to their parents' marital conflict and disruptions in their sleep. While doing so, we present conceptual considerations that may be useful as researchers begin to address the question, "Why does marital conflict relate to children's sleep?" Our second objective is to present a conceptual model in which children's sleep operates as a pathway or moderating variable linking their exposure to marital conflict with their developmental outcomes (see Figure 1.1).

Marital psychological and verbal conflict/aggression refer to threats, insults, and throwing objects (not at a partner). Marital physical conflict/aggression indicates physical assault on a partner's body (Jouriles, Norwood, & McDonald, 1996). The terms marital conflict and aggression are used interchangeably in this chapter and refer to either psychological/verbal or physical aggression unless further specificity is needed.

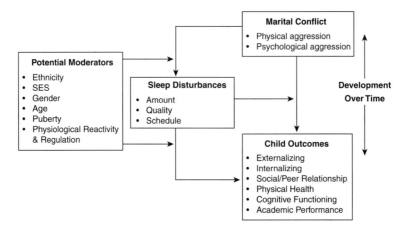

FIGURE 1.1   Conceptual Model Linking Parental Marital Conflict and Children's Sleep and Development

We also use "sleep problems" interchangeably with "sleep disruptions," and the terms do not refer to clinically diagnosed sleep disorders (e.g., sleep apnea); almost all published studies that connect sleep with marital conflict have examined sleep parameters in typically developing children. Sleep problems are conceptualized along a continuum, and are indicated by shorter than average sleep times, higher activity during sleep, several extended night wakings, or sleep schedules that are more variable from night to night, relative to other participants. Chronic partial sleep deprivation and erratic sleep schedules may be the most prevalent forms of sleep problems in otherwise typically developing children, and assessing these sleep parameters along the normative continuum is important for understanding developmental outcomes of many children in the population.

We begin the chapter with a discussion of marital conflict and its effects on children, including the small yet expanding literature linking interparental conflict and sleep problems. In subsequent sections of the chapter, we present our conceptual model in which sleep carries, exacerbates, or attenuates the effects of marital conflict on developmental outcomes in children (see Figure 1.1). Although links between marital conflict and child maladjustment are well-established across multiple domains, child adjustment varies widely in the context of exposure to marital conflict. Examining processes, intervening variables, and moderators in the connection between parental marital conflict and child adaptation is critical to explicate *why* and *for whom* marital conflict is related to negative outcomes. Our discussion of the model will also include the role of other potential moderators (e.g., socioeconomic status (SES), ethnicity) in relation to marital aggression, sleep, and child functioning. Finally, future directions for investigations of sleep and marital conflict will be discussed.

Marital Conflict and Child Functioning

Marital psychological, verbal, and physical conflict and aggression are prevalent in U.S. families. While it is difficult to know the exact number of children exposed to marital aggression, such exposure is recognized internationally as a public health problem, and surveys indicate that some form of marital aggression occurs in as many as 12% of American households (National Institutes of Health, 2003, PAR-03-096). Surveys also show that children younger than 12 years of age live in about 50% of the maritally aggressive homes. Recent work has documented that 49% of couples with at least one child experience some form of physical marital conflict, with 24% of these couples experiencing severe physical conflict such as choking, hitting, burning, or using a gun or knife (Smith Slep & O'Leary, 2005). Given the high prevalence of marital aggression in homes with young children, examining the effects of such aggression on child functioning is imperative.

Marital Conflict and Children's Adjustment, Physical Health, and Cognitive Functioning

Marital conflict is an important family stressor linked cross-sectionally and longitudinally to negative outcomes in children across multiple domains including psychological and social adjustment, physical health, and cognitive functioning. For example, exposure to verbal or physical marital conflict has been associated with children's externalizing problems (El-Sheikh, Cummings, Kouros, Elmore-Staton, & Buckhalt, 2008; Marks, Glaser, Glass, & Horne, 2001), and internalizing symptoms, including depression (Grych, Fincham, Jouriles, & McDonald, 2000; Shelton & Harold, 2007) and anxiety (Bogels & Brechman-Toussaint, 2006; Grych et al., 2000; Katz & Low, 2004). Similarly, increased exposure to parental marital conflict has been linked with children's social and peer relationship problems (Du Rocher Schudlich, Shamir, & Cummings, 2004; Lindsey, MacKinnon-Lewis, Campbell, Frabutt, & Lamb, 2002; Marks et al., 2001), physical health difficulties (El-Sheikh et al., 2008; El-Sheikh, Harger, & Whitson, 2001; Saltzman, Holden, & Holahan, 2005), poor cognitive functioning (Koenen, Moffitt, Caspi, Taylor, & Purcell, 2003; Ybarra, Wilkens, & Lieberman, 2007) and academic problems (Harold, Aitken, & Shelton, 2007; Sturge-Apple, Davies, Winter, Cummings, & Schermerhorn, 2008).

Marital Conflict and Children's Sleep: Empirical Evidence

Initial Inquiries

While numerous studies have linked marital conflict with a range of child outcomes, thorough examinations of relations between parental marital conflict and children's sleep are novel in the literature. However, several initial studies have examined associations between general family stressors and sleep in children. For example, Van Tassel (1985) found that family stress, which included unemployment, serious family illness, and marital problems within the last six months, was associated with parent-reported infant sleep disturbances. Further, in the first study to examine associations between family stress and objective measures of children's sleep, Sadeh, Raviv, and Gruber (2000) found that poorer sleep quality, as indexed by actigraphic measures of sleep percentage and number of night awakenings, was more likely to occur among children from families that experienced loss, illness, hospitalization, relocation, and emotional turmoil compared to children from families that experienced lower levels of stress. Furthermore, parental divorce and separation have been linked with parent-reported child sleep disruptions, including long sleep latency and frequent night awakenings (Kahn et al., 1989). In high conflict homes, children may experience fear during the night, waiting for the next violent episode to occur between their parents (Jaffe, Wolfe, & Wilson, 1990), which can result in nighttime hyperarousal and hyperactivity (Perry, 1997). Among infants and children residing in shelters for battered women, Layzer, Goodson, and Delange (1986) found that sleep problems were highly prevalent, based on case worker assessments. Taken together, these findings shed light on the importance of considering family stress when examining sleep disruptions in children.

Recent Inquiries

While various familial stressors have been examined collectively in initial studies linking them with children's sleep, more recent work has begun to pinpoint specific types of family stressors, including marital conflict, as they relate to disruptions in children's sleep. In addition, newer research has generally utilized more sophisticated methodologies and rigorous statistical testing to explicate associations between exposure to parental marital conflict and children's sleep problems. Next, literature linking children's sleep parameters specifically with marital aggression will be reviewed.

In our cross-sectional study of 54 normally developing school-aged children, the frequency of parental marital conflict was examined through mothers', fathers', and children's reports, and sleep was assessed via actigraphy as well as through children's and mothers' reports (El-Sheikh, Buckhalt, Mize, & Acebo, 2006). Results indicated that, even in a community sample, a considerable amount of physical and verbal conflict occurred between parents, which is consistent with the high prevalence of marital aggression in the United States (Straus & Gelles, 1990). For instance, within the prior year, 23% of couples in the El-Sheikh and colleagues' (2006) study of community-recruited families experienced physical marital conflict, as reported by at least one spouse. Higher levels of physical and verbal marital conflict were associated with subjective reports of sleepiness in children as well as actigraphically derived sleep measures including sleep duration, sleep efficiency, and nighttime activity. Findings illustrated that, in comparison to children from lower-conflict homes, those from higher-conflict homes had shorter sleep durations, and worse quality sleep as indexed by activity or restlessness during the night.

Exposure to conflict during childhood may have a long-lasting impact on children's sleep. Gregory, Caspi, Moffitt, and Poulton (2006) examined whether family conflict during childhood is directly linked to symptoms of insomnia at 18 years of age, measured via self-report, while controlling for childhood sleep problems. Mothers reported on general family conflict via self-report items that assessed expressed anger, aggression, and conflict between all family members (e.g., "Family members sometimes hit each other," and "In our family, we believe you don't ever get anywhere by raising your voice"). Findings revealed that higher levels of family conflict during childhood were linked with increased insomnia symptoms when children were 18 years of age.

Findings from Gregory and colleagues' (2006) study build on previous findings connecting marital conflict with sleep disruptions cross-sectionally (i.e., El-Sheikh et al., 2006), and further indicate that high-conflict homes may contribute to disruptions in children's sleep years later. Although this study did not examine marital conflict specifically, the implication is clear: high-conflict homes are not conducive to sleep and may lead to long-term symptoms of insomnia.

Of importance is that the studies reviewed in this chapter were mostly conducted with community samples characterized by normative levels of conflict and aggression. Thus, even with normative levels of interparental aggression, children's sleep duration was shorter and sleep quality (e.g., nighttime activity) was less optimal (El-Sheikh et al., 2006) in the context of higher conflict exposure. It is very likely, yet unconfirmed by scientific investigation, that sleep disruptions in children would be more pronounced in families experiencing frequent and/or intense marital violence. Furthermore, a caveat in cross-sectional studies (e.g., El-Sheikh et al., 2006) establishing a connection between marital conflict and children's sleep is that directionality of effects cannot be ascertained (e.g., sleep problems in children may have an impact on marital conflict between parents). Next, we review preliminary evidence that children's sleep disruptions predict parental marital conflict over time. We hope that by doing so, we underscore the need for longitudinal assessments and transactional conceptualizations of sleep and family functioning.

Reciprocal Relations

Research evidence is suggestive of reciprocal relations between family stress and children's sleep. That is, in addition to studies where family stress predicted the quantity and quality of children's sleep, disruption in children's sleep has also served as a predictor of different facets of the marital relationship including marital satisfaction and conflict. For instance, findings from intervention studies have shown that parental marital satisfaction improved after treatment was provided to children who experienced chronic sleep problems (Durand & Mindell, 1990; Mindell & Durand, 1993); see Meltzer and Westin, chapter 6 in this volume for a more thorough discussion of the impact of children's sleep on parents' functioning.

In one of our studies (Kelly et al., 2008), actigraphic measures of children's sleep when they were eight years of age predicted mother-reported physical and verbal marital conflict two years later, while controlling for initial levels of conflict. Results indicated that more variability in children's sleep onset time and delayed child morning wake times were each predictive of increases in mothers' psychological and physical aggression toward the father as well as fathers' psychological aggression toward the mother over time. Although we did not test mediators, we considered several potential explanations for the effects (Kelly et al., 2008). For example, child sleep disruptions often result in parent sleep disruptions (Meltzer & Mindell, 2007), which in turn can have a negative impact on the marital relationship (Troxel, Robles, Hall, & Buysse, 2007). In addition, the negative consequences that children experience from sleep problems, such as externalizing and internalizing symptoms as well as poor academic performance, can create a stressful home environment, which can strain the marital relationship. These explanations are speculative and empirical investigations are needed to address mechanisms of effects and protective and vulnerability factors in the connection between children's sleep disruptions and parental marital conflict.

Marital Conflict and Children's Sleep: Conceptual Considerations

An important question to consider in this developing literature is, "Why do children experience sleep problems in high conflict homes?" There are several conceptual frameworks supportive of the proposition that familial stressors, including marital conflict, can generate levels of distress that disrupt children's sleep: Dahl's (1996) propositions regarding security, vigilance, and sleep; the Cognitive-Contextual Framework (Grych & Fincham, 1990; McDonald & Grych, 2006); and the Emotional Security Theory (Cummings & Davies, 1996, 2010; Davies & Cummings, 1994). Although these frameworks are not explicitly focused on marital conflict, child sleep, and child adjustment together, we believe that they can be easily expanded to address the connections between marital conflict, sleep problems, and developmental outcomes at a conceptual level. We also believe that these frameworks can be further utilized in empirical endeavors that attempt to elucidate the marital aggression-sleep problems connection. We do not view these frameworks as the only ones that could be used effectively in this emerging literature linking sleep and family processes. Rather, we focus on them because they are either the leading theories in the marital conflict–child development literature (Cognitive-Contextual and Emotional Security) or are widely accepted in the sleep community (Dahl's conceptualization). We hope that integrating existing and well-recognized propositions will facilitate the out-branching of current viewpoints and empirical investigations to incorporate both family and sleep processes.

Dahl (1996) proposed a model in which sleep and vigilance are conceptualized as opponent processes. Feeling safe is a prerequisite to falling asleep and returning to sleep after normal awakenings; perceived threat and corresponding vigilance impede sleep (Dahl & Lewin, 2002; Dahl et al., 1996). Empirical research supports this proposition. Cognitive and somatic pre-sleep arousal in children has been linked to sleep problems, broadly defined, as well as insomnia symptoms specifically (Gregory, Willis, Wiggs, Harvey, & the STEPS team, 2008). Because the family is perhaps the most salient environment of child development, families characterized by frequent, intense, or unpredictable hostility and aggression may generate levels of distress that disrupt children's sleep. Indeed, leading theories concerning marital conflict and child adjustment attempt to explain why and how marital conflict can produce levels of arousal, vigilance, and insecurity that interfere with children's sleep.

The Cognitive-Contextual Framework proposes that exposure to marital conflict often triggers children's attributions of self-blame for such conflict and perceptions of threat to the self and the family; such negative cognitive representations, in turn, contribute to child maladjustment (Grych & Fincham, 1990; Grych et al., 2000). Supportive of this theory, children's cognitive representations of their parents' conflict (e.g., self-blame, perceived threat) function as mediators of risk and pathways in the association between children's exposure to conflict and their internalizing and externalizing problems (e.g., Fosco & Grych, 2008; Grych & Fincham, 1990; McDonald & Grych, 2006). Our recent work also provides empirical evidence that marital conflict may contribute to children's sleep problems via negative cognitive representations of the conflict. We examined the link between children's perceptions of marital conflict and their sleep disturbances as mediated by children's appraisals of their parents' marital disputes (Kelly & El-Sheikh, 2009). Two hundred and seventeen school-aged children reported on their appraisals of the parents' marital conflict and mothers reported on children's sleep problems. Results revealed that children who perceived marital conflict as intense, unresolved, threatening, or blamed themselves for the conflict, were more likely to experience sleep problems than those who did not have such negative perceptions and attributions about the conflict. Thus, findings extend supportive empirical evidence for the cognitive-contextual framework by demonstrating that children's understanding, awareness, and appraisals of marital conflict are salient not only for their adjustment but also for their sleep.

The Emotional Security Theory proposes that marital relationships shape children's sense of safety, stability, and security within the home (Cummings & Davies, 1996, 2010; Davies & Cummings, 1994). Whereas warm and supportive marital relationships promote children's emotional security, highly conflictual relationships can undermine emotional security. Emotional insecurity is characterized by children's concerns about their own and their family's well-being and stability, as well as by elevated levels of fear, vigilance, and distress. An important component of the Emotional Security Theory is the sensitization hypothesis (Cummings & Cummings, 1988; Cummings & Davies, 2002), which proposes that frequent exposure to marital conflict results in increased vigilance and reactivity to conflict, which in turn can lead to increased emotional and behavioral problems. Supportive of children's sensitization to conflict at a biobehavioral level, repeated exposure to marital conflict has been found to impact children's vagal suppression to stressors (El-Sheikh et al., 2001), electrodermal responding (El-Sheikh & Cummings, 1992; El-Sheikh, 2005), cortisol levels (Pendry & Adam, 2003), and disruptions in the quality and duration of children's sleep (e.g., El-Sheikh et al., 2006). Thus, the Cognitive-Contextual Framework and Emotional Security Theory offer propositions regarding how marital conflict can produce levels of cognitive and emotional distress that are incompatible with children's sleep.

Link between Marital Conflict and Children's Adaptation: The Role of Sleep Problems

Important advances in the literature linking marital conflict with children's adjustment have been made. These advances include the identification of several mediators such as cognitive appraisals (e.g., Fosco & Grych, 2008) and emotional insecurity (e.g., Cummings & Davies, 2010), as well as vulnerability and protective factors (e.g., physiological regulation; El-Sheikh et al., 2009). However, investigations of children's sleep as an intervening variable, mediator, or moderator of risk in the association between parental marital aggression and children's adaptation and maladaptation have just begun. In both a mediation model and intervening variable model, the independent variable shares a significant association with the mediator or intervening variable, which in turn is significantly related to the dependent variable (MacKinnon, Lockwood, Hoffman, West, & Sheets, 2002). In other words, mediating and intervening variables serve as bridges to connect the predictor and the outcome variable (MacKinnon, 2008). In addition to mediating risk, sleep can interact with marital conflict and function as a moderator of risk for children's functioning. A moderating variable affects the relationship between the independent and dependent variable, such that the relationship between the predictor and outcome is more pronounced for one group, in comparison to another group (Holmbeck, 1997). Within this model, more optimal sleep may function as a protective factor against negative outcomes for children exposed to higher levels of marital aggression. Conversely, poor sleep may exacerbate the effects of conflict on children's adaptation, operating as a vulnerability factor.

Chronic sleep problems in otherwise typically developing children can disrupt their adjustment and jeopardize their well-being across many domains. As reflected in Figure 1.1, various sleep parameters, including amount, quality (e.g., sleep activity, sleep efficiency), and schedule (e.g., inconsistent from day to day or weekday to weekend nights), have been associated with a range of child difficulties including externalizing problems (Aronen, Paavonen, Fjallberg, Soininen, & Torronen, 2000; El-Sheikh, Erath, & Keller, 2007), internalizing symptoms (El-Sheikh, Kelly, Buckhalt, & Hinnant, 2010; Fredriksen, Rhodes, Reddy, & Way, 2004; Gregory et al., 2005), as well as social and peer relationship problems (Goetz, Shin, Krzysik, Wingo, & Vaughn, 2009). Similarly, sleep problems have been associated with children's physical health problems (Lumeng et al., 2007; Snell, Adam, & Duncan, 2007), diminished cognitive functioning (Buckhalt, El-Sheikh, & Keller, 2007; Buckhalt, El-Sheikh, Keller, & Kelly, 2009; Sadeh, Gruber, & Raviv, 2002; Steenari et al., 2003), and poorer academic performance (Fallone, Acebo, Seifer, Carskadon, 2005; Meijer, Habekothe, & van den Wittenboer, 2000); other chapters in this volume provide a more thorough discussion of associations between sleep problems and negative outcomes in young children (Staples & Bates, chapter 7), older children (Buckhalt & Staton, chapter 11), and preadolescents (Wolfson & Richards, chapter 12).

As shown in our model (Figure 1.1) and discussed above, marital conflict and sleep problems have been associated with negative child outcomes across several similar domains. Further, marital conflict is directly associated with sleep disruptions. These empirical associations and corresponding theoretical frameworks support our proposition that sleep problems may function as pathways of risk or intervening variables in the connection between exposure to interparental conflict and child adaptation. Similar to our mediation hypothesis, Spilsbury (2009) recently proposed that the trauma and stress that accompany exposure to violent circumstances are likely to result in sleep disruptions; in turn children are put at risk for health and behavioral problems. Thus, on a conceptual level, Spilsbury's (2009) propositions support the idea that sleep disruptions might serve as important mechanisms of effects in the link between a family stressor like marital conflict and children's adjustment problems.

Consistent with our conceptualization (Figure 1.1), findings stemming from recent empirical work provide initial evidence that sleep may play a key intervening role in the well-studied association between marital conflict and children's developmental outcomes. Specifically, in several published reports (e.g., El-Sheikh, Buckhalt, Keller, Cummings, &

Acebo, 2007; Hall, Zubrick, Silburn, Parsons, & Kurinczuk, 2007), sleep problems served as either mediators or intervening variables linking marital conflict with children's emotional, behavioral, and academic problems.

In a three-year longitudinal study starting when children were two years old, Hall and colleagues (2007) found that parent-reported child sleep problems mediated associations between interparental conflict and children's aggressive behavior. That is, higher levels of conflict were linked with increased sleep problems in children, which in turn were associated with an increase in children's aggression over time. Interparental conflict included disagreements about how to respond to the child's behavioral problems, arguments about parenting tactics, and conflict about undermining one another's relationship with the child. Hall and colleagues (2007) proposed that interparental conflict about parenting skills might result in inconsistencies regarding house rules and limit setting, variability in sleep schedules, fragmented sleep, and the handling of nighttime awakenings. In turn, sleep problems stemming from interparental conflict increased the risk for daytime aggression in children.

El-Sheikh, Buckhalt, Cummings, and Keller (2007) examined children's emotional insecurity regarding parents' marital conflict and sleep problems as pathways of effects in the relation between marital conflict and children's adjustment (parent- and teacher-reported) and teacher-reported academic functioning (see Figure 1.2). The sample was composed of 166 third-grade boys and girls. Findings supported a complex pathway, in which emotional security served as an intervening variable in the association between marital conflict and children's sleep (see Figure 1.2). Furthermore, sleep mediated the relation between emotional insecurity and child functioning. Taken together, higher levels of physical and verbal conflict between parents were associated with greater emotional insecurity in children, which in turn was related to lower sleep efficiency, shorter sleep duration, and more minutes awake during the night, as measured by actigraphy. Finally, sleep problems were linked with emotional and behavioral problems reported by parents and teachers and poor academic functioning. As proposed by the emotional security theory, exposure to marital conflict can result in elevated levels of anxiousness, alertness, and hypervigilance, as well as children's concerns and ruminations over the future of the family (Cummings & Davies, 1996,

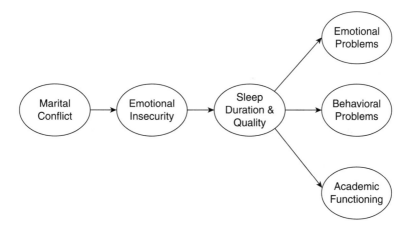

FIGURE 1.2   Emotional Insecurity and Sleep Problems as Pathways of Effects between Parental Marital Conflict and Children's Adaptation

2010; Davies & Cummings, 1994). Furthermore, biological regulatory systems can become adversely impacted. Given that sleep and vigilance are opponent processes (Dahl, 1996; Dahl & Lewin, 2002), elevated levels of hypervigilance and concern about family functioning may result in increased nighttime awareness and alertness, making sleep difficult to attain.

In another report with the aforementioned sample, El-Sheikh, Buckhalt, Keller, et al. (2007) examined children's sleep as an intervening variable in the connection between emotional insecurity in the marital relationship and academic achievement. The results illustrate that acti-graph measures of sleep efficiency and child-reported sleepiness and sleep/wake problems each served as an intervening variable linking children's emotional insecurity about the marital relationship with children's achievement on standardized tests [the Stanford Achievement Tests 10th ed. (SAT; 2005), and the Otis Lennon School Ability Test 8th ed.(OLSAT; Otis & Lennon, 2003)].

Collectively, findings from these studies enhance understanding of marital conflict and emotional insecurity as family functioning parameters that can interrupt the amount and quality of children's sleep, which consequently can influence children's adjustment and academic achievement. A limitation of these studies, however, is that most were cross-sectional, limiting inferences about causality. Hopefully, initial empirical evidence will encourage future investigations with longitudinal designs that will explicate relations between multiple parameters of family functioning, sleep, and child development.

Despite the relatively robust association between marital conflict and children's adaptation, not all children exposed to such conflict develop problems. Individual differences in children's physiological reactivity and regulation have been acknowledged as important moderators of risk in the connection between exposure to parental marital conflict and child outcomes across many domains (e.g., El-Sheikh, 2005; El-Sheikh et al. 2001). Sleep is a potential moderator at a bioregulatory level. The prefrontal cortex (PFC), in particular, is sensitive to the effects of sleep disturbance, and the PFC is a key regulator of behavioral and emotional functioning (Dahl, 1996). Indeed, reduced sleep amount and poor sleep quality have been linked with externalizing problems (Sadeh et al., 2002), as well as anxiety (Gregory et al., 2005) and depression (Fredriksen, Rhodes, Reddy, & Way, 2004). As a foundation for cognitive and emotion regulation, sleep may affect how children function in the general context of marital aggression as well as how they respond to specific parental altercations, which has implications for their adjustment. Adolescents whose sleep has been disrupted respond to negative emotion cues with more anger, sadness, and fear (Leotta, Carskadon, Acebo, Seifer, & Quinn, 1997). It is possible that optimal sleep promotes children's capacity to regulate negative thoughts and feelings (e.g., guilt, anxiety) in the context of interparental conflict. Conversely, negative self-regard and upset feelings may flourish if poor sleep compromises children's capacity to cope with marital disputes via adaptive regulation strategies such as cognitive reappraisal, distraction, or problem-solving.

We have conducted preliminary examinations of sleep problems as potential moderators of the associations between either parental marital conflict (unpublished data; El-Sheikh, 2007) or child-parent attachments (Keller, El-Sheikh, & Buckhalt, 2008) and children's adjustment and academic achievement. Although support was found for sleep as a moderator of risk in the context of parent–child attachments and children's academic functioning (Keller et al., 2008), not much support was found for the proposition that sleep interacts with marital conflict to exacerbate children's adjustment and cognitive outcomes (El-Sheikh, 2007).

However, we view these findings as preliminary. Many variables including sample characteristics and outcome measures may have contributed to the lack of significant effects. Thus, before minimizing the role of sleep as a potential moderator of the link between marital conflict and child adjustment, more empirical investigations should be conducted, ideally across several labs and with varied child outcomes.

As shown in Figure 1.1, child age, gender, physiological and biological regulation, pubertal status as well as broader socio-milieu variables (ethnicity, SES) may function as moderators of risk affecting the relations between (a) marital conflict and children's sleep, and/or (b) sleep parameters and children's adjustment. These potential moderators are exemplars of the extant proximal and distal variables that may exacerbate or ameliorate negative child outcomes in the context of risk associated with family functioning or poor sleep. It is beyond the scope of this chapter to review literature on each of these moderators as they relate to model variables. However, we review the small empirical literature that addresses whether the association between marital conflict and children's sleep is moderated by the broader socio-cultural milieu (SES and ethnicity). Our objective is to offer examples that highlight the value of examining moderators of risk in studies that focus on family functioning, sleep, and child adaptation.

With an aforementioned sample of elementary school children, we examined moderated mediation effects by assessing whether ethnicity (controlling for SES) and SES (controlling for ethnicity) moderate the pathway linking children's emotional insecurity about parental marital conflict with sleep problems and academic achievement (Figure 1.2; El-Sheikh, Buckhalt, Keller, et al., 2007). Moderated mediation occurs when a variable (e.g., sleep) functions as a mediator only (or especially strongly) under certain conditions (e.g., membership in a particular ethnic group; Muller, Judd, & Yzerbyt, 2005). Examination of these moderators rests on the assumption that although emotional insecurity in the family may be related to sleep disruptions, the impact of family functioning on children's sleep, and the impact of sleep on children's achievement, may vary based on the child's ethnic and SES context. We found evidence that sleep disruptions functioned as intervening variables linking emotional insecurity about marital conflict with children's academic performance more robustly for African American children in comparison to European American children (controlling for SES), and for children from lower SES families in comparison to higher SES families (controlling for ethnicity).

The aforementioned findings lend support to the health disparities view (Carter-Pokras & Baquet, 2002), which suggests that specific populations, such as minorities and lower SES families, may experience increased burden of adverse conditions (National Institutes of Health, 2006). For example, the disruption of a primary biological function like sleep may differentially impact individuals based on their economic or cultural milieu and associated processes (e.g., discrimination, poorer living conditions, unhealthy/inadequate diets, reduced health care benefits).

Conclusions and Future Directions

Marital conflict is highly prevalent and has been associated robustly with negative outcomes across many domains; however, only recently has marital conflict been examined in relation to children's sleep problems. Likewise, although many advances have been made to understand the negative sequelae of insufficient and poor quality sleep for children's adaptation and development, literature linking sleep with family processes including marital conflict is in its infancy. Nevertheless, the small yet rapidly growing body of literature that we reviewed suggests that concurrent investigations of marital conflict and children's sleep parameters could advance understanding of child functioning and development. In addition to reviewing empirical evidence in this chapter, we discussed some conceptual considerations that may explain the link between marital aggression and children's sleep problems. Furthermore, we advanced our conceptual model and initial supporting empirical evidence in which sleep may operate as a pathway or moderator linking children's exposure to interparental aggression with their developmental outcomes. It is important to indicate that we consider much of the current empirical evidence preliminary, and we hope that existing work will stimulate future work in this area.

One direction for future research is to extend investigations of sleep as an intervening variable to outcomes other than internalizing and externalizing behaviors and academic performance. As discussed previously in this chapter, associations have been established between either marital conflict or child sleep problems and a wide range of developmental outcomes including social functioning, physical health, and cognitive functioning. This provides a rationale for examining whether sleep disruptions might bridge the link between marital aggression and children's developmental outcomes across multiple domains. In addition, future investigations utilizing longitudinal designs would be instrumental for assessing the understudied bidirectional and cyclical relationship between marital conflict and children's sleep.

Sampling issues need to be addressed. Almost all studies that have conducted thorough assessments of interparental aggression in relation to children's sleep have utilized community samples. Considering that exposure to normative levels of marital conflict is linked with disruptions in children's sleep, it seems highly plausible that sleep disruptions might be more intense or prevalent in the context of severe marital abuse and domestic violence. There is a critical need to empirically address sleep patterns among both adults and children exposed to intense and frequent domestic aggression and violence. Recent research has linked parental sleep disruptions with negative marital processes, including marital conflict (e.g., Troxel et al., 2007; Humphreys & Lee, 2005). Fuller clarification of disruptions in sleep in various family members in the context of domestic and community violence is warranted.

The majority of studies that have investigated children's sleep disruptions in the context of marital aggression have utilized actigraphic, self-report, or parental reports to measure children's sleep. Whereas actigraphy is generally affordable and serves as a good proxy for the quantity and quality of sleep (e.g., sleep efficiency, sleep activity), and questionnaires provide important subjective reports of sleep, they each lack the capability to examine sleep architecture (Sadeh, 2008). The use of polysomnography could reveal whether exposure to marital aggression disrupts sleep architecture and sleep staging among children. Explicating disruptions in sleep architecture that may accompany exposure to familial stressors including marital conflict is of importance for enhanced understanding of mechanisms of effects connecting family functioning, sleep, and children's well-being.

Another methodological consideration is the examination of the timing of marital conflict (e.g., during the evening when children may either be asleep or trying to fall asleep) and children's awareness of late night disputes. It is plausible that some parents may wait until the child goes to bed to engage in conflict. Hearing such conflict could have direct ramifications for children's sleep.

Considering that the majority of samples in studies examining relations between marital conflict and children's sleep have consisted of pre-pubescent children, important questions remain regarding developmental and pubertal effects. Although developmental effects have been reported for children's responses to interparental aggression (Cummings & Davies, 2010), and puberty has pronounced effects on children's sleep (Carskadon, 2002), little is known about whether the effects of marital aggression on children's sleep are more pronounced for children of specific developmental or pubertal stages. Likewise, gender-related effects have been reported in the literatures on marital conflict and child adjustment (e.g., Davies & Lindsay, 2001, 2004), and on children's sleep (e.g., in terms of sleep quantity and quality; Buckhalt et al., 2007; Fredriksen et al., 2004). However, whether the association between marital conflict and children's sleep differs for boys and girls has not been examined.

Studies on marital conflict and children's sleep have not assessed the role of the perpetrator of marital aggression and violence. Although a majority of studies have focused on aggression against the mother in relation to children's adjustment, research in the marital conflict field has supported the importance of marital aggression against both the father and the mother in relation to children's emotional insecurity and negative adjustment outcomes (e.g., El-Sheikh et al., 2008). Furthermore, there is evidence that mother-initiated conflict, in comparison to father-initiated conflict, may differentially impact children's adjustment outcomes (Crockenberg & Langrock, 2001; Goeke-Morey, Cummings, Harold, & Shelton, 2003; Shelton, Harold, Goeke-Morey, & Cummings, 2006). For example, witnessing aggression against the mother may be more distressing to children than watching aggression against the father (Goeke-Morey et al., 2003). Thus, it is plausible that perpetration of aggression against the mother may have a more negative effect on children's sleep than aggression directed at the father.

Individual differences at the physiological level can modulate the type and degree of maladjustment among children exposed to stress (Steinberg & Avenevoli, 2000). However, little is known about physiological systems that increase vulnerability or provide protection against the effects of either (a) marital conflict on sleep problems, or (b) sleep problems on children's developmental outcomes (see Figure 1.1 for physiological reactivity and regulation as potential moderators of risk). Using a biopsychosocial conceptualization, work in our laboratory has demonstrated that children's physiological responses [e.g., respiratory sinus arrhythmia (RSA), a marker of parasympathetic nervous system activity (PNS) and skin conductance level, an index of sympathetic nervous system activity (SNS)], moderate the link between marital conflict and children's psychological adjustment (El-Sheikh et al., 2009; El-Sheikh & Whitson, 2006) and physical health (El-Sheikh et al., 2001; Whitson & El-Sheikh, 2003). Yet, there are many open scientific questions regarding whether children's physiological regulation (e.g., evidenced in PNS activity) exacerbates or attenuates the impact of marital conflict on children's sleep.

Providing very preliminary support for the importance of individual differences in physiological regulation, we found that sleep disturbances examined through self-report and actigraphy were associated with less optimal RSA in children (El-Sheikh & Buckhalt, 2005). In another study, RSA interacted with sleep problems (actigraphically derived sleep duration and quality) to predict children's adjustment problems (El-Sheikh et al., 2007). Sleep disruptions can negatively affect neurobiological regulatory systems and impair executive functions largely governed by the prefrontal cortex (PFC; Archbold, Giordani, Ruzicka, & Chervin, 2004) and disrupt PNS regulatory functions (Irwin, 2008). Prefrontal and PNS regulatory systems are not only both affected by sleep, but are overlapping systems that regulate one another (Gianaros, Van Der Veen, & Jennings, 2004). Given that RSA functions as a protective factor against adjustment, cognitive, and physical health problems in the context of family stress (e.g., El-Sheikh et al., 2001), it may allow children to compensate for the negative effects of poor sleep.

According to Dahl (1996), sleep is not only affected by arousal and vigilance, but itself affects the ability to modulate arousal and regulate emotions during waking hours. Thus, sleep and physiological regulation can facilitate or impede regulation of arousal, affect, and attention. Future research in these directions could further illuminate associations and interactions among familial stressors including marital conflict, sleep problems, and various physiological reactivity and regulation parameters.

REFERENCES

Archbold, K. H., Giordani, B., Ruzicka, D. L., & Chervin, R. D. (2004). Cognitive executive dysfunction in children with mild sleep-disordered breathing. *Biological Research for Nursing, 5*, 168–176.

Aronen, E. T., Paavonen, E. J., Fjallberg, M., Soininen, M., & Torronen, J. (2000). Sleep and psychiatric symptoms in school-age children. *Journal of the American Academy of Child and Adolescent Psychiatry, 39*, 502–508.

Bogels, S. M., & Brechman-Toussaint, M. L. (2006). Family issues in child anxiety: Attachment, family functioning, parental rearing and beliefs. *Clinical Psychology Review, 26*, 834–856.

Buckhalt, J. A., El-Sheikh, M., & Keller, P. (2007). Children's sleep and cognitive functioning: Race and socioeconomic status as moderators of effects. *Child Development, 78*, 213–231.

Buckhalt, J. A., El-Sheikh, M., Keller, P. S., & Kelly, R. J. (2009). Concurrent and longitudinal relationships between children's sleep and cognitive functioning: The moderating role of parent education. *Child Development, 80*, 875–892.

Carskadon, M. A. (2002). Factors influencing sleep patterns of adolescents. In M. A. Carskadon (Ed.), *Adolescent sleep patterns: Biological, social, and psychological influences* (pp. 4–26). New York: Cambridge University Press.

Carter-Pokras, O., & Baquet, C. (2002). What is a "health disparity"? *Public Health Reports, 117*, 426–434.

Crockenberg, S., & Langrock, A. (2001). The role of specific emotions in children's responses to interparental conflict: A test of the model. *Journal of Family Psychology, 15*, 163–182.

Cummings, E. M., & Cummings, J. L. (1988). A process-oriented approach to children's coping with adults' angry behavior. *Developmental Review, 8*, 296–321.

Cummings, E. M., & Davies, P. (1996). Emotional security as a regulatory process in normal development and the development of psychopathology. *Development and Psychopathology, 8*, 123–139.

Cummings, E. M., & Davies, P. T. (2002). Effects of marital conflict on children: Recent advances and emerging themes in process-oriented research. *Journal of Child Psychology and Psychiatry, 43*, 31–63.

Cummings, E. M., & Davies, P. T. (2010). *Marital conflict and children: An emotional security perspective*. New York, NY: The Guilford Press.

Dahl, R. E. (1996). The regulation of sleep and arousal: Development and psychopathology. *Development and Psychopathology, 8*, 3–27.

Dahl, R. E., & Lewin, D. S. (2002). Pathways to adolescent health sleep regulation and behavior. *Journal of Adolescent Health, 31*, 175–184.

Dahl, R. E., Ryan, N. D., Matty, M. K., Birmaher, B., Al-Shabbout, M., Williamson, D. E., & Kupfer, D. J. (1996). Sleep onset abnormalities in depressed adolescents. *Biological Psychiatry, 39*, 400–410.

Davies, P. T., & Cummings, E. M. (1994). Marital conflict and child adjustment: An emotional security hypothesis. *Psychological Bulletin, 116*, 387–411.

Davies, P. T., & Lindsay, L. L. (2001). Does gender moderate the effects of marital conflict on children? In J. Grych & F. Fincham (Eds.), *Child development and interparental conflict* (pp. 64–97). New York: Cambridge University Press.

Davies, P. T., & Lindsay, L. L. (2004). Interparental conflict and adolescent adjustment: Why does gender moderate early adolescent vulnerability? *Journal of Family Psychology, 18*, 160–170.

Durand, V. N., & Mindell, J. A. (1990). Behavioral treatment of multiple childhood sleep disorders. *Behavior Modification, 14*, 37–49.

Du Rocher Schudlich, T. D., Shamir, H., & Cummings, E. M. (2004). Marital conflict, children's representations of family relationships, and children's dispositions towards peer conflict strategies. *Social Development, 13*, 171–192.

El-Sheikh, M. (2005). The role of emotional responses and physiological reactivity in the marital conflict-child functioning link. *The Journal of Child Psychology and Psychiatry, 46*, 1191–1199.

El-Sheikh, M. (2007). [Sleep problems as potential moderators of effects in the associations between parental marital conflict and children's adjustment]. Unpublished raw data.

El-Sheikh, M., & Buckhalt, J. (2005). Vagal regulation and emotional intensity predict children's sleep problems. *Developmental Psychobiology, 46*, 307–317.

El-Sheikh, M., Buckhalt, J. A., Cummings, E. M., & Keller, P. (2007). Sleep disruptions and emotional insecurity are pathways of risk for children. *Journal of Child Psychology and Psychiatry, 48*, 88–96.

El-Sheikh, M., Buckhalt, J. A., Keller, P. S., Cummings, E. M., & Acebo, C. (2007). Child emotional insecurity and academic achievement: The role of sleep disruptions. *Journal of Family Psychology, 21*, 29–38.

El-Sheikh, M., Buckhalt, J. A., Mize, J., & Acebo, C. (2006). Marital conflict and disruption of children's sleep. *Child Development, 77*, 31–43.

El-Sheikh, M., & Cummings, E. M. (1992). Availability of control and preschoolers' responses to interadult anger. *International Journal of Behavioral Development, 15*, 207–226.

El-Sheikh, M., Cummings, E. M., Kouros, C. D., Elmore-Staton, L., & Buckhalt, J. A. (2008). Marital psychological and physical aggression and children's mental and physical health: Direct, mediated, and moderated effects. *Journal of Consulting and Clinical Psychology, 76*, 138–148.

El-Sheikh, M., Erath, S. A., & Keller, P. S. (2007). Children's sleep and adjustment: The moderating role of vagal regulation. *Journal of Sleep Research, 16*, 396–405.

El-Sheikh, M., Harger, J., & Whitson, S. M. (2001). Exposure to interparental conflict and children's adjustment and physical health: The moderating role of vagal tone. *Child Development, 72*, 1617–1636.

El-Sheikh, M., Kelly, R. J., Buckhalt, J. A., & Hinnant, J. B. (2010). Children's sleep and adjustment over time: The role of socioeconomic context. *Child Development, 81*, 870–883.

El-Sheikh, M., Kouros, C. D., Erath, S., Keller, P., Cummings, E. M., & Staton, L (2009). Marital conflict and children's externalizing behavior: Interactions between parasympathetic and sympathetic nervous system activity. *Monographs of the Society for Research in Child Development, 74* (1, Serial No. 292).

El-Sheikh, M., & Whitson, S. A. (2006). Longitudinal relations between marital conflict and child adjustment: Vagal regulation as a protective factor. *Journal of Family Psychology, 20,* 30–39.

Fallone, G., Acebo, C., Seifer, R., & Carskadon, M. A. (2005). Experimental restriction of sleep opportunity in children: Effects on teacher ratings. *Sleep, 28,* 1561–1567.

Fosco, G. M., & Grych, J. H. (2008). Emotional, cognitive, and family systems mediators of children's adjustment to interparental conflict. *Journal of Family Psychology, 22,* 843–854.

Fredriksen, K., Rhodes, J., Reddy, R., & Way, N. (2004). Sleepless in Chicago: Tracking the effects of adolescent sleep loss during the middle school years. *Child Development, 75,* 84–95.

Gianaros, P. J., Van Der Veen, F. M., & Jennings, R. (2004). Regional cerebral blood flow correlates with heart period and high-frequency heart period variability during working-memory tasks: Implications for the cortical and subcortical regulation of cardiac autonomic activity. *Psychophysiology, 41,* 521–530.

Goeke-Morey, M. C., Cummings, E. M., Harold, G. T., & Shelton, K. H. (2003). Categories and continua of destructive and constructive marital conflict tactics from the perspective of U.S. and Welsh children. *Journal of Family Psychology, 17,* 327–338.

Goetz, S. E., Shin, N., Kryzysik, L., Wingo, B. N., & Vaughn, B. E. (2009, April). *Social benefits of a good night's sleep for preschool-age children.* Poster presented at the biennial meeting of the Society for Research in Child Development, Denver, CO. Gregory, A. M., Caspi, A., Eley, T. C., Moffitt, T. E., O'Conner, T. G., & Poulton, R. (2005). Prospective longitudinal associations between persistent sleep problems in childhood and anxiety and depression disorders in adulthood. *Journal of Abnormal Child Psychology, 33,* 157–163.

Gregory, A. M., Caspi, A., Moffitt, T. E., & Poulton, R. (2006). Family conflict in childhood: A predictor of later insomnia. *Sleep, 29,* 1063–1067.

Gregory, A. M., Willis, T. A., Wiggs, L., Harvey, A. G., & the STEPS team. (2008). Presleep arousal and sleep disturbances in children. *Sleep, 31,* 1745–1747.

Grych, J. H., & Fincham, F. D. (1990). Marital conflict and children's adjustment: A cognitive-contextual framework. *Psychological Bulletin, 108,* 267–290.

Grych, J. H., Fincham, F. D., Jouriles, E. N., & McDonald, R. (2000). Interparental conflict and child adjustment: Testing the mediational role of appraisals in the cognitive-contextual framework. *Child Development, 71,* 1648–1661.

Hall, W. A., Zubrick, S. R., Silburn, S. R., Parsons, D. E., & Kurinczuk, J. J. (2007). A model for predicting behavioural sleep problems in a random sample of Australian pre-schoolers. *Infant and Child Development, 16*, 509–523.

Harold, G. T., Aitken, J. J., & Shelton, K. H. (2007). Inter-parental conflict and children's academic attainment: A longitudinal analysis. *Journal of Child Psychology, and Psychiatry, 48*, 1223–1232.

Holmbeck, G. N. (1997). Toward terminological, conceptual, and statistical clarity in the study of mediators and moderators: Examples from the child-clinical and pediatric psychology literatures. *Journal of Consulting and Clinical Psychology, 65*, 599–610.

Humphreys, J., & Lee, K. (2005). Sleep disturbance in battered women living in transitional housing. *Issues in Mental Health Nursing, 26*, 771–780.

Irwin, M. (2008). Human psychoneuroimmunology: twenty years of discovery. *Brain, Behavior and Immunity, 22*, 129–139.

Jaffee, P. G., Wolfe, D. A., & Wilson, S. K. (1990). *Children of battered women.* Newbury Park, CA: Sage.

Jouriles, E. N., Norwood, W. D., & McDonald, R. (1996). Physical violence and other forms of marital aggression: Links with children's behavior problems. *Journal of Family Psychology, 10*, 223–234.

Kahn, A., Van de Merckt, C., Rebuffat, E., Mozin, M. J., Sottiaux, M., Blum, D., & Hennart, P. (1989). Sleep problems in healthy preadolescents. *Pediatrics, 84*, 542–546.

Katz, L. F., & Low, S. M. (2004). Marital violence, co-parenting, and family-level processes in relation to children's adjustment. *Journal of Family Psychology, 18*, 372–382.

Keller, P. S., El-Sheikh, M., & Buckhalt, J. A. (2008). Children's attachment to parents and their academic functioning: Sleep disruptions as moderators of effects. *Journal of Developmental and Behavioral Pediatrics, 29*, 441–449.

Kelly, R. J., & El-Sheikh, M. (2009, April). *Children's appraisals of marital conflict and their sleep disruptions.* Poster presented at the biennial meeting of the Society for Research in Child Development, Denver, CO.

Kelly, R. J., Keller, P., Staton, L., Reinecke, D., Buckhalt, J. A., & El-Sheikh, M. (2008, March). *Children's sleep as a predictor of marital conflict: A longitudinal study.* Poster presented at the Pediatric Sleep Medicine Conference, Amelia Island, FL.

Koenen, K. C., Moffitt, T. E., Caspi, A., Taylor, A., & Purcell, S. (2003). Domestic violence is associated with environmental suppression of IQ in young children. *Development and Psychopathology, 15*, 297–311.

Layzer, J. I., Goodson, B. D., & Delange, C. (1986). Children in shelters. *Response to the Victimization of Women and Children, 9*, 2–5.

Leotta, C., Carskadon, M. A., Acebo, C., Seifer, R., & Quinn, B. (1997). Effects of acute sleep restriction on affective response in adolescents: Preliminary results. *Sleep Research, 26*, 201.

Lindsey, E. W., MacKinnon-Lewis, C., Campbell, J., Frabutt, J. M., & Lamb, M. E. (2002). Marital conflict and boys' peer relationships: The mediating role of mother-son emotional reciprocity. *Journal of Family Psychology, 16,* 466–477.

Lumeng, J. C., Somashekar, D., Appugliese, D., Kaciroti, N., Corwyn, R. F., & Bradley, R. H. (2007). Shorter sleep duration is associated with increased risk for being overweight at ages 9 to 12 years. *Pediatrics, 120,* 1020–1029.

MacKinnon, D. P. (2008). *Introduction to statistical mediation analyses* (pp. 1–22). New York, NY: Lawrence Erlbaum.

MacKinnon, D. P., Lockwood, C. M., Hoffman, J. M., West, S. G., & Sheets, V. (2002). A comparison of methods to test mediation and other intervening variable effects. *Psychological Methods, 7,* 83–104.

Marks, C. R., Glaser, B. A., Glass, J. B., & Horne, A. M. (2001). Effects of witnessing severe marital discord on children's social competence and behavioral problems. *The Family Journal, 9,* 94–101.

McDonald, R., & Grych, J. H. (2006). Young children's appraisals of interparental conflict: Measurement and links with adjustment problems. *Journal of Family Psychology, 20,* 88–99.

Meijer, A. M., Habekothe, H. T., & van den Wittenboer, G. L. H. (2000). Time in bed, quality of sleep and school functioning of children. *Journal of Sleep Research, 9,* 145–153.

Meltzer, L. J., & Mindell, J. A. (2007). Relationship between child sleep disturbances and maternal sleep, mood, and parenting stress: A pilot study. *Journal of Family Psychology, 21,* 67–73.

Mindell, J. A., & Durand, V. M. (1993). Treatment of childhood sleep disorders: Generalization across disorders and effects on family members. *Journal of Pediatric Psychology, 18,* 731–750.

Muller, D., Judd, C. M., & Yzerbyt, V. Y. (2005). When moderation is mediated and mediation is moderated. *Journal of Personality and Social Psychology, 89,* 852–863.

National Institutes of Health. (2003). *Research on children exposed to violence.* Research program announcement PAR-03-096. Retrieved from http://grants2.nih.gov/grants/guide/pa-files/PAR-03-096.html

National Institutes of Health. (2006). NIH strategic plan to reduce and ultimately eliminate health disparities. Retrieved from http://www.nih.gov/about/hd/strategicplan.pdf

Otis, A. S., & Lennon, R. T. (2003). *The Otis-Lennon School Ability Test* (8th ed.). San Antonio, TX: Harcourt.

Pendry, P., & Adam, E. K. (2003, April). *Hush-a-bye hormones: Parent behavior, parent emotional and marital functioning, and child cortisol.* Poster presented at the biennial meeting of the Society for Research in Child Development, Tampa, FL.

Perry, B. D. (1997). Incubated in terror: Neurodevelopmental factors in the "cycle of violence." In J. D. Osofsky (Ed.), *Children in a violent society* (pp. 124–149). New York: Guilford.

Sadeh, A. (2008). Commentary: Comparing actigraphy and parental report as measures of children's sleep. *Journal of Pediatric Psychology, 33,* 406–407.

Sadeh, A., Gruber, R., & Raviv, A. (2002). Sleep, neurobehavioral functioning, and behavior problems in school-age children. *Child Development, 73,* 405–417.

Sadeh, A., Raviv, A., & Gruber, R. (2000). Sleep patterns and sleep disruptions in school-age children. *Developmental Psychology, 36,* 291–301.

Saltzman, K. M., Holden, G. W., & Holahan, C. J. (2005). The psychobiology of children exposed to marital violence. *Journal of Clinical Child and Adolescent Psychology, 34,* 129–139.

Shelton, K. H., & Harold, G. T. (2007). Marital conflict and children's adjustment: The mediating and moderating role of children's coping strategies. *Social Development, 16,* 497–512.

Shelton, K. H., Harold, G. T., Goeke-Morey, M. C., & Cummings, E. M. (2006). Children's coping with marital conflict: The role of conflict expression and gender. *Social Development, 15,* 232–247.

Smith Slep, A. M., & O'Leary, S. G. (2005). Parent and partner violence in families with young children: Rates, patterns, and connections. *Journal of Consulting and Clinical Psychology, 73,* 435–444.

Snell, E. K., Adam, E. K., & Duncan, G. J. (2007). Sleep and the body mass index and overweight status of children and adolescents. *Child Development, 78,* 309–323.

Spilsbury, J, C. (2009). Sleep as a mediator in the pathway from violence-induced traumatic stress to poorer health and functioning: A review of the literature and proposed conceptual model. *Behavioral Sleep Medicine, 7,* 223–244.

Stanford Achievement Test Series, 10th Edition. (2005). San Antonio, TX: Harcourt.

Steenari, M. R., Vuontela, V., Paavonen, E. J., Carlson, S., Fjallberg, M., & Aronen, E. T. (2003). Working memory and sleep in 6- to 13-year-old school children. *Journal of the American Academy of Child and Adolescent Psychiatry, 42,* 85–92.

Steinberg, L., & Avenevoli, S. (2000). The role of context in the development of psychopathology: A conceptual framework and some speculative propositions. *Child Development, 71,* 66–74.

Straus, M. A., & Gelles, R. J. (1990). How violent are American families? Estimates from the national family violence resurvey and other studies. In M. A. Straus & R. J. Gelles (Eds.), *Physical violence in American families: Risk factors and adaptations to violence in 8,145 families* (pp. 95–112). New Brunswick, NJ: Transaction Publishers.

Sturge-Apple, M. L., Davies, P. T., Winter, M. A., Cummings, E. M., & Schermerhorn, A. (2008). Interparental conflict and children's school adjustment: The explanatory role of children's internal representations of interparental and parent–child relationships. *Developmental Psychology, 44,* 1678–1690.

Troxel, W. M., Robles, T. F., Hall, M., & Buysse, D. J. (2007). Marital quality and the marital bed: Examining the covariation between relationship quality and sleep. *Sleep Medicine Reviews, 11*, 389–404.

Van Tassel, E. B. (1985). The relative influence of child and environmental characteristics on sleep disturbances in the first and second years of life. *Developmental and Behavioral Pediatrics, 6*, 81–85.

Whitson, S., & El-Sheikh, M. (2003). Marital conflict and health: Processes and protective factors. *Aggression and Violent Behavior, 8*, 283–312.

Ybarra, G. J., Wilkens, S. L., & Lieberman, A. F. (2007). The influence of domestic violence on preschooler behavior and functioning. *Journal of Family Violence, 22*, 33–42.

2

The Parenting Context of Children's Sleep

Stephen A. Erath and Kelly M. Tu

Introduction

Sufficient, high-quality sleep is necessary for optimal social and psychological adjustment; conversely, sleep disturbances can impair functioning across critical domains of child development. Unfortunately, sleep problems in childhood are prevalent, affecting around 25% of children (e.g., Meltzer & Mindell, 2006; Mindell, Owens, & Carskadon, 1999). Rates and effects of sleep disturbances are relatively well-documented (e.g., Buckhalt, Wolfson, & El-Sheikh, 2009). In contrast, the social correlates of sleep problems are understudied, despite an important fact: children's sleep occurs in the social context of the family (Dahl & El-Sheikh, 2007). Parents play a critical role in the primary domains of children's lives (e.g., social, school), and parental involvement in children's sleep is no exception.

This chapter is organized around a conceptual model which contends that children's sleep is influenced by (and influences) parental sleep-related cognitions and behaviors as well as the general context of the parent–child relationship. Our conceptual model is selectively focused on some key aspects of parenting and children's sleep that have been the subject of empirical work, but is not a comprehensive model of parenting or children's sleep (see conceptual model in Figure 2.1). We begin the chapter by discussing parental sleep-related cognitions and behaviors in terms of the balance between parental sensitivity and the need to facilitate children's independent sleep competence. In this section, we

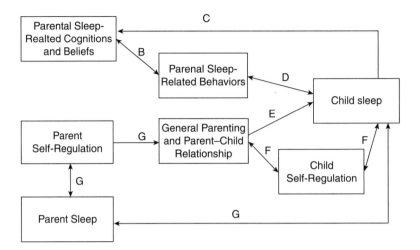

FIGURE 2.1   Conceptual Model Linking Parenting and Children's Sleep

consider a perspective in which sleep problems are conceptualized like other behavioral problems, motivated, in part, by inadvertent positive reinforcement from parents (France & Blampied, 1999). Next, we discuss the parent–child relationship as a context that may promote or undermine children's psychological comfort (e.g., level of anxiety at night), and thereby establish better or poorer conditions for children's sleep. In this section, we highlight evolutionary biology (Dahl, 1996) and emotional security (Cummings & Davies, 2002) perspectives as potential explanatory mechanisms linking negative features of the parent–child relationship with children's psychological unrest and sleep problems. Following this, we consider the reciprocal nature of the connection between parenting and children's sleep, emphasizing the effects of children's sleep on parents' sleep and their capacity to regulate emotions and behaviors that support positive parent–child interactions and relationships (see Meltzer & Westin, chapter 6 in this volume, for more information about child effects). Finally, we discuss directions for future research that would accelerate understanding of the interface between parenting and children's sleep.

The research we review generally concerns typically developing children (with some exceptions noted below), and our coverage of topics reflects the focus in the existing literature on parental sleep-related cognitions and behaviors in early childhood and more general parenting strategies in later childhood. We use the general phrases "sleep problems" or "sleep disturbances" to refer to reduced sleep duration or quality (e.g., sleep latency, night waking) and less consistent sleep schedules (e.g., bedtime) that range from greater than average to clinically significant.

Parental Sleep-Related Cognitions and Behaviors

Parental sleep-related cognitions and behaviors refer to how parents think and act about their children's sleep. These sleep-specific features of parenting probably overlap with, but are not redundant with, more general features of parenting and parent–child relationships (path A in Figure 2.1), which are discussed in more detail below. Until recently, relatively few empirical studies considered associations among parental sleep-related constructs and children's sleep (beyond infancy). Parental sleep-related cognitions and behaviors may be especially intertwined with children's sleep during infancy, when parents and children co-establish behavioral patterns for falling asleep and night waking (e.g., sleeping together, physical soothing). Sleep difficulties, such as initiating and maintaining sleep, are common in infants and toddlers, and parental responses may influence whether these normative difficulties persist and become sleep problems in childhood (Sheldon, 2001). In addition to supporting basic sleep skills during infancy, parents may continue to play an important role in children's sleep, and parents encounter new challenges in later childhood, such as scheduling consistent sleep routines and alleviating nighttime fears and bedtime resistance (Blader, Koplewicz, Abikoff, & Foley, 1997). However, many more studies have examined parental sleep-related cognitions and behaviors during infancy compared to later childhood.

Parental cognitions that favor active intervention in children's sleep are linked with more sleep problems in infancy and childhood, and the converse is also well-documented (Morrell, 1999; Sadeh, Flint-Ofir, Tirosh, & Tikotzky, 2007; Tikotzky & Sadeh, 2009). For example, maternal beliefs that they should limit involvement in infant sleep at night were associated with fewer sleep problems and more consolidated sleep over time in infants (as measured by actigraphy; Tikotzky & Sadeh, 2009).

Likewise, parental beliefs that infants should learn to self-soothe at night were linked with less night waking among infants (Sadeh et al., 2007). In a longitudinal study, Tikotzky and Sadeh (2009) found that greater maternal beliefs that infants experienced distress upon waking at night were associated with higher objective and subjective reports of night waking. Furthermore, parents of sleep-disturbed infants (clinical group) reported more difficulties with limit-setting and were less able to resist infants' demands at night, compared to parents whose infants did not have sleep problems (Morrell, 1999; Sadeh et al., 2007). It is important to note that the extent to which these associations are parent-driven (parental sleep-related cognitions contribute to children's sleep problems; via path B in Figure 2.1) or child-driven (children's sleep problems contribute to parental sleep-related cognitions; path C in Figure 2.1) is not established, and it seems most plausible that the effects are bidirectional.

Parental sleep-related beliefs or cognitions may affect children's sleep because they underlie parental behaviors and parent–child interactions at night (path B in Figure 2.1). Beliefs about the importance of direct parental involvement in children's sleep and distress about night waking are linked with more active physical comforting to soothe children at night (Morrell & Cortina-Borja, 2002; Morrell & Steele, 2003; Tikotzky & Sadeh, 2009). In turn, children of parents who actively soothe their children back to sleep have more sleep problems than children of parents who provide lower levels of active physical soothing (Morrell & Cortina-Borja, 2002). In addition, parents who have more problems with limit-setting and more doubts about their abilities to help their children with sleep tend to engage more actively with their preschool-aged children at bedtime. In turn, higher levels of parental active engagement during sleep time are associated with children's sleep problems. Active parent–child interactions at bedtime may mediate the association between parental sleep-related cognitions and children's sleep (Johnson & McMahon, 2008).

Other studies have focused more exclusively on parental sleep-related *behaviors* as predictors of children's sleep, or on children's sleep as a predictor of parental sleep-related behaviors (path D in Figure 2.1). Interestingly, parental behaviors indicative of *investment* in children's sleep (e.g., check on child, assign bedtime) are linked with longer time in bed on school nights, an estimate of sleep duration (Meijer, Habekothe, & Van Den Wittenboer, 2001). On the other hand, as noted, greater parental involvement in children's sleep (e.g., active physical comforting) is linked with children's sleep problems, such as resisting bedtime, difficulties falling asleep alone, and waking at night (Johnson & McMahon, 2008; Morrell, 1999; Morrell & Cortina-Borja, 2002; Sadeh, Mindell, Luedtke, & Wiegand, 2009; Tikotzky & Sadeh, 2009). For example, Morrell and Cortina-Borja (2002) found that mothers who identified no significant sleep-settling or sleep-waking problems in their children at one-year-old and two-year-old assessments reported that they engaged in lower levels of active physical comforting, compared to mothers who identified sleep problems in their children at both assessments; across these groups, parental use of active physical comforting significantly declined over time (for additional evidence of age-related declines in active physical comforting, see Sadeh et al., 2009).

Parental behaviors that encourage children's autonomy and independence are linked with fewer sleep problems and more consolidated sleep (Morrell & Cortina-Borja, 2002; Sadeh et al., 2009). For example, parental encouragement of school-aged children's maturity at home (e.g., self-care such as cleaning room, enforcing rules such as bedtime) was associated with longer sleep duration and decreased likelihood of late bedtime, as well as lower nightly variation in sleep duration among girls (Spilsbury et al., 2005). In addition, Morrell and Cortina-Borja (2002) reported that parents of infants without sleep-settling or sleep-waking problems engaged in higher levels of autonomy encouragement than parents of infants with persistent sleep problems (i.e., mother-reported sleep problems at one-year-old and two-year-old assessments). Interestingly, parents of both subgroups (i.e., no sleep problem and persistent sleep problem) engaged in active physical comforting. However, parents of infants without sleep problems used autonomy encouragement and active physical comforting equally, whereas parents of infants with persistent sleep problems used active physical comforting much more frequently than autonomy encouragement. Across groups, parental use of strategies to encourage autonomy significantly increased as infants got older.

Children's sleep problems have been viewed from a behavior problem perspective (e.g., France & Blampied, 1999). That is, like many childhood behavior problems (e.g., temper tantrums), sleep problems often involve interactions between parents and children, and sleep problems may emerge or escalate by attracting parental attention and inadvertent reinforcement. For example, Blampied and France (1993) suggested that parents may reinforce children's night waking and attempts to seek comfort when they respond intensively to soothe their children back to sleep (e.g., feeding, picking up, rocking). Conversely, parents who respond less intensively may avoid reinforcing night waking and encourage children to engage in self-soothing behaviors, thus reducing the risk of escalating sleep disturbance (France, Blampied, & Henderson, 2003). France and colleagues (2003) suggested that *monitoring* children without actively engaging them may be well-advised.

The behavior problem perspective appears to have some support from studies examining parental sleep-related cognitions and behaviors, which suggest that excessive parental involvement in children's sleep may limit children's self-regulation and exacerbate their sleep problems (Morrell & Cortina-Borja, 2002; Sadeh et al., 2009). However, it is very likely that children who have greater sleep problems (independent of parenting) elicit more active parental involvement; the relative directions of effect between parental involvement and children's sleep problems have not been clarified in the existing literature. Furthermore, both excessive parental involvement in children's sleep (Morrell & Cortina-Borja, 2002; Sadeh et al., 2009) and low parental sensitivity or responsiveness (e.g., Bell & Belsky, 2008) may interfere with children's sleep. Co-sleeping, which is covered more extensively elsewhere (see Burnham & Gaylor, chapter 9 in this volume; and Worthman, chapter 8 in this volume), is illustrative: Whereas co-sleeping based on values may reflect sensitive investment in children's sleep and promote sleep, co-sleeping in response to sleep problems may attenuate immediate problems, yet impede children's independent sleep in the long-term (Germo, Chang, Keller, & Goldberg, 2007; Goldberg & Keller 2007; Polimeni, Richdale, & Francis, 2007; Ramos, Youngclarke, & Anderson, 2007). Optimal parental sleep-related behaviors may be conceptualized as a balance between parental sensitivity and responsiveness on one hand, and attempts to foster the child's independence and self-regulation, on the other.

General Context of the Parent–Child Relationship

Aside from parental beliefs and behaviors that are specifically related to children's sleep, the broader context of parenting, including parent–child relationships and parent–child interactions, may shape the amount or quality of children's sleep (path E in Figure 2.1). As discussed in further detail below, the existing literature is somewhat mixed, with some studies providing evidence for independent connections between parenting and children's sleep (Adam, Snell, & Pendry, 2007; Bell & Belsky, 2008; Brand, Hatzinger, Beck, and Holsboer-Trachsler, 2009; Liu et al., 2000; Spilsbury et al., 2005). Other studies have not found independent associations between parenting and children's sleep when mediators (e.g., psychological distress; Cousins, Bootzin, Stevens, Ruiz, & Haynes, 2007) or covariates (e.g., family stress; Bates, Viken, Alexander, Beyers, & Stockton, 2002) were included in analytic models.

Despite some inconsistencies, several recent studies provide evidence linking parent–child interactions and relationships with children's sleep. In a large, nationally representative sample, Adam et al. (2007) reported that parent-reported warmth was linked positively with school-aged children's sleep hours, recorded by children or their parents in time diaries, and parent-reported family rules were linked with more sleep hours in adolescents. Analyses included statistical control for a variety of demographic, family, and daily activity (e.g., television, sports, socializing) variables. Bell and Belsky (2008) found that less observed sensitivity in mother-child interactions and more negative mother-child relationships (e.g., lower parent-reported closeness and more conflict) predicted increased mother-reported sleep problems over time in a large sample of school-aged children. Reciprocally, sleep problems predicted adverse changes in maternal negative emotionality, maternal sensitivity, and mother-child closeness and conflict. Brand, Hatzinger and colleagues (2009) reported that adolescent-reported positive parenting (e.g., support and commendation) was associated with adolescent-reported lower sleepiness and higher daytime concentration. Negative parenting (e.g., reproach, restriction, and inconsistency) was associated with sleepiness and poorer sleep quality. Finally, in a longitudinal, auto-regressive model, Kelly, Hinnant, and El-Sheikh (2009) found that parental psychological control predicted decreased sleep duration in school-aged children one year later.

These recent findings are consistent with the broader parenting literature, indicating that parental warmth, sensitivity, involvement, and consistent structure (e.g., rules, expectations) are linked with positive child adjustment, whereas parental harshness, psychological control, and negative emotionality, as well as parent–child conflict, are linked with child maladjustment across behavioral, psychological, and health domains (Grusec & Davidov, 2007). However, there are some exceptions to the evidence for independent associations linking positive parenting with children's sleep amount and quality, such as studies in which parental or family stress appeared to account for the effects of parenting on children's sleep (Bates et al., 2002; Cousins et al., 2007). Furthermore, Scher (2001) reported that more positive mother-child play interactions were linked with more night waking in young children. Perhaps an alternative route to sleep problems involves children's desire for continued interaction with parents at night and parental receptivity or (over)responsivity to night waking that stems, in part, from warm parent–child relationships (Sadeh, Tikotzky, & Scher, 2009). The results from Scher's (2001) study reinforce the idea that parents who balance warmth and responsiveness with consistent structure and limits may provide optimal support for children's sleep.

Although investigators have not fully tested or established any particular theoretical framework linking general parenting and children's sleep, existing conceptual models and relevant research should inform future work on the subject. Dahl (1996) advanced a conceptualization of sleep based in evolutionary biology. According to this model, sleep involves diminished attentiveness and responsiveness; as such, it is most adaptive for sleep to occur at times and places that are relatively free of threat. Indeed, vigilance and sleep are incompatible, and threat inhibits sleep (Dahl, 1996). Paired with the emotional security model (Cummings & Davies, 2002), which posits that feelings of emotional security are derived from family relationships that children perceive as safe and stable, negative parent–child interactions or relationships may be expected to interfere with children's sense of security, and thus, undermine their sleep.

One potential mechanism linking parenting with children's sleep is that negative parent–child relationships may produce psychological discomfort (i.e., arousal and vigilance), and thereby disrupt children's sleep (path F in Figure 2.1). For example, a large body of research has linked negative parenting (e.g., harsh parenting, psychological control, low warmth and availability) with children's symptoms of anxiety and depression (e.g., Barber & Harmon, 2002). In turn, internalizing symptoms are associated with sleep disruptions (Dahl, 1996; Dahl & Lewin, 2002; El-Sheikh & Buckhalt, 2005; Patten, Choi, Gillin, & Pierce, 2000), perhaps due to cognitive distress (e.g., worry while trying to fall asleep), negative mood (e.g., lack of motivation to prevent oversleep or inconsistent sleep), and physiological arousal (e.g., racing heart while trying to fall asleep). Cousins et al. (2007) reported that adolescents' psychological distress (e.g., depression, anxiety, self-esteem, somatic symptoms) mediated the association between lower levels of parental involvement and adolescents' lower sleep efficiency. Thus, internalizing symptoms may mediate the association between negative parent–child interactions and children's sleep problems.

A closely related mechanism that may link parenting with children's sleep problems involves children's feelings of emotional insecurity in the context of negative parent–child interactions. Research on marital conflict, for example, has demonstrated that children's exposure to marital conflict can produce emotional insecurity in the family, which is marked by feelings of anxiety and anger as well as sensitivity to cues of conflict (Cummings & Davies, 2002), all of which are incompatible with the psychological calm necessary for sleep (El-Sheikh, Buckhalt, Mize, & Acebo, 2006; see El-Sheikh and Kelly, chapter 1 in this volume, for more information about the association between marital conflict and children's sleep). In one study, marital conflict was associated with children's emotional insecurity about the marital relationship (e.g., emotional and behavioral arousal in response to parental arguments, negative representations about the interparental relationship) which, in turn, was linked with lower sleep quality and duration (El-Sheikh, Buckhalt, Cummings, & Keller, 2007). Emotional security is not derived exclusively from children's perceptions of marital quality, but also from children's sense of positive parent–child relationships. Studies linking parental warmth, sensitivity, and involvement with better sleep in childhood, as well as studies linking negative parenting with poorer sleep (e.g., Adam et al., 2007; Bell & Belsky, 2008; Brand, Hatzinger, et al., 2009; Cousins et al., 2007), suggest that a similar mechanism (i.e., emotional security) may exist in the parent–child domain (see Keller, chapter 3 in this volume, for more information about the association between attachment insecurity in the parent–child relationship and children's sleep). It would be very informative for future research to investigate emotional insecurity specifically as a mediator of the association between negative parent–child interactions and children's sleep disruptions (path F in Figure 2.1).

In addition to the broader temporal context of parent–child interactions, positive or negative interactions that occur specifically around bedtime may affect sleep. Parents and school-age children are perhaps most likely to spend extended time in close proximity to each other in the evening hours after work and school. Negative parent–child interactions (e.g., disagreements about homework, social life, or bedtime) may produce feelings of guilt, threat, or anger that disrupt children's sleep. More specifically, harsh parent–child interactions, which involve verbal or physical aggression, are likely to produce feelings of threat and anger, whereas parenting characterized by psychological control may produce feelings of guilt and sadness. When these forms of negative parent–child interactions occur around bedtime, children (and parents) may find it particularly difficult to sleep well. The effect of the timing of positive and negative parent–child interactions on children's sleep is another fruitful direction for future research. In addition, to strengthen confidence in the conceptual propositions discussed above, it will be important for future research to further examine mediation models, such as the possibility that negative parent–child relationships contribute to children's internalizing problems or emotional insecurity which, in turn, contribute to children's sleep problems (e.g., Cousins et al., 2007).

Reciprocal Association between Parenting and Children's Sleep

Appropriate longitudinal models must be tested before we can conclude that negative parenting and children's sleep have reciprocal or transactional effects on one another. However, on the basis of existing research on parenting and child adjustment (Pettit & Arsiwalla, 2008), including research focused on children's sleep (Bell & Belsky, 2008), it seems reasonable to speculate that parenting has at least some effect on children's sleep (paths B, D, E, and F in Figure 2.1), and that children's sleep has at least some effect on parenting (paths C, D, F, and G in Figure 2.1). We have discussed potential explanations for the effects of negative parenting on children's sleep. Much less research is available to explain the potential effects of children's sleep on parenting, but we propose that children and parents' emotion regulation has central importance.

One mechanism through which children's sleep may influence parenting is via the effects of children's sleep on children's self-regulation and behavior that, in turn, shapes parenting in a reciprocal manner (path F in Figure 2.1). Sleep promotes or undermines children's capacity to regulate emotions and exercise executive control over thoughts and behaviors (Dahl, 1996; Sadeh, Gruber, & Raviv, 2003). Indeed, sleep disruptions are linked with children's internalizing problems (Fredriksen, Rhodes, Reddy, & Way, 2004; Gregory & Eley, 2005; Gregory & O'Connor, 2002), as well as externalizing behavior problems, including aggression, conduct problems, and ADHD symptoms (Aronen, Paavonen, Fjallberg, Soininen, & Torronen, 2000; Paavonen, 2004). Thus, sleep may affect how children function across contexts, including how they behave in parent–child contexts. For example, adolescents whose sleep has been disrupted respond to negative emotion cues with more anger, sadness, and fear (Leotta, Carskadon, Acebo, Seifer, & Quinn, 1997). It is likely that optimal sleep promotes children's capacity to regulate negative thoughts and feelings in the context of parent–child interactions, particularly when these interactions are characterized by disagreement or conflict. In turn, well-regulated child behavior may elicit more positive parenting, whereas reactive, dysregulated child behavior may elicit more negative parenting.

In addition, children's sleep may influence parenting through parents' own sleep and corresponding self-regulatory capacity (path G in Figure 2.1). It is well known that parents' sleep is affected by their children's sleep. Most parents of infants (80%), toddlers (70%), preschoolers (64%), and school-aged children (46%) report that they are awakened by their child at least once per week (National Sleep Foundation, 2004). Parents are often kept awake or awakened by their children's sleep problems, and they often attempt to soothe or otherwise intervene when their children are awake at night, potentially contributing to both parental sleep deprivation and psychological distress. For example, sleep problems (e.g., night waking) in infants have been linked with maternal depressive symptoms (Bayer, Hiscock, Hampton, & Wake, 2007; Karraker & Young, 2007) and poorer general health in mothers and fathers (Martin, Hiscock, Hardy, Davey, & Wake, 2007). In preschool- and school-aged samples, children's sleep problems have been linked with poorer maternal sleep quality, and poorer maternal sleep quality has been linked with maternal negative mood, stress, and fatigue (Meltzer & Mindell, 2007; Polimeni et al., 2007). Parents also report more daytime sleepiness when their school-aged children have multiple sleep disorders (Boergers, Hart, Owens, Streisand, & Spirito, 2007). Even in adolescence, maternal and adolescent sleep problems co-occur (Brand, Gerber, Hatzinger, Beck, & Holsboer-Trachsler, 2009).

Thus, children's sleep problems may not only affect parenting via direct effects on children's dysregulated emotions and behaviors (Sadeh, Gruber, & Raviv, 2002), but also via effects on parents' ability to regulate their own emotions and behaviors in the context of their own sleep deprivation. Consistent with this logic, Bell and Belsky (2008) reported that school-aged children's sleep problems predict parental negativity and parents' ability to regulate negative emotions. In addition, Brand, Gerber, and colleagues (2009) reported that maternal sleep problems were linked with adolescent perceptions of negative parenting character-ized by reproach, restriction, and inconsistency. Thus, children's sleep dis-ruptions may doubly diminish positive parent–child interactions, by contributing directly to children's dysregulated emotions and behaviors in the parent–child context, and by limiting parents' sleep and under-mining parents' capacity to regulate emotions in a manner that supports positive parenting.

Conclusions and Future Directions

Childhood sleep problems are prevalent and potentially impairing, yet surprisingly little is known about the effects of parenting and parent–child relationships on children's sleep, particularly during middle child-hood through adolescence, despite the proximity of parenting to children's sleep. There is a relatively small but growing body of evidence suggesting that parenting and parent–child relationships are potentially influential contexts for children's sleep. In particular, we reviewed evidence that parental sleep-related cognitions and behaviors, as well as parent–child interactions that support or undermine children's psychological well-being, may affect children's sleep. We also noted that children's sleep probably affects parenting in a reciprocal manner, by influencing children and parents' self-regulatory capacities in parent–child interaction contexts. Though important, finding associations among dimensions of parenting and children's sleep is perhaps not surprising, and requires more longitudinal and experimental designs to demonstrate causality. Among the challenges ahead are to increase the specificity of parenting and sleep variables examined, elucidate mechanisms and moderators that link parenting and children's sleep, and contextualize associations between parenting and children's sleep in developmental and ecological domains.

One important direction for future research is to identify more specific dimensions of parenting and parent–child relationships (e.g., warmth, conflict) that are most predictive of children's sleep schedule, amount, and quality. In particular, further research on parental involvement and monitoring would be informative because parental monitoring may support sleep hygiene, such as consistent sleep routine and schedule, which are linked with children's daytime emotional, behavioral, and academic functioning (Wolfson & Carskadon, 1998). Identifying characteristics of parents (e.g., mental health, substance use) linked with children's sleep would also shed new light on the parenting context of children's sleep. Parent gender may be an important characteristic to consider, in part, because mothers and fathers may play different roles in children's sleep and because fathers have received so little attention in this literature. Investigating multiple dimensions of parenting (or characteristics of parents) within single studies will be necessary to achieve these objectives.

Characteristics of children may mediate or moderate the effects of parenting and parent–child relationships on children's sleep (see Staples and Bates, chapter 7 in this volume, for relations between children's temperament and sleep). We have identified internalizing symptoms and emotional security as potential mediators, but these hypotheses must be tested empirically. In addition, a substantial body of research has demonstrated that emotional and physiological reactivity can operate as vulnerability or protective factors for behavioral maladjustment in the context of family and parent–child conflict (e.g., El-Sheikh, Kouros, et al., 2009; Erath, El-Sheikh, & Cummings, 2009). Emotional and physiological responses that support adaptive coping may also allow children to preserve adequate sleep in stressful parent–child contexts. In addition, children's sleep may operate as a vulnerability or protective factor in the context of environmental adversity, such as negative parenting. For example, maternal psychological control was associated with anxiety and depression symptoms among children with either objectively examined sleep disturbances or lower SES, but not among children with both higher sleep efficiency and higher SES (El-Sheikh, Hinnant, Kelly, & Erath, 2009). That is, children with higher sleep quality from higher SES families were protected against internalizing symptoms in the context of maternal psychological control. Thus, it may be productive to conceptualize children's sleep not only as an outcome of parenting and parent–child relationships, but also as an individual bioregulatory variable that can provide protection or exacerbate risk.

Future research should also investigate the developmental and cultural context of parenting and children's sleep. Clearly, parents' roles in their children's sleep changes developmentally, yet age-specific information about parenting practices that support or undermine children's sleep has not been well-documented. It is likely, for example, that a developmental shift occurs in the optimal level of active parental involvement (e.g., physical soothing) in children's sleep during childhood, but limited research suggests when this shift may occur or how steep the change ought to be. Greater precision about the developmentally-appropriate balance of responsiveness and autonomy encouragement for children's sleep would be very useful for parents. Studies that chart general parenting and parental sleep-related cognitions and behaviors, as well as children's sleep, over multiple years and across developmental transitions (e.g., transition to school, puberty) will be especially informative.

It is also critical that we advance understanding of whether and how cultural or ecological factors predict children's sleep and moderate associations between parenting and children's sleep. For example, stressful life events have been linked with children's disrupted sleep schedules (e.g., Bates et al., 2002), and social-ecological factors have been documented as moderators of the association between dimensions of parenting and other indices of children's adjustment (e.g., Lansford et al., 2005). Just as children's sleep occurs in the context of parenting, family processes occur in a broader ecological context, and models that incorporate these broader influences would be most informative.

REFERENCES

Adam, E. K., Snell, E. K., & Pendry, P. (2007). Sleep timing and quantity in ecological and family context: A nationally representative time-diary study. *Journal of Family Psychology, 21*, 4–19.

Aronen, E. T., Paavonen, E. J., Fjallberg, M., Soininen, M., & Torronen, J. (2000). Sleep and psychiatric symptoms in school-age children. *Journal of the American Academy of Child and Adolescent Psychiatry, 39*, 502–508.

Barber, B. K., & Harmon, E. L. (2002). Violating the self: Parental psychological control of children and adolescents. In B. K. Barber (Ed.), *Intrusive parenting: How psychological control affects children and adolescents* (pp. 15–52). Washington, DC: American Psychological Association.

Bates, J. E., Viken, R. J., Alexander, D. B., Beyers, J., & Stockton, L. (2002). Sleep and adjustment in preschool children: Sleep diary reports by mothers relate to behavior reports by teachers. *Child Development, 73*, 62–74.

Bayer, J. K., Hiscock, H., Hampton, A., & Wake, M. (2007). Sleep problems in young infants and maternal mental and physical health. *Journal of Paediatrics and Child Health, 43*, 66–73.

Bell, B. G., & Belsky, J. (2008). Parents, parenting, and children's sleep problems: Exploring reciprocal effects. *British Journal of Developmental Psychology, 26*, 579–593.

Blader, J. C., Koplewicz, H. S., Abikoff, H., & Foley, C. (1997). Sleep problems of elementary school children. *Archives of Pediatrics & Adolescent Medicine, 151*, 473–480.

Blampied, N. M., & France, K. G. (1993). A behavioral model of infant sleep disturbance. *Journal of Applied Behavioral Analysis, 26*, 477–492.

Boergers, J., Hart, C., Owens, J. A., Streisand, R., & Spirito, A. (2007). Child sleep disorders: Associations with parental sleep duration and daytime sleepiness. *Journal of Family Psychology, 21*, 88–94.

Brand, S., Gerber, M., Hatzinger, M., Beck, J., & Holsboer-Trachsler, E. (2009). Evidence for similarities between adolescents and parents in sleep patterns. *Sleep Medicine, 10*, 1124–1131. doi:10.1016/j.sleep.2008.12.013.

Brand, S., Hatzinger, M., Beck, J., & Holsboer-Trachsler, E. (2009). Perceived parenting styles, personality traits and sleep patterns in adolescents. *Journal of Adolescence, 32*, 1189–1207. doi:10.1016/j.adolescence.2009.01.010.

Buckhalt, J. A., Wolfson, A. R., & El-Sheikh, M. (2009). Children's sleep and school psychology practice. *School Psychology Quarterly, 24*, 60–69.

Cousins, J. C., Bootzin, R. R., Stevens, S. J., Ruiz, B. S., & Haynes, P. L. (2007). Parental involvement, psychological distress, and sleep: A preliminary examination in sleep-disturbed adolescents with a history of substance abuse. *Journal of Family Psychology, 21,* 104–113.

Cummings, E. M., & Davies, P. T. (2002). Effects of marital conflict on children: Recent advances and emerging themes in process-oriented research. *Journal of Child Psychology and Psychiatry, 43,* 31–63.

Dahl, R. E. (1996). The regulation of sleep and arousal: Development and psychopathology. *Development and Psychopathology, 8,* 3–27.

Dahl., R. E., & El-Sheikh, M. (2007). Considering sleep in a family context: Introduction to the special issue. *Journal of Family Psychology, 21,* 1–3.

Dahl, R. E., & Lewin, D. S. (2002). Pathways to adolescent health: Sleep regulation and behavior. *Journal of Adolescent Health, 31,* 175–184.

El-Sheikh, M., & Buckhalt, J. A. (2005). Vagal regulation and emotional intensity predict children's sleep problems. *Developmental Psychobiology, 46,* 307–317.

El-Sheikh, M., Buckhalt, J. A., Cummings, E. M., & Keller, P. (2007). Sleep disruptions and emotional insecurity are pathways of risk for children. *Journal of Child Psychology and Psychiatry, 48,* 88–96.

El-Sheikh, M., Buckhalt, J. A., Mize, J., & Acebo, C. (2006). Marital conflict and disruption of children's sleep. *Child Development, 77,* 31–43.

El-Sheikh, M., Hinnant, J. B., Kelly, R. J., & Erath, S. A. (2009). Maternal psychological control and child internalizing symptoms: Vulnerability and protective factors across bioregulatory and ecological domains. *Journal of Child Psychology and Psychiatry.* doi:10.1111/j.1469-7610.2009.02140.x

El-Sheikh, M., Kouros, C. D., Erath, S., Cummings, E. M., Keller, P., & Staton, L. (2009). Marital conflict and children's externalizing behavior: Interactions between parasympathetic and sympathetic nervous system activity. *Monographs of the Society for Research in Child Development, 74* (1, Serial No. 231).

Erath, S. A., El-Sheikh, M., & Cummings, E. M. (2009). Harsh parenting and child externalizing behavior: Skin conductance level reactivity as a moderator. *Child Development, 80,* 578–592.

France, K. G., & Blampied, N. M. (1999). Infant sleep disturbance: Description of a problem behaviour process. *Sleep Medicine Reviews, 3,* 265–280.

France, K. G., Blampied, N. M., & Henderson, J. M. T. (2003). Infant sleep disturbance. *Current Paediatrics, 13,* 241–246.

Fredriksen, K., Rhodes, J., Reddy, R., & Way, N. (2004). Sleepless in Chicago: Tracking the effects of adolescent sleep loss during the middle school years. *Child Development, 75,* 84–95.

Germo, G. R. Chang, E. S., Keller, M. A., & Goldberg, W. A. (2007). Child sleep arrangements and family life: Perspectives from mothers and fathers. *Infant and Child Development, 16,* 433–456.

Goldberg, W. A., & Keller, M. A. (2007). Co-sleeping during infancy and early childhood: Key findings and future directions. *Infant and Child Development*, *16*, 457–469.

Gregory, A. M., & Eley, T. C. (2005). Sleep problems, anxiety and cognitive style in school-aged children. *Infant and Child Development*, *14*, 435–444.

Gregory, A. M., & O'Connor, T. G. (2002). Sleep problems in childhood: A longitudinal study of developmental change and association with behavioral problems. *Journal of the American Academy of Child and Adolescent Psychiatry*, *41*, 964–971.

Grusec, J. E., & Davidov, M. (2007). Socialization in the family: The roles of parents. In J. E. Grusec & P. D. Hastings (Eds.), *Handbook of socialization: Theory and research* (pp. 284–308). New York: The Guilford Press.

Johnson, N., & McMahon, C. (2008). Preschoolers' sleep behavior: Associations with parental hardiness, sleep-related cognition and bedtime interactions. *Journal of Child Psychology and Psychiatry*, *49*, 765–773.

Karraker, K. H., & Young, M. (2007). Night waking in 6-month-old infants and maternal depressive symptoms. *Journal of Applied Developmental Psychology*, *28*, 493–498.

Kelly, R. J., Hinnant, J. B., & El-Sheikh, M. (2009). Parenting, children's sleep, and academic functioning: A mediated relationship. Poster session presented at the biennial meeting of the Society for Research on Child Development, Denver, CO.

Lansford, J. E., Chang, L., Dodge, K. A., Malone, P. S., Oburu, P., Palmerus, K.,… Quinn, N. (2005). Physical discipline and children's adjustment: Cultural normativeness as a moderator. *Child Development*, *76*, 1234–1246.

Leotta, C., Carskadon, M. A., Acebo, C., Seifer, R., & Quinn, B. (1997). Effects of acute sleep restriction on affective response in adolescents: Preliminary results. *Sleep Research*, *26*, 201.

Liu, X., Sun, Z., Uchiyama, M., Shibui, K., Kim, K., & Okawa, M. (2000). Prevalence and correlates of sleep problems in Chinese schoolchildren. *Sleep*, *23*, 1053–1062.

Martin, J., Hiscock, H., Hardy, P., Davey, B., & Wake, M. (2007). Adverse associations of infant and child sleep problems and parent health: An Australian population study. *Pediatrics*, *119*, 947–955.

Meijer, A. M., Habekothe, R. T., & Van Den Wittenboer, G. L. H. (2001). Mental health, parental rules and sleep in pre-adolescents. *Journal of Sleep Research*, *10*, 297–302.

Meltzer, L. J., & Mindell, J. A. (2006). Sleep and sleep disorders in children and adolescents. *Psychiatric Clinics of North America*, *29*, 1059–1076.

Meltzer, L. J., & Mindell, J. A. (2007). Relationship between child sleep disturbances and maternal sleep, mood, and parenting stress: A pilot study. *Journal of Family Psychology*, *21*, 67–73.

Mindell, J. A., Owens, J. A., & Carskadon, M. A. (1999). Developmental features of sleep. *Child and Adolescent Psychiatric Clinics of North America, 8*, 695–725.

Morrell, J. M. B. (1999). The role of maternal cognitions in infant sleep problems as assessed by a new instrument, the Maternal Cognitions about Infant Sleep questionnaire. *Journal of Child Psychology and Psychiatry, 40*, 247–258.

Morrell, J., & Cortina-Borja, M. (2002). The developmental change in strategies parents employ to settle young children to sleep, and their relationship to infant sleeping problems, as assessed by a new questionnaire: The Parental Interactive Bedtime Behaviour Scale. *Infant and Child Development, 11*, 17–41.

Morrell, J., & Steele, H. (2003). The role of attachment security, temperament, maternal perception, and care-giving behavior in persistent infant sleeping problems. *Infant Mental Health Journal, 24*, 447–468.

National Sleep Foundation. (2004). *Sleep in America Poll*. Washington, DC: National Sleep Foundation.

Paavonen, J. (2004). *Sleep disturbances and psychiatric symptoms in school-aged children.* (Doctoral dissertation, University of Helsinki, Finland), Retrieved from http://ethesis.helsinki.fi/julkaisut/laa/kliin/vk/paavonen/sleepdis.pdf

Patten, C. A., Choi, W. S., Gillin, J. C., & Pierce, J. P. (2000). Depressive symptoms and cigarette smoking predict development and persistence of sleep problems in US adolescents. *Pediatrics, 106*, 1–9.

Pettit, G. S., & Arsiwalla, D. D. (2008). Commentary on special section on "bidirectional parent–child relationships": The continuing evolution of dynamic, transactional models of parenting and youth behavior problems. *Journal of Abnormal Child Psychology, 36*, 711–718.

Polimeni, M., Richdale, A., & Francis, A. (2007). The impact of children's sleep problems on the family and behavioural processes related to their development and maintenance. *Journal of Applied Psychology, 3*, 76–85.

Ramos, K. D., Youngclarke, D., & Anderson, J. E. (2007). Parental perceptions of sleep problems among co-sleeping and solitary sleeping children. *Infant and Child Development, 16*, 417–431.

Sadeh, A., Flint-Ofir, E., Tirosh, T., & Tikotzky, L. (2007). Infant sleep and parental sleep-related cognitions. *Journal of Family Psychology, 21*, 74–87.

Sadeh, A., Gruber, R., Raviv, A. (2002). Sleep, neurobehavioral functioning, and behavior problems in school-age children. *Child Development, 73*, 405–417.

Sadeh, A., Gruber, R., Raviv, A. (2003). The effects of sleep restriction and extension on school-age children: What a difference an hour makes. *Child Development, 74*, 444–455.

Sadeh, A., Mindell, J. A., Luedtke, K., & Wiegand, B. (2009). Sleep and sleep ecology in the first 3 years: A web-based study. *Journal of Sleep Research, 18*, 60–73.

Sadeh, A., Tikotzky, L., & Scher, A. (2009). Parenting and infant sleep. *Sleep Medicine Reviews.* doi: 10.1016/j.smrv.2009.05.003.

Scher, A. (2001). Attachment and sleep: A study of night waking in 12-month-old infants. *Developmental Psychobiology, 38*, 274–285.

Sheldon, S. H. (2001). Insomnia in children. *Current Treatment Options in Neurology, 3*, 37–50.

Spilsbury, J. C., Storfer-Isser, A., Drotar, D., Rosen, C. L., Kirchner, H. L., & Redline, S. (2005). Effects of the home environment on school-aged children's sleep. *Sleep, 28*, 1419–1427.

Tikotzky, L., & Sadeh, A. (2009). Maternal sleep-related cognitions and infant sleep: A longitudinal study from pregnancy through the 1st year. *Child Development, 80*, 860–874.n

Wolfson, A. R., & Carskadon, M. A. (1998). Sleep schedules and daytime functioning in adolescents. *Child Development, 69*, 875–887.

3

Sleep and Attachment

Peggy S. Keller

Introduction

Both sleep and attachment are critical domains of human functioning and development. Sleep is necessary for health and adjustment, and disruptions to sleep may jeopardize the individual's immune system, cognitive functioning, and emotion and behavior regulation (Dahl & Lewin, 2002; Pilcher & Ott, 1998; Tanaka et al., 2002). The attachment relationship is a familial relationship that is also necessary for health, and an insecure attachment early in life may place children at risk for physical and mental health problems across the lifespan (Diamond & Hicks, 2004; Maunder & Hunter, 2008; Mikulincer & Shaver, 2007). Sleep-wake regulation undergoes significant development during infancy and early childhood, and sleep is often consolidated by the first year of life (Anders, Halpern, & Hua, 1992). During this same period, primary attachment bonds form, and these bonds can typically be classified as secure or insecure (Colin, 1996). Thus, the development of sleep regulation and attachment appear to overlap, raising important questions about their influence on each other (Sagi, Tirosh, Ziv, Guttman, & Lavie, 1998). Despite the importance of both sleep and attachment to development and adaptation, there has been relatively little study of the relations between them. Investigation of relations between sleep and attachment parameters will likely enhance understanding of the individual's adaptation and maladaption processes. Increased study of the role of sleep may augment understanding of a wider range of outcomes associated with insecure attachments (Keller, Buckhalt, El-Sheikh, 2008). Likewise, investigating the role of family functioning, including security of attachment toward significant others, will likely enhance understanding of familial processes that may disrupt children's sleep (Dahl & El-Sheikh, 2007).

The purpose of this chapter is to review studies examining the link between various sleep parameters and attachment across the lifespan, consider various plausible conceptual frameworks that might explain relations between the two domains, and suggest directions for future research. Although the chapter focuses on relations between attachment and sleep in infancy and childhood, attachment relationships are important throughout adulthood. Therefore, relations between sleep and attachment among adults will also be reviewed for a more comprehensive coverage of the topic.

Attachment Theory

Attachment refers to the emotional bond between child and caregiver—usually one or both parents (Bowlby, 1969). Attachment theory was first proposed by Bowlby (1969; 1973; 1980), and has become one of the cornerstone theories of the social sciences (this overview of attachment theory is based on Bowlby, 1969; Bowlby, 1988; Cassidy & Shaver, 1999; Colin, 1996; and Kerns & Richardson, 2005). According to the theory, the attachment bond serves the function of maintaining proximity between young children and their adult caregivers and providing security to the child. As human young are far less developed than the young from many other species, this proximity is necessary for survival. Thus, the classic expressions of the attachment bond are those in which infants make bids for contact with their caregivers, such as by crying, calling out, reaching out, holding onto, or moving toward. As children develop (for example, by becoming more mobile), they use their attachment figures as a secure base from which to explore their environment. In the face of uncertainty, threat, or danger, children quickly return to their attachment figures or look toward them for reassurance. Eventually, children develop internal working models (a set of beliefs and expectations) of their attachment bond, and longer and greater separations from caregivers become normative. For example, a child in school who is picked on by a bully may be able to rely on past experiences of warmth and support from a mother and the resulting internalized view that he or she is loved and valuable, rather than needing the mother's immediate assurance for comfort. In adulthood, romantic partners often become primary attachment figures. However, the quality of the attachment bond during childhood may influence and be similar to the quality of the romantic attachment bond in adulthood.

The development of the attachment bond is based heavily on infants' and children's experience of their caregivers as warm, consistent, and sensitive in meeting their needs, or as cold, unpredictable, and insensitive to their needs. Attachments can generally be classified as secure or insecure. Infants and children who are securely attached view their parents as supportive and consistent, feel comfortable exploring their environment, and seek proximity with their caregivers during times of uncertainty, threat, or danger. The Strange Situation (Ainsworth, Blehar, Waters, & Wall, 1978) is the gold standard procedure for assessing attachment in infancy wherein infants and young children are separated from caregivers, left with a stranger, and reunited with caregivers. During the Strange Situation, secure children are distressed when their caregivers leave them alone or with a stranger, but approach caregivers and are easily soothed by caregivers upon their return.

Children who are insecurely attached view their caregivers as unsupportive and inconsistent; they may have difficulty exploring their environments on their own, but may also have difficulties maintaining proximity with their caregivers. For example, physically or emotionally abused children may be fearful of their environment, but may be wary of seeking comfort from a potentially dangerous parent. Within the broad classification of insecurity, attachment can be further classified as anxious/ambivalent or as avoidant. During the Strange Situation (Ainsworth et al., 1978), anxious/ambivalent children are preoccupied with their caregivers, they may appear either angry or passive during separation or reunion, and their caregivers are unable to sooth them upon reunion. Children who are avoidant show little distress upon separation from their caregivers, they often distract themselves with toys or other activities during separation and reunion, and during reunion they ignore or actively avoid contact with their caregivers. For example, they may pull away from parents when approached. A fourth classification, disorganized or disoriented, originally included children who were not able to be classified in any of the other attachment categories. However, it has since been observed that many of these children exhibit unusual behavior reflecting serious problems within the attachment relationship, and it is now considered a substantive insecure classification (Main & Solomon, 1990).

Similar categories are available for the description of attachment in adulthood. Specifically, adult attachment styles are typically classified as secure, dismissing (similar to avoidant attachment in childhood), pre-occupied (similar to anxious/ambivalent attachment in childhood), or unresolved-disorganized (similar to disoriented/disorganized in child-hood). These classifications may be derived from the Adult Attachment Interview (George, Kaplan, & Main, 1996), which retrospectively assesses childhood attachment to parental figures, or through questionnaires such as the Experiences in Close Relationships Scale (Brennan, Clark, & Shaver, 1998), which assesses current attachment style in reference to romantic partners. Individuals who are dismissing feel uncomfortable with close relationships and have difficulty trusting others. Individuals who are preoccupied tend to view themselves as unworthy of love, feel that their relationships are not as close as they would like them to be, and may be perceived as "clingy" by others. Although it is possible to change attachment classifications over time, it is often the case that insecurely attached children retain their insecure attachment status over the long term (Hamilton, 2000).

Attachment theory can be thought of as part of the broader frame-work of emotion regulation theory. Emotion regulation refers to the identification and modulation of emotional states (such as the intensity or expression of emotion), especially in service of goals (Cole, Martin, & Dennis, 2004; Thompson, 1994). For example, the experience of fear may serve the function of enhancing vigilance to potential threats, or moti-vating adaptive fight or flight responses to danger. Similarly, anger may need to be expressed in socially acceptable ways, and frequently serves the goal of getting attention to one's needs or frightening off adversaries. Emotion may be regulated through neuropsychological processes, atten-tion, cognitive attributions of events, and behavioral responses. With regard to emotion regulation, individuals who are anxiously attached to their caregivers or partners, focus their attention on attachment figures, maintain and express high levels of anxiety or distress in order to achieve proximity to caregivers, and have difficulties down-regulating negative affect after difficult situations have been resolved (Pietromonaco & Feldman Barrett, 1997; Hazan & Shaver, 1987). Individuals who are avoidantly attached focus their attention away from attachment figures, are emotionally inexpressive, and may have difficulties up-regulating affect in order to engage in social interactions (Bartholomew & Horowitz, 1991; Hazan & Shaver, 1987; Pietromonaco & Feldman Barrett, 1997). In contrast, individuals who are securely attached can easily down-regulate their distress once a difficult situation has been resolved, especially through temporarily increased attention and contact with an attachment figure, and are also able to adapt their emotional expression to the demands of various situations. In this way, attachment styles may also be viewed as emotion regulation styles (Mikulincer, Orbach, & Iavnieli, 1998; Pietromonaco, Feldman Barrett, & Powers, 2006). As will be discussed later in the chapter, attachment classification as emotion regulation style will be especially relevant to understanding relations between attachment and sleep. In the section that follows, associations between attachment security and individuals' mental and physical health will be highlighted.

Attachment security is strongly associated with physical and mental health. For example, insecure attachments are associated with self-ratings of poor health in adults (Ciechanowski, Walker, Katon, & Russo, 2002; Fortenberry & Wiebe, 2007). One important reason that insecure attachment may adversely affect physical health is the link between psychological distress and physiological systems, such as the immune system (Diamond & Hicks, 2004; Maunder & Hunter, 2008). Insecurity is also associated with poor coping in patients suffering from chronic disease such as breast cancer (Schmidt, Nachtigall, Wuethrich-Martone, & Strauss, 2002). Insecurely attached children and adults are also at risk for mental health problems such as anxiety disorders (Cassidy, Lichtenstein-Phelps, Sibrava, Thomas, & Borkovec, 2009), depression (Lee & Hankin, 2009), conduct problems (Vando, Rhule-Louie, McMahon, & Spieker, 2008), antisocial behaviors (Bekker, Bachrach, & Croon, 2007), and substance abuse problems (Kassel, Wardle, & Roberts, 2007). Further, interventions designed to enhance attachment security have been found to have positive effects on mental health (Mikulincer & Shaver, 2007).

In sum, a secure attachment with a caregiver or partner is of great importance with far ranging implications for physical and mental health across the lifespan. Later in the chapter, it will be clarified how a better understanding of the development of sleep regulation and sleep problems is likely to be enhanced by taking into account the potential role of attachment relationships.

Empirical Studies of Sleep and Attachment

Despite the critical importance of both sleep and attachment for human development, there has been relatively little empirical investigation of relations between them. The goal of this section is to provide a comprehensive review of studies linking attachment and sleep. Toward that goal, studies that have examined relations between attachment and any sleep parameter (e.g., duration, quality, bedtime resistance) will be reviewed.

Sleep and Attachment in Infancy and Childhood

One of the earliest studies of sleep and attachment examined the attachment of mothers in relation to toddler sleep (Benoit, Zeanah, Boucher, & Minde, 1992). In this study, toddlers were classified as having or not having a sleep disorder based on Richman's (1981) criteria of having settling or waking problems five or more nights per week and at least one of the following: taking more than 30 minutes to settle, waking three or more times per night, awaking for more than 20 minutes during the night, or sleeping in parents' bed because of being upset. All toddlers who had been diagnosed with a sleep problem had mothers who exhibited insecure attachment style as adults in comparison to only 57% of toddlers who had no sleep disorder. Interestingly, children with and without sleep disorders were matched on socioeconomic status (SES), child and mother age, mother marital status, and family size, and there were no group differences in maternal defensiveness, maternal self-esteem, or maternal social support. Thus, only maternal attachment style distinguished between the sleep disordered and non-sleep disordered groups. However, the attachment styles of the toddlers themselves were not examined.

Some studies of attachment and sleep in childhood have examined the impact of sleeping arrangements on the development of the attachment bond. Sagi and colleagues (1994) compared the attachment classifications of infants living in two types of Israeli kibbutzim. Kibbutzim are Jewish communes in which the responsibilities of caregiving are shared on a rotating basis among a group of adults, and have often been the subject of attachment research. Sagi and colleagues (1994) compared infants (aged 14 to 22 months) from kibbutzim in which children and their biological parents spent the night in the same, private living quarters to infants from kibbutzim in which children from several families were placed together for sleep in one room and were watched over by adults who were strangers to them. Infants living in the latter type of kibbutzim therefore did not have access to their primary attachment figures during the night, and any bids for contact with attachment figures were inconsistently met by strangers. The attachments of infants were classified using the Strange Situation procedure, and findings indicated that infants in the communal sleep kibbutzim were more likely to be anxiously attached to their mothers than infants in the private sleep kibbutzim. These differences were observed despite similar background (e.g., SES) characteristics and parenting skills across the two groups. These findings are consistent with results from an earlier study, which suggested that communal, non-parental sleeping arrangements are a risk factor for anxious attachments in infants (Sagi et al., 1985). Sagi and colleagues (1994) suggest that although communal kibbutzim mothers may be warm, sensitive, and consistent with their children during the day, their absence and inability to attend to their children's needs during the night is experienced as dramatically inconsistent parenting on the part of children, leading to attachment insecurity.

More recently, there have been studies of links between children's sleep duration and quality in relation to attachment security with primary caregivers. One notable study was conducted by Scher (2001), in which the Strange Situation procedure was administered to a sample of 12-month-old infants in Israel. Almost all infants were classified as either securely or anxiously attached (there are few infants classified as avoidant in Israeli samples). Scher (2001) distinguished a subgroup of secure infants, those classified as dependent-secure, from the remaining secure infants. Dependent-secure infants are infants who are considered secure but who tend to exhibit some traits of anxious attachment, such as increased intensity of distress during separation from attachment figures. Rates of maternal-reported and actigraphy-assessed infant night waking were similar across infants of various attachment classifications, with infants across all attachment categories showing relatively high levels of night waking. However, mothers of anxiously attached infants or secure-dependent infants reported greater bedtime resistance from their infants than mothers of securely attached infants. Further, infants who exhibited increased night waking scored higher on ratings of proximity seeking behavior toward their mothers during the Strange Situation.

Similar findings were reported in a more recent study of Israeli mother-infant dyads from a different sample (Scher & Asher, 2004). In this study, mothers provided assessments of 12-month-old infants' attachment using a Q-sort method, in which respondents are asked to sort attachment-related statements into those that are or are not characteristic of the child. The Q-sort is a well-established alternative to the Strange Situation (van Ijzendoorn, Vereijken, Bakermans-Kranenburg, & Riksen-Walraven, 2004). Infant sleep was assessed via maternal report, and also with actigraphy. Infants were classified as having a sleep problem if they met Richman's (1981) criteria. Findings indicated that infants who were classified as having a sleep problem were just as likely to be insecurely attached as were infants who did not have a sleep problem. Attachment security of the infant toward the mother was also unrelated to maternal reports of her responsiveness to the infant's night wakings. However, in comparison to insecurely attached infants, infants who were rated as more secure exhibited shorter night waking, based on actigraphy measures of sleep.

Morrell and Steele (2003) conducted a study of 100 infants aged 14 to 16 months (T1). Children's attachment was classified using the Strange Situation and sleep was assessed via maternal questionnaire reports and a two-week maternal diary. One year following T1 participation, children's sleep was reassessed during a second study wave (T2). Using maternal reports, infants were classified as having or not having a sleep problem based on Richman's (1981) criteria. Infants exhibiting sleep problems at T1 were significantly more likely to be anxiously attached at T1, even after controlling for maternal limit setting, infant temperament, and maternal anxiety and depression. Further, severity of night waking at T1 was significantly greater in anxiously attached infants than in avoidantly or securely attached infants. Finally, T1 anxious attachment status significantly predicted T2 sleep problems, even after controlling for T1 sleep problems, infant temperament, maternal limit setting, and maternal anxiety and depression.

Data from the National Institute of Child Health and Human Development Study of Early Child Care (NICHD SECC) also support relations between sleep disruptions and insecure attachments in infants (McNamara, Belsky, & Fearon, 2003). McNamara and colleagues (2003) made use of the large sample provided by the SECC to compare anxiously and avoidantly attached infants at 6 months and 15 months. Infants' attachments were classified using the Strange Situation at 15 months. Infants were classified as having a sleep problem if they met Zuckerman, Stevenson, and Bailey's (1987) maternal report criteria of waking three or more times per night, being awake for an hour or more per night, or the mother's perception of a severe sleep disruption in her infant. Anxiously attached infants were more likely than avoidantly attached infants to have sleep problems at both 6 and 15 months. Further, in comparison to anxiously attached infants, avoidantly attached infants exhibited fewer night wakings based on maternal report at 6 months and shorter night wakings at 15 months.

Only one study to date has examined relations between sleep and attachment in children older than two years. Keller, El-Sheikh, and Buckhalt (2008) assessed sleep and perceived attachment security in a large sample of third-grade children. Children's perceived attachment to parents was assessed via the Inventory of Parent and Peer Attachment (IPPA; Armsden & Greenberg, 1987); the IPPA is one of the most widely used assessments of attachment security for middle childhood. Children's sleep was assessed via self-report on a well-established questionnaire (Sleep Habits Survey; Wolfson & Carskadon, 1998) and seven nights of actigraphy. This study is notable for providing the first examination of both mother–child and father–child attachment security in relation to children's sleep. Findings indicate that greater security in the child's relationship with either the mother or the father was associated with fewer self-reported sleep–wake problems and less self-reported sleepiness. No significant relations between attachment security and objective measures of child sleep were observed. However, significant interactions between objective sleep measures and children's perceived attachments were found in the prediction of children's academic functioning. Specifically, the combination of attachment insecurity and poor objective sleep problems (reduced sleep amount and efficiency) was associated with especially low mathematics achievement scores on standardized tests.

Taken together, these studies suggest that there are links between infants' and children's attachment security to caregivers and various sleep parameters. The majority of studies indicate that anxious attachment security in particular is associated with sleep disruptions. These disruptions include bedtime resistance, night waking, and subjective daytime sleepiness. However, there are a number of gaps in research. Most studies included infants and there is therefore little understanding of relations in middle childhood or adolescence. Further, studies have primarily been cross-sectional and thus shed no light on the direction of relations between these two constructs. Finally, most studies examine attachment in infancy or early childhood, often with small sample sizes and reliance on subjective measures of sleep. There is therefore a critical need for additional research.

Attachment and Sleep in Adulthood

Attachment is important throughout the lifespan, and consideration of adult attachment is therefore required for a comprehensive treatment of relations between attachment and sleep. Notably, while attachment in childhood is in reference to a specific person (e.g., a parent), attachment in adulthood involves approaches to close relationships more generally. Typically, romantic partners will serve as attachment figures, but the attachment style of individuals who are not in romantic relationships can also be evaluated. Common measures of adult attachment ask respondents to rate what they believe and how they feel about close relationships whether they are in one or not.

There are only four known studies of relations between sleep and attachment in adulthood. Scharfe and Eldredge (2001) examined relations between adult attachment style and sleep problems in a sample of college undergraduates. For those students who were in committed romantic relationships, higher ratings of preoccupied or fearful attachments toward romantic partners were associated with greater sleep difficulties; avoidant and dismissive attachments were unrelated to sleep. For those students who were not in committed relationships, the opposite pattern was observed: higher scores on avoidant attachment were associated with sleep problems, while anxious attachment was unrelated to sleep. One possible explanation for these findings is that individuals with more severe anxious attachments may be more likely to always ensure that they are in a romantic relationship, while those individuals with more severe avoidant attachments are less likely to be in romantic relationships; thus, it may be the degree of insecurity, rather than the classification per se, that is relevant to sleep.

A study of married couples offers further support for relations between anxious attachments and sleep problems. Carmichael and Reis (2005) examined scores on the standard measure of adult attachment security (Experiences in Close Relationships Scale; Fraley, Waller, & Brennan, 2000) and also a well-established self-report measure of sleep (Pittsburgh Sleep Quality Index; Buysse, et al., 1991) in a sample of 78 married couples. They found that anxious attachment in the spousal relationship was related to poorer sleep quality for both husbands and wives, even after controlling for depression and general anxiety. Avoidant attachment was unrelated to sleep measures.

Two studies have examined adult sleep using polysomnography in relation to attachment. Troxel and colleagues (2007) considered sleep and attachment in a sample of approximately 100 clinically depressed women. Attachment style was assessed via self-report; participants read descriptions of each attachment classification and chose the one that best represented them. Previously married women with anxious attachment spent the lowest amount of time in stage 3 and stage 4 sleep (these stages are known as deep sleep or slow wave sleep, and are believed to be restorative). Women with anxious attachment also exhibited longer sleep latency than other women. Finally, Sloan and colleagues (2007) examined alpha-EEG anomaly in a small sample of adults referred to a sleep clinic. Alpha-EEG anomaly is the superimposition of alpha waves (which are predominant during wakefulness) on the typical low voltage waves that occur during sleep, and indicates maladaptive arousal levels during the sleep state. The attachment security of participants was assessed via self-report on the Experiences in Close Relationships Scale. Attachment anxiety was associated with greater alpha-EEG anomaly, even after controlling for age. Further, attachment anxiety was not associated with general anxiety or symptoms of depression, suggesting that it is anxiety specific to attachment relationships that is associated with disrupted sleep. Attachment avoidance was not associated with alpha-EEG anomaly.

There are fewer studies investigating relations between sleep and attachment security in adulthood than in infancy and childhood. Nevertheless, existing studies with adults further support relations between anxious attachments and sleep disruptions, and expand sleep parameters examined in relation to attachment security to include sleep architecture problems (e.g., time spent in sleep stages). Further, the only study to find that avoidantly attached individuals have increased sleep problems was conducted with adults. Note that many studies of sleep and attachment concern only those individuals who are in current attachment relationships. Results of Scharfe and Eldrige (2001) suggest that additional research should consider individuals who are not in current relationships and that for such individuals, avoidant attachment may be more strongly linked to sleep.

Relations between Sleep and Attachment: Conceptual Frameworks

It is possible to develop several possible conceptual and theoretical explanations for the relations between sleep and attachment. This section will propose four possible models and evaluate them based on current empirical evidence. Some of these theoretical viewpoints have been explicitly proposed by researchers, others are implicit, while others are being proposed here for the first time. Because there has been relatively little empirical investigation of relations between sleep and attachment, particularly in relation to theory testing and comparison, it is difficult to draw firm conclusions about possible theoretical models. However, it is possible to consider the empirical evidence to date in light of these different conceptual frameworks. These include (1) sleep disruptions as a manifestation of attachment behavior; (2) attachment insecurity as a predictor of sleep disruptions; (3) sleep disruptions as predictors of attachment insecurity; and (4) sleep and attachment as dual products of parenting (see Fig. 1). These conceptualizations and the evidence in support of them are described below.

Sleep Disruptions as Attachment Behavior

One possible conceptual approach to understanding relations between attachment and sleep is to incorporate sleep-wake regulation into the repertoire of attachment behaviors (see Model 1 in Figure 3.1). According to this view, bedtime resistance, night wakings, and similar sleep disruptions are simply manifestations of attachment behavior in much the same way as behavioral and emotional reactions to separation and reunion with the attachment figure (Anders, 1994; Sadeh & Anders, 1993; Moore, 1989; Scher, 2001). In Western nations, infants and children are typically expected to sleep in locations separate from their caregivers (McKenna, 1996); and even in co-sleeping contexts, the unconscious state and darkness associated with sleep represents a condition of significant vulnerability and psychological separation from caregivers. Thus, sleep requires separation from caregivers and represents a potentially dangerous situation. Consistent with attachment theory, this would be expected to elicit proximity-seeking behavior on the part of the infant, such as resistance

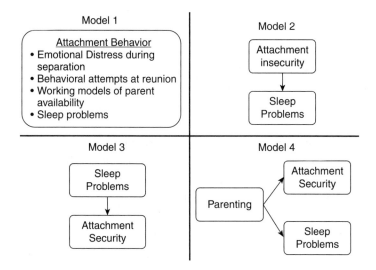

FIGURE 3.1   Possible Conceptual Frameworks for the Relations between Sleep and Attachment. Model 1 pertains to sleep disruptions as a manifestation of attachment behavior. Model 2 and 3 pertain to directional associations between attachment and sleep. Finally, model 4 refers to attachment and sleep disruptions as dual products of parenting.

to being left alone and crying out for the caregiver after being left alone or waking up to find herself alone.

In this sense, sleep disruptions may be viewed as "normal" behavior, exhibited by the majority of children, particularly during developmental periods (such as infancy) when children are highly vulnerable and dependent on caregivers, and have not yet developed internal working models of attachment figures that allow them to be more independent. As children become older, however, the need to maintain close proximity to caregivers diminishes and sleep problems of this nature should resolve. Securely attached children understand that parents are still readily accessible if needed, and feel safe in their sleeping environment (Colin, 1996). On the other hand, anxiously attached children may continue to manifest sleep disruptions, as their experience of inconsistent and insensitive parenting leads to concerns about the availability of parents and drives them to be highly insistent on contact with their caregivers. For these children, bedtime separation from caregivers is likely to continue to be distressing throughout childhood. In adulthood, anxiously attached individuals may continue to have concerns about the security of their environment and the stability of their relationships; these worries may prevent them from relaxing and falling asleep at night.

Interestingly, a much different pattern would be expected for avoidantly attached children. These children respond to inconsistent and insensitive parenting with reduced bids for proximity, as they have come to fear the rejection with which such bids are often met. Thus, even early in their development, avoidant children may exhibit little bedtime resistance or calling out for parents during the night. In adulthood, this pattern of reduced likelihood for sleep disruptions may continue. For example, it is possible that individuals with avoidant attachments fail to form significant relationships, and therefore worry little about their relationships as they are trying to fall asleep. For those avoidant individuals who do have significant relationships, they may use cognitive or other strategies to avoid worrying about them while trying to fall asleep.

The view that sleep disruptions are a manifestation of attachment behavior has been one of the more prominent views espoused by researchers (e.g., Anders, 1994; Sadeh & Anders, 1993; Moore, 1989; Scher, 2001), and has been supported by findings. First, research on the development of sleep regulation demonstrates that sleep disruptions such as night wakings requiring parental intervention routinely occur in almost all infants during the first few months of life (Marcus, Carroll, Donnelly, & Loughlin, 2008), but the prevalence of sleep disruptions rapidly declines as children approach toddlerhood (Anders, Halpern, & Hua, 1992; Zuckerman, Stevenson, & Bailey, 1987). This is consistent with the view that sleep disruptions are an expectable effort to maintain proximity to caregivers during the most vulnerable period of development and subsequently resolve themselves as the attachment relationship matures. Some studies support this model by showing no differences in sleep problems among infants with various attachment classifications during developmental periods involving intense stranger anxiety and proximity-seeking toward caregivers (typically around 12 to 18 months) (Scher, 2001; Scher & Asher, 2004).

Previously reviewed findings supportive of associations between anxious attachments and sleep problems are also consistent with the conceptual view that sleep disruptions constitute manifestations of attachment behavior. Scher (2001), Scher and Asher (2004), as well as Morrell and Steele (2003) each found evidence for anxious attachment being a risk factor for sleep problems in early childhood, especially with sleep problems that persist into toddlerhood; findings were consistent across subjective and objective sleep assessments. Particularly relevant is the McNamara and colleagues study (2003) in which anxious toddlers were more likely to exhibit sleep problems than avoidant toddlers. Keller, El-Sheikh, and Buckhalt (2008) found support for insecure attachment as a risk factor for subjective sleep problems in middle childhood, but this study did not distinguish between anxious and avoidant attachment insecurity. Finally, the results of studies of adult attachment consistently report sleep disruptions for individuals high in anxious but not avoidant attachments (Carmichael & Reis, 2005; Scharfe & Eldredge, 2001; Sloan et al, 2007; Troxel et al, 2007). In sum, empirical evidence is consistent with the view that sleep disruptions are attachment behaviors by showing that night waking and similar sleep disruptions are common in infants of all attachment classifications. At the same time, anxiously attached infants may be at special risk for continued sleep disruptions, including those which may persist into adulthood.

Attachment Insecurity as a Predictor of Sleep Disruptions

A variant on the view that sleep disruptions are a form of attachment behavior is the view that sleep disruptions are the result of attachment insecurity (see Model 2 in Figure 3.1). Because attachment is a product of parent–child interaction, adherents to this view would likely propose that attachment serves as a mediator of, or intervening variable in, relations between parenting and children's sleep. However, there have been no studies of this possible mediation effect. This model differs from the former (Model 1) in that sleep disruptions are considered another one of the many mental and physical health problems that are a consequence of attachment insecurity, rather than an aspect of attachment insecurity per se. This model (Model 2) follows from the framework developed by Dahl (1996), in which sleep and vigilance are considered opponent processes. In other words, one needs to be able to relax in order to fall asleep, whereas in order to maintain awareness of the environment and vigilance to any potential threats or dangers, one must be awake. Thus, anything that promotes feelings of worry or concerns for personal well-being are expected to lead to problems falling and staying asleep because the individual will be overly vigilant and unable to relax.

Attachment insecurity, which is characterized by fears of being alone and unable to access a caregiver, worries that significant others are untrustworthy and unreliable, and unfulfilled desires for closeness with significant others, is therefore a likely factor in the development of sleep problems. In contrast, individuals who feel secure in their attachment relationships likely have fewer relationship worries, and may also worry less about their work, finances, health, or other problems if they believe that their attachment figures can provide reliable social and instrumental support. Securely attached individuals may therefore experience high quality sleep and reduced risk for sleep problems in comparison to their insecurely attached counterparts.

The link between attachment and sleep in this model (Model 2) makes clear the benefits of understanding attachment as part of the broader framework of emotion regulation, as it is the emotion dysregulation aspects of insecurity that are proposed to influence sleep. Specifically, anxiously attached individuals experience high intensity negative affect (often fear and anxiety) and thus have difficulties down-regulating.

The inability to down-regulate negative affect at bedtime may prevent reaching a relaxed sleep state and may lead to increased night wakings and additional problems returning to sleep. Therefore, a reasonable prediction is that anxious attachments are especially detrimental to sleep, while secure and avoidant attachments may be associated with fewer sleep problems. Accordingly, predictions that would be likely made from the attachment as a predictor of sleep disruptions model (Model 2) are similar to the predictions from the sleep disruptions as attachment behavior model (Model 1). It is not surprising that some researchers offer both models as a rationale for relations between children's attachment and sleep, and use both models to explain empirical findings (Benoit et al., 1992). In fact, Model 2 is one of the most frequently used conceptual frameworks (Carmichael & Reis, 2005; Sloan et al., 2007; Troxel et al, 2007).

There is empirical evidence to support the second model. Individuals who are insecurely attached do exhibit high levels of emotional arousal, including physiological arousal. Anxiously attached individuals have been found to report greater emotional distress in response to traumatic events, while avoidant individuals report greater hostility and trauma-related avoidance (Mikulincer, Florian, & Weller, 1993). Some studies indicate that both anxious and avoidant attachments are related to physiological arousal (Carpenter & Kirkpatrick, 2005; Spangler & Grossmann, 1993), while others suggest that anxious but not avoidant attachments are associated with greater physiological arousal. For example, avoidantly attached adults show decreased physiological arousal when suppressing attachment-related thoughts (Fraley & Shaver, 1997). Further, psychological and physiological arousal during the wake to sleep transition is associated with sleep problems such as insomnia (Morin, Rodrigue, & Ivers, 2003; Robertson, Broomfield & Espie, 2007) and poor sleep quality (Smith, Perlis, Smith, Giles, Carmody, 2000). Taken together, these findings offer support for relations between attachment insecurity and increased arousal and vigilance, and suggest that this increased arousal may disrupt sleep.

The reviewed studies linking attachment security with sleep can be interpreted as supportive of the model of attachment as a predictor of sleep problems (Model 2). For example, Troxel and colleagues (2007), Sloan and colleagues (2007), and Carmichael and Reis (2005) each report significant associations between anxious attachments and sleep disruptions in adults. However, a key to establishing attachment insecurity as a predictor of sleep disruptions is to demonstrate the temporal precedence of attachment security. In other words, attachment security must be shown to predict the development of sleep problems over time, rather than simply be associated with sleep disruptions concurrently. In this respect, Morrell & Steele (2003) offer the strongest evidence to date for attachment as a predictor of sleep problems. In this longitudinal study, attachment insecurity predicted greater sleep problems over time, even controlling for earlier sleep problems. Not all current empirical evidence supports Model 2, however. McNamara and colleagues' (2003) findings stemming from their longitudinal study suggest that sleep problems may precede attachment insecurity, although this study did not control for prior attachment insecurity. Further, Scher (2001) and Scher and Asher (2004) report more similarities than differences in sleep across attachment classifications, which is not very consistent with the view that attachment insecurity is a predictor of sleep disruptions. Thus, additional research, and specifically longitudinal research, is needed in order to fully evaluate this model.

Sleep Disruptions as a Predictor of Insecure Attachment

In considering possible explanations for associations between sleep and attachment, it is also important to examine whether sleep disruptions may be a predictors of insecure attachment (Model 3). This direction of association would not be consistent with attachment theory, which proposes that the quality of the attachment relationship is determined almost entirely by the quality of care giving. That is, insecure attachments are the result of insensitive and inconsistent parenting, which then persist into adulthood. However, it is possible to develop a model in which sleep disruptions may be expected to play a causal role in the development of attachment insecurity.

Sleep has been shown to impact daily emotion regulation (Blagrove & Akehurst, 2001), and it has been proposed that one of the functions of sleep is to regulate mood (Roth, Kramer, & Lutz, 1976). For example, earlier sleep onset is associated with better mood and more positive social interactions the next day (Totterdell, Reynolds, Parkinson, & Briner,

1994). Shorter sleep duration has also been linked to symptoms of hypomania in adults diagnosed with bipolar disorder (Leibenluft, Albert, Rosenthal, & Wehr, 1996). Because attachment involves emotion regulation, it is possible that children who do not have adequate sleep are less able to cope with separations from caregivers, have difficulties downregulating their negative affect after achieving contact with caregivers, and are therefore at greater risk for developing insecure attachments.

McNamara, Belsky, and Fearon (2003) also propose that sleep, specifically REM sleep, plays an important role in the formation of social bonds such as the attachment relationship. They cite evidence from several lines of sleep research. For example, during REM sleep, parts of the brain involved in the experience of emotion are highly activated (e.g., Maquet et al., 1996). REM sleep also appears to regulate hormonal systems that are key to mother-child bonding (Van Cauter & Speigel, 1999). Studies have found that REM (as compared to non-REM sleep) is disrupted in rat and monkey infants following separation from mothers (e.g., McKenna & Mosko, 1994). Further, REM sleep is predominant (approximately 60% of sleep) in infancy, during the period when attachment relationships are formed, but subsequently decreases such that adults spend only about 23% of their sleep in REM sleep (Zepelin, 2000). Taken together, these findings do suggest that REM sleep may support the formation of the attachment relationship, and that sleep disruptions may contribute to attachment insecurity at least in part.

Just as cross-sectional studies showing relations between insecure attachment and sleep problems can be interpreted as supportive of a model in which attachment can contribute to sleep disruptions (Model 2), they can also be interpreted as supportive of a model in which sleep disruptions contribute to insecure attachments (Model 3). As previously noted, Morrell and Steele (2003), Keller, El-Sheikh, and Buckhalt (2008), Troxel and colleagues (2007), Sloan and colleagues (2007), as well as Carmichael and Reis (2005) among others do present such cross-sectional findings, and in particular suggest relations between sleep disruptions and anxious attachments. Therefore, a key to establishing sleep problems as a predictor of attachment insecurity is to demonstrate that sleep problems precede the development of insecure attachments, evidence that cross-sectional studies cannot provide. McNamara and colleagues (2003) did find that clinically significant sleep problems based on Zuckerman et al.'s

(1987) criteria and greater night wakings at 6 months were associated with anxious attachments at 15 months. Attachment security was not assessed at 6 months, as the attachment bond is not formally developed until closer to 12 months. This provides evidence that sleep disruptions may precede the development of insecure attachments; however, whether fully formed insecure attachments predict subsequent sleep problems is still a possibility, and this alternative direction of effects is supported by the findings of Morrell and Steele (2003). It should also be noted again that Scher (2001) and Scher and Asher (2004) found few differences in sleep problems across attachment classifications, which is not consistent with the view that sleep problems predict attachment insecurity. Finally, the only study that has examined sleep stages (Troxel et al., 2007) found significant differences in the amount of time insecure and secure adults spend in non-REM sleep, although the amount of time spent in REM sleep was similar across the two groups. Thus, the current evidence for sleep disruptions as a predictor of insecure attachment is equivocal, and future longitudinal research is required to more directly establish the direction of relations between sleep problems and attachment insecurity.

Attachment and Sleep Disruptions as Dual Products of Poor Parenting

A fourth possible model of relations between attachment security/insecurity and sleep disruptions (among children and adults) would posit that they are both predicted by the same variable, namely poor parenting (Figure 3.1). Thus, it is poor parenting that accounts for any observed relations between attachment and sleep problems. In this model, attachment and sleep disruptions are not causally related to each other, after considering the role of parenting. Morrell and Steele (2003) propose a similar view in discussion of their findings. Specifically, they implicate the inconsistency in parenting that produces anxious attachment as the source of sleep problems, noting that inconsistent attention to the cries of infants in their cribs will serve as an intermittent reinforcer of those cries. Accordingly, infants are unsure of whether their bids for crib removal will be met with success, and learn to increase the intensity and frequency of these bids to optimize their success. Thus, the same mechanism is operating on sleep behavior (intermittent reinforcement) that is operating on attachment behavior.

According to attachment theory, caregiver consistency and sensitivity in responding to child needs are the fundamental underpinnings of the development of secure attachment (Colin, 1996). Empirical research supports sensitivity as a moderately strong predictor of attachment security, but also supports the roles of mutuality (harmonious interaction), synchrony (coordinated interaction), stimulation (providing stimuli and encouragement), and positive support (warmth and involvement) on the part of caregivers (De Wolff & van Ijzendoorn, 1997) as predictors of attachment security. The attachment styles then persist into adulthood. There has been relatively little research on whether these aspects of parenting are associated with sleep-wake regulation in children (see Erath and Tu, chapter 2 in this volume, for relations between parenting and children's sleep; Sadeh, Tikotzky, & Scher, 2010, for a recent review on parenting and infant sleep; and Keller, Buckhalt, & El-Sheikh, 2008, for a review on family functioning and children's sleep). Harsh and abusive parenting, lack of parental involvement, and low parental warmth have each been associated with poor sleep in children, including greater night waking and more restless sleep (Glod, Teicher, Hartman, & Harakal,1997; Cousins, Bootzin, Stevens, Ruiz, & Haynes, 2007; Adam, Snell, & Pendry, 2007). There is also a series of studies showing that nighttime limit setting with young children is an especially important parenting skill for promoting the development of healthy sleep-wake regulation (e.g., Burnham, Goodlin-Jones, Gaylor, & Anders, 2002; Sadeh, Flint-Ofir, Tirosh, & Tikotsky, 2007). These studies may be taken as evidence that there are sleep-specific aspects of parenting that are important for children's sleep, while at the same time supporting more general parenting skills as also important. It is currently unknown if these sleep-specific parenting skills and more general parenting skills are related to each other.

Empirical support for the model of children's sleep and attachment as dual products of parenting is, like that of the other models, equivocal. The model can be used to interpret (a) cross-sectional relations between anxious attachments and sleep problems across the lifespan, (b) findings that communal infant sleeping arrangements are associated with insecure attachments, and (c) the longitudinal relations between sleep and attachment identified by McNamara and colleagues (2003) and Morrell and Steele (2003). A strong test of this model (Model 4) would require longitudinal data in which parenting behaviors are shown to precede and predict both sleep and attachment; further, the association between sleep and attachment would be nonsignificant after controlling for parenting. However, Morrell and Steele (2003) found that anxious attachment was associated with risk for sleep problems even after controlling for maternal limit setting, and other studies suggest that parenting does not account for the association between sleep and attachment (Benoit et al., 1992). Note also that inconsistent and insensitive parenting is associated with all insecure attachment classifications (anxious, avoidant, and disorganized). If it is inconsistent parenting rather than attachment that predicts sleep problems, then any attachment classification associated with inconsistent parenting would be expected to be correlated with sleep problems. Yet, the majority of studies implicate anxious attachments rather than avoidant or disorganized attachment classifications in associations with sleep problems. Thus, among the different models considered as plausible explanations for relations between attachment and sleep, the dual products of the parenting model has received the least support. At the same time, none of the reviewed studies have included measures of current parenting received by children or prior parenting received by adults. Thus, this model has yet to receive adequate investigation.

Conclusions and Future Directions

Attachment and sleep are both critical to human adaptation and development, yet there has been remarkably little research on relations between them. There are only a handful of known studies with adults, and a slightly larger number of studies with infants/children, most of which are cross-sectional. The few studies that have been conducted suggest that during the period when the attachment bond is first forming, the necessary separation from caregivers that occurs during sleep may be experienced as distressing for children, resulting in bedtime resistance and night wakings. Securely attached children are eventually able to become more independent of their caregivers and have an easier time settling and falling asleep, while those who have anxious attachments may continue to experience sleep-related distress and be at risk for sleep problems, which may persist into adulthood. Evidence has been found that night waking, subjective sleep problems, and altered sleep structure may be the most likely sleep disruptions. However, possible disruptions such as difficulty falling asleep have yet to be investigated, and additional research is needed to improve understanding of the specific sleep problems that may arise.

There are a variety of possible conceptual models for explaining the findings of studies of sleep and attachment, including (1) sleep disruptions as a manifestation of attachment behavior; (2) attachment as a predictor of sleep disruptions; (3) sleep disruptions as predictors of insecure attachment; and (4) sleep and attachment as dual products of parenting. Each of these models has received some empirical support, but none has undergone rigorous testing. Current research has been weak in the development of conceptual models, including the consideration of alternative models. There is therefore a critical need for additional research on relations between attachment and sleep, especially with objective measures of sleep, and longitudinal investigations that attempt to evaluate the possible theoretical models. Further, future research concurrently investigating attachment and sleep as interactive or intervening predictors of mental and physical health outcomes will advance research beyond establishing simple bivariate relations between sleep and attachment. Keller, El-Sheikh, and colleague (2008) represents the first such attempt at process-oriented research, and suggests that the impact of attachment security on children's functioning may depend on whether they obtain adequate, high-quality sleep. Thus, sleep may serve as a protective factor against negative familial influences on child development and therefore represent an important target for prevention and intervention efforts.

REFERENCES

Adam, E. K., Snell, E. K., & Pendry, P. (2007). Sleep timing and quantity in ecological and family context: A nationally representative time-diary study. *Journal of Family Psychology*, 21, 4–19.

Ainsworth, M., Blehar, M., Waters, E., & Wall, S. (1978). *Patterns of attachment*. Hillsdale, NJ: Lawrence Erlbaum.

Anders, T. F. (1994). Infant sleep, nighttime relationships, and attachment. *Psychiatry: Interpersonal and Biological Processes*, 57, 11–21.

Anders, T. F., Halpern, L. F., & Hua, J. (1992). Sleeping through the night: A developmental perspective. *Pediatrics*, 90, 554–560.

Armsden, G. C., & Greenberg, M. T. (1987). The inventory of parent and peer attachment: Individual differences and their relationship to psychological well-being in adolescence. *Journal of Youth and Adolescence, 16*, 427–454.

Bartholomew, K., & Horowitz, L. M. (1991). Attachment styles among young adults: A test of a four-category model. *Journal of Personality and Social Psychology, 61*, 226–244.

Bekker, M. H. J., Bachrach, N., & Croon, M. A. (2007) The relationship of antisocial behavior with attachment styles, autonomy-connectedness, and alexithymia. *Journal of Clinical Psychology, 63*, 507–527.

Benoit, D., Zeanah, C. H., Boucher, C., & Minde, K. K. (1992). Sleep disorders in early childhood: Association with insecure maternal attachment. *Journal of the American Academy of Child and Adolescent Psychiatry, 31*, 86–93.

Blagrove, M., & Akehurst, L. (2001). Personality and the modulation of effects of sleep loss on mood and cognition. *Personality and Individual Differences, 30*, 819–828.

Bowlby, J. (1969). *Attachment and loss: Vol. 1. Attachment.* New York: Basic Books.

Bowlby, J. (1973). *Attachment and loss: Vol. 2. Separation: Anxiety and anger.* New York: Basic Books.

Bowlby, J. (1980). *Attachment and loss: Vol. 3. Loss: Sadness and depression.* New York: Basic Books.

Bowlby, J. (1988). *A secure base: Parent–child attachment and healthy human development.* New York: Basic Books.

Brennan, K. A., Clark, C. L., & Shaver, P. R. (1998). Self-report measurement of adult attachment: An integrative overview. In J. A. Simpson & W. S. Rholes (Eds.). *Attachment theory and close relationships* (pp. 46–76). New York: Guilford Press.

Burnham, M. M., Goodlin-Jones, B. L., Gaylor, E. E., & Anders, T. F. (2002). Nighttime sleep-wake patterns and self-soothing from birth to one year of age: A longitudinal intervention study. *Journal of Child Psychology and Psychiatry, 43*, 713–725.

Buysse, D. J., Reynolds, C. F., Monk, T. H., Hoch, C. C., Yeager, A. L., & Kupfer, D. J. (1991). Quantification of subjective sleep quality in healthy elderly men and women using the Pittsburgh Sleep Quality Index (PSQI). *Sleep: Journal of Sleep Research and Sleep Medicine, 14*, 331–338.

Carmichael, C. L., & Reis, H. T. (2005). Attachment, sleep quality, and depressed affect. *Health Psychology, 24*, 526–531.

Carpenter, E. M., & Kirkpatrick, L. A. (2005). Attachment style and presence of a romantic partner as moderators of psychophysiological responses to a stressful laboratory situation. *Personal Relationships, 3*, 351–367.

Cassidy, J., Lichtenstein-Phelps, J., Sibrava, N. J., Thomas, C. L., & Borkovec, T. D. (2009). Generalized anxiety disorder: Connections with self-reported attachment. *Behavior Therapy, 40*, 23–38.

Cassidy, J., & Shaver, P. (Eds.). (1999). Handbook of attachment: Theory, research, and clinical applications. New York: Guilford Press.

Ciechanowski, P. S., Walker, E. A., Katon, W. J., & Russo, J. E. (2002). Attachment theory: A model for health care utilization and somatization. *Psychosomatic Medicine, 64*, 660–667.

Cole, P. M., Martin, S. E., & Dennis, T. A. (2004). Emotion regulation as a scientific construct: Methodological challenges and directions for child development research. *Child Development, 75*, 317–333.

Colin, V. L. (1996). *Human attachment*. Philadelphia, PA: Temple University Press.

Cousins, J. C., Bootzin, R. R., Stevens, S. J., Ruiz, B. S., & Haynes, P. L. (2007). Parental involvement, psychological distress, and sleep: A preliminary examination in sleep-disturbed adolescents with a history of substance abuse. *Journal of Family Psychology, 21*, 104–113.

Dahl, R. E. (1996). The regulation of sleep and arousal: Development and psychopathology. *Development and Psychopathology, 8*, 3–27.

Dahl, R. E., & El-Sheikh, M. (2007). Considering sleep in a family context: Introduction to the special issue. *Journal of Family Psychology, 21*, 1–3.

Dahl, R. E., & Lewin, D. S. (2002). Pathways to adolescent health sleep regulation and behavior. *Journal of Adolescent Health, 31*, 175–184.

De Wolff, M. S., & van Ijzendoorn, M. H. (1997). Sensitivity and attachment: A meta-analysis on parental antecedents of infant attachment. *Child Development, 68*, 571–591.

Diamond, L. M., & Hicks, A. M. (2004) Psychobiological perspectives on attachment: Implications for health over the lifespan. In W. S. Rholes & J. A. Simpson (Eds.), *Adult attachment: Theory, research, and clinical implications* (pp. 240–263). New York, NY: Guilford Press.

Fortenberry, K. T., & Wiebe, D. J. (2007). Medical excuse making and individual differences in self-assessed health: The unique effects of anxious attachment, trait anxiety, and hypochondriasis. *Personality and Individual Differences, 43*, 83–94.

Fraley, R. C., & Shaver, P. R. (1997). Adult attachment and the suppression of unwanted thoughts. *Journal of Personality and Social Psychology, 73*, 1080–1091.

Fraley, R. C., Waller, N. G., & Brennan, K. A. (2000). An item response theory analysis of self-report measures of adult attachment. *Journal of Personality and Social Psychology, 78*, 350–365.

George, C., Kaplan, N., & Main, M. (1996). The adult attachment interview protocol (3rd ed.). Unpublished Manuscript, Department of Psychology, University of California at Berkeley.

Glod, C. A., Teicher, M. H., Hartman, C. R., & Harakal, T. (1997). Increased nocturnal activity and impaired sleep maintenance in abused children. *Journal of the American Academy of Child and Adolescent Psychiatry, 36*, 1236–1243.

Hamilton, C. E. (2000). Continuity and discontinuity of attachment from infancy through adolescence. *Child Development, 71*, 690–694.

Hazan, C., & Shaver, P. R. (1987). Romantic love conceptualized as an attachment process. *Journal of Personality and Social Psychology, 52*, 511–524.

Kassel, J. D., Wardle, M., & Roberts, J. E. (2007). Adult attachment security and college student substance use. *Addictive Behaviors, 32*, 1164–1176.

Keller, P. S., Buckhalt, J. A., & El-Sheikh, M. (2008). Links between family functioning and children's sleep. In A. Ivanenko (Ed.), *Sleep and psychiatric disorders in children and adolescents*. New York, NY: U.S. Books.

Keller, P. S., El-Sheikh, M., & Buckhalt, J. A. (2008). Children's attachment to parents and their academic functioning: Sleep disruptions as moderators of effects. *Journal of Developmental and Behavioral Pediatrics, 29*, 441–449.

Kerns, K. A., & Richardson, R. A. (Eds.). (2005). *Attachment in middle childhood.* New York: Guilford Press.

Lee, A., & Hankin, B. L. (2009). Insecure attachment, dysfunctional attitudes, and low self-esteem predicting prospective symptoms of depression and anxiety during adolescence. *Journal of Clinical Child and Adolescent Psychology, 38*, 219–231.

Leibenluft, E., Albert, P. S., Rosenthal, N. E., & Wehr, T. A. (1996). Relationship between sleep and mood in patients with rapid-cycling bipolar disorder. *Psychiatry Research, 63*, 161–168.

Main, M., & Solomon, J. (1990). Procedures for identifying infants as disorganized/disoriented during the Ainsworth Strange Situation. In M. T. Greenberg, D. Cicchetti, & E. M. Cummings (Eds.), *Attachment in the preschool years: Theory, research, and intervention* (pp. 121–160). Chicago: University of Chicago Press.

Maquet, P., Peters, J., Aerts, J., Delfiore, G., Degueldre, C., Luxen, A., & Franck, G. (1996). Functional neuroanatomy of human rapid-eye-movement sleep and dreaming. *Nature, 383*, 163–166.

Marcus, C. L., Carroll, J. L., Donnelly, D. F., & Loughlin, G. M. (Eds.) (2008). *Sleep in children: Developmental changes in sleep patterns*. New York, NY: Informal Health Care.

Maunder, R. G., & Hunter, J. J. (2008). Attachment relationships as determinants of physical health. *The Journal of the American Academy of Psychoanalysis and Dynamic Psychiatry, 36*, 11–32.

McKenna, J. J. (1996). Sudden Infant Death Syndrome in cross-cultural perspective: Is infant-parent cosleeping protective? *Annual Review of Anthropology, 25*, 201–216.

McKenna, J. J., & Mosko, S. S. (1994). Sleep and arousal, synchrony and independence, among mothers and infants sleeping apart and together (same bed): An experiment in evolutionary medicine. *Acta Paediatrica Supplement, 397*, 94–102.

McNamara, P., Belsky, J., & Fearon, P. (2003). Infant sleep disorders and attachment: Sleep problems in infants with insecure-resistant versus insecure-avoidant attachments to mother. *Sleep and Hypnosis, 5,* 7–16.

Mikulincer, M., Florian, V., & Weller, A. (1993). Attachment styles, coping strategies, and posttraumatic psychological distress: The impact of the Gulf War in Israel. *Journal of Personality and Social Psychology, 64,* 817–826.

Mikulincer, M., Orbach, I., & Iavnieli, D. (1998). Adult attachment style an affect regulation: Strategic variations in subjective self-other similarity. *Journal of Personality and Social Psychology, 75,* 436–448.

Mikulincer, M., & Shaver, P. R. (2007). Boosting attachment security to promote mental health, prosocial values, and inter-group tolerance. *Psychologial Inquiry, 18,* 139–156.

Moore, M. S. (1989). Disturbed attachment in children: A factor in sleep disturbance, altered dream production and immune dysfunction: 1. Not safe to sleep: Chronic sleep disturbance in anxious attachment. *Journal of Child Psychotherapy, 15,* 99–111.

Morin, C. M., Rodrigue, S., Ivers, H. (2003). Role of stress, arousal, and coping skills in primary insomnia. *Psychosomatic Medicine, 65,* 259–267.

Morrell, J., & Steele, H. (2003). The role of attachment security, temperament, maternal perception, and care-giving behavior in persistent infant sleeping problems. *Infant Mental Health Journal, 24,* 447–468.

Pietromonaco, P. R., & Feldman Barrett, L. (1997). Working models of attachment and daily social interactions. *Journal of Personality and Social Psychology, 73,* 1409–1423.

Pietromonaco, P. R., Feldman Barrett, L., & Powers, S. I. (2006). Adult attachment theory and affective reactivity and regulation. In D. K. Snyder, J. A. Simpson, & J. N. Hughes (Eds.), *Emotion regulation in couples and families: Pathways to dysfunction and health* (pp. 57–74). Washington DC: American Psychological Association.

Pilcher, J. J., & Ott, E. S. (1998). The relationships between sleep and measures of health and well-being in college students: A repeated measures approach. *Behavioral Medicine, 23,* 170–178.

Richman, N. (1981). A community survey of characteristics of one-to-two year olds with sleep disruptions. *Journal of the American Academy of Child Psychiatry, 20,* 281–291.

Robertson, J. A., Broomfield, N. M., Espie, C. A. (2007). Prospective comparison of subjective arousal during the pre-sleep period in primary sleep-onset insomnia and normal sleepers. *Journal of Sleep Research, 16,* 230–238.

Roth, T., Kramer, M., & Lutz, T. (1976). The effects of sleep deprivation on mood. *The Psychiatric Journal of the University of Ottawa, 1,* 136–139.

Sadeh, A., Tikotzky, L., & Scher, A. (2010). Parenting and infant sleep. *Sleep Medicine Reviews, 14,* 89–96.

Sadeh, A. & Anders, T. F. (1993). Infant sleep problems: Origins, assessment, interventions. *Infant Mental Health Journal, 14,* 17–34.

Sadeh, A., Flint-Ofir, E., Tirosh, T. & Tikotsky, L. (2007). Infant sleep and parental sleep-related cognitions. *Journal of Family Psychology, 21,* 74–87.

Sagi, A., Donnell, F., van Ijzendoorn, M. H., Mayseless, O., & Aviezer, O. (1994). Sleeping out of home in a kibbutz communal arrangement: It makes a difference for infant-mother attachment. *Child Development, 65,* 992–1004.

Sagi, A., Lamb, M. E., Lewkowicz, K., Shoham, R., Dvir, R., & Estes, E. (1985). Security of infant-mother, -father, and -metapelet attachments among kibbutz-reared Israeli children. In I. Bretherton & E. Waters (Eds.), Growing points in attachment theory and research (pp. 257–275). *Monographs of the Society for Research in Child Development, 50* (1–2, Series no. 209).

Sagi, A., Tirosh, E., Ziv, Y. Guttmann, S., & Lavie, P. (1998). Attachment and sleep patterns in the first two years of life. *Infant Behavior and Development, 21,* 665.

Scharfe, E., & Eldredge, D. (2001). Association between attachment representations and health behaviors in late adolescence. *Journal of Health Psychology, 6,* 295–307.

Scher, A. (2001). Attachment and sleep: A study of night waking in 12-month-old infants. *Developmental Psychobiology, 38,* 274–285.

Scher, A., & Asher, R. (2004). Is attachment security related to sleep-wake regulation? Mothers' reports and objective sleep recordings. *Infant Behavior and Development, 27,* 288–302.

Schmidt, S., Nachtigall, C., Wuethrich-Martone, O., & Strauss, B. (2002). Attachment and coping with chronic disease. *Journal of Psychosomatic Research, 53,* 763–773.

Sloan, E. P., Maunder, R. G., Hunter, J. J., & Moldofsky, H. (2007). Insecure attachment is associated with the alpha-EEG anomaly during sleep. *Biopsychosocial Medicine, 1,* 20–25.

Smith, M. T., Perlis, M. L., Smith, M. S., Giles, D. E., Carmody, T. P. (2000). Sleep quality and presleep arousal in chronic pain. *Journal of Behavioral Medicine, 23,* 1–13.

Spangler, G., & Grossmann, K. E. (1993). Biobehavioral organization in securely and insecurely attached infants. *Child Development, 64,* 1439–1450.

Tanaka, H., Taira, K., Arakawa, M., Masuda, A., Yamamoto, Y., Komoda, Y., … Shirakawa, S. (2002). An examination of sleep health, lifestyle and mental health in junior high school students. *Psychiatry and Clinical Neurosciences, 56,* 235–236.

Thompson, R. A. (1994). Emotion regulation: A theme in search of a definition. *Monographs of the Society for Research in Child Development, 59* (2–3), 25–52.

Totterdell, P., Reynolds, S., Parkinson, B., & Briner, R. B. (1994). Associations of sleep with everyday mood, minor symptoms and social interaction experience. *Sleep, 17,* 466–475.

Troxel, W. M., Cyranowski, J. M., Hall, M., Frank, E., & Buysse, D. J. (2007). Attachment anxiety, relationship context, and sleep in women with recurrent major depression. *Psychosomatic Medicine, 69,* 692–699.

Van Cauter, E. S. & Speigel, K. (1999). Circadian and sleep control of hormonal secretions. In F. Turek & P. C. Zee (Eds.). *Regulation of sleep and circadian rhythms* (pp. 397–421). New York, NY: Marcel Dekker.

van Ijzendoorn, M. H., Vereijken, C. M. J. L., Bakermanns-Kranenburg, J., & Riksen-Walraven, J. M. (2004). Assessing attachment security with the attachment Q-set: Meta-analytic evidence for the validity of the observer AQS. *Child Development, 75,* 1188–1213.

Vando, J., Rhule-Louie, D. M., McMahon, R. J., & Spieker, S. J. (2008). Examining the link between infant attachment and child conduct problems in grade 1. *Journal of Child and Family Studies, 17,* 615–628.

Wolfson, A. R., & Carskadon, M. A. (1998). Sleep schedules and daytime functioning in adolescents. *Child Development, 69,* 875–887.

Zepelin, H. (2000). Mammalian sleep. In M. H. Kryger, T. Roth, & W. C. Dement (Eds.). *Principles and practice of sleep medicine,* (3rd ed) (pp. 82–92). Philadelphia, PA: Saunders.

Zuckerman, B., Stevenson, J., & Bailey, V. (1987). Sleep problems in early childhood: Continuities, predictive factors, and behavioral correlates. *Pediatrics, 80,* 664–671.

4

Parental Psychopathology and Children's Sleep

Ronald Seifer

Introduction

Children's sleep may be viewed from multiple perspectives. First and foremost, we can strive to understand the quality of children's sleep, as it has downstream effects on individual daytime functioning, health, and psychological well-being. In addition, children's sleep may be understood regarding how characteristics of the family and the broader social context affect its quality. In turn, variation in children's sleep quality may be helpful in understanding effects they have on other family members. These multiple perspectives are particularly germane to the focus of this chapter—the association of parental psychopathology and children's sleep.

Parental psychopathology is a well-identified risk factor for children's development in many domains. The epidemiology of cross-generational occurrence of mental illness was established decades ago, and our basic understanding has remained unchanged. Many diagnoses, when present in the parent generation (G1), are seen more frequently in the child generation (G2). For example, schizophrenia has a 1% prevalence in the general population; in children with one schizophrenic, the prevalence is about 10%. Other more common diagnoses (such as depression or anxiety) also reveal increases over population norms in the G2 offspring of affected parents (Seifer, 1995).

Cross-generational transmission of specific disorders tells only a small part of the story, which if far more complicated than simple familial transmission would imply. The intergenerational pattern of mental illness is a field where nature-nurture debates are intense (Gotlib & Hammen, 2009). Furthermore, the specificity of cross-generational patterns is weak. That is, G2 children are at risk not only for the specific condition found in the G1 parents, but for other mental illness, sub-threshold manifestations of disorders, impaired psychological functioning, and generally poor psychosocial adaptation (Seifer, 1995). The complexity of these cross-generational influences has led researchers to examine a wide variety of behavioral characteristics in both parents and children in the search for clues regarding the mechanisms by which G2 children succumb to the risks conferred by the G1 parents.

Sleep Characteristics

As would be expected, the large majority of studies examining children's sleep in the context of parental psychopathology are concerned with the specific measures of sleep, such as bedtime, rise time, efficiency, or duration (as opposed to more functional consequences of sleep, such as emotional lability or poor performance). Furthermore, the existing literature is dominated by questionnaire and activity-based measures of sleep. I will begin with the largest portion of this literature—sleep characteristics during infancy and early childhood. Following this will be shorter sections on middle childhood and adolescence (reflective of the smaller base of studies in the literature). I will follow these descriptions of the empirical literature with integrative material on methodolgic issues (such as sleep assessment strategies, informant confounds, and psychopathology assessment), as well as theoretical integration of the available literature.

Infancy and Early Childhood

Early in the life of children, maternal depression is a focus of study for two reasons. First, depression is the most common serious manifestation of psychopathology, affecting 25–40% of women by the time they have completed their childbearing years (Gotlib & Hammen, 2009). Second, depression is a particular problem during the perinatal period; although diagnosis of major depression is no more common around pregnancy and childbirth than at other times during young adulthood (Murray & Cooper, 1997). The literature on children's sleep follows this lead.

The early report of Zuckerman, Stevenson, and Bailey (1987) is indicative of many studies that follow in this domain. Data were obtained from surveys during pediatric visits of mothers in the United Kingdom who had participated in a trial of mother's informational and support groups following the birth of their child. The main finding was that maternal depressive symptoms, measured by a 30-item general health questionnaire, was associated with child sleep problems (assessed by maternal report) at eight months of age. About twice as many children of depressed mothers (using a cutoff indicating mild to moderate symptom levels) were reported to have sleep problems compared with nondepressed mothers. Follow-up at 30 months of age did not reveal a depression-sleep association. Data about depression and sleep problems were both obtained via mother report.

Three reports from a large-scale survey conducted in Australian health centers (initiated at the time of hearing screening at seven to nine months of age) also indicate an association of depression and child sleep problems. About half of the 738 mothers reported sleep problems in their infants around eight months of age—apparently defined by frequent night wakings (Hiscock & Wake, 2001). Like the Zuckerman and colleagues' (1987) report, the rate of reported infant sleep problems was nearly doubled among the women reporting high levels of depression symptoms (on the Edinburgh Postnatal Depression Scale; Cox, Holden, Sagovsky, 1987), which accounted for about one-third of the sample. Specific sleep characteristics, such as longer time to fall asleep, higher number and longer duration of night wakings, less co-sleeping, and more nursing child to sleep were associated with higher depression symptoms (Hiscock & Wake, 2001). There was some indication (although no statistical tests) that among mothers above the depression symptom cutoff, those with higher symptom levels reported more sleep problems in their infants (Hiscock & Wake, 2001).

Following the initial survey assessment, 156 of the mother-infant pairs who reported sleep problems were enrolled in a randomized trial to test the efficacy of a three-week sleep intervention (based on increasing time to respond to infant distress during the sleep period; Hiscock & Wake, 2002). The intervention was effective in reducing both reported infant sleep problems and mothers' depression symptoms (Hiscock & Wake, 2002). When the children were three to four years of age, 114 of the 156 intervention families were followed up with questionnaires (Lam, Hiscock, & Wake, 2003). About one-third of the children were reported to have sleep problems. Mothers' depression symptoms were higher in the group reporting sleep problems than in the group not reporting such problems. Unlike the initial report, data were not presented in terms of depression cutoff scores, but rather as mean values within the sleep problem groups (Lam et al., 2003). In these reports, mothers were the informant for both depression and child sleep problems.

The Avon Longitudinal Study of Parents and Children (ALSPAC) included more than 11,000 births over a 20-month period in the United Kingdom. Sleep data were collected at 6, 18, and 30 months of age. Analyses were conducted on total sleep time, night wakings, and sleep problems (e.g., bedtime refusal, nightmares, early awakening—18 and 30 months only). Depression and anxiety were measured prenatally (18 and 32 weeks gestation) and postnatally (8 weeks, 8 months). Prenatal depression and anxiety was unrelated to reported infant sleep at six months of age. In contrast, all prenatal indicators of depression and anxiety were associated with more night wakings and sleep problems (but not total sleep time) in infants and young children at 18 and 30 months of age. Postnatal depression and anxiety were associated with child sleep problems at all ages, but the patterns were more varied. Eight-*week* anxiety was associated with all indicators of sleep disturbance in infants except number of night wakings at six months and total sleep time at 18 months. Similarly, eight-*week* anxiety was associated with all indicators of sleep disturbance except number of night wakings at six months. Eight-*month* anxiety was associated with all sleep disturbance indicators in infants except total sleep time at six and 18 months of age. Eight-*month* depression was associated with all indictors of sleep disturbance at all ages. Additional analyses indicated that prenatal anxiety and depression were strong indicators of infant sleep after controlling for postnatal anxiety/depression and other social-demographic variables; postnatal depression and anxiety were less robust in predicting sleep when prenatal and social-demographic factors were controlled (O'Connor et al., 2007). As in the prior studies described, mothers were the source of both mood (depression, anxiety) and child sleep data.

Data from the Canadian National Longitudinal Study of Child and Youth employed survey data to examine more complex associations of parent/family characteristics, children's sleep, and behavioral outcomes when children were two to three years of age (Reid, Hong, & Wade, 2009). A four-item sleep problems aggregate was used (trouble falling asleep, bedtime resistance, problems staying asleep, and restless sleep). Sleep problems were predicted by internalizing and externalizing behavior problems after controlling for child characteristics, social-demographic variables, family functioning, and parenting practices. When structural models were examined, direct paths from parent depression to child sleep problems and from sleep problems to child internalizing/externalizing behavior were significant. Furthermore, indirect paths (generally mediated by parental depression) for demographics, family dysfunction, and negative parenting to sleep problems were also significant. Again, data regarding depression, child sleep problems, and child behavioral problems were all provided by the mother.

In previous work in our own lab, we identified mothers with diagnosed depression, bipolar disorder, anxiety disorder, other illness, and no mental illness (Seifer, Sameroff, Dickstein, Hayden, & Schiller, 1996). When children were two and a half years of age, mothers completed a sleep habits questionnaire developed in our laboratory. Family functioning (e.g., problem solving, communication, affective involvement and responsiveness) was assessed by both structured interview and observation of family meals. Specific diagnosis in mothers was unrelated to any of the child sleep measures. Presence of any mental illness was associated with reported daytime sleepiness, and higher functional impairment was associated with more bedtime problems. Overall family functioning was associated with fewer bedtime problems and longer sleep periods in children. In this study mothers provided information about children's sleep, their own mental health status, and participated in the interview portion of family functioning; the observation portion of family functioning was coded by trained observers.

In another study in our lab (unpublished data), mothers were diagnosed with psychopathology (depression, anxiety, no illness) during pregnancy with the study child (12–30 months of age). Child sleep was measured by a sleep habits questionnaire, diary methods, and actigraphy. Family functioning was assessed by direct interview and observation.

As in the previous study from our laboratory (Seifer, Sameroff, Dickstein, Hayden, & Schiller, 1996), maternal diagnosis was not associated with child sleep, but symptom level was related to bedtime problems and daytime sleepiness indexed by questionnaire. Poorer family functioning measured by structured interview with all family members (Dickstein et al., 1998) was also associated with more bedtime problems on the questionnaire and more diary night wakings. For neither symptoms nor family functioning was there any association with children's sleep examined via actigraphy. The maternal psychopathology, child sleep questionnaire/ diary, and interview portion of family functioning all involved information from the mother; actigraphy and observed family functioning were collected by objective methods.

Secondary data analysis of the NICHD Study of Early Child Care and Youth Development examined maternal depression and child sleep (Warren, Howe, Simmens, & Dahl, 2006). Data for children between 1 month and 36 months of age were used—four measures of child sleep (6, 15, 24, and 36 months) and five measures of maternal depression (1, 6, 15, 24, and 36 months). Sleep was indexed by frequency and duration of night wakings, while depression was measured using the Center of Epidemiological Studies Depression scale (CES-D; Radloff, 1977). The primary focus of these analyses was (1) the correspondence between the trajectories of sleep and depression, and (2) cross-lag type analyses used to infer direction of effect. The trajectory analyses revealed no correspondence between the slope of maternal depression (estimated using SEM growth modeling strategy) and the slope of child sleep (neither frequency nor duration had an association). The initial level of maternal depression was, however, positively associated with the slope of child night waking duration; no effect was evident for the slope of the number of night wakings. For the cross-lagged models, the pattern indicated that prior maternal depressive symptoms predicted subsequent child sleep variables, while the reverse was typically not found. In fact, the only significant parameter for child sleep predicting subsequent maternal depression was the opposite of expectation (greater duration of night wakings predicted lower maternal depression). When examining simple correlations, the significant effects were all small in this sample of more than 1,100 families—the largest was .17 and most centered around .10. All data in this study was obtained via maternal report.

Families seeking help for children 10 to 42 months of age with sleep problems were recruited at parenting centers in Australia (n = 45); a sample of children with no reported problems was also recruited (n = 45) (Gelman & King, 2001). These families were studied on general health factors and parenting stress. Maternal depression, anxiety, somatic symptoms, and parenting stress were all higher in the group presenting with sleep problems. Mothers reported on health and stress, and were responsible for seeking help with child sleep.

Families identified by maternal diagnosis of affective disorder (unipolar and bipolar) and enrolled in a longitudinal study provided information about sleep on the Child Behavior Checklist (CBCL; Achenbach, 1991) (Stoleru, Nottelmann, Belmont, & Ronsaville, 1997). Two subsamples of children were identified, those between one and a half and three and a half years of age, and those between five and eight years of age. For the younger group, mothers with affective disorders (versus those with no diagnosed illness) reported more sleep problems across several assessment points. In this study, mothers provided information about child sleep and were the subject of the clinical interviews that established affective disorder diagnoses.

Two reports provide data on the association of maternal depression and child sleep during the first year of life within the context of an intervention designed to promote self-soothing by infants following night wakings. The intervention was to provide a t-shirt worn by the mother to the infant in his or her crib, so that maternal odor cues would be available during night waking. Infant sleep was measured by maternal report and time-lapse video, and the Beck Depression Inventory (Beck, Ward, Mendelson, Mock, & Erbaugh, 1961) was used to measure maternal depression. In the first study (21 infants and mothers), there was an association at six months of age between maternal depression and infants who did not self-sooth during night-wakings (Goodlin-Jones, Eiben, & Anders, 1997). It was also noted that mothers with higher depression scores were less likely to interact with their infants at bedtime, but more likely to intervene during night wakings. In the second study (n=80), maternal depression was again associated with less infant self-soothing at 12 months of age (Burnham, Goodlin-Jones, Gaylor, & Anders, 2002). It should be noted that (1) in neither case did the sleep aid intervention affect infant self-soothing, and (2) the depression associations with self-soothing were examined and interpreted in a larger context of infant and mother characteristics. Unlike all of the studies previously described, these two studies used objective measures of infant sleep (time-lapse video) compared with mothers' reports of depression.

Indirect Predictors Related to Psychopathology—Parent Cognitions

The studies described above all examine direct associations of maternal psychopathology symptoms (almost exclusively depression) and child sleep characteristics. In this section, I will describe a few examples of studies that seek child sleep associations with indicators known to be strongly associated with parental psychopathology, thus providing indirect evidence that parental psychopathology may be implicated in child sleep difficulties.

Several studies have examined maternal cognitions, some studies focused on sleep-specific cognitions, and others assessed more general cognitions. Such studies are relevant because of the well-established relation between dysfunctional thinking and mood disorders (Gotlib & Hammen, 2009).

Sleep-related cognitions in mothers and fathers were the focus of a study of Israeli infants referred to a sleep clinic (problems in the realm of night waking), as well as infants without identified sleep problems (Sadeh, Flint-Ofir, Tirosh, & Tikotzky, 2007). Questionnaire and vignette interpretation methods were used to assess parental cognitions. Actigraphy and maternal reports were used to measure infant sleep characteristics. Parental cognitions indicating difficulty with limit setting were associated with reported night wakings (but not with actigraphy indicators of night waking); doubts about parental competency were associated with actigraphy indicators of night waking (but not with the reported night waking). The cognitions about limit setting were also indicative of those parents whose infants were referred to the sleep clinic. Sadeh and colleagues (2007) measured cognitions by parent report and sleep by both parent report and objective actigraph recording.

A group of 99 mothers and two-year-old children recruited in a pediatric practice in the United Kingdom were divided into a group with (n = 40) and without (n = 59) sleep problems based on maternal diary (Morrell & Cortina-Borja, 2002). They also completed a sleep cognitions questionnaire (as well as behavioral strategies around sleep and infant temperament questionnaires). Although the focus of the report was the development of the questionnaire assessing behavioral strategies, information about parental cognitions was also presented. Reported cognitions regarding difficulty with limit setting, parenting competence, and anger at child were associated with child sleep problems indicated in the sleep diary. Furthermore, these cognitions interacted with reports of temperament in predicting sleep problems. As noted, mothers were the source of both cognition and child sleep data. In a follow-up report, these cognitions were associated with child sleep problems one year later, and were predicted by maternal depression (Morrell & Steele, 2003). In addition, ambivalent attachment (measured in the Strange Situation; Ainsworth, Blehar, Waters, & Wall, 1978) was predictive of sleep problems at two years of age. The data in these reports were provided by mothers (sleep problems, cognitions, depression) and direct observation (attachment status).

Indirect Predictors Related to Psychopathology—Family Context

Following on the themes of maternal cognitions and attachment, adult attachment measured in mothers has been related to children's sleep problems. These cognitions of the mother are not about children's sleep, but instead are about their own family relationship history. There is evidence that insecure adult attachment is more frequent among those with psychopathology (e.g., Atkinson et al., 2000). In this study of 20 children with sleep disorders (excessive night waking) and 21 without sleep problems, insecure adult attachment was found for all mothers of the sleep-disordered children, but only for half of those without sleep disorders (Benoit, Zeanah, Boucher, & Minde, 1992). In this study, identification of sleep disorders were based on parent report as was classification of adult attachment.

A group of 127 families in the Netherlands participated in a longitudinal study of marital quality and problem solving, parents' sleep, and children's sleep in the first year of life (Meijer & van den Wittenboer, 2007). Marital quality has been associated with depression and other psychopathology in many studies (Dickstein et al., 1998). Although the authors reported many indirect effects, there was no direct association of marital quality and children's sleep. All data were provided via parent report.

Families of children from four preschools in different parts of Indiana (213 participants) were studied on child sleep, family functioning, family stress, family management, and child adaptation (Bates, Viken, Alexander, Byers, & Stockton, 2002). As with marital quality, family functioning has been associated with parental psychopathology (Dickstein et al., 1998). Child sleep disruption (nighttime sleep variability, bedtime variability) was consistently associated with family stress measures, but not with whether families accomplished tasks of daily life or management of child behavior. These associations were modest in size, however. Structural models indicated that child sleep disruption mediated associations of family stress and child preschool adjustment. Parents provided information about family characteristics and child sleep, and teachers provided preschool adjustment information.

Middle Childhood

Moving from infancy and early childhood to middle childhood, the literature on parent psychopathology and child sleep thins out dramatically. There is no clear theoretical reason for the lesser interest in child sleep and parent psychopathology during this developmental period, nor are there obvious pragmatic barriers to conducting such research.

In the Stoleru and colleagues' (1997) study described earlier, the affectively ill mothers provided information about child sleep on the Child Behavior Checklist (CBCL). As for the younger subsample of one and a half and three and a half year olds, the ill mothers of children between five and eight years of age (versus those with no diagnosed illness) reported more child sleep problems on the CBCL across several assessment points. As noted above, mothers provided information about child sleep and were the subject of the clinical interviews that established affective disorder diagnoses.

In a pilot investigation, 25 children were examined in terms of parent-reported sleep using the Children's Sleep Habits Questionnaire (CSHQ; Owens, Spirito, & McGuinn, 2000) and mothers' depression using the CES-D (Radloff, 1977). Using cutoffs for clinical sleep disturbance on the CSHQ, maternal depression, fatigue, sleep quality, overload, and parental distress were all more prevalent in the children with significant sleep disruptions (Meltzer & Mindell, 2007). Mothers completed the questionnaires about sleep and about maternal distress.

Indirect Predictors Related to Psychopathology

Children with early onset bipolar symptomatology provide indirect evidence regarding parental psychopathology owing to the strong familial transmission of bipolar disorder. It is likely that a high percentage of these children have a parent with bipolar disorder, or some other diagnosed mental illness. In one such study of 133 children, sleep was measured using instruments otherwise designed to assess depression and mania in the children. Although there was no control group in this study, the rate of any sleep problem reports (96%) indicates at least some signal associating child bipolar spectrum disorders and reported sleep problems (Lofthouse, Fristad, Splaingard, & Kelleher, 2007). There are some interesting method characteristics in this study. Child sleep was assessed by one parent and by the children, but parent-child correspondence was very low. Also, given the measurement of sleep was a subset of mania and depression items, most of the relevant comparisons involved part-whole correlation. As with the sleep measures, the assessment of diagnosis, as well and mania and depression scales, was completed by both parents and children.

A group of 161 U.S. schoolchildren, with no identified sleep or behavioral problems, were examined for sleep characteristics and family factors. Sleep was measured by actigraphy, and family factors were measured by child report (reported marital conflict, and perceived emotional insecurity related to inter-parental conflict). Multiple indicators of family conflict and emotional insecurity in the context of the parental marital relationship were associated with percent sleep and, to a lesser extent, night waking in children. All of these associations were small in magnitude (El-Sheikh, Buckhalt, Cummings, & Keller, 2007; El-Sheikh, Buckhalt, Keller, Cummings, & Acebo, 2007; see also El-Sheikh, Buckhalt, Mize, & Acebo, 2006). Attachment insecurity did not show such association. Children provided family conflict and emotional insecurity information, and sleep was measured via actigraphy.

In a large survey study in the United States, about 3,500 children (in 2,400 families) were reported on, and about 2,900 of these children were followed five years later (Adam, Snell, & Pendry, 2007). The children were nearly evenly divided between middle childhood and adolescence. Time diaries for two 24-hour periods provided data about child sleep (on weekdays and weekends) and surveys developed for this study measured several components of family functioning. For the children, longer weekday sleep time was associated with stronger family rules; later weekend wake time was associated with more family economic strain. These effects were small in magnitude and in the context of many other comparisons (about 1 in 18 comparisons were significant). Time diaries were completed by varying combinations of mother and child, and the mother apparently completed the family functioning survey (although the report is somewhat vague on this point).

Adolescence

The literature on adolescence is even smaller than that for middle childhood, with only a couple of studies available. In the Meltzer and Mindell (2007) report described above, there were nine adolescents in the sample. Although the data for these adolescents were not presented separately, there was little evidence that age was an important moderator of the associations found (most notably between child sleep problems and maternal depression).

In the Adam et al. (2007) study described above, the adolescent group had different family functioning predictors associated with child sleep. Stronger family rules were associated with longer sleep times and earlier bedtimes on weekdays; no associations were found for family functioning variables and weekend sleep. Again, effects were small and few in number compared with the number of significance tests examined.

Methodologic and Conceptual Issues

The studies reviewed above point to a modest but consistent signal relating some aspects of parental psychopathology with children's sleep. This general statement must, however, be substantially qualified by many characteristics of the methods and research designs used in the data collection for these studies.

Sleep Assessment

None of the studies reviewed employed polysomnography (PSG), and we thus have no data that includes the gold standard in the field for assessing sleep. PSG is, of course, a labor intensive procedure, typically conducted in laboratory settings. As most of the studies have been conducted during infancy and early childhood, the subject population is ill-suited to this method (although home-based PSG is becoming more feasible for the research community). There is also a poor match with the parent population in this area (by definition, many will have psychopathology) as there is non-trivial burden on the families when PSG is used in either laboratory or home settings.

The alternative for obtaining objective data in this population is actigraphy methods. Actigraphy has the advantage of easy utility in the field combined with long durations of assessment. This method does, however, require good diary-keeping by the participant or parent (Acebo et al., 2005), which again can be a challenge if the parent or family is compromised by mental health issues. Actigraphy may also be confounded with co-sleeping, which is particularly prevalent in the younger infants and toddlers who have been the focus of many studies (Burnham, 2007). There is a minimal amount of evidence suggesting the activity of the co-sleeper will not affect the infant's actigraph assessment, but this remains an open question regarding the validity of sleep-wake assignment in the context of co-sleeping.

Most sleep researchers would agree that parental questionnaire would be the method associated with the most error of measurement. Yet, this is the most prevalent method employed in the literature on child sleep and parental psychopathology. This issue is especially relevant because much of the information about parental psychopathology is provided by the same informant. Thus, in addition to the generic measurement error inherent in questionnaire assessment of sleep, there may be systematic error because of informant confounds (which is discussed in more detail below). The result is the potential for two error sources to be combined in much of the literature reviewed above.

In this same vein, it should be recognized that clinic referral for a child sleep problem is a variant of parental report on sleep. Although this may appear on the surface as a professional's assessment of sleep, most studies using this approach have relied on simple referral to a clinic, rather than an objectively assessed and documented sleep problem.

The majority of studies reviewed herein relied on questionnaire assessment of child sleep problems, with a small minority employing actigraphy or clinic referral. This characteristic should be noted as a limitation on broad interpretations of the data, owing to the multiple sources of error (some potentially systematic) inherent in the method.

Psychopathology Assessment

Psychopathology can have many meanings. The most accepted standard is individuals identified as qualifying for a specific diagnosis (usually according to the Diagnostic and Statistical Manual of the American Psychiatric Association, 1994). This standard is stringent in the sense that it applies to a minority of the general population.

Symptoms associated with diagnostic syndromes are also used to characterize individuals in terms of their psychopathology. When symptoms are used, some researchers employ cutoff values, often in the interest of employing a proxy for a specific diagnosis. Others employ continuous symptom counts (or scores on a scale), with less interest in using the symptom measure to index diagnostic status. Furthermore, both the symptom cutoff scores and continuous scores may be in the range where there is no likelihood that the individuals would meet diagnostic criteria.

Finally, psychological distress is employed in the literature on psychopathology. Rather than indexing specific symptoms, distress measures tap into multiple indicators related to diagnostic syndromes and their symptoms. As in the case of symptom measures, both cutoff scores and continuous scores are employed.

In the studies reviewed above, only a few included parents who had been identified with diagnosed psychopathology. Instead, the vast majority employed symptom measures, and the majority of these studies were of parents whose symptom levels were in a range not indicative of diagnosable illness. This sub-syndromal level of symptoms should not be viewed as mis-measurement of psychopathology. In fact, it is often the case that symptom indexes are better predictors of associated behavioral and functional problems than are diagnostic classification (Seifer, 1995). Rather, this characteristic of the studies provides a limit to generalizability of the findings to certain levels of psychopathology assessed in particular ways.

Informant Confounds

Throughout this chapter, I have noted characteristics of studies relevant to the overlap of informants for the various domains of functioning associated in the reports. Two substantial issues are raised. The first is the generic issue of method overlap. This simply refers to the fact that two conceptually distinct pieces of data emanate from a common source. Thus, any feature of that common source (in this case the same informant) could contribute to an observed association. This portion of the association would not be attributable to the target individual (the child) but would be attributable to the information source (the parent).

The second issue is additional systematic variance related to the fact that the informant has some degree of psychopathology. This characteristic may serve to increase the degree of method overlap attributable to the common source of information, in this case the parent with psychopathology. For example, depression is associated with a general negative cognitive attribution to general events happening in one's daily life. When asked to report on their own symptoms, or their child's sleep characteristics, the informant with depression may overlay a negative response set on top of any other similarities of response he or she brings to the research setting. Some have refuted this position, but the potential biasing influence of psychopathology of an informant remains an open question (Richters, 1992).

It is also the case that informants may have difficulty reporting accurately on individuals with whom they are in close relationships. This has been well documented in the field of infant temperament, where a minimal level of correspondence between parent reports and observations of children is the norm (Seifer, Sameroff, Barrett, & Krafchuck, 1994). Furthermore, mothers have the capacity to be accurate reporters, but this capacity is minimally evident when they are asked to report about their own child (Seifer, Sameroff, Dickstein, Schiller, & Hayden, 2004).

As was evident in the studies reviewed above, the large majority included informant confounds in the form of a parent (almost always the mother) reporting about both his or her own psychopathology and the child's sleep. In similar fashion, the parental psychopathology was almost exclusively in the mother as well. In most cases, the dimension of psychopathology in question included depression. In the instances when this informant confound was not present, the results of studies were less consistent than for those including such confounds.

Mutual Influences of Parent, Child, and Context

One of the basic tenets of current theories of human development is that influences among parents and children are bidirectional. In the case of child sleep, the parent to child direction of effect might be manifest in genetic transmission, organization provided by the parent with respect to sleep hygiene, or the imposition of a parent's own sleep schedule on the child. Child to parent influences might be manifest in terms of how early sleep organization (or lack thereof) might influence parent behavior. Much of the research on parent psychopathology and child sleep has little flavor of this bidirectionality. Instead, the studies typically examine levels of association, often with an implicit message that the direction of effect is from parent to child.

A related issue is that the unfolding of child development in relation to a parent (with or without psychopathology) does not occur in isolation. Larger contextual factors are typically involved in understanding children's development. Psychopathology is often associated with lower socioeconomic status, more family disruption and dissolution, more substance use, lower quality neighborhood environments, and poorer overall relationship functioning. Psychopathology is but one element of this complex set of contextual influences on a child's development, and it is well established that as the negative influences accumulate in a child's context, developmental adaptation is adversely affected (Sameroff, Seifer, Baldwin, & Baldwin, 1993).

In the realm of child sleep, the organizing influences of families and contexts may be compromised in the presence of parental psychopathology. The parent-to-child effects would most obviously be problematic in multiple-risk contexts. There would, however, likely also be difficulties with maladaptive child-to-parent influences as well. Children with relatively mild variations from optimal norms of sleep may trigger far more negative response in parents who are stressed by their own psychopathology in concert with multiple contextual stressors.

At its core, development of sleep organization is a relationship process that occurs within families. Similarly, psychopathology has fundamental relationship implications. To the extent that complex relationship processes are subject to individual and contextual pressures, childhood functions such as sleep organization can be impaired. The future task of researchers in this domain is to more clearly identify the sensitive points in development where parental influences on children, and child influences on parents, may be altered by the presence of parental psychopathology and its correlated contextual risks. Furthermore, these studies will also require investigation with more rigorous methods and designs, which eliminate some of the qualifications that exist in the current literature.

REFERENCES

Acebo, C., Sadeh, A., Seifer, R., Tzischinsky, O., Hafer, A., & Carskadon, M. A. (2005). Sleep/wake patterns derived from activity monitoring and maternal report for healthy 1- to 5-year-old children. *Sleep, 28,* 1568–1577.

Achenbach, T. M. (1991). Manual for the Child Behavior Checklist/4-18 and 1991 profile. Burlington: University of Vermont, Department of Psychiatry.

Adam, E. K., Snell, E. K., & Pendry, P. (2007). Sleep timing and quantity in ecological and family context: A nationally representative time-diary study. *Journal of Family Psychology, 21,* 4–19.

Ainsworth, M., Blehar, M., Waters, E., & Wall, S. (1978). *Patterns of attachment.* Hillsdale, NJ: Lawrence Erlbaum.

American Psychiatric Association (1994). *Diagnostic and statistical manual of mental disorders* (4th ed.). Arlington, VA: American Psychiatric Association.

Atkinson, L., Paglia, A., Coolbear, J., Niccols, A., Parker, K. C. H., & Guger, S. (2000). Attachment security: A meta-analysis of maternal mental health correlates. *Clinical Psychology Review, 20,* 1019–1040.

Bates, J. E., Viken, R. J., Alexander, D. B., Byers, J., & Stockton, L. (2002). Sleep and adjustment in preschool children: Sleep diary reports by mothers relate to behavior reports by teachers. *Child Development, 73*, 62–74.

Beck, A. T., Ward, C. H., Mendelson, M., Mock, J. E., & Erbaugh, J. K. (1961). An inventory for measuring depression. *Archives of General Psychology, 4*, 561–571.

Benoit, D., Zeanah, C. H., Boucher, C., & Minde, K. K. (1992). Sleep disorders in early childhood: Association with insecure maternal attachment. *Journal of the American Academy of Child & Adolescent Psychiatry, 31*, 86–93.

Burnham, M. M., Goodlin-Jones, B. L., Gaylor, E. E., & Anders, T. F. (2002). Nighttime sleep-wake patterns and self-soothing from birth to one year of age: A longitudinal intervention study. *Journal of Child Psychology and Psychiatry, 43*, 713–725.

Burnham, M. M. (2007). The ontogeny of diurnal rhythmicity in bed-sharing and solitary-sleeping infants: A preliminary report. *Infant and Child Development, 16*, 341–357.

Cox, J. L., Holden, J. M., & Sagovsky, R. (1987). Detection of postnatal depression: Development of the 10-item Edinburgh Postnatal Depression Scale. *British Journal of Psychiatry, 150*, 782–786.

Dickstein, S., Seifer, R., Hayden, L. C., Schiller, M., Sameroff, A. J., Keitner, G., ... Magee, K. D. (1998). Levels of family assessment II: Impact of maternal psychopathology on family functioning. *Journal of Family Psychology, 12*, 23–40.

El-Sheikh, M., Buckhalt, J. A., Cummings, E. M., & Keller, P. (2007). Sleep disruptions and emotional insecurity are pathways of risk for children. *Journal of Child Psychology and Psychiatry, 48*, 88–96.

El-Sheikh, M., Buckhalt, J. A., Keller, P. S., Cummings, E. M., & Acebo, C. (2007). Child emotional insecurity and academic achievement: The role of sleep disruptions. *Journal of Family Psychology, 21*, 29–38.

El-Sheikh, M., Buckhalt, J. A., Mize, J., & Acebo, C (2006). Marital conflict and disruption of children's sleep. *Child Development, 77*, 31–43.

Gelman, V. S., & King, N. J. (2001). Wellbeing of mothers with children exhibiting sleep disturbance. *Australian Journal of Psychology, 53*, 18–22.

Goodlin-Jones, B. L., Eiben, L. A., & Anders, T. F. (1997). Maternal well-being and sleep-wake behaviors in infants: An intervention using maternal odor. *Infant Mental Health Journal, 18*, 378–393.

Gotlib, I. H., & Hammen, C. L. (2009). *Handbook of depression* (2nd ed.). New York: Guilford.

Hiscock, H., & Wake, M. (2001). Infant sleep problems and postnatal depression: A community-based study. *Pediatrics, 107*, 1317–1322.

Hiscock, H., & Wake, M. (2002). Randomised controlled trial of behavioural infant sleep intervention to improve infant sleep and maternal mood. *British Medical Journal, 324*, 1062–1067.

Lam, P., Hiscock, H., & Wake, M. (2003). Outcomes of infant sleep problems: A longitudinal study of sleep, behavior, and maternal well-being. *Pediatrics, 111*, e203–e207.

Lofthouse, N., Fristad, M., Splaingard, M., & Kelleher, K. (2007). Parent and child reports of sleep problems associated with early-onset bipolar spectrum disorders. *Journal of Family Psychology, 21*, 114–123.

Meijer, A. M., & van den Wittenboer, G. L. H. (2007). Contribution of infants' sleep and crying to marital relationships of first-time parent couples in the 1st year after childbirth. *Journal of Family Psychology, 21*, 49–57.

Meltzer, L. J., & Mindell, J. A. (2007). Relationship between child sleep disturbances and maternal sleep, mood, and parenting stress: A pilot study. *Journal of Family Psychology, 21*, 67–73.

Morrell, J., & Cortina-Borja, M. (2002). The developmental change in strategies parents employ to settle young children to sleep, and their relationship to infant sleeping problems, as assessed by a new questionnaire: The Parental Interactive Bedtime Behaviour Scale. *Infant and Child Development, 11*, 17–41.

Morrell, J., & Steele, H. (2003). The role of attachment security, temperament, maternal perception, and care-giving behavior in persistent infant sleeping problems. *Infant Mental Health Journal, 24*, 447–468.

Murray, L., & Cooper, P. J. (1997). *Postpartum depression and child development.* New York: Guilford.

O'Connor, T. G., Caprariello, P., Blackmore, E. R., Gregory, A. M., Glover, V., Fleming, P., & the ALSPAC Team. (2007). Prenatal mood disturbance predicts sleep problems in infancy and toddlerhood. *Early Human Development, 83*, 451–458.

Owens, J. A., Spirito, A., & McGuinn, M. (2000). The Children's Sleep Habits Questionnaire (CSHQ): Psychometric properties of a survey instrument for school-aged children. *Sleep, 23*, 1043–1051.

Radloff, L. S. (1977). The CES-D scale: A self-report depression scale for research in the general population. *Applied Psychological Measurement, 1*, 385–401.

Reid, G. J., Hong, R. Y., & Wade, T. J. (2009). The relation between common sleep problems and emotional and behavioral problems among 2- and 3-year-olds in the context of known risk factors for psychopathology. *Journal of Sleep Research, 18*, 49–59.

Richters, J. E. (1992). Depressed mothers as informants about their children: A critical review of the evidence for distortion. *Psychological Bulletin, 112*, 485–499.

Sadeh, A., Flint-Ofir, E., Tirosh, T., & Tikotzky, L. (2007). Infant sleep and parental sleep-related cognitions. *Journal of Family Psychology, 21*, 74–87.

Sameroff, A. J., Seifer, R., Baldwin, A., & Baldwin, C. (1993). Stability of intelligence from preschool to adolescence: The influence of social and family risk factors. *Child Development, 64*, 80–97.

Seifer, R. (1995). Perils and pitfalls of high-risk research. *Developmental Psychology*, *31*, 420–424.

Seifer, R., Sameroff, A. J., Barrett, L. C., & Krafchuk. E. (1994). Infant temperament measured by multiple observations and mother report. *Child Development*, *65*, 1478–1490.

Seifer, R., Sameroff, A. J., Dickstein, S., Hayden, L. C., & Schiller, M. (1996). Parental psychopathology and sleep variation in children. In R. Dahl (Ed.), *Child and adolescent psychiatric clinics: Sleep disorders* (Vol 5., No 3, pp. 715–728). Philadelphia: W. B. Saunders.

Seifer, R., Sameroff, A., Dickstein, S., Schiller, M., & Hayden, L. C. (2004). Your own children are special: Clues to the sources of reporting bias in temperament assessments. *Infant Behavior & Development*, *27*, 323–341.

Stoleru, S., Nottelmann, E. D., Belmont, B., & Ronsaville, D. (1997). Sleep problems in children of affectively ill mothers. *Journal of Child Psychology, Psychiatry*, *38*, 831–841.

Warren, S. L., Howe, G., Simmens, S. J., & Dahl, R. E. (2006). Maternal depressive symptoms and child sleep: Models of mutual influence over time. *Development and Psychopathology*, *18*, 1–16.

Zuckerman, B., Stevenson, J., & Bailey, V. (1987). Sleep problems in early childhood: Continuities, predictive factors, and behavioral correlates. *Pediatrics*, *80*, 664–671.

5

Effects of Trauma on Children's Sleep

Carol Glod

Introduction

Sleep disturbance has been suggested as the "hallmark of posttraumatic stress disorder" (Ross, Ball, Sullivan, & Caroff, 1989, p. 697). The sleep of children who have been exposed to trauma and/or maltreatment is disrupted, from problems with sleep onset to terrifying dreams. Sexual and physical abuse are linked with many negative child outcomes, including sleep disturbances. Likewise, wars and natural disasters have been associated with sleep disruption, and there is some initial evidence that cuddly objects, behavioral sleep interventions, and family environment may alleviate sleep disturbances in children following such trauma.

Both the long- and short-term effects of trauma on children depend on a variety of factors. These include age of exposure to the traumatic event, duration of exposure, level of psychological maturity and temperament, directness and severity of exposure, type and nature of the trauma and its context, parental response to the trauma, degree of social support, and positive community influences. Traumatic reactions may emerge immediately and develop into acute stress disorder or be delayed and/or prolonged, as in posttraumatic stress disorder (PTSD). In addition, a myriad of psychological sequelae and psychiatric disorders may result, ranging from externalizing behaviors (including aggressive behaviors, conduct problems, and reenactment of the trauma) to attentional problems and school avoidance to underlying mood changes (e.g., anxiety, depression, fear, and irritability). Sleep disturbances in the context of trauma exposure have only more recently been investigated; such sleep problems may include frightening dreams, nightmares, re-experiencing symptoms, as well as difficulties in sleep onset or maintenance.

In this chapter, available evidence indicating that traumatized children are hypervigilant not only during the day but also during the night, resulting in disrupted sleep, will be reviewed. Most of the extant literature to date has focused on trauma resulting from emotional, physical, or sexual abuse, or witnessing domestic violence, torture, war, or terrorist attacks. Research on traumatized children includes mostly subjective and descriptive investigations of sleep in children and adolescent samples, with a paucity of studies that use objective sleep methods. Studies that have utilized subjective sleep assessments will first be reviewed, followed by investigations that have included objective evaluation of sleep. The chapter will conclude with an examination of the limited data on pertinent interventions with children and adolescents.

Effects of Abuse on Sleep

Subjective Reports of Sleep Disruption

Averse traumatic experiences during childhood can take many forms, including verbal, emotional, physical, or sexual abuse, as well as witnessing domestic violence. These types of trauma pose unique challenges for clinicians and researchers. Documentation of the trauma with clear duration, severity, and age of onset is foundational. However, even with clear substantiation of the abuse and its associated characteristics, relating it directly to sleep difficulties, particularly in children and adolescents, is difficult. Given the small number of child clinicians and researchers interested in pediatric sleep in the context of trauma, along with potential concerns about protection of human subjects and vulnerable populations such as these, the research on sleep of abused children is meager and limited. Although some investigators have explored the effects of traumatic abuse experiences during childhood on adults and their current sleep problems (Bader, Schäfer, Schenkel, Nissen, & Schwander, 2007; Caldwell & Redeker, 2005), it is difficult to extend and relate current sleep disruptions with past abuse due to the retrospective nature of the events. Nonetheless, there are several studies, reviewed below, that have

examined the role and relationship of abuse to sleep in younger populations, including prepubertal and adolescent samples. The methods have
ranged from parental or self-reports using surveys or established instruments (reviewed first in the chapter) to more objective evaluation of
sleep using ambulatory activity monitoring (e.g., actigraphy) to determine nocturnal activity and sleep onset, duration, and maintenance.

Wells, McCann, Adams, Voris, and Ensign (1995) examined the
results of a structured parent interview for Signs Associated with Sexual
Abuse (SASA) in young girls. They compared three matched samples of
prepubescent girls: 68 who were not abused, 68 from a sexual abuse clinic
in which a perpetrator confessed, and 68 seen at the same clinic who
did not have a perpetrator confession (Allegedly Abused). Parents of girls
in both the sexual abuse and alleged abuse groups reported increased
sleep problems along with fearfulness, emotional and behavioral changes,
concentration problems, and more sexual curiosity and knowledge.
Compared with the non-abused girls, 63% of the girls with documented
sexual abuse experienced significant problems falling asleep as well as
self-consciousness and fear of being left alone. Nonsignificant increases
also emerged between groups in reported nightmare frequency: 39% of
sexually abused girls reported nightmares compared with 30% and 17%
of the girls in the alleged abused and non-abused groups, respectively.

Noll, Trickett, Susman, and Putnam (2006) compared the sleep of
74 adolescent girls who were sexually abused 10 years after the disclosure
of substantiated abuse with 69 comparison girls. Self-reported sleep
disruption included items on sleeping patterns (n = 6), and items from
the Child Behavioral Checklist (n = 4) and the Brief Symptom Inventory
(n = 2), resulting in a 12-item composite score. Sleep disturbances correlated moderately with depression and modestly with PTSD symptoms
domains (arousal symptoms, reexperiencing symptoms, and avoidant
symptoms). Hierarchical regression analysis showed that sexually abused
participants reported significantly more sleep disturbances than comparison participants independent of the effects of comorbid depression
and PTSD. No differences emerged in percent hours asleep, insomnia
(defined as less than seven hours of sleep per night) or hypersomnia
(more than 10 hours of sleep per night). Sleep disturbances were not
related to individual characteristics of sexual abuse, such as age of onset,
duration, severity, and identity of the perpetrator.

Agargun, Kara, Özer, Selvi, Kiran, and Kiran (2003) examined nightmares and dissociative experiences of 292 young adult undergraduates.
The rate of childhood traumatic experiences was higher in nightmare
sufferers than in those who did not have nightmares. Over one-half
(55%) of subjects who reported nightmares "often" also endorsed at least
one of four traumatic symptoms that included maternal loss or separation, and physical or sexual abuse. Nightmare frequency was not associated with sexual abuse. The rate of nightmares were, however, significantly
greater in those with physical abuse; 35% of subjects who reported experiencing nightmares frequently were physically abused.

Runyon, Faust, and Orvaschel (2002) explored factors that discrim-
inated three groups of children: abused with PTSD, non-abused with
major depression (MDD), and abused with PTSD and MDD. Interestingly,
the symptoms of sleep disruption and flashbacks differed between groups,
with the abused group with both disorders having the greatest problems.
"Trouble sleeping" occurred in 64% of children in the PTSD/MDD
group versus 29% in those with PTSD. Curiously, the other major dis-
criminating factor, psychogenic amnesia, emerged more frequently in
the PTSD group compared with the PTSD/MDD group (43% vs. 13%,
respectively).

Two studies have used qualitative methods to evaluate sleep disruption in children exposed to domestic violence. Lemmey, McFarlane,
Willson, and Malecha (2001) explored mothers' impressions (n = 72)
of the impact of witnessing domestic violence on their children. Overall,
72% reported negative behaviors in their children. Some of the patterns
and themes were coded into distressing behaviors that included clinging,
crying, and fretful behaviors, and commonly, sleep problems such as
nighttime wakening, refusal to sleep alone, and recurrent nightmares.
Using focus groups, Humphreys, Lowe, and Williams (2008) interviewed
17 mothers of 28 young children and adolescents exposed to domestic
violence to assess the organization, management, and constraints on sleep,
and the impact of risk and safety. Mothers reported disruption to their
children's sleep resulting from fear of living with domestic violence.
Frequent sleep problems included difficulty settling to sleep, enuresis,
and nightmares, and the presentation of sleep symptoms in children was

phasic or delayed. Specifically, sleep disruptions may arise at key developmental periods or their onset may emerge many years post-trauma.

These studies using parent report and youth self-report suggest that nightmares and difficulty falling asleep are predominant symptoms associated with severe abuse and domestic violence in children and adolescents. Although some data on the presence of nightmares and their prevalence has emerged, little information is available on the nature of these dreams. In the one published study that examined the content of nightmares in 220 traumatized children and adolescents with enduring interpersonal violence compared with their non-traumatized counterparts, traumatized children's dreams were associated with greater content of trauma and a much higher proportion of aggressive objects (Kamphuis, Tuin, Timmermans, & Punamäki, 2008).

Objective Reports of Sleep Disruption

Other studies have focused on more objective assessments of sleep in children who have experienced maltreatment, particularly severe forms of abuse. Sadeh and colleagues (1995) measured sleep-wake patterns using actigraphy in 39 abused children (mean age = 9.5 years) hospitalized in a psychiatric inpatient unit. They were monitored for one to three consecutive nights with wrist activity monitors to determine sleep-wake patterns. Children's self-ratings of depression, hopelessness, and low self-esteem were significantly correlated with objective sleep measures indicating poorer sleep quality for children with increased adjustment problems. Physically abused children had significantly worse sleep quality than non-abused and sexually abused inpatients. Specifically, those who experienced physical abuse had somewhat lower sleep efficiencies and lower percent time spent in quiet sleep (Sadeh et al., 1995).

In determining whether intense averse stimulation, in the form of physical and/or sexual abuse, leads to disruption of sleep and nocturnal activity, Glod, Teicher, Hartman, and Harakal (1997) compared three groups of children. Nineteen prepubertal children with documented abuse were compared with 15 non-abused normal controls and 10 non-abused depressed children. Actigraphy was used to evaluate sleep-related activity for three consecutive nights using algorithmic estimation of sleep initiation and continuity. The authors found that abused children were twice as active at night as normal or depressed children. Further, greater amounts of abused children's total daily activity occurred during the night. Specifically, children in the abused group exhibited twice the percentage of nocturnal activity compared with children in both the non-abused control group and the non-abused depressed group (7.4% vs. 3.6%, 3.7%, respectively). Actigraph-derived sleep measures suggested that abused children had increased nocturnal activity, prolonged sleep latency, and decreased sleep efficiency compared with children in the other non-abused groups. Specifically, abused children were about twice as active during the night compared with children in the non-abused groups. Abused children also took about three times as long to fall asleep (mean sleep onset latency = 33.9 minutes) in comparison to the control groups. Physically abused children had more impaired sleep efficiency than sexually abused children (89.0% vs. 92.9%, respectively). Interestingly, PTSD failed to exert significant effects on sleep; abused children *without* PTSD had more sleep and activity disruption.

Glod and Teicher (1996) also examined this sample, comparing the 19 children with documented abuse histories to the 15 normal control children, to examine relations between early severe abuse, PTSD, and circadian rest/activity rhythms. Abuse status was associated with 10% greater diurnal activity compared with non-abuse, which was largely accounted for by PTSD. Earlier onset of abuse was significantly associated with greater levels of hyperactivity and PTSD in children. Thus, in addition to increased nocturnal activity and sleep disruption, severe maltreatment in the form of physical and sexual abuse appears to be related to increased daytime activity (suggestive of hyperactivity) and PTSD.

These actigraphy studies, using more objective means of sleep evaluation, found higher levels of nocturnal activity, difficulty falling asleep, and somewhat less efficient sleep in abused compared with normal control or depressed children. Some preliminary data also suggest that physical abuse may have the most marked effects on sleep. Specifically, physical abuse appears to be the salient factor rather than posttraumatic stress disorder or other forms of abuse. Although disrupted sleep may be a hallmark of PTSD, emerging data suggests that sleep and activity disturbances may be more of a consequence of abuse *per se* rather than

PTSD. In addition to impaired sleep, daytime restlessness and hyperactivity may be a consequence of abuse as well. Taken together, the studies on abuse and exposure to domestic violence point to subjective reports and observations of disrupted sleep and nightmares, with difficulty falling asleep, decreased sleep efficiency, and increased nocturnal activity emerging in objective studies. Thus these traumatized children display prominent delays in sleep onset and enhanced nighttime movement with significant nightmares.

War-Related and Terrorist Trauma Effects on Sleep

In their survey documenting symptoms of distress after the September 11 attacks, Schlenger and colleagues (2002) investigated the nature of children's reactions to the event, including sleep disturbances. Adult households that included children younger than 18 years were queried as to whether any children were "upset" by the events and about the presence of three specific distress symptoms: difficulty sleeping; being irritable or easily upset; and fear of separation from parents. The 729 adults reporting about their children indicated that at least one child per family was upset by the events. No differences emerged in the association between children being upset by the event and geographical proximity to the attacks (between the New York City metropolitan area [60.7%], other major metropolitan areas [57.3%], Washington, DC [54.9%], and the rest of the United States [48.0%]). Thus, children who lived nearby or closer to Manhattan did not experience more symptoms than those residing in other areas in the United States. Adult reports indicated that 20% of the most upset children were having trouble sleeping; other prominent reactions included being irritable, grouchy, easily upset (30%), and fears of parental-separation (26.5%).

In another investigation of the effects of September 11 attacks, Klein, Devoe, Miranda-Julian, and Linas (2009) examined young children's responses to the terrorists' attacks. Using focus groups of 67 parents with 104 children (five years of age or younger), parents reported chronic sleep disruptions, fearful reactions, development of new fears, and increased clingy and separation anxiety behaviors in their children, eight months after the attacks. Specifically, young children's sleep was characterized by inability or refusal to go to sleep or to sleep alone, frequent wakenings, crying during the night, and nightmares.

Other studies suggest that sleep disruption is associated with trauma in refugees. In an investigation of 50 newly resettled refugee Chilean children, 36 had persecutory experiences (Hjern, Angel, & Höjer, 1991). For the purposes of this study, persecution included direct physical assault, arrest of the child or parent, witnessing violence in home or riots in the streets, or parental loss (because of death, disappearance, parental arrest, need to change homes). Using parental interviews and observed behaviors in children ages 2 to 15 years, sleep disturbances and dependency emerged as behaviors that were most associated with persecution. Seventy-five percent of persecuted children had sleep disturbances. Similarly, among 311 recent refugee children from the Middle East, ages 3 to 15 years, Montgomery and Foldspang (2001) conducted structured interviews with parents to assess the effects of exposure to war, organized violence, and human rights violation. Family history of violence (such as grandparent's violent death, parental exposure to torture) and current stressful family interactions (father scolding child) were the strongest predictors of their children's prevalent sleep disturbance. Parents reported that 15% of children experienced nightmares, 28% had difficulty falling asleep, while 35% had difficulty staying asleep. Sleep disruption was mediated by family environment, particularly the presence of both parents during relocation. This suggests that child refugees who experienced sleep problems after the violent death and torture of family members may have less sleep disturbance when both parents accompany the child during relocation.

In a study designed to assess stress reactions in young children during and after war, Sadeh, Hen-Gal, and Tikotzky (2008) assessed sleep and stress of 74 young children (two to seven years of age) in a sheltered camp during the second Israel-Lebanon war (July to August 2006). Symptoms were evaluated through parental reports during the last week of the war. Parents reported sleep difficulties in their children; specifically, over 50% of children experienced nightmares/anxious arousals and 49% experienced fear or difficulty falling asleep. Separation fears, anxiety, and nervous agitation were also highly endorsed. In addition, these investigators assessed the efficacy of group administration of a novel intervention, the "Huggy-Puppy" to 191 young children, compared with 101 control participants. The Huggy-Puppy intervention "encourag[ed] children to care for a needy Huggy-Puppy doll that was given to them as a gift" (Sadeh et al., 2008, p. 46). This intervention was associated with significant reductions in children's stress reactions during the postwar assessment. A higher level of attachment and involvement with the doll was associated with better outcomes. Specifically, number of severe overall stress symptoms was reduced, although the effects on sleep were not reported specifically. In the follow-up period, 71% of the children in the intervention group were symptom-free (i.e., not presenting any severe symptom) three weeks later, compared with only 39% of the children in the control group.

Treatment Interventions for Sleep Difficulties in Children and Adolescents Exposed to Traumatic Events

Controlled trials are very limited in specifically treating sleep disturbances in traumatized youth. One preliminary study investigated the effects over time (12 months) of an integrated behavioral sleep intervention in a small sample of 20 adolescents with substance abuse and traumatic stress severity, using sleep diaries and an index of trauma severity (Stevens, Haynes, Ruiz, & Bootzin, 2007); the nature of trauma was not specified. The intervention consisted of sleep education (including encouragement to leave the bedroom if unable to sleep and to delay bedtime), natural bright light therapy, and mindfulness-based stress reduction strategies. Those adolescents who spent increased time in bed and greater amounts of total sleep time at baseline showed greater improvement in severity trauma symptoms at the 12-month follow-up.

A recent review of 21 psychosocial treatments for children and adolescents who experienced trauma found that trauma-focused Cognitive behavior therapy (CBT) was effective, while school-based CBT might possibly be effective (Silverman et al., 2008). While the meta-analysis revealed that CBT had modest yet positive effects on overall trauma (particularly posttraumatic stress, depressive, anxiety, and externalizing symptoms), the specific effects on sleep improvement have had little systematic study. Since this publication, Sadeh and colleagues' evaluation (2008) of using cuddly stuffed animals is one of the first to systematically evaluate an intervention to improve sleep in very young children exposed to traumatic violence. Systematic controlled pharmacological trials aimed at improving documented sleep abnormalities in traumatized children have yet to be conducted.

Conclusion

Early adverse experience in the form of severe abuse or exposure to violence may potentially lead to the development of posttraumatic stress and other psychiatric disorders in both children and adults. A recently published conceptual model postulates that sleep disturbance mediates the relationship between violence-induced trauma in children and health and psychiatric outcomes (Spilsbury, 2009), suggesting that poor sleep quality and quantity may lead to poorer mental health response and outcomes. Sleep disturbance, labeled as the "hallmark" of PTSD, is one of several key symptoms of the disorder. PTSD is characterized by a triad of symptom clusters, namely re-experiencing the event, avoidant behaviors, and hyperarousal symptoms. Re-experiencing symptoms include prominent nightmares, flashbacks, and other symptoms. Difficulty falling or staying asleep is one of the symptoms of hyperarousal, along with irritability or anger, difficulty concentrating, exaggerated startle, and feeling "on guard." Arousal, a necessary condition for survival, is essential for sustaining basic life functions and serves to protect humans and animals under dangerous conditions and defend against sudden attacks. Persons exposed to sustained, severe trauma may develop a state of constant fear, activating arousal, which fails to extinguish. For children, exposure during key developmental periods during childhood may have salient neurobiological consequences and has the potential to affect neurogenesis and dysregulation in neurotransmitters, or lead to structural or functional brain changes.

Some emerging evidence from neuroimaging and animal studies suggests that posttraumatic stress is associated with noradrenergic dysregulation and abnormal functioning of key brain areas, including the amygdala and prefrontal cortex. In particular, studies of PTSD in adults using polysomnography have found REM abnormalities (Kobayashi, Boarts, & Delahanty, 2007) that are hypothesized to result from hyperactive functioning of the amygdala and increased noradrenergic levels, which lead to nightmares during REM sleep (Germain, Buysse, & Nofzinger, 2008; Spoormaker & Montgomery, 2008). Amygdalar hyperactivity and attenuated medial prefrontal cortex activity during non-REM sleep may lead to arousal and insomnia. Thus, a confluence of neurobiological and brain dysfunction may help to explain and understand the pathogenesis of sleep difficulties in traumatized children.

Overall it appears that trauma, in the form of severe maltreatment or exposure to terror and relocation as refugees, has significant effects on the sleep of children and adolescents. Most of the investigations to date, however, have explored "sleep difficulties" as a generic and nonspecific symptom and as one of the myriad consequences of the trauma. Some research exists to suggest that parents and children report nightmares and difficulty falling asleep along with clinging, fearful, and/or dependent behaviors as the predominant problems of children exposed to trauma. In studies utilizing actigraphic assessments of children's sleep, physical abuse appears to have more significant effects on sleep than sexual abuse or depression in children. These actigraphy-based studies also found several sleep difficulties in physically abused children including difficulty falling asleep, increased sleep onset latency, and increased nocturnal as well as diurnal activity. No published studies emerged using more detailed methods for sleep assessment such as polysomnography (PSG) to determine disruption in sleep stages, REM, nightmares, and other parameters for more detailed evaluation of sleep in traumatized children. There is very limited data on what interventions improve sleep in traumatized children and adolescents, except for perhaps the presence of a comforting object and parental presence. Lacking are studies that examine the specific nature and type of sleep disturbance on traumatized children at different ages, or what developmentally specific effects on sleep emerge.

REFERENCES

Agargun, M. Y., Kara, H., Özer, Ö. A., Selvi, Y., Kiran, Ü., & Kiran, S. (2003). Nightmares and dissociative experiences: The key role of childhood traumatic events. *Psychiatry and Clinical Neurosciences, 57*, 139–145.

Bader, K., Schäfer, V., Schenkel, M., Nissen, L., & Schwander, J. (2007). Adverse childhood experiences associated with sleep in primary insomnia. *Journal of Sleep Research, 16*, 285–296.

Caldwell, B. A., & Redeker, N. (2005). Sleep and trauma: An overview. *Issues in Mental Health Nursing, 26*, 721–738.

Germain, A., Buysse, D. J., & Nofzinger, E. (2008). Sleep-specific mechanisms underlying posttraumatic stress disorder: Integrative review and neurobiological hypotheses. *Sleep Medicine Reviews, 12*, 185–195.

Glod, C. A., & Teicher, M. H. (1996). Relationship between early abuse, posttraumatic stress disorder, and activity levels in prepubertal children. *Journal of the American Academy of Child and Adolescent Psychiatry, 35*, 1384–1393.

Glod, C. A., Teicher, M. H., Hartman, C. R., & Harakal, T. (1997). Increased nocturnal activity and impaired sleep maintenance in abused children. *Journal of the American Academy of Child and Adolescent Psychiatry, 36*, 1236–1243.

Hjern, A., Angel, B., & Höjer, B. (1991). Persecution and behavior: A report of refugee children from Chile. *Child Abuse & Neglect, 15*, 239–248.

Humphreys, C., Lowe, P., & Williams, S. (2008). Sleep disruption and domestic violence: Exploring the interconnections between mothers and children. *Child & Family Social Work, 14*, 6–14.

Kamphuis, J. H., Tuin, N., Timmermans, M., & Punamäki, R. L. (2008). Extending the Rorschach trauma content index and aggression indexes to dream narratives of children exposed to enduring violence: An exploratory study. *Journal of Personality Assessment, 90*, 578–584.

Klein, T. P., Devoe, E. R., Miranda-Julian, C., & Linas, K. (2009). Young children's responses to September 11th: The New York City experience. *Infant Mental Health Journal, 30*, 1–22.

Kobayashi, I., Boarts, J. M., & Delahanty, D. L. (2007). Polysomnographically measured sleep abnormalities in PTSD: A meta-analytic review. *Psychophysiology, 44*, 660–669.

Lemmey, D., McFarlane, J., Willson, P., & Malecha, A. (2001). Intimate partner violence: Mothers' perspectives of effects on their children. *MCN: The American Journal of Maternal/Child Nursing, 26*, 98–103.

Montgomery, E., & Foldspang, A. (2001). Traumatic experience and sleep disturbance in refugee children from the Middle East. *European Journal of Public Health, 11*, 18–22.

Noll, J. G., Trickett, P. K., Susman, E. J., Putnam, F. W. (2006). Sleep disturbances and childhood sexual abuse. *Journal of Pediatric Psychology, 31*, 469–480.

Ross, R. J., Ball, W. A., Sullivan, K. A., & Caroff, S. N. (1989). Sleep disturbance as the hallmark of posttraumatic stress disorder. *American Journal of Psychiatry, 146*, 697–707.

Runyon, M. K., Faust, J., & Orvaschel, H. (2002). Differential symptom pattern of post-traumatic stress disorder (PTSD) in maltreated children with and without concurrent depression. *Child Abuse & Neglect, 26*, 39–53.

Sadeh, A., McGuire, J. P. D., Sachs, H., Seifer, R., Tremblay, A., Civita, R., Hayden, R. M. (1995). Sleep and psychological characteristics of children on a psychiatric inpatient unit. *Journal of the American Academy of Child and Adolescent Psychiatry, 34,* 813–819.

Sadeh, A., Hen-Gal, S., & Tikotzky, L. (2008). Young children's reactions to war-related stress: A survey and assessment of an innovative intervention. *Pediatrics, 121,* 46–53.

Schlenger, W. E., Caddell, J. M., Ebert, L., Jordan, K., Rourke, K. M., Wilson, D., … Kulka, R. A. (2002). Psychological reactions to terrorist attacks: Findings from the National Study of Americans' reactions to September 11. *The Journal of the American Medical Association, 288,* 581–588.

Silverman, W. K., Ortiz, C. D., Viswesvaran, C., Burns, B. J., Kolko, D. J., Putnam, F. W., & Amaya-Jackson, L. (2008). Evidence-based psychosocial treatments for children and adolescents exposed to traumatic events. *Journal of Clinical Child and Adolescent Psychology, 37,* 156–183.

Spilsbury, J. C. (2009). Sleep as a mediator in the pathway from violence-induced traumatic stress to poorer health and functioning: A review of the literature and proposed conceptual model. *Behavioral Sleep Medicine, 7,* 223–244.

Spoormaker, V. I., & Montgomery, P. (2008). Disturbed sleep in post-traumatic stress disorder: Secondary symptom or core feature? *Sleep Medicine Reviews, 12,* 169–184.

Stevens, S., Haynes, P. L., Ruiz, B., & Bootzin, R. R. (2007) Effects of a behavioral sleep medicine intervention on trauma symptoms in adolescents recently treated for substance abuse. *Substance Abuse, 28,* 21–31.

Wells, R. D., McCann, J., Adams, J., Voris, J., Ensign, J. (1995). Emotional, behavioral, and physical symptoms reported by parents of sexually abused, nonabused, and allegedly abused prepubescent females. *Child Abuse & Neglect, 19,* 155–163.

6

Impact of Child Sleep Disturbances on Parent Sleep and Daytime Functioning

Lisa J. Meltzer and Anna M. L. Westin

Introduction

Sleep problems across development are common, from infancy through adolescence (Meltzer & Mindell, 2006a). Further, the consequences of disrupted or insufficient sleep are numerous, impacting growth, learning, development, and mood (Fallone, Owens, & Deane, 2002). However, youth do not live in isolation, but rather are a part of a family system that is dynamic and interactive. One consequence of sleep problems in youth that has only recently received increasing attention is how sleep disorders or sleep disruptions in youth affect parent sleep and daytime functioning. The purpose of this chapter is to review the existing literature in this area. We will begin with a review of the relationship between sleep in children and their parents using a developmental framework from pregnancy through adolescence. This will be followed by a review of the complex relationship among a child's illness or developmental disorder, the child's sleep, and both parental sleep and daytime functioning. Throughout we will highlight how the treatment of sleep problems in children is essential, resulting in the improvement of not only the child's sleep but also parent sleep and daytime functioning.

Because the literature is not consistent in its terminology, and for simplicity, in this chapter we will refer to "parents," with the understanding that (unless otherwise stated) this includes any primary adult caregivers, including mothers, fathers, and/or grandparents. Further, unless specified, sleep disruptions and sleep problems will refer to sleep issues with a behavioral etiology such as bedtime problems (e.g., difficulties falling asleep, bedtime stalling) and night wakings, while sleep disorders will refer to sleep issues with a physiological etiology (e.g., obstructive sleep apnea, parasomnias).

Family Systems and Sleep

Family systems are dynamic, with reciprocal interactions among family members, including interactions at night and during the day. When children are having problems sleeping, they often wake a parent, impacting parent sleep and subsequent parent functioning. Completing the cycle, when parents are obtaining insufficient sleep or experiencing external stressors (e.g., work or marital problems), this can result in an increase in sleep problems in children. Different aspects of this dynamic relationship between child sleep and family functioning will be explored in several chapters in this volume. While we recognize and support these dynamic and reciprocal relationships, for this chapter we will view the literature through a unidirectional lens, namely that child sleep problems or sleep disorders impact parent sleep, resulting in increased negative daytime functioning in parents. Most studies reviewed here utilized a cross-sectional methodology, limiting the ability to make such a causal conclusion, but in many cases, in particular with infants or young children, as well as children with chronic illnesses or developmental disorders, parental sleep and daytime functioning are less likely to impact child sleep than child sleep is to impact parent sleep and daytime functioning.

Sleep in Children and Families across Development

Pregnancy and Infancy

Children begin to impact parent sleep in utero. Compared to her regular sleep pattern, a mother's sleep starts to change by the second trimester due to changes in hormone levels along with an increasing discomfort lying down as a result of the growing fetus (Gay, Lee, & Lee, 2004). Although total sleep time tends to increase early in the pregnancy (Gay et al., 2004), actigraphic and polysomnographic data show that women in their third trimester have less total sleep, lower sleep efficiency, more frequent night wakings, and less deep sleep than they did prior to their pregnancy (Kang, Matsumoto, Shinkoda, Mishima, & Seo, 2002; Lee, Zaffke, & McEnany, 2000). Although the pregnancy only has a direct effect on the mother's sleep, father's sleep is likely indirectly affected as well because one partner's sleep problems have been shown to influence the other partner's sleep (Meijer & van den Wittenboer, 2007). Still, the changes in sleep patterns that occur during pregnancy are less pronounced compared to those that parents experience postpartum.

With the birth of a baby, parents report getting considerably less sleep than they did both before and during the pregnancy (Gay et al., 2004). Actigraphic and polysomnographic data support such parent reports showing that mothers have less total nighttime sleep, more daytime sleep, and more frequent night wakings postpartum (Gay et al., 2004; Lee et al., 2000). Disruptions to parental sleep during the months immediately following childbirth are unavoidable due to the lack of a circadian rhythm in newborns. The need for parents to respond to their newborn infant's needs consequently results in irregular sleep patterns for the caregiver as well.

By six months of age, sleep begins to consolidate for most infants, establishing a more regular sleep pattern. Nonetheless, some parents continue to perceive difficulties with sleep onset and prolonged night wakings as problematic. A large population-based study found that approximately 17% of parents reported that their infant had a moderate or severe sleep problem (Martin, Hiscock, Hardy, Davey, & Wake, 2007). Other studies have reported that 20–30% of infants have sleep problems (Mindell, Kuhn, Lewin, Meltzer, & Sadeh, 2006). Moreover, infant sleep problems commonly persist into childhood if they are not treated (Lam, Hiscock, & Wake, 2003). Thus, although many parents will be able to return to a more normal sleep schedule after the infant's sleep consolidates, a significant number of parents have infants with continuous sleep problems, which may result in more chronic sleep loss for caregivers.

Insufficient sleep, whether caused by developmentally appropriate infant sleep patterns or an infant sleep problem, places caregivers at risk for a number of adverse outcomes, including fatigue, distress, and poor mental and physical health (Bayer, Hiscock, Hampton, & Wake, 2007; Dennis & Ross, 2005; Goodlin-Jones, Eiben, & Anders, 1997; Martin et al., 2007; Thunstrom, 1999). When daytime functioning becomes impaired, it may be difficult for parents to provide appropriate care for their infant as well as interact positively with other members of the family. It has been suggested that infant sleep problems may contribute to marital problems (Meijer & van den Wittenboer, 2007) and may put infants at risk of physical abuse (Chavin & Tinson, 1980).

The association between infant sleep problems and maternal depression is particularly well established (Armstrong, O'Donnell, McCallum, & Dadds, 1998; Dennis & Ross, 2005; Goodlin-Jones et al., 1997; Hiscock & Wake, 2001; Karraker & Young, 2007). In fact, mothers of infants with severe sleep problems are twice as likely to report clinically significant levels of depression as mothers of infants without sleep problems (Karraker & Young, 2007). Although the relationship between child sleep and maternal depression is likely complex and reciprocal, longitudinal studies provide support for infant sleep problems contributing to the development of maternal symptoms of depression (Karraker & Young, 2007; Lam et al., 2003). Moreover, maternal sleep quality has been supported to be a mediator of the relationship between infant sleep problems and maternal mental health (Bayer et al., 2007; Hiscock & Wake, 2001).

Although the majority of studies have found that disruptions in children's sleep have a great impact on mothers, who are likely to be the primary caregivers during the day and night, fathers also experience sleep disruptions in the postpartum period. For example, fathers have less total sleep than mothers as measured by actigraphy (Gay et al., 2004), likely due to less sleep for fathers during the day compared to mothers. An infant's sleep postpartum also impacts both mothers' and fathers' level of fatigue equally (Damato & Burant, 2008; Elek, Hudson, & Fleck, 2002; Gay et al., 2004). Still, due to infant nursing and the fact that women are less likely to return to work in the first 8-12 weeks after delivery, mothers' sleep is more fragmented than fathers', which likely results in a greater impact of infant sleep disruptions on the mother than the father (Gay et al., 2004). However, working mothers experience less sleep and higher levels of fatigue postpartum than nonworking mothers, whereas working fathers experience an equal or greater amount of sleep than nonworking fathers (Gay et al., 2004).

Additional support for infant sleep problems contributing to adverse caregiver outcomes comes from sleep intervention trials. Such behavioral interventions can include teaching the infant how to self-soothe, facilitating sleep entrainment, and removing sleep associations that reinforce problematic sleep patterns. Several studies evaluating behavioral sleep interventions show that when infant sleep problems are reduced, parent sleep quality also improves (Hiscock, Bayer, Gold, Hampton, Ukoumunne, & Wake, 2007; Stremler et al., 2006). For example, one randomized controlled trial resulted in an average of 46 and 57 more minutes of nighttime sleep for infants and mothers respectively as compared to the control group (Stremler et al., 2006). In addition to increasing sleep duration, interventions have also been found to improve maternal depression (Eckerberg, 2004; Hall, Clauson, Carty, Janssen, & Saunders, 2006; Hiscock, Bayer, Hampton, Ukoumunne, & Wake, 2008; Hiscock & Wake, 2002), decrease levels of caregiver fatigue (Eckerberg, 2004; Hall et al., 2006), and reduce both maternal and paternal distress (Thome & Skuladottir, 2005). More research is needed on whether these positive effects are maintained long-term, but one study evaluating infant intervention success at two years of age found that while the improvements in child sleep were no longer significantly different between the treatment and control groups, maternal depression was significantly lower in the treatment group (Hiscock et al., 2008).

In addition to reducing already existing sleep problems and improving poor maternal health, behavioral sleep interventions can be used to prevent these problems from occurring in the first place. When behavioral sleep programs are implemented to mothers before and soon after birth, infants show fewer problems with sleep at 6–9 weeks of age than do control infants and their mothers who did not participate in the prevention program (Wolfson, Lacks, & Futterman, 1992). In addition, whereas caregivers in the control group reported increased levels of stress postpartum, parents in the prevention group maintained the same stress level they had before birth (Wolfson et al., 1992). Thus, behavioral sleep interventions have the potential to both prevent sleep problems and reduce sleep problems in infants (see Johnson & Mindell, chapter 16 in this volume, for family based interventions for sleep problems of infants and children).

Unfortunately, physicians often consider infant sleep problems normative and provide little support for parents who express distress and fatigue related to their infants' sleep (Bayer et al., 2007). It has been suggested that primary care may present a golden opportunity for health professionals to screen for and address problems with sleep (Martin et al., 2007). Behavioral interventions for infant sleep problems, although not widely implemented, are effective in preventing or reducing adverse outcomes, such as maternal depression, and are feasible, cost-effective, and welcomed by families (Hiscock et al., 2007; Hiscock et al., 2008; Hiscock & Wake, 2002).

Toddlers, Preschoolers, and School-Age Children

Sleep problems in young children and school-age children can also have a negative impact on parent sleep and daytime functioning. In a national survey of American children's sleep, over half of parents reported being awakened at least once per week by their children, resulting in parents losing an average of 30 minutes of sleep per night (National Sleep Foundation, 2004). Further, almost 20% of respondents reported daytime sleepiness so significant that it interfered with daytime functioning.

Two population-based research studies have also shown a negative association between child sleep disruptions and parent sleep and health. A large Australian study of almost 5,000 preschoolers reported that child sleep problems were associated with psychological distress in mothers and poor general health in both mothers and fathers (Martin et al., 2007). Another study of 500 Swedish children (ages 5.5–6 years) found that 22% of mothers and 12% of fathers reported that their sleep worsened after becoming a parent (Smedje, Broman, & Hetta, 1998); children with frequent night wakings had mothers who reported more sleep problems, while children with difficulties falling asleep or sleep disordered breathing had fathers who reported more sleep problems. Although not a causal result, it is a logical conclusion based on the reported parent outcomes (e.g., early morning wakings in mothers, difficulty falling asleep in fathers, not feeling rested, and daytime sleepiness in both parents) that the child's sleep was disrupting parent sleep as opposed to parent sleep disrupting the child's sleep.

Going beyond sleep problems in children and parents, Leonhard and Randler (2009) examined how children may influence the circadian rhythm and synchronization of social rhythms in four groups of mothers: nonpregnant women without children, pregnant women without children, nonpregnant women with children, and pregnant women with children. The authors reported that children have a significant influence on maternal chronotype. In particular, women with children, regardless of pregnancy status, had the earliest chronotype (Leonhard & Randler, 2009). Further, women with children had earlier weekend wake times, with their biological clock in synchrony with their children more so than with their partners.

In contrast, Gau and Merikangas (2004) examined the association between sleep-wake patterns in school-aged children and their parents, reporting no relationship. Child age likely accounts for much of this contradiction in findings, with the Gau study reporting on older children than the Leonhard study (Gau & Merikangas, 2004; Leonhard & Randler, 2009). As children get older, parents become less involved with sleep routines, and children require less supervision when they wake in the morning. Thus as children transition from preschool to school-age, their sleep schedules have less of an influence on parent sleep schedules and parent sleep amount. However, child sleep disorders and sleep disruptions during the night do not cease with development, thus parental nocturnal sleep disruptions are also likely to continue into school-age and adolescence.

Two recent studies that included both pre-school and school-aged children examined the impact of children's sleep disorders and sleep disturbances on parent sleep and parent functioning (Boergers, Hart, Owens, Streisand, & Spirito, 2007; Meltzer & Mindell, 2007). Boergers and colleagues (2007) surveyed 107 families who presented to a pediatric sleep disorders clinic, and found that parental daytime sleepiness was significantly associated with child sleep problems, child sleep duration, and child daytime sleepiness. Further, having a child with more than one sleep disorder was associated with increased daytime sleepiness for both mothers and fathers. Notably, parent sleep duration was not associated with parent daytime sleepiness. Similar to findings in the National Sleep Foundation's survey (National Sleep Foundation, 2004), Boergers and colleagues (2007) suggested that their finding of mothers having more significant daytime sleepiness than fathers is a result of mothers being the primary caregiver during the night.

In a study of 47 mothers of typically developing children, Meltzer and Mindell (2007) found that mothers of children with significant sleep disturbances reported poorer sleep quality, decreased mood, increased parenting stress, more fatigue, and more daytime sleepiness than mothers of children without significant sleep disruptions. The study also reported an indirect relationship between child sleep disruptions and maternal daytime functioning. Namely child sleep disruptions were found to be a significant predictor of maternal sleep quality, while in turn maternal sleep quality significantly predicted all aspects of negative daytime functioning in mothers (e.g., depression, parenting stress, etc.).

Although no studies have examined treatment benefits of sleep problems in typically developing school-age children, several studies have found behavioral interventions for younger children (toddlers and preschoolers) to not only be effective in improving the child's sleep, but also multiple aspects of family functioning (Mindell et al., 2006). In particular, the use of graduated extinction has been associated with decreased depression, increased marital satisfaction, and decreased parenting stress (Adams & Rickert, 1989; Eckerberg, 2004; Mindell & Durand, 1993). Further, the implementation of a consistent bedtime routine was associated with changes in maternal functioning, including decreased tension, anger, and fatigue (Mindell, Telofski, Wiegand, & Kurtz, 2009). Finally, 84% of mothers reported that a brief behavioral intervention for sleep resulted in a more positive relationship with their child one year after the treatment ended (Hiscock et al., 2008). Together these studies demonstrate the effectiveness and durability of changes to the child's sleep, parent's sleep, and family functioning.

Adolescents

Adolescence is a time of increased independence, as well as increased academic, social, and extracurricular demands. If you add in the biological shift of the circadian rhythm that occurs during puberty, the result is a lot of sleepy adolescents (Crowley, Acebo, & Carskadon, 2007; Moore & Meltzer, 2008). In a representative national survey of American adolescents, the average reported total sleep time was 7.6 hours, significantly less than the needed 9.2 hours (National Sleep Foundation, 2006). Although much of this sleep loss is due to a late bedtime and early rise time, the result is that over 10% of adolescents are late or miss school due to insufficient sleep. Further, more than 50% of adolescents reported driving while drowsy in the previous year, with 15% reporting drowsy driving at least once a week (National Sleep Foundation, 2006). Together the causes and consequences of adolescent insufficient sleep may also impact parent sleep, with parents having to pick adolescents up late at night after extracurricular activities or social events end. Alternatively, many parents may have a difficult time initiating or maintaining sleep if they are worried about their teenager driving at night. Parent sleep also may be disturbed by teenagers' nighttime activities (e.g., watching television, playing video games, talking on the phone). Finally, during the day, parents may also be negatively affected if they have to miss work to drive a sleepy adolescent who missed the bus to school.

The three studies that have looked at adolescent and parent sleep have included only adolescents' report of their own and their parents' sleep (Brand, Gerber, Hatzinger, Beck, & Holsboer-Trachsler, 2009; Tynjala, Kannas, Levalahti, & Valimaa, 1999; Vignau et al., 1997). Together these studies have suggested a dynamic relationship between adolescent and parent sleep, with adolescent sleep affected by poor parenting or family functioning. In turn, poor parenting may result from poor parent sleep, which may be a result of poor or insufficient adolescent sleep. Clearly more research on the relationship between adolescent sleep, parent sleep, and subsequent parent and family functioning is needed.

Sleep in Families of Children with Chronic Conditions

Chronic Illness

Approximately 13% of children have a chronic illness or health condition (National Center for Health Statistics, 2006). Caring for a child with a chronic illness goes above and beyond typical parenting, requiring parents to become medical caregivers within the home. This additional caregiving occurs not only during the day, but also at night, as children with chronic illnesses have more night wakings than healthy children due to disease symptoms such as wheezing, itching, or pain

(Chamlin et al., 2005; Diette et al., 2000; Fiese, Winter, Sliwinski, & Anbar, 2007; Gedaly-Duff, Lee, Nail, Nicholson, & Johnson, 2006; Hinds et al., 2007; Moore, David, Murray, Child, & Arkwright, 2006).

A recent review reported that up to 86% of parents of children with chronic illnesses also have sleep disruptions (Meltzer & Moore, 2008). Prevalence rates varied based on disease type, study methodology (including the lack of control groups), and the time of assessment (current, past, or during a flare or acute episode). For example, during an eczema flare, 86% of parents reported having sleep disruptions due to caregiving (Reid & Lewis-Jones, 1995), but the prevalence of sleep disruptions was not reported when children's eczema was under control. In terms of control groups, one study found significant differences in the prevalence of sleep disruptions for mothers of ventilator-assisted children compared to mothers of healthy children, but no difference was found between mothers of children with cystic fibrosis and mothers of healthy children (Meltzer & Mindell, 2006b).

A child's illness and subsequent sleep disruptions affect parental sleep in multiple ways. First, parents of children with chronic illnesses obtain insufficient sleep. Mothers of ventilator-assisted children obtain almost one hour less of sleep than mothers of healthy children, with almost 50% of the mothers of ventilator-assisted children obtaining less than six hours of sleep (Meltzer & Mindell, 2006b). Parents of children with epilepsy reported an average of only 4.5 hours of sleep at night (Cottrell & Khan, 2005), while parents whose child was hospitalized reported an average of only 4.6 hours of sleep the previous night (McCann, 2008). Finally, mothers and fathers of children with eczema reported losing 39 minutes and 45 minutes (respectively) per night due to their child's illness, compared to parents of children with asthma who reported no sleep loss due to their child's illness (Moore et al., 2006).

This lack of sleep in parental caregivers is alarming, as research has shown that after 18 hours of wakefulness, adults experience deficits in behavioral alertness and working memory (Van Dongen, Maislin, Mullington, & Dinges, 2003). Further, studies of residents and nurses have reported an increase in medical errors following chronic sleep loss (Balas, Scott, & Rogers, 2006; Richardson et al., 1996; Scott, Hwang, & Rogers, 2006). Thus parents' ability to make decisions regarding their child's medical care may be compromised by the very fact that they are required to provide nighttime medical care.

Other consequences of chronic partial sleep loss include changes to mood, health, and emotion regulation (Dinges, Rogers, & Baynard, 2005). These changes have been seen in parental caregivers of children with chronic illnesses. In parents of children with epilepsy, the frequency of night wakings was associated with increased symptoms of maternal depression, as well as poorer sleep quality, less marital satisfaction, and poorer health in both parents (Cottrell & Khan, 2005). Similarly, poor sleep quality was associated with anxiety and depression in mothers of children with asthma or cystic fibrosis (Yilmaz et al., 2008). Finally, a study of parents of children with type 1 diabetes reported that parents who performed nighttime caregiving (nocturnal blood glucose monitoring) had significantly higher anxiety and stress compared to parents who did not engage in regular nighttime caregiving (Monaghan, Hilliard, Cogen, & Streisand, 2009). The authors of this study concluded that perhaps parental sleep mediates the relationship between parenting a chronically ill child and negative daytime functioning found in parents.

Two studies have supported this mediation hypothesis. Moore and colleagues (2006) found that elevated depression and anxiety in mothers and fathers of children with eczema was a result of sleep disruptions, independent of the child's illness. Similarly, Meltzer and Mindell (2006b) found that maternal sleep quality mediated the relationship between child health status and both maternal depression and fatigue.

Other areas of family functioning that are affected by a child's illness and sleep disruptions include poorer parental health-related quality of life (Hatzmann, Heymans, Ferrer-i-Carbonell, van Praag, & Grootenhuis, 2008), changes to less independent sleeping arrangements (Chamlin et al., 2005; Williams et al., 2000), and more frequent parental absence from work (Diette et al., 2000). Hatzmann and colleagues (2008) found that across chronic illnesses, parents of ill children had significantly poorer health-related quality of life compared to parents of healthy children, with sleep being one of the most impaired domains. An increase in co-sleeping has been reported in families of children with epilepsy, diabetes, and eczema (Chamlin et al., 2005; Williams et al., 2000), in particular for newly diagnosed and younger children. Changes to sleeping arrangements most commonly resulted from the parental desire to provide additional nocturnal supervision for the child's illness. Finally, parents who were awakened during the night by their child's asthma reported more missed days of work than parents of children who did not awaken from asthma (Diette et al., 2000).

While it appears that poor sleep quality provides one mechanistic explanation for the increased rates of negative functioning found in parents of children with chronic illnesses, more research is needed in this area. This includes studies that utilize objective assessments of sleep (i.e., actigraphy), longitudinal designs to detect differences during fluctuations of the child's health, the inclusion of appropriate control groups, and intervention studies that focus on improving sleep in children with chronic illnesses. In addition, all aspects of family life are disrupted by a child's illness, including daily routines and a sense of safety, both of which can affect sleep (Gedaly-Duff et al., 2006). Thus it is important to examine siblings' sleep and daytime functioning, which may also be disrupted by a child's illness, frequent night wakings, or a parent's negative daytime functioning.

Developmental Disorders

Sleep problems are common in children with developmental disorders, including intellectual disabilities (ID), autism spectrum disorder (ASD), and attention-deficit/hyperactivity disorder (ADHD). This includes difficulties falling asleep, multiple night wakings, and/or early morning sleep termination (Didden, Korzilius, van Aperlo, van Overloop, & De Vries, 2002; Owens, 2005; Patzold, Richdale, & Tonge, 1998; Robinson & Richdale, 2004; Wiggs, Montgomery, & Stores, 2005; Wiggs & Stores, 1996). Because children with developmental disorders often require increased supervision compared to typically developing children, one can assume that when children with developmental disorders are not sleeping, neither are their parents.

This suggestion has been supported by multiple studies. Robinson and Richdale (2004) found that 45% of parents of children with an ID reported sleep disruptions due to the child's sleep problems, with more parents reporting disrupted sleep when their child had night wakings or early sleep termination. Another study of children with development disorders found that child sleep disturbances accounted for 22% of the variance in maternal sleep quality, independent of child daytime behavior problems (Chu & Richdale, 2009). Similarly, sleep problems in parents of children with ASDs were found to be significantly associated with the child's sleep problems, but not the severity of the child's ASD symptoms (Lopez-Wagner, Hoffman, Sweeney, Hodge, & Gilliam, 2008). Finally, a different study of parents of children with ASDs that used actigraphy found that parents slept on average one hour less per night than parents of typically developing children (Meltzer, 2008). Together these studies demonstrate that parent sleep is negatively affected by sleep disruptions in children with developmental disorders.

Parental daytime functioning has also been found to be associated with sleep disruptions in children with developmental disorders. Two studies have reported more parenting stress and hassles for parents of children with IDs or pervasive developmental disorders (Doo & Wing, 2006; Richdale, Francis, Gavidia-Payne, & Cotton, 2000). Further, sleep problems in children with ADHD were found to be associated with poorer maternal health, including depression, anxiety, and stress (Sung, Hiscock, Sciberras, & Efron, 2008). In addition, this same study reported a negative impact on parental work attendance and family functioning when children with ADHD also had sleep problems.

Behavioral treatments for sleep problems in children with IDs have been shown to not only improve parental satisfaction with their own sleep, but also their ability to cope with their child's sleep problems (Wiggs & Stores, 1998; 2001). One conclusion drawn from these behavioral treatment studies is that improvements in the child's sleep may not be the only important outcome of interventions. In fact, the improvements in parental total sleep time and ability to cope with a child's sleep problems may be as significant, if not an even more important benefit of these treatments (Wiggs & Stores, 1998; 2001). Including parent sleep, daytime functioning, and coping is important for all treatment studies examining the benefits of behavioral interventions for sleep problems in children with developmental disorders.

Conclusions

Sleep problems are common in youth, affecting children of all ages, including those with chronic illnesses or developmental disorders.

In turn, children's sleep disruptions can have a significant impact on parental sleep and daytime functioning, including depression, fatigue, parenting stress, and marital satisfaction. However, behavioral treatments for sleep problems, as well as improved disease management for children with chronic illnesses, can result in improved child sleep, parent sleep, and family functioning.

The relationship between child sleep and family functioning is complex and dynamic. However, even when viewed through a unidirectional lens, as we have done in this chapter, it is clear that all health care providers who work with children and families should be educated about the causes and consequences of sleep problems in children, providing interventions or treatment referrals as appropriate. In addition, more research is needed to examine the relationship between child sleep disruptions and family functioning in all developmental stages, including school-age children and adolescents. Further, researchers need to include parent sleep and daytime functioning as outcomes for any treatment study that focuses on sleep in youth, fully capturing both direct and indirect effects of the intervention on family functioning.

REFERENCES

Adams, L. A., & Rickert, V. I. (1989). Reducing bedtime tantrums: Comparison between positive routines and graduated extinction. *Pediatrics, 84*, 756–761.

Armstrong, K. L., O'Donnell, H., McCallum, R., & Dadds, M. (1998). Childhood sleep problems: Association with prenatal factors and maternal distress/depression. *Journal of Pediatrics and Child Health, 34*, 263–266.

Balas, M. C., Scott, L. D., & Rogers, A. E. (2006). Frequency and type of errors and near errors reported by critical care nurses. *Canadian Journal of Nursing Research, 38*, 24–41.

Bayer, J. K., Hiscock, H., Hampton, A., & Wake, M. (2007). Sleep problems in young infants and maternal mental and physical health. *Journal of Pediatrics and Child Health, 43*, 66–73.

Boergers, J., Hart, C., Owens, J. A., Streisand, R., & Spirito, A. (2007). Child sleep disorders: Associations with parental sleep duration and daytime sleepiness. *Journal of Family Psychology, 21*, 88–94.

Brand, S., Gerber, M., Hatzinger, M., Beck, J., & Holsboer-Trachsler, E. (2009). Evidence for similarities between adolescents and parents in sleep patterns. *Sleep Medicine.* Advance online publication. doi:10.1016/j.sleep.2008.12.013

Chamlin, S. L., Mattson, C. L., Frieden, I. J., Williams, M. L., Mancini, A. J., Cella, D., Chren, M. M. (2005). The price of pruritus: Sleep disturbance and cosleeping in atopic dermatitis. *Archives of Pediatrics and Adolescent Medicine, 159*, 745–750.

Chavin, W., & Tinson, S. (1980). Children with sleep difficulties. *Health Visitor, 53*, 477–480.

Chu, J., & Richdale, A. L. (2009). Sleep quality and psychological wellbeing in mothers of children with developmental disabilities. *Research in Developmental Disabilities, 30*, 1512–1522.

Cottrell, L., & Khan, A. (2005). Impact of childhood epilepsy on maternal sleep and socioemotional functioning. *Clinical Pediatrics, 44*, 613–616.

Crowley, S. J., Acebo, C., & Carskadon, M. A. (2007). Sleep, circadian rhythms, and delayed phase in adolescence. *Sleep Medicine, 8*, 602–612.

Damato, E. G., & Burant, C. (2008). Sleep patterns and fatigue in parents of twins. *Journal of Obstetric, Gynecologic, and Neonatal Nursing, 37*, 738–749.

Dennis, C. L., & Ross, L. (2005). Relationships among infant sleep patterns, maternal fatigue, and development of depressive symptomatology. *Birth, 32*, 187–193.

Didden, R., Korzilius, H., van Aperlo, B., van Overloop, C., & De Vries, M. (2002). Sleep problems and daytime problem behaviours in children with intellectual disability. *Journal of Intellectual Disability Research, 46*, 537–547.

Diette, G. B., Markson, L., Skinner, E. A., Nguyen, T. T., Algatt-Bergstrom, P., & Wu, A. W. (2000). Nocturnal asthma in children affects school attendance, school performance, and parents' work attendance. *Archives of Pediatrics and Adolescent Medicine, 154*, 923–928.

Dinges, D. F., Rogers, N. L., & Baynard, M. D. (2005). Chronic sleep deprivation. In M.H. Kryger, T. Roth, & W. C. Dement (Eds.), *Principles and practice of sleep medicine* (4th ed., pp. 67–76). Philadelphia, PA: Elsevier Saunders.

Doo, S., & Wing, Y. K. (2006). Sleep problems of children with pervasive developmental disorders: Correlation with parental stress. *Developmental Medicine and Child Neurology, 48*, 650–655.

Eckerberg, B. (2004). Treatment of sleep problems in families with young children: Effects of treatment on family well-being. *Acta Paediatrica, 93*, 126–134.

Elek, S. M., Hudson, D. B., & Fleck, M. O. (2002). Couples' experiences with fatigue during the transition to parenthood. *Journal of Family Nursing, 8*, 221–240.

Fallone, G., Owens, J. A., & Deane, J. (2002). Sleepiness in children and adolescents: Clinical implications. *Sleep Medicine Reviews, 6*, 287–306.

Fiese, B. H., Winter, M. A., Sliwinski, M., & Anbar, R. D. (2007). Nighttime waking in children with asthma: An exploratory study of daily fluctuations in family climate. *Journal of Family Psychology, 21*, 95–103.

Gau, S. S., & Merikangas, K. R. (2004). Similarities and differences in sleep-wake patterns among adults and their children. *Sleep, 27,* 299–304.

Gay, C. L., Lee, K. A., & Lee, S. Y. (2004). Sleep patterns and fatigue in new mothers and fathers. *Biological Research for Nursing, 5,* 311–318.

Gedaly-Duff, V., Lee, K. A., Nail, L. M., Nicholson, S., & Johnson, K. P. (2006). Pain, sleep disturbance, and fatigue in children with Leukemia and their parents: A pilot study. *Oncology Nursing Forum, 33,* 641–646.

Goodlin-Jones, B. L., Eiben, L. A., & Anders, T. F. (1997). Maternal well-being and sleep- wake behaviors in infants: An intervention using maternal odor. *Infant Mental Health Journal, 18,* 378–393.

Hall, W. A., Clauson, M., Carty, E. M., Janssen, P. A., & Saunders, R. A. (2006). Effects on parents of an intervention to resolve infant behavioral sleep problems. *Pediatric Nursing, 32,* 243–250.

Hatzmann, J., Heymans, H. S. A, Ferrer-i-Carbonell, A., van Praag, B. M. S, & Grootenhuis, M. A. (2008). Hidden consequences of success in pediatrics: Parental health-related quality of life results from the Care Project. *Pediatrics, 122,* e1030–e1038.

Hinds, P. S., Hockenberry, M., Rai, S. N., Zhang, L., Razzouk, B. I., McCarthy, K., Rodriguez-Galindo, C. (2007). Nocturnal awakenings, sleep environment interruptions, and fatigue in hospitalized children with cancer. *Oncology Nursing Forum, 34,* 393–402.

Hiscock, H., Bayer, J., Gold, L., Hampton, A., Ukoumunne, O. C., & Wake, M. (2007). Improving infant sleep and maternal mental health: A cluster randomised trial. *Archives of Disease in Childhood, 92,* 952–958.

Hiscock, H., Bayer, J. K., Hampton, A., Ukoumunne, O. C., & Wake, M. (2008). Long-term mother and child mental health effects of a population-based infant sleep intervention: Cluster-randomized, controlled trial. *Pediatrics, 122,* e621–e627.

Hiscock, H., & Wake, M. (2001). Infant sleep problems and postnatal depression: A community-based study. *Pediatrics, 107,* 1317–1322.

Hiscock, H., & Wake, M. (2002). Randomised controlled trial of behavioural infant sleep intervention to improve infant sleep and maternal mood. *British Medical Journal, 324,* 1062–1067.

Kang, M. J., Matsumoto, K., Shinkoda, H., Mishima, M., & Seo, Y. J. (2002). Longitudinal study for sleep-wake behaviours of mothers from pre-partum to post-partum using actigraph and sleep logs. *Psychiatry and Clinical Neurosciences, 56,* 251–252.

Karraker, K. H., & Young, M. (2007). Night waking in 6-month-old infants and maternal depressive symptoms. *Journal of Applied Developmental Psychology, 28,* 493–498.

Lam, P., Hiscock, H., & Wake, M. (2003). Outcomes of infant sleep problems: A longitudinal study of sleep, behavior, and maternal well-being. *Pediatrics, 111,* 203–207.

Lee, K. A., Zaffke, M. E., & McEnany, G. (2000). Parity and sleep patterns during and after pregnancy. *Obstetrics and Gynecology, 95*, 14–18.

Leonhard, C., & Randler, C. (2009). In sync with the family: Children and partners influence the sleep-wake circadian rhythm and social habits of women. *Chronobiology International, 26,* 510–525.

Lopez-Wagner, M. C., Hoffman, C. D., Sweeney, D. P., Hodge, D., & Gilliam, J. E. (2008). Sleep problems of parents of typically developing children and parents of children with autism. *Journal of Genetic Psychology, 169,* 245–259.

Martin, J., Hiscock, H., Hardy, P., Davey, B., & Wake, M. (2007). Adverse associations of infant and child sleep problems and parent health: An Australian population study. *Pediatrics, 119,* 947–955.

McCann, D. (2008). Sleep deprivation is an additional stress for parents staying in hospital. *Journal for Specialists in Pediatric Nursing, 13,* 111–122.

Meijer, A. M., & van den Wittenboer, G. L. H. (2007). Contribution of infants' sleep and crying to marital relationship of first-time parent couples in the 1st year after childbirth. *Journal of Family Psychology, 21,* 49–57.

Meltzer, L. J. (2008). Brief report: Sleep in parents of children with autism spectrum disorders. *Journal of Pediatric Psychology, 33,* 380–386.

Meltzer, L. J., & Mindell, J. A. (2006a). Sleep and sleep disorders in children and adolescents. *Psychiatric Clinics of North America, 29,* 1059–1076.

Meltzer, L. J., & Mindell, J. A. (2006b). Impact of a child's chronic illness on maternal sleep and daytime functioning. *Archives of Internal Medicine, 166,* 1749–1755.

Meltzer, L. J., & Mindell, J. A. (2007). Relationship between child sleep disturbances and maternal sleep, mood, and parenting stress: A pilot study. *Journal of Family Psychology, 21,* 67–73.

Meltzer, L. J., & Moore, M. (2008). Sleep disruptions in parents of children and adolescents with chronic illnesses: Prevalence, causes, and consequences. *Journal of Pediatric Psychology, 33,* 279–291.

Mindell, J. A., & Durand, V. M. (1993). Treatment of childhood sleep disorders: Generalization across disorders and effects on family members. *Journal of Pediatric Psychology, 18,* 731–750.

Mindell, J. A., Kuhn, B., Lewin, D. S., Meltzer, L. J., & Sadeh, A. (2006). Behavioral treatment of bedtime problems and night wakings in infants and young children. *Sleep, 29,* 1263–1276.

Mindell, J. A., Telofski, L. S., Wiegand, B., & Kurtz, E. S. (2009). A nightly bedtime routine: Impact on sleep in young children and maternal mood. *Sleep, 32,* 599–606.

Monaghan, M. C., Hilliard, M. E., Cogen, F. R., & Streisand, R. (2009). Nighttime caregiving behaviors among parents of young children with Type 1 diabetes: Associations with illness characteristics and parent functioning. *Families, Systems, and Health, 27,* 28–38.

Moore, K., David, T. J., Murray, C. S., Child, F., & Arkwright, P. D. (2006). Effect of childhood eczema and asthma on parental sleep and well-being: A prospective comparative study. *British Journal of Dermatology, 154*, 514–518.

Moore, M., & Meltzer, L. J. (2008). The sleepy adolescent: Causes and consequences of sleepiness in teens. *Paediatric Respiratory Reviews, 9*, 114–121.

National Center for Health Statistics (2006). *Health, United States, 2006 with Chartbook on Trends in the Health of Americans*. Hyattsville, MD: U.S. Government Printing Office.

National Sleep Foundation (2004). Sleep in America Poll. Retrieved May 11, 2007, from http://www.sleepfoundation.org/.

National Sleep Foundation (2006). Sleep in America Poll. Retrieved March 31, 2006, from http://www.sleepfoundation.org/.

Owens, J. A. (2005). The ADHD and sleep conundrum: A review. *Journal of Developmental and Behavioral Pediatrics, 26*, 312–322.

Patzold, L. M., Richdale, A. L., & Tonge, B. J. (1998). An investigation into sleep characteristics of children with autism and Asperger's disorder. *Journal of Paediatrics and Child Health, 34*, 528–533.

Reid, P., & Lewis-Jones, M. S. (1995). Sleep difficulties and their management in preschoolers with atopic eczema. *Clinical and Experimental Dermatology, 20*, 38–41.

Richardson, G. S., Wyatt, J. K., Sullivan, J. P., Orav, E. J., Ward, A. E., Wolf, M. A., & Czeisler, C. A. (1996). Objective assessment of sleep and alertness in medical house staff and the impact of protected time for sleep. *Sleep, 19*, 718–726.

Richdale, A., Francis, A., Gavidia-Payne, S., & Cotton, S. (2000). Stress, behaviour, and sleep problems in children with an intellectual disability. *Journal of Intellectual and Developmental Disability, 25*, 147–161.

Robinson, A. M., & Richdale, A. L. (2004). Sleep problems in children with an intellectual disability: Parental perceptions of sleep problems, and views of treatment effectiveness. *Child: Care, Health and Development, 30*, 139–150.

Scott, L. D., Hwang, W. T., & Rogers, A. E. (2006). The impact of multiple care giving roles on fatigue, stress, and work performance among hospital staff nurses. *Journal of Nursing Administration, 36*, 86–95.

Smedje, H., Broman, J. E., & Hetta, J. (1998). Sleep disturbances in Swedish preschool children and their parents. *Nordic Journal of Psychiatry, 52*, 59–67.

Stremler, R., Hodnett, E., Lee, K., MacMillan, S., Mill, C., Ongcangco, L., & Willan, A. (2006). A behavioral-educational intervention to promote maternal and infant sleep: A pilot randomized, controlled trial. *Sleep, 29*, 1609–1615.

Sung, V., Hiscock, H., Sciberras, E., & Efron, D. (2008). Sleep problems in children with attention-deficit/hyperactivity disorder: Prevalence and the effect on the child and family. *Archives of Pediatrics and Adolescent Medicine, 162*, 336–342.

Thome, M., & Skuladottir, A. (2005). Evaluating a family-centred intervention for infant sleep problems. *Journal of Advanced Nursing, 50*, 5–11.

Thunstrom, M. (1999). Severe Sleep Problems among Infants: Family and infant characteristics. *Ambulatory Child Health*, *5*, 27–41.

Tynjala, J., Kannas, L., Levalahti, E., & Valimaa, R. (1999). Perceived sleep quality and its precursors in adolescents. *Health Promotion International*, *14*, 155–166.

Van Dongen, H. P. A., Maislin, G., Mullington, J. M., & Dinges, D. F. (2003). The cumulative cost of additional wakefulness: Dose-response effects on neurobehavioral functions and sleep physiology from chronic sleep restriction and total sleep deprivation. *Sleep*, *26*, 117–126.

Vignau, J., Bailly, D., Duhamel, A., Vervaecke, P., Beuscart, R., & Collinet, C. (1997). Epidemiologic study of sleep quality and troubles in French secondary school adolescents. *Journal of Adolescent Health*, *21*, 343–350.

Wiggs, L., Montgomery, P., & Stores, G. (2005). Actigraphic and parent reports of sleep patterns and sleep disorders in children with subtypes of attention-deficit hyperactivity disorder. *Sleep*, *28*, 1437–1445.

Wiggs, L., & Stores, G. (1996). Severe sleep disturbance and daytime challenging behaviour in children with severe learning disabilities. *Journal of Intellectual Disability Research*, *40*, 518–528.

Wiggs, L., & Stores, G. (1998). Behavioural treatment for sleep problems in children with severe learning disabilities and challenging daytime behaviour: Effect on sleep patterns of mother and child. *Journal of Sleep Research*, *7*, 119–126.

Wiggs, L., & Stores, G. (2001). Behavioural treatment for sleep problems in children with severe intellectual disabilities and daytime challenging behaviour: Effect on mothers and fathers. *British Journal of Health Psychology*, *6*, 257–269.

Williams, J., Lange, B., Sharp, G., Griebel, M., Edgar, T., Haley, T.,… Dykman, R. (2000). Altered sleeping arrangements in pediatric patients with epilepsy. *Clinical Pediatrics*, *39*, 635–642.

Wolfson, A., Lacks, P., & Futterman, A. (1992). Effects of parent training on infant sleeping patterns, parents' stress, and perceived parental competence. *Journal of Consulting and Clinical Psychology*, *60*, 41–48.

Yilmaz, O., Sogut, A., Gulle, S., Can, D., Ertan, P., & Yuksel, H. (2008). Sleep quality and depression-anxiety in mothers of children with two chronic respiratory diseases: Asthma and cystic fibrosis. *Journal of Cystic Fibrosis*, *7*, 495–500.

7

Children's Sleep Deficits and Cognitive and Behavioral Adjustment

Angela D. Staples and John E. Bates

Introduction

Sadeh (2007) recently observed that research on the consequences of children's sleep deficits lags behind research about the consequences of adults' sleep deficits. We would further note that research on consequences of young children's sleep deficits lags behind research about the consequences of adolescents' sleep deficits. This chapter has benefited from research on adolescents and adults, but its focus is on consequences of sleep deficits for children between one and 10 years of age. Research on adolescents and adults strongly suggests that sleep plays important roles in learning and behavior (Dahl, 2002; Walker & Stickgold, 2006). Recent reviews suggest that less than optimal nighttime sleep is associated with less than optimal functioning during the day, particularly with respect to adults' learning (Stickgold, 2005), adolescents' academic performance (Curcio, Ferrara, & De Gennaro, 2006; Wolfson & Carskadon, 2003), and attention deficit disorders in children (Owens, 2005). Likewise, sleep disordered breathing has been linked with cognitive functioning and emotions and behavior problems in children between ages four and 16 years (Beebe, 2006).

Following Dahl (1996; 2002), we view sleep, daytime behavior, and affect as part of a larger, transactional system involving the child, family, community, and culture. Deficiencies in sleep-wake regulation may have a complex etiology. In this way, sleep problems would be quite similar to behavior problems, which have a complex etiology that includes genetic predispositions, prenatal exposure to stress or toxins, other environmental factors such as family stress, school and neighborhood quality, and importantly, the quality of parenting that the child receives.

Complex transactional processes linking sleep and behavioral adjustment begin even before a child is born. Pesonen and colleagues (2009) recently demonstrated that low birth weight children had lower sleep efficiency and greater parent-reported sleep problems at age eight years even after controlling for other potential confounds such as current health status or parent socioeconomic status. Feldman (2009) showed that greater regularity of sleep-wake states in pre-term infants at 32 and 34 weeks gestational age was predictive of better emotion regulation during the first year, increased attention regulation in the second year of life, and better executive function, self-restraint, and fewer behavior problems at age five. Moreover, Feldman (2009) showed that the association between sleep-wake regularity at 32 and 34 weeks gestational age and behavioral adjustment at age five developed through the mediating effects of relatively good emotion and attention regulation in the first two years of life.

Developing a regular sleep pattern is part of the development of a larger regulatory system according to Goodlin-Jones, Burnham, and Anders (2000). In general, poorer self-regulation is associated with more behavior problems (Eisenberg et al., 2009; Fox & Calkins, 2003; Nigg, 2006). In the present chapter, we will review the evidence that sleep deficits may play an active role in shaping the development of behavior problems in young children. We have chosen the term sleep deficits to reflect the myriad of ways sleep problems have been defined as well as the variety of ways children's sleep might be compromised (e.g., deficits in quantity, quality, consistency). However, because we also note that the relation between sleep and behavior problems is typically of modest to moderate size, we consider other factors that could complement or moderate the sleep-adjustment association. One likely factor, considered briefly in the chapter, is parenting (for a more in-depth review of parenting and sleep, see Erath and Tu, chapter 2 in this volume). Parenting could affect how children transition from wakefulness to sleep at the beginning of the night, and parental responses to nighttime awakenings could influence children's sleep. The same parenting practices that are associated with children's sleep problems may also be associated with daytime behavior problems. Numerous studies link poor parenting with poor daytime adjustment (Maccoby & Martin, 1983; Patterson, Reid, & Dishion, 1992; Rothbaum & Weisz, 1994), therefore we highlight studies that account for parenting practices when linking sleep and adjustment.

Another likely factor, considered here in more detail, is temperament. Temperament constructs describe early appearing differences in reactivity and regulation that result in behavioral expressions of negative emotionality, impulsivity, and fearfulness (Rothbart & Bates, 2006). Temperament traits have been shown to differentially predict later adjustment (Bates, 1989a; Rothbart & Bates, 2006; Janson & Mathiesen, 2008). Specifically, measures of impulsivity are more strongly associated with later externalizing than internalizing behavior problems, while measures of fearfulness are more strongly associated with later internalizing than externalizing behavior problems. In comparison, measures of negative emotionality, which reflect both frustration and other forms of distress, are equally associated with later externalizing and internalizing behavior problems. In addition, the link between temperament and adjustment has been shown to vary with differences in parenting and vice versa—the link between parenting and adjustment varies with child temperament (Bates & Pettit, 2007). For example, resistant temperament predicted later externalizing problems more strongly for children whose mothers were less controlling than for children whose mothers were more controlling (Bates, Pettit, Dodge, & Ridge, 1998). As another example, harsh parenting was associated with slower development of internalized self-control for temperamentally fearful children than for fearless children (Kochanska, 1997). Prior to exploring how children's sleep and behavioral adjustment are related, we consider the development of sleep itself in childhood.

Development of Sleep Patterns in Childhood

One of the major changes in young children's sleep from ages one to five years is the consolidation of sleep into a single nighttime period (Crowell, Keener, Ginsburg, & Anders, 1987; Ottaviano, Giannotti, Cortesi, Bruni, & Ottaviano, 1996). In addition, physiological aspects of children's sleep begin to resemble those of adults' sleep around age five (Kahn, Fisher, Edwards, & Davis, 1973). However, total amount of sleep in a 24-hour period seems to be relatively stable—it tends to only decline about one hour from toddlerhood to school entry (Iglowstein, Jenni, Molinari, & Largo, 2003). In general, children who sleep more at night tend to sleep less during the day and vice versa (Acebo et al., 2005; Kaplan, McNicol, Conte, & Moghadam, 1987; Koch, Soussignan, & Montagner, 1984). Children who do not nap tend to get the same amount of sleep over 24-hours as children who do nap (Ward, Gay, Alkon, Anders, & Lee, 2008). By the time children are five years of age, most have stopped napping, however the transition appears to be a decline in the frequency of naps as opposed to a gradual shortening of the length of the nap (Iglowstein et al., 2003; Koch et al., 1984). From kindergarten through sixth grade, children's total sleep time declines from approximately 10.5 to 9.5 hours per night (Jenni, Molinari, Caflisch, & Largo, 2007; Sadeh, Raviv, & Gruber, 2000; Spruyt, O'Brien, Cluydts, Verleye, & Ferri, 2005) and continues to decline into adolescence (Iglowstein et al., 2003). Overall, the average one-year-old sleeps roughly two hours more per 24-hours than the average 12-year-old.

In addition to changes in the timing and amount of sleep, the quality of children's sleep changes dramatically between ages one and 12 years. Around age one, approximately 35% of children wake one or more times per night. This percentage declines to approximately 5% by age 12 (Beltramini & Hertzig, 1983; Fricke-Oerkermann et al., 2007). In one of the few studies that objectively measured sleep in elementary school children, one in five children were classified as sleeping poorly, which was characterized by a combination of the frequency of night awakenings and spending more than 10% of the night awake (Sadeh et al., 2000). Direct comparisons between sleep as reported by parents and sleep indexed by actigraphs (motion-detection devices) in a sample of kindergarten children revealed that 41% of children met the criteria for poor sleep (spending more than 10% of the night awake following sleep onset or waking three times per night for at least five minutes per waking) according to actigraphic sleep measures (Tikotzky & Sadeh, 2001). Yet none of the children met the criteria for poor sleep according to the parent daily diaries. Nevertheless, even though parents underreported the number of night awakenings detected by actigraphy, there was a significant association between the numbers of nighttime awakenings as reported by parents and as recorded by actigraphy.

Despite the overall trend toward more mature sleep patterns with increasing age, frequent night waking and difficulties going to sleep remain relatively common problems reported by parents of preschool and elementary school children. Studies have found that night awakenings at least once a week are normal among three- to five-year-olds (Beltramini & Hertzig, 1983; Gaylor, Burnham, Goodlin-Jones, & Anders, 2005; Lam, Hiscock, & Wake, 2003). Large, population-based studies suggest that approximately 20% of children between five and seven years of age experience frequent night awakenings (Ottaviano et al., 1996; Smedje, Broman, & Hetta, 2001). At the same time, longitudinal studies do suggest a decline in the number of night awakenings from infancy through age five (Beltramini & Hertzig, 1983; Gaylor et al., 2005; Scher, Epstein, & Tirosh, 2004). Longitudinal studies also suggest that children who do not sleep through the night relatively early in life are at greater risk for continued sleep disruptions throughout early childhood. For example, one-third of five month olds who were not sleeping six consecutive hours at night continued to have disrupted sleep at two and a half years of age (Touchette et al., 2005). When the definition of a sleep problem also included prolonged latency to fall back to sleep, 41% of eight month olds with sleep problems continue to have sleep problems at age three (Zuckerman, Stevenson, & Bailey, 1987). Additionally, 13%–45% of infants who woke at least once a night per week continued to have nighttime waking problems through ages four and five (Beltramini & Hertzig, 1983; Gaylor et al., 2005; Zuckerman et al., 1987). In short, children's night waking tendencies show continuity from infancy into the preschool ages, and parents often regard this as a problem. Moreover, occasional night wakening is quite common even as late as age five.

Even more common in early childhood are problems associated with going to sleep. From age one to five years, there is an increase in the length of the bedtime routine; more "curtain calls" after the child has been put to bed; and longer time to fall asleep once in bed (Beltramini & Hertzig, 1983; Crowell et al., 1987; Zuckerman et al., 1987). There also appears to be some stability in average rates of these behaviors, at least during the preschool years. For example, Gaylor et al. (2005) found no evidence of change in the number of children ages two to four who took longer than 20 minutes to fall asleep or the number of children calling their parent back after being put to bed.

Recent research suggests that parenting practices play the largest role in the persistence of sleep problems (Spilsbury et al., 2005; Van Tassel, 1985). Parenting practices such as putting the child to bed asleep, removing the child from bed after a nighttime awakening, and giving food at night are associated with chronic and persistent sleep problems (Johnson & McMahon, 2008; Simard, Nielsen, Tremblay, Boivin, & Montplaisir, 2008). One viewpoint is that such parenting practices hinder the child's ability to learn how to fall asleep alone, which is carried over as a need for parental intervention when the child awakes in the middle of the night (Weissbluth, 1989). Furthermore, global assessments of parenting style have shown that more lax or less autonomy-supporting parenting styles were associated with current and persistent sleep problems (Owens-Stively et al., 1997; Spilsbury et al., 2005; Staples & Bates, 2009). For a more detailed treatment of the role of parenting in children's sleep see Erath and Tu (Chapter 2, this volume).

To summarize, evidence suggests that children's sleep tends to improve from infancy into early school age, with more consolidated and better quality of nighttime sleep occurring over time. While sleep shows improvement from infancy through age five, there are increased problems associated with going to sleep. However, both of these findings rest largely on parent reports and there is some evidence that parents may differ in the types of child sleep behaviors that they consider problematic. For example, Crowell and colleagues (1987) found that only 12% of parents reported that their toddler had a sleep problem, yet twice as many reported that their child frequently woke at night or took longer than 30 minutes to fall asleep. Similarly, Lam and colleagues (2003) found only 32% of parents considered their three- to four-year-old children's frequent night awakenings to be a problem, but 78% of parents reported that their child woke at least one night each week and 43% of parents reported their child woke several nights each week. In addition to potential confounds associated with parent-report measures of sleep, other methodological issues such as a lack of standardized criteria for determining whether a child has a clinically significant sleep problem (Archbold, Pituch, Panahi, & Chervin, 2002; Gaylor et al., 2005; Goodlin-Jones & Anders, 2004) and the conflation of multiple types of sleep problems into a single overall index of poor sleep will be considered in the context of linking sleep and adjustment.

Sleep and Adjustment

Current theories have identified two ways that poor sleep may affect daytime behavior (Dahl, 1996; Owens, 2008; Sadeh, 2007). The first is through disrupting neural processes during sleep that have been shown to be critical for learning (Ellenbogen, Hulbert, Stickgold, Dinges, & Thompson-Schill, 2006; Walker & Stickgold, 2006). The second is through disruptions in executive functioning, emotion regulation, and behavioral control as a result of decreased alertness due to daytime sleepiness (Anderson, Storfer-Isser, Taylor, Rosen, & Redline, 2009; Fallone, Owens, & Deane, 2002; Gradisar, Terrill, Johnston, & Douglas, 2008). Our general conclusion is that research is broadly supportive of the conceptual links between sleep and differences in adaptive functioning among young children. However, before detailing the evidence, we list some methodological issues.

The majority of studies examining the association between sleep and daytime adjustment have tended to use a single index of sleep problems (i.e., a single questionnaire item or the total score from a series of questions) without distinguishing between disrupted sleep (e.g., night awakenings, restlessness, irregular schedule) and insufficient sleep (e.g., due to resisting bedtime or too short time in bed). Consequently, there is little information about the relation between specific forms of sleep problems and adjustment. There is evidence that some types of sleep problems are associated with poor daytime functioning while others appear to result from difficulties in daytime functioning. In the first case, frequent night awakenings as a consequence of sleep disordered breathing are thought to interfere with learning (e.g., difficulty consolidating memories) and the ability to regulate behavior (e.g., poor impulse control due to the effects of fatigue; Beebe, 2006). In the second case, difficulty falling asleep has been associated with higher levels of anxiety, perhaps due to separation anxiety (Cortesi, Giannotti, Sebastiani, Vagnoni, & Marioni, 2008) or heightened vigilance that "intereferes with the feelings of safety that are critical to the onset of sleep" (Forbes et al., 2008, p. 154). Therefore, studies that index sleep problems with a composite including both frequent nighttime awakenings and prolonged latency to sleep onset may obscure the process by which sleep affects daytime adjustment.

Furthermore, the majority of relevant studies have used parent reports of children's sleep and behavioral problems. Parent reports of sleep differ from objective measures of sleep or child reports of sleep (Fricke-Oerkermann et al., 2007; Sadeh, 2008; Tikotzky & Sadeh, 2001). In general, parent reports have complex, incompletely unpacked meanings (Bates, 1989b). Parent reports could overestimate, on average, some problems and underestimate others, depending partly on how the questions are formulated and on characteristics of parents (Bates, 1989b). For example, parent reports have been shown to underestimate the number of night awakenings that children experience (Tikotzky & Sadeh, 2001), which could affect conclusions about the effects of night waking on children's adjustment. Finally, the majority of studies have been cross-sectional and correlational, thereby limiting conclusions regarding directionality of effects.

Nonetheless, despite methodological limitations, there is considerable convergence across studies in showing a relation between sleep and daytime functioning in both cognitive and behavioral domains. In our review of the evidence that poor sleep affects cognitive and behavioral functioning, we give experimental and longitudinal studies special consideration, because of their methodological advantages.

Sleep and Cognitive Functioning

Research on adolescents and adults has found that fewer minutes and poorer quality of sleep are associated with worse performance on tests of executive functioning, memory, and planning (Beebe, 2006; Fulda & Schulz, 2001; Sadeh, 2007). Similar patterns are emerging in research on children. For example, children between the ages of three and five who were at higher risk for sleep-disordered breathing performed poorly on a series of laboratory tests of inhibition, working memory, and planning (Karpinski, Scullin, & Montgomery-Downs, 2008).

Several studies have shown more minutes of nighttime sleep and better quality of sleep to be concurrently associated with higher scores on standardized tests of general cognitive ability in elementary school–aged children (Buckhalt, El-Sheikh, & Keller, 2007; El-Sheikh, Buckhalt, Keller, Cummings, & Acebo, 2007; Meijer, 2008; Ravid, Afek, Suraiya, Shahar, & Pillar, 2009). The association between better sleep and greater cognitive ability has been found in children as young as 10 months (Scher, 2005) and in preschoolers (Jung, Molfese, Beswick, Jacobi-Vessels, & Molnar, 2009).

Such findings raise important questions about the long-term consequences of poor sleep on children's general cognitive functioning along with their later academic achievement. A recent study found differences in sleep quality, measured via parent report and actigraphy, between children who were and those who were not promoted to first grade (Ravid et al., 2009). Specifically, children who were not promoted to first grade slept less at night and had more nighttime awakenings than children who were promoted to first grade. Also, children not promoted to first grade were rated by parents as having poorer sleep hygiene, more movement while sleeping, and more behaviors consistent with insomnia and parasomnias (such as night terrors and sleepwalking), compared to children promoted to first grade. Additionally, children who were not promoted had lower scores on a standardized test of cognitive function than children who were promoted. The decision to retain a child in kindergarten may be based on both socio-emotional and academic behaviors, and it seems likely that chronic sleep deficits could affect both kinds of behavior. One possible interpretation is that children who were sleeping poorly were unable to learn as efficiently as children who were sleeping well, because of deficits in memory consolidation as a consequence of interrupted and insufficient sleep. Another interpretation is that children who were sleeping poorly were more dysregulated in their behaviors and attention, which may have interfered with their acquisition of important information in the first place.

Although the findings of Ravid and colleagues (2009) provide evidence that children who are not reaching academic and likely, socio-emotional developmental milestones by first grade differ in their sleep from children reaching these milestones, the cross-sectional nature of the design limits our understanding of the active role sleep may play in this process. For example, the evidence does not distinguish causal directions (i.e., children's sleep problems led to their poorer academic functioning or children's behavioral dysregulation led to both sleep problems and poorer academic functioning). Longitudinal studies of sleep and later cognitive functioning do not settle questions about causality, but they do provide evidence for sequences, and thus, they provide stronger evidence for the effect of poor sleep quality on reductions in general cognitive functioning than do cross-sectional studies.

Longitudinal studies provide support that regulated sleep patterns as well as the amounts of nighttime sleep are associated with later cognitive outcomes. Feldman (2009) showed that more regular sleep-wake states observed at 32 and 37 weeks gestational age in a sample of preterm infants were predictive of better performance at age five years on a series of standardized tests for neuropsychological functioning. Dearing, McCartney, Marshall, and Warner (2001) also found that more regular sleep at 7 and 19 months was predictive of higher general cognitive functioning at 24 months and higher language scores at 36 months. Similarly, Touchette et al. (2007) found that children who were reported to sleep less than 8.5 hours per night from age two and a half to five years had lower vocabulary and nonverbal skills than children who were reported to sleep 11 or more hours per night. Over a shorter period, Jung and colleagues (2009) found that preschool children who regularly slept seven hours a night according to parent report had lower general cognitive ability scores on a standardized assessment at the beginning of the school year and showed slower gains in cognitive ability over the academic year compared to children who regularly slept eight or more hours each night. Longitudinal studies of sleep and cognitive abilities are not numerous, but they offer important support to the possibility that insufficient sleep at one age impairs cognitive development at later stages.

Another way in which longitudinal designs can be important is in considering the impact of continuity of sleep problems. Children whose sleep problems persisted from age five to seven years were subsequently reported to have poorer parent reported language skills and more behavior problems and difficulty learning as reported by teachers, compared to ratings of children whose sleep problems were resolved or were not present at either five or seven years of age (Quach, Hiscock, Canterford, & Wake, 2009). Interestingly, however, there was a lack of concurrent association between sleep problems at age seven and adjustment, and there was no concurrent relation between parent-reported sleep difficulty and standardized tests of vocabulary, literacy skills, or nonverbal skills when these children were five (Hiscock, Canterford, Ukoumunne, & Wake, 2007). Thus, the persistence of sleep problems over time rather than episodic problems may account for behavior problems and learning difficulties. Similarly, Friedman, Corley, Hewitt, and Wright (2009) found that initial levels of sleep problems at age four were not related to later cognitive functioning. However, children whose sleep problems declined over time performed better on laboratory tests of executive functioning at age 17. The longitudinal link between sleep and academic functioning in the absence of concurrent associations might suggest that chronic sleep deficits pose a greater problem for children's academic development than more intermittent sleep deficits.

The strongest evidence for the causal effect of sleep on children's cognitive function is from an experimental study with children between 9 and 12 years of age in which half of the sample restricted and the other half extended their time in bed by one hour for three days (Sadeh, Gruber, & Raviv, 2003). Children's baseline sleep and performance on a series of neurobehavioral functioning tasks (e.g., finger-tap, continuous performance task) were assessed before and after the sleep manipulation. Objective sleep measures confirmed that approximately two-thirds of the children were able to extend or restrict their sleep by at least 30 minutes. Reaction times on the continuous performance task and correct responses on digit forward tasks were improved in the sleep-extension and unchanged in the no-modification and sleep-restriction groups from pre- to post-intervention. In the simple reaction-time task where children were instructed to push a button as many times as possible, the average reaction time declined for the sleep-restriction and no-change groups and was unchanged in the sleep-extension group from pre- to post-intervention. Therefore, sleep restriction does not result in a uniform decrease in performance, nor does sleep extension result in a uniform increase in performance. It is also important to note that cognitive functioning decrements due to experimental sleep restrictions do not necessarily correspond to cognitive functioning decrements over longer periods of time. Chronic sleep deficits may have a different effect than acute ones, and immediate effects of a sleep deficit may or may not correspond to problems in cognitive development over the longer term.

To our knowledge there are no full-length, published sleep restriction studies with children younger than 10 years of age, however, there are some encouraging published abstracts with preschool-age children (Berger, Cares, Miller, Seifer, & LeBourgeois, 2009) and seven- to eight-year-old children (Fonaryova Key, Ivanenko, O'Brien, Gozal, & Molfese, 2003).

Although the sleep restriction studies even in older children are few in number, they do suggest that sleep loss can cause deficits in cognitive and behavioral functioning. However, because of methodological differences, the studies do not firmly establish parameters of the effects of sleep deficits. The sleep restriction studies conducted with older children have generally used some portion of a single night of sleep restriction and each used different outcome measures (Carskadon, Harvey, & Dement, 1981; Fallone, Acebo, Arnedt, Seifer, & Carskadon, 2001; Randazzo, Muehlbach, Schweitzer, & Walsh, 1998). Additionally, two of the studies had very small samples ($N = 9$, Carskadon et al., 1981; $N = 16$, Randazzo et al., 1998) making generalizations about the effects of sleep loss difficult. However, in a larger sample of children 8–15 years of age, Fallone et al. (2001) found that children in the sleep-restricted group had more commission errors on a vigilance task and waited longer to respond on a delayed response task compared to the children in the control group. Additionally, observers blind to the sleep condition rated children who had only four hours of sleep as showing more inattentive and sleepiness behaviors in a task designed to simulate an academic situation, compared to children who had nine hours of sleep. However, other more general aspects of cognitive-behavioral functioning such as impulsive or hyperactive behavior did not differ between the children who experienced the single night of restricted sleep and those who did not.

Both longitudinal and experimental studies show that a shorter sleep duration and lower sleep quality have measurable consequences for children's cognitive performance. The relative scarcity of studies with young children limits strong conclusions about the extent to which processes of poor sleep result in long-term cognitive problems. At the same time, the general convergence between studies, despite their differences in definition of sleep problems, methodology, and type of cognitive outcome, strengthens the argument that sleep plays an important role in children's cognitive development.

Sleep and Behavior Problems

Closely related to questions of sleep and cognitive development are questions of sleep and behavioral adjustment. Perhaps sleep loss contributes to too few supportive opportunities for acquiring positive skills and too many opportunities to learn skills that may turn out to be dysfunctional in socio-emotionally and behaviorally demanding settings, such as school. In contrast to the small number of studies on sleep and cognitive functioning in young children, more studies have considered the role of sleep in children's externalizing and internalizing behavior problems. Such studies have looked at whether sleep problems predicted behavior problems or vice versa. Sleep problems have typically been assessed by parent report. Less often, studies have used actigraphy or polysomnographic (measurement of sleep with psychophysiological recordings) estimates of sleep problems. Even fewer studies have examined the longitudinal association between sleep and behavior problems. However, it should be noted that while there is still much to be done, there is now sufficient evidence to suggest some general relations between sleep and behavior problems in both community and clinical samples.

In general, parental ratings of sleep problems in children between the ages of two and six years have been associated positively with parental ratings of aggressive behavior (Cortesi et al., 2008; Lam et al., 2003), problems of inattentiveness and hyperactivity (DeVincent, Gadow, Delosh, & Geller, 2007; Hiscock et al., 2007), and emotional problems (DeVincent et al., 2007; Hiscock et al., 2007; Owens-Stively et al., 1997). In a large study of children between the ages of two and five years, less parent-reported nighttime sleep and less objectively measured sleep in a 24-hour period were associated with higher parent ratings of total behavior problems and externalizing behavior problems after controlling for child age (Lavigne et al., 1999). In particular, children between two and three years of age who slept less than 10 hours per night or in a 24-hour period were rated much higher on behavior problems than same aged children who got more sleep.

There have also been consistent findings of relations between objective measurements of poor quality sleep and greater negative emotionality in toddlerhood and early childhood, although the findings are limited in number (Nixon et al., 2008; Ravid et al., 2009; Sadeh, Lavie, & Scher, 1994; Scher, Epstein, Sadeh, Tirosh, & Lavie, 1992; Ward et al., 2008). Montgomery-Downs and Gozal (2006) found that emotion regulation in 14-month-olds was affected by their quality of sleep during a single night of polysomnography the night before. However, the effect was not related to the quality of sleep during the polysomnography assessment per se, but rather to the extent to which the child's sleep was more active compared to their previous four nights of actigraphy. During the administration of a standardized test following their night in the sleep lab, children whose sleep was more restless in the lab compared to their typical sleep at home were observed to be less emotionally regulated than children whose sleep patterns were similar at home and in the lab. Analogous findings were reported in a much older sample of eight-year-olds in which poor quality of sleep was also determined by polysomnography (Mulvaney et al., 2006). However, the cross-sectional nature of these studies leaves open the possibility that nighttime regulation stems from daytime regulation.

In studies presented in this alternate causal direction—daytime regulation difficulties cause nighttime regulation difficulties—higher ratings of behavior problems were concurrently predictive of more problematic sleep (Shang, Gau, & Soong, 2006; Smedje et al., 2001; Stein, Mendelsohn, Obermeyer, Amromin, & Benca, 2001). For example, children who reported more sleep problems also reported greater levels of anxiety (Gregory & Eley, 2005). In particular, greater anxiety was associated with nightmares, being fearful of the dark, and being fearful of sleeping alone. El-Sheikh, Buckhalt, Cummings, and Keller (2007) found that higher self-reported emotional insecurity in response to marital discord was associated with poorer sleep quality, which in turn was predictive of greater emotional and behavior problems as reported by both mothers and fathers. A similar pattern emerged with teacher-reported emotional and academic problems, but not externalizing behavior problems. Poor sleep quality was associated with higher teacher ratings of internalizing problems. These findings are consistent with those of another study in which more sleep problems, based on children's own reports of sleep as well as actigraphic measurements of poor sleep, were associated with greater negative emotionality (El-Sheikh & Buckhalt, 2005).

In light of the concurrent associations between sleep and adjustment, questions remain about the developmental processes involved in the sleep-adjustment relation across months and years. Longitudinal studies have shown that sleep problems in the first year of life are predictive of behavior problems in preschool (Feldman, 2009; Scher, Zukerman, & Epstein, 2005). Sleep problems in the preschool years have been linked with higher ratings of behavior problems in early school age as rated by both parents and teachers (Hall, Zubrick, Silburn, Parsons, & Kurinczuk, 2007; Quach et al., 2009). Although these studies establish a longitudinal link between sleep problems and later behavior problems, they did not control for initial levels of behavior problems. This raises questions about whether sleep problems are associated with increases in behavior problems or whether the presence of both sleep and daytime behavior problems reflect a common underlying deficit in self-regulation, which was indexed by sleep problems at time one and behavior problems at time two.

Several recent longitudinal studies have found that later behavior problems were predicted by earlier sleep problems after controlling for earlier behavior problems. Specifically, Gregory and O'Connor (2002) found that sleep problems at age four years predicted parent-reported anxiety, aggression, and attention problems at age 14, even after controlling for age-four levels of anxiety, aggression, and attention problems. Similarly, age-four sleep problems predicted anxiety, conduct, and hyperactivity problems at age seven after controlling for the continuity of these behavior problems (Gregory, Eley, O'Connor, & Plomin, 2004). In addition, Goodnight, Bates, Staples, Pettit, & Dodge (2007) found that a sleep problem trajectory predicted trajectories of teacher-rated externalizing behavior problems from age five to nine years. Specifically, increases in sleep problems from age five to nine years were significantly associated with increases in externalizing behavior problems.

Supplementing the handful of longitudinal studies linking sleep problems to increases in behavior problems, clinical interventions have shown that improvements in children's sleep result in improved daytime functioning. Mindell, Kuhn, Lewin, Meltzer, and Sadeh (2006) systematically reviewed the efficacy of several sleep interventions and found that in studies in which children's sleep improved, parents also reported improvement in children's daytime behavior. Similarly, in a review of the studies following the effect of surgery to correct obstructive sleep apnea, Beebe (2006) found that improved sleep was directly related to improvements in children's self-regulation from pre- to post-surgery. However, most of the research reviewed by both Mindell and colleagues (2006) and Beebe (2006) utilized parent reports of daytime adjustment. Improvement of the child's sleep could have produced improved daytime functioning not only because of improved child self-regulation, but also because of changes in the parent's view of the child. One possibility is that parents reported improved daytime behavior because they expected such improvement following surgery. Another possibility is that improvement in the parents' own sleep (since they were no longer being awakened by their child) allowed them to be less distressed by the child's daytime behavior (see Meltzer and Westin, chapter 6 in this volume for a detailed discussion of the effect of children's sleep on parental functioning).

The strongest evidence for the causal role of sleep problems in children's daytime adjustment comes from an experimental study. Fallone, Acebo, Seifer, and Carskadon (2005) restricted and extended 10-year-old children's time in bed for one week each, counter-balanced, following a week of baseline sleep assessment. The children were all healthy and in the normative range for problem behaviors on the CBCL prior to beginning the study. The average difference in children's time in bed from baseline to restricted sleep was approximately two hours and 45 minutes and corresponded to an average reduction of two hours of objectively measured sleep. Teachers, who were not informed whether the child's sleep was restricted or extended, rated children's academic performance lower, total behavior problems higher, and attention problems more severe during the week of restricted sleep compared to the weeks of baseline and extended sleep.

Although the Fallone and colleagues' (2005) study provides strong empirical evidence that a reduction in sleep affects children's behavior, there are still several questions that need further research. For example, the children in the Fallone et al. (2005) study were typically developing, healthy children who were largely from middle- to upper-middle-class homes. Presumably, these children were living in relatively calm, orderly homes with supportive parents. One may question whether the effects of restricted sleep on classroom behavior would have been detectable with a less severe reduction in sleep, as is somewhat more common in naturally occurring sleep problems. In addition, the presumably supportive environments at home and at school experienced by the children in the Fallone and colleagues' (2005) study may have attenuated some of the potential for increases in conflict with caregivers following a week of restricted sleep that would presumably occur if the home and/or school environments were less supportive. Of course, effects of sleep restriction might also be less pronounced, once family characteristics are accounted for.

In fact, there is some evidence that sleep problems are independently associated with adjustment even after controlling for family environment in preschool. In a preschool sample of predominantly low-income families, Bates, Viken, Alexander, Beyers, and Stockton (2002) showed that disrupted sleep patterns were associated with poorer preschool adjustment as rated by teachers, even after accounting for family stress and optimal family management. Reid, Hong, and Wade (2009), in three large cohorts of two- to three-year-old children, found that more sleep problems were associated with higher levels of internalizing and externalizing behavior problems after controlling for family background, family functioning, negative parenting style, and parental depressive symptomatology.

To summarize, there is a wide body of evidence suggesting relations between children's sleep and their cognitive and behavioral adjustment. Worse sleep, whether indexed by parent reports of sleep problems, sleep problem trajectories, diary measures of disrupted sleep patterns, or experimental or clinical alterations of sleep, is associated with worse cognitive and behavioral adjustment. Furthermore, the effects of poor sleep are detectable even after accounting for familial and socio-cultural factors.

Temperament, Sleep, and Adjustment

Temperamental characteristics reflect early-appearing differences in reactivity and self-regulation (Rothbart & Bates, 2006). Temperament, sleep problems, and behavior problems might be linked in several different ways—as confounded relationships, mediated relationships, independent main effects, and as interaction effects. In the confounded relationship possibility, sleep problems and cognitive or behavior problems could both share a common underlying feature such as difficulty in regulation of behavior/emotion, which may appear in early infancy as temperamental difficulty in regulation of negative emotionality or being less adaptable to change. In the mediated relationships, temperamentally difficult or unadaptable children may contribute to an early family process in which, to avoid child distress, parents do things that maintain a sleep problem and/or allow it to be transformed into a more severe problem. For example, parents may form the habit of putting the child to bed

asleep and providing lots of physical comfort in response to night awakenings, two predictors that are linked to the persistence of sleep problems
(Johnson & McMahon, 2008; Morrell & Steele, 2003; Van Tassel, 1985). In
the case of independent main effects, a temperament trait might predict
behavior problems over and above other variables such as parenting and
family stress. Finally, in interaction effects, the temperament trait might
amplify risks, such as poor parenting, for behavior problems.

By far, the most commonly investigated link between temperament
and sleep in young children has been the relation between temperamental difficultness (basically attributable to negative emotionality, although
operational definitions vary) and frequent nighttime awakenings. In general, higher ratings of difficultness have been associated concurrently and
longitudinally with both parent reported and objective measures of poor
sleep (Atkinson, Vetere, & Grayson, 1995; Keener, Zeanah, & Anders,
1988; Reid et al., 2009; Scher et al., 2005; Weissbluth, 1984). For example,
Weissbluth (1984) found that higher ratings of negative mood, unadaptability, activity, and intensity at eight months were longitudinally associated at age three years with less sleep in a 24-hour period. Specific to
temperamental difficultness, infants rated as difficult slept less during the
day at age three compared to infants rated as easy. Although temperamentally difficult children slept one hour less during the daytime hours,
their total amount of sleep in a 24-hour period did not differ from that
of temperamentally easy children. Ward and colleagues (2008) also found
no difference in 24-hour sleep between children rated high on negative
mood compared to children rated low on negative mood. However, children who were observed to have trouble napping (e.g., trouble settling,
being disruptive) while at childcare had higher parent-ratings of negative
mood and also slept less during the day than children with lower ratings
of negative mood. The association between greater infant difficultness
and poor sleep has been found with children between six months and six
years in both community (Atkinson et al., 1995; Palmstierna, Sepa, &
Ludvigsson, 2008) and clinical samples (Owens-Stively et al., 1997;
Schaefer, 1990). Although reported less extensively, lower ratings of
adaptability (basically distress in response to novel situations, but as with
difficultness, operational definitions vary) have also been associated with
more problematic sleep (Fisher & Rinehart, 1990; Sadeh, Lavie, et al.,
1994; Scher et al., 1992; Scher, Tirosh, & Lavie, 1998). In addition, low

adaptable infants showed less daytime sleep and more frequent night waking in toddlerhood.

However, the pattern of findings between temperament and sleep has not been totally consistent. For example, neither maternal ratings of adaptability nor negative mood were associated with objective sleep measures in a small sample of 12-month-olds (Scher et al., 1998). In addition, in a study that asked if there was an unconfounded, independent effect of temperament on sleep in a relatively large sample of children two to five years of age, Johnson and McMahon (2008) found that neither parent nor teacher ratings of temperamental difficultness were associated with children's sleep after controlling for parenting style, parental thoughts about their child's sleep, and parenting practices at bedtime. Additionally, Van Tassel (1985) found no relation between ratings of infant negative emotionality and sleep disturbances at 9 or 21 months after accounting for other factors such as nighttime feedings, sleeping location, and maternal behavior following an awakening. It thus appears plausible that the bivariate association between temperamental unadaptability or negative mood and disrupted sleep may result because children who have these temperamental characteristics may evoke parental responses to their sleep onset delay and nighttime awakenings that inadvertently lead to persistent sleep problems. If so, this would support a mediation model of the temperament-sleep association.

More clearly supporting a mediation model, in a longitudinal study of sleep problems, Morrell and Steele (2003) examined the links between temperament, parenting, and attachment on the persistence of sleep problems from 15 months to 27 months of age. They found that temperamental negative emotionality was associated with the persistence of sleep problems through its effect on mother's use of active physical comforting. Although this study needs replication, the findings are consistent with earlier observations that temperamentally difficult infants may evoke different parental responses (Weissbluth, 1989). Further research would be needed to see if the same or related parenting responses to child aversive behavior resulting from sleep deficits are involved in further development of more general behavior problems.

In addition to the possibility that temperament traits may lead to sleep problems, it could also be that sleep problems lead to the pattern of waking behavior that marks temperament. A small videosomnography study of 21 infants found that infants who were awake more at three weeks of age were observed to be more irritable and inhibited at three months (Halpern, Anders, Garcia Coll, & Hua, 1994). There is also some evidence that early appearing difficulties in sleep-wake regulation are associated with behaviors typically found in temperamentally difficult infants. In a study of sleep in the first two days of life, infants who showed more active sleep and shorter sleep-wake transitions than average and who also showed, somewhat paradoxically, fewer arousals during quiet sleep and longer average sleep periods in the first 24 hours, had the highest ratings of difficult temperament eight months later (Novosad, Freudigman, & Thoman, 1999). The authors speculated that this mix of immature and mature sleep patterns in the first days of life might forecast infants who are especially susceptible to becoming dysregulated in stressful situations. While the results from both Halpern and colleagues (1994) and Novosad and colleagues (1999) provide support for longitudinal links between early sleep and later temperamental traits, these findings are from relatively small, homogenous samples, which calls for further replication. Furthermore, the relation between early-appearing sleep patterns and later temperament traits are likely to be influenced by the broader parent-child context of those first months of life (Sadeh, Tikotzky, & Scher, 2010; Erath & Tu, Chapter 2, in this volume). It is with this idea of context that we return to temperament as a particular context in which the nature of the association between sleep and adjustment may be linked.

Only a handful of studies have considered temperament, sleep, and adjustment simultaneously. Reid and colleagues (2009) found that sleep problems and temperamental difficultness independently predicted both internalizing and externalizing problems in toddlers. Bruni et al. (2006) found that temperamental emotionality as rated by teachers and sleep problems as rated by parents independently predicted lower teacher-rated school achievement. Longitudinally, temperamental difficultness and sleep problems in the first year of life were both independently associated with more behavior problems at three and a half years (Scher et al., 2005). Thus, research suggests that sleep and temperament predict adjustment in parallel.

However, perhaps not all children are equally affected by poor sleep. In addition to the possibility of effects of temperament in parallel to those of sleep, it seems possible that there could be interactions between temperament and sleep in predicting behavior problems. Such moderating effects of temperament have been found frequently for family factors in recent research (Bates & Pettit, 2007). Perhaps children with challenging temperaments are more susceptible to the effects of poor sleep. Goodnight et al. (2007) used a cross-domain growth-curve model to link changes in sleep problems and changes in behavior problems from age five to nine years. They found that temperamental unmanageability (resisting parental control) served as a moderator of the relation between sleep and adjustment. Specifically, temperamentally unmanageable children whose sleep problems declined slower than average from age five to nine years showed an increase in behavior problems over the same period. In a follow-up analysis of the Bates et al. (2002) paper, Bates, Viken, Staples, and Williams (in prep.) tested whether parent-rated temperamental unmanageability and negative emotionality moderated the relation between sleep and teacher-rated adjustment in preschool. They found that poor sleep was especially problematic for children high in temperamental unmanageability and that there was a trend for a similar effect with children high in temperamental negative emotionality. Note that this moderated effect of sleep was independent of family management, which had its own moderated association with child adjustment, such that family management mattered more for temperamentally unmanageable children. Thus, children who show an early predisposition to dysregulated behavior may be particularly vulnerable to the effects of poor sleep. Moreover, it is also possible that the links between temperament, sleep, and parenting, such as acceding to coercive demands, are interactive, too. For example, it may be that temperamentally difficult infants who receive certain types of parenting are more likely to develop and have persistent sleep problems. These same parenting behaviors may also contribute to the development of behavior problems more so for temperamentally difficult or unmanageable as opposed to temperamentally easy or manageable children.

Conclusion

In this chapter, we have considered several common child sleep problems and their association with cognitive and behavioral adjustment. Research to date has established that the various kinds of sleep problems—including slow maturation of independent sleeping through the night, resistance at bedtime, sleep disorders due to breathing problems, and short and variable patterns of sleep—are all associated with children's difficulties in daily function, both in terms of their cognitive-academic and social functioning. The evidence for a sleep-adjustment association is impressively broad, coming from cross-sectional correlations in community and clinical samples, longitudinal correlations, experimental manipulations of sleep, and clinical interventions. Compelling theories of how sleep and adjustment variables are related in terms of psychological and biological processes are also emerging. The most plausible mechanisms through which sleep affects adjustment involve disruptions in attentional processes, memory consolidation, and other executive functions as a consequence of sleep problems.

However, there is still a great deal to be learned about how sleep and adjustment are related. It is not yet clear how particular types of sleep problems might be differentially related to the various kinds of adjustment such as basic cognitive, academic, relationships with peers, caregivers, and teachers, regulation of emotion, and regulation of both externalizing and internalizing behaviors. Nor is it sufficiently clear what roles the sleep variables play in relation to the many other factors that are involved in the development of individual differences in adjustment, such as children's temperament and intellectual ability, family stress, and parenting practices. Studies are just beginning to address these more complex, developmental questions.

We can offer several suggestions for further research on how sleep and adjustment are related in development. First, in recognition of the advances in identification of sleep disorders in children (Goodlin-Jones & Anders, 2004), as well as research suggesting that not all sleep problems are attributable to the same cause, we recommend that researchers consider sleep problems associated with falling asleep (e.g., bedtime resistance, being afraid of the dark) separate from those that are associated with night awakenings (e.g., trouble breathing, nightmares). If these are not different in their implications, they can be combined. However, if they are different in systematic ways—for example, problems going to sleep may be more strongly associated with externalizing problems, while problems staying asleep may be more strongly associated with internalizing problems—independent assessments of various sleep parameters in relation to adjustment outcomes may be warranted. Second, where possible, we encourage researchers to include an objective measure of sleep such as actigraphy. We refer the interested reader to Tryon (2004) for an extended review of issues accompanying the use of actigraphy (also see Acebo et al., 1999; Sadeh, Sharkey, & Carskadon, 1994; Sadeh, 2008; Sitnick, Goodlin-Jones, & Anders, 2008; Werner, Molinari, Guyer, & Oskar, 2008).

Third, given the established links between sleep disordered breathing and poor cognitive, behavioral, and emotional outcomes (Beebe, 2006) we also recommend that researchers include an assessment of children's breathing problems while asleep to account for disruptions due to physiological origins as opposed to those due to psychological and behavioral origins (e.g., nightmares, anxiety). We refer the interested reader to Goodwin and colleagues (2003) and Gozal (1998) for examples of parent-report questionnaires for sleep disordered breathing.

Fourth, we encourage experimental research with toddlers, pre-school, and early elementary school-age children to more precisely assess the impact of restricted daytime (i.e., naps) or nighttime sleep on cognitive, emotional, and/or behavioral functioning. Fifth, there is a need for more longitudinal studies that assess both sleep deficits and adjustment at multiple time points to better understand the short- and long-term consequences of sleep deficits in early childhood. Finally, we urge researchers to consider a range of possible moderators and confounds such as child temperament, parenting practices, and family environment. We think this is especially important given the evidence for the moderating effects of temperament predicting children's sleep problems *and* daytime adjustment. It has been established that parenting is related to children's sleep and it seems likely that children's temperament would moderate the effect of parenting on sleep. Sleep problems arise within a social and environmental context that if left unmeasured will reduce our ability to uncover the ways in which sleep may exert an independent effect on children's adjustment.

In conclusion, we have been excited by the remarkable growth in empirical work on how children's sleep and their cognitive and behavioral adjustment are related. We are also eager to see the further advances in both the quantity and methodological quality that will emerge in the near future.

REFERENCES

Acebo, C., Sadeh, A., Seifer, R., Tzischinsky, O., Hafer, A., & Carskadon, M. A. (2005). Sleep/wake patterns derived from activity monitoring and maternal report for healthy 1-to 5-year-old children. *Sleep, 28,* 1568–1577.

Acebo, C., Sadeh, A., Seifer, R., Tzischinsky, O., Wolfson, A. R, Hafer, A., & Carskadon, M. A. (1999). Estimating sleep patterns with activity monitoring in children and adolescents: How many nights are necessary for reliable measures? *Sleep, 22,* 95–103.

Anderson, B., Storfer-Isser, A., Taylor, H. G., Rosen, C. L., & Redline, S. (2009). Associations of executive function with sleepiness and sleep duration in adolescents. *Pediatrics, 123,* E701–E707.

Archbold, K. H., Pituch, K. J., Panahi, P., & Chervin, R. D. (2002). Symptoms of sleep disturbances among children at two general pediatric clinics. *Journal of Pediatrics, 140,* 97–102.

Atkinson, E., Vetere, A., & Grayson, K. (1995). Sleep disruption in young children. The influence of temperament on the sleep patterns of pre-school children. *Child: Care, Health and Development, 21,* 233–246.

Bates, J. E. (1989a). Applications of temperament concepts. In G. A. Kohnstamm, J. E. Bates, & M. K. Rothbart (Eds.), *Temperament in childhood* (pp. 322–355). Chichester, England: Wiley.

Bates, J. E. (1989b). Concepts and measures of temperament. In G. A. Kohnstamm, J. E. Bates, & M. K. Rothbart (Eds.), *Temperament in childhood* (pp. 3–26). Chichester, England: Wiley.

Bates, J. E., & Pettit, G. S. (2007). Temperament, parenting, and socialization. In J. E. Grusec & P. D. Hastings (Eds.), *Handbook of socialization: Theory and research* (pp. 153–177). New York, NY: Guilford Press.

Bates, J., Pettit, G., Dodge, K., & Ridge, B. (1998). Interaction of temperamental resistance to control and restrictive parenting in the development of externalizing behavior. *Developmental Psychology, 34,* 982–995.

Bates, J. E., Viken, R. J., Alexander, D. B., Beyers, J., & Stockton, L. (2002). Sleep and adjustment in preschool children: Sleep diary reports by mothers relate to behavior reports by teachers. *Child Development, 73,* 62–74.

Bates, J. E., Viken, R. J., Staples, A. D., & Williams, N. (in prep). Children's temperament moderates the relationship between sleep and preschool adjustment.

Beebe, D. W. (2006). Neurobehavioral morbidity associated with disordered breathing during sleep in children: A comprehensive review. *Sleep, 29,* 1115–1134.

Beltramini, A. U., & Hertzig, M. E. (1983). Sleep and bedtime behavior in pre-school-aged children. *Pediatrics, 71,* 153–158.

Berger, R. H., Cares, S. R., Miller, A. L., Seifer, R., & LeBourgeois, M. K. (2009). Sleep restriction (nap deprivation) impacts emotional responses in 2-3 year-old children. *Sleep, 32,* A94–A95.

Bruni, O., Ferini-Strambi, L., Russo, P. M., Antignani, M., Innocenzi, M., Ottaviano, P.,… Ottaviano, S. (2006). Sleep disturbances and teacher ratings of school achievement and temperament in children. *Sleep Medicine, 7*, 43–48.

Buckhalt, J. A., El-Sheikh, M., & Keller, P. (2007). Children's sleep and cognitive functioning: Race and socioeconomic status as moderators of effects. *Child Development, 78*, 213–231.

Carskadon, M. A., Harvey, K., & Dement, W. C. (1981). Acute restriction of nocturnal sleep in children. *Perceptual and Motor Skills, 53*, 103–112.

Cortesi, F., Giannotti, F., Sebastiani, T., Vagnoni, C., & Marioni, P. (2008). Cosleeping versus solitary sleeping in children with bedtime problems: Child emotional problems and parental distress. *Behavioral Sleep Medicine, 6* (2), 89–105.

Crowell, J., Keener, M., Ginsburg, N., & Anders, T. (1987). Sleep habits in toddlers 18 to 36 months old. *Journal of the American Academy of Child & Adolescent Psychiatry, 26*, 510–515.

Curcio, G., Ferrara, M., & De Gennaro, L. (2006). Sleep loss, learning capacity and academic performance. *Sleep Medicine Reviews, 10*, 323–337.

Dahl, R. E. (1996). The regulation of sleep and arousal: Development and psychopathology. *Development and Psychopathology, 8*, 3–27.

Dahl, R. E. (2002). The regulation of sleep-arousal, affect, and attention in adolescence: Some questions and speculations. In M. A. Carskadon (Ed.), *Adolescent sleep patterns: Biological, social, and psychological influences* (pp. 269–284). Cambridge, England: Cambridge University Press.

Dearing, E., McCartney, K., Marshall, N. L., & Warner, R. M. (2001). Parental reports of children's sleep and wakefulness: Longitudinal associations with cognitive and language outcomes. *Infant Behavior & Development, 24*, 151–170.

DeVincent, C. J., Gadow, K. D., Delosh, D., & Geller, L. (2007). Sleep disturbance and its relation to DSM-IV psychiatric symptoms in preschool-age children with pervasive developmental disorder and community controls. *Journal of Child Neurology, 22*, 161–169.

Eisenberg, N., Valiente, C., Spinrad, T. L., Cumberland, A., Liew, J., Reiser, M., … Losoya, S. H. (2009). Longitudinal relations of children's effortful control, impulsivity, and negative emotionality to their externalizing, internalizing, and co-occurring behavior problems. *Developmental Psychology, 45*, 988–1008.

El-Sheikh, M., & Buckhalt, J. A. (2005). Vagal regulation and emotional intensity predict children's sleep problems. *Developmental Psychobiology, 46*, 307–317.

El-Sheikh, M., Buckhalt, J. A., Cummings, E. M., & Keller, P. (2007). Sleep disruptions and emotional insecurity are pathways of risk for children. *Journal of Child Psychology and Psychiatry, 48*, 88–96.

El-Sheikh, M., Buckhalt, J. A., Keller, P. S., Cummings, E. M., & Acebo, C. (2007). Child emotional insecurity and academic achievement: The role of sleep disruptions. *Journal of Family Psychology, 21*, 29–38.

Ellenbogen, J. M., Hulbert, J. C., Stickgold, R., Dinges, D. F., & Thompson-Schill, S. L. (2006). Interfering with theories of sleep and memory: Sleep, declarative memory, and associative interference. *Current Biology, 16*, 1290–1294.

Fallone, G., Acebo, C., Arnedt, J. T., Seifer, R., & Carskadon, M. A. (2001). Effects of acute sleep restriction on behavior, sustained attention, and response inhibition in children. *Perceptual and Motor Skills, 93*, 213–229.

Fallone, G., Acebo, C., Seifer, R., & Carskadon, M. A. (2005). Experimental restriction of sleep opportunity in children: Effects on teacher ratings. *Sleep, 28*, 1561–1567.

Fallone, G., Owens, J. A., & Deane, J. (2002). Sleepiness in children and adolescents: Clinical implications. *Sleep Medicine Reviews, 6*, 287–306.

Feldman, R. (2009). The development of regulatory functions from birth to 5 years: Insights from premature infants. *Child Development, 80*, 544–561.

Fisher, B. E., & Rinehart, S. (1990). Stress, arousal, psychopathology and temperament: A multidimensional approach to sleep disturbance in children. *Personality and Individual Differences, 11*, 431–438.

Fonaryova Key, A. P., Ivanenko, A., O'Brien, L. M., Gozal, D., & Molfese, D. M. (2003). Mild sleep restriction affects cognitive functioning in young children: Evidence from brain recordings. Abstract of presentation at the annual meeting of the Associated Professional Sleep Societies Chicago. *Sleep, 26*, Abstract Issue, A174.

Forbes, E. E., Bertocci, M. A., Gregory, A. M., Ryan, N. D., Axelson, D. A., Birmaher, B., & Dahl, R. E. (2008). Objective sleep in pediatric anxiety disorders and major depressive disorder. *Journal of the American Academy of Child and Adolescent Psychiatry, 47*, 148–155.

Fox, N. A., & Calkins S. D. (2003). The development of self-control of emotion: Intrinsic and extrinsic influences. *Motivation and Emotion, 27*, 7–26.

Fricke-Oerkermann, L., Pluck, J., Schredl, M., Heinz, K., Mitschke, A., Wiater, A., & Lehmkuhl, G. (2007). Prevalence and course of sleep problems in childhood. *Sleep, 30*, 1371–1377.

Friedman, N. P., Corley, R. P., Hewitt, J. K., & Wright K. P., Jr. (2009). Individual differences in childhood sleep problems predict later cognitive executive control. *Sleep, 32*, 323–333.

Fulda, S., & Schulz, H. (2001). Cognitive dysfunction in sleep disorders. *Sleep Medicine Reviews, 5*, 423–445.

Gaylor, E. E., Burnham, M. M., Goodlin-Jones, B. L., & Anders, T. F. (2005). A longitudinal follow-up study of young children's sleep patterns using a developmental classification system. *Behavioral Sleep Medicine, 3*(1), 44–61.

Goodlin-Jones, B. L., & Anders, T. F. (2004). Sleep disorders. In R. DelCarmen-Wiggins & A. Carter (Eds.), *Handbook of infant, toddler, and preschool mental health assesment* (pp. 271–288). New York, NY: Oxford University Press.

Goodlin-Jones, B. L., Burnham, M. M., & Anders, T. F. (2000). Sleep and sleep disturbances: Regualtory processes in infancy. In A. J. Sameroff, M. Lewis, & S. M. Miller (Eds.), *Handbook of developmental psychopathology* (2nd ed., pp. 309–325). New York, NY: Kluwer Academic/Plenum.

Goodnight, J. A., Bates, J. E., Staples, A. D., Pettit, G. S., & Dodge, K. A. (2007). Temperamental resistance to control increases the association between sleep problems and externalizing behavior development. *Journal of Family Psychology, 21*, 39–48.

Goodwin, J. L., Babar, S. I., Kaemingk, K. L., Rosen, G. M., Morgan, W. J., Sherrill, D. L., & Quan, S. F. (2003). Symptoms related to sleep-disordered breathing in White and Hispanic children: The Tucson Children's Assessment of Sleep Apnea Study. *Chest, 124*(1), 196–203.

Gozal, D. (1998). Sleep-disordered breathing and school performance in children. *Pediatrics, 102*, 616–620.

Gradisar, M., Terrill, G., Johnston, A., & Douglas, P. (2008). Adolescent sleep and working memory performance. *Sleep and Biological Rhythms, 6*, 146–154.

Gregory, A. M., & Eley, T. C. (2005). Sleep problems, anxiety and cognitive style in school-aged children. *Infant and Child Development, 14*, 435–444.

Gregory, A. M., Eley, T. C., O'Connor, T. G., & Plomin, R. (2004). Etiologies of associations between childhood sleep and behavioral problems in a large twin sample. *Journal of the American Academy of Child & Adolescent Psychiatry, 43*, 744–751.

Gregory, A. M., & O'Connor, T. G. (2002). Sleep problems in childhood: A longitudinal study of developmental change and association with behavioral problems. *Journal of the American Academy of Child & Adolescent Psychiatry, 41*, 964–971.

Hall, W. A., Zubrick, S. R., Silburn, S. R., Parsons, D. E., & Kurinczuk, J. J. (2007). A model for predicting behavioural sleep problems in a random sample of Australian pre-schoolers. *Infant and Child Development, 16*, 509–523.

Halpern, L. F., Anders, T. F., Garcia Coll, C., & Hua, J. (1994). Infant temperament: Is there a relation to sleep-wake states and maternal nighttime behavior? *Infant Behavior and Development, 17*, 255–263.

Hiscock, H., Canterford, L., Ukoumunne, O. C., & Wake, M. (2007). Adverse associations of sleep problems in Australian preschoolers: National population study. *Pediatrics, 119*, 86–93.

Iglowstein, I., Jenni, O. G., Molinari, L., & Largo, R. H. (2003). Sleep duration from infancy to adolescence: Reference values and generational trends. *Pediatrics, 111*, 302–307.

Janson, H., & Mathiesen, K. S. (2008). Temperament profiles from infancy to middle childhood: Development and associations with behavior problems. *Developmental Psychology, 44*, 1314–1328.

Jenni, O. G., Molinari, L., Caflisch, J. A., & Largo, R. H. (2007). Sleep duration from ages 1 to 10 years: Variability and stability in comparison with growth. *Pediatrics*, *120*, e769–e776.

Johnson, N., & McMahon, C. (2008). Preschoolers' sleep behaviour: Associations with parental hardiness, sleep-related cognitions and bedtime interactions. *Journal of Child Psychology and Psychiatry*, *49*, 765–773.

Jung, E., Molfese, V. J., Beswick, J., Jacobi-Vessels, J., & Molnar, A. (2009). Growth of cognitive skills in preschoolers: Impact of sleep habits and learning-related behaviors. *Early Education and Development*, *20*, 713–731.

Kahn, E., Fisher, C., Edwards, A., & Davis, D. M. (1973). 24-Hour sleep patterns: A comparison between 2- to 3-year-old and 4- to 6-year-old children. *Archives of General Psychiatry*, *29*, 380–385.

Kaplan, B. J., McNicol, J., Conte, R. A., & Moghadam, H. K. (1987). Sleep disturbance in preschool-aged hyperactive and nonhyperactive children. *Pediatrics*, *80*, 839–844.

Karpinski, A. C., Scullin, M. H., & Montgomery-Downs, H. E. (2008). Risk for sleep-disordered breathing and executive function in preschoolers. *Sleep Medicine*, *9*, 418–424.

Keener, M. A., Zeanah, C. H., & Anders, T. F. (1988). Infant temperament, sleep organization, and nighttime parental interventions. *Pediatrics*, *81*, 762–771.

Koch, P., Soussignan, R., & Montagner, H. (1984). New data on the wake-sleep rhythm of children aged from 2 1/2 to 4 1/2 years. *Acta Paediatrica*, *73*, 667–673.

Kochanska, G. (1997). Multiple pathways to conscience for children with different temperaments: From toddlerhood to age 5. *Developmental Psychology*, *33*, 228–240.

Lam, P., Hiscock, H., & Wake, M. (2003). Outcomes of infant sleep problems: A longitudinal study of sleep, behavior, and maternal well-being. *Pediatrics*, *111*, e203–e207.

Lavigne, J. V., Arend, R., Rosenbaum, D., Smith, A., Weissbluth, M., Binns, H. J., & Christoffel, K. K. (1999). Sleep and behavior problems among preschoolers. *Journal of Developmental & Behavioral Pediatrics*, *20*, 164–169.

Maccoby, E. E., & Martin, J. A. (1983). Socialization in the context of the family: Parent-child interaction. In P. H. Mussen (Ed.-in-chief) & E. M. Hetherington (vol. Ed.), *Handbook of child psychology: Vol. 4. Socialization, personality, and social development* (pp. 1–101). New York, NY: Wiley.

Meijer, A. M. (2008). Chronic sleep reduction, functioning at school and school achievement in preadolescents. *Journal of Sleep Research*, *17*, 395–405.

Mindell, J. A., Kuhn, B., Lewin, D. S., Meltzer, L. J., & Sadeh, A. (2006). Behavioral treatment of bedtime problems and night wakings in infants and young children. *Sleep*, *29*, 1263–1276.

Montgomery-Downs, H. E., & Gozal, D. (2006). Toddler behavior following polysomnography: Effects of unintended sleep disturbance. *Sleep*, *29*, 1282–1287.

Morrell, J., & Steele, H. (2003). The role of attachment security, temperament, maternal perception, and care-giving behavior in persistent infant sleeping problems. *Infant Mental Health Journal*, *24*, 447–468.

Mulvaney, S. A., Goodwin, J. L., Morgan, W. J., Rosen, G. R., Quan, S. F., & Kaemingk, K. L. (2006). Behavior problems associated with sleep disordered breathing in school-aged children—The Tucson Children's Assessment of Sleep Apnea Study. *Journal of Pediatric Psychology*, *31*, 322–330.

Nigg, J. T. (2006). Temperament and developmental psychopathology. *Journal of Child Psychology and Psychiatry*, *47*, 395–422.

Nixon, G. M., Thompson, J. M. D., Han, D. Y., Becroft, D. M., Clark, P. M., Robinson, E., . . . Mitchell, E. A. (2008). Short sleep duration in middle childhood: Risk factors and consequences. *Sleep*, *31*, 71–78.

Novosad, C., Freudigman, K., & Thoman, E. B. (1999). Sleep patterns in newborns and temperament at eight months: A preliminary study. *Journal of Developmental and Behavioral Pediatrics*, *20*, 99–105.

Ottaviano, S., Giannotti, F., Cortesi, F., Bruni, O., & Ottaviano, C. (1996). Sleep characteristics in healthy children from birth to 6 years of age in the urban area of Rome. *Sleep*, *19*, 1–3.

Owens, J. A. (2005). The ADHD and sleep conundrum: A review. *Journal of Developmental and Behavioral Pediatrics*, *26*, 312–322.

Owens, J. A. (2008). Classification and epidemiology of childhood sleep disorders. *Primary Care*, *35*, 533–546.

Owens-Stively, J., Frank, N., Smith, A., Hagino, O., Spirito, A., Arrigan, M., & Alario, A. (1997). Child temperament, parenting discipline style, and daytime behavior in childhood sleep disorders. *Journal of Developmental and Behavioral Pediatrics*, *18*, 314–321.

Palmstierna, P., Sepa, A., & Ludvigsson, J. (2008). Parent perceptions of child sleep: A study of 10,000 Swedish children. *Acta Paediatrica*, *97*, 1631–1639.

Patterson, G. R., Reid, J. B., & Dishion, T. J. (1992). *Antisocial boys: A social interactional approach* (Vol. 4). Eugene, OR: Castalia.

Pesonen, A. K., Raikkonen, K., Matthews, K., Heinonen, K., Paavonen, J. E., Lahti, J., . . . Strandberg, T. (2009). Prenatal origins of poor sleep in children. *Sleep*, *32*, 1086–1092.

Quach, J., Hiscock, H., Canterford, L., & Wake, M. (2009). Outcomes of child sleep problems over the school-transition period: Australian population longitudinal study. *Pediatrics*, *123*, 1287–1292.

Randazzo, A. C., Muehlbach, M. J., Schweitzer, P. K., & Walsh, J. K. (1998). Cognitive function following acute sleep restriction in children ages 10–14. *Sleep*, *21*, 861–868.

Ravid, S., Afek, I., Suraiya, S., Shahar, E., & Pillar, G. (2009). Kindergarten children's failure to qualify for first grade could result from sleep disturbances. *Journal of Child Neurology*, *24*, 816–822.

Reid, G. J., Hong, R. Y., & Wade, T. J. (2009). The relation between common sleep problems and emotional and behavioral problems among 2- and

3-year-olds in the context of known risk factors for psychopathology. *Journal of Sleep Research, 18*, 49–59.

Rothbart, M. K., & Bates, J. E. (2006). Temparment. In N. Eisenberg, W. Damon, & R. M. Lerner (Eds.), *Handbook of child psychology: Social, emotional, and personality development* (6th ed., Vol. 3, pp. 99–166). Hoboken, NJ: John Wiley & Sons.

Rothbaum, F., & Weisz, J. R. (1994). Parental caregiving and child externalizing behavior in nonclinical samples: A meta-analysis. *Psychological Bulletin, 116*, 55–74.

Sadeh, A. (2007). Consequences of sleep loss or sleep disruption in children. *Sleep Medicine Clinics, 2*, 513–520.

Sadeh, A. (2008). Commentary: Comparing actigraphy and parental report as measures of children's sleep. *Journal of Pediatric Psychology, 33*, 406–407.

Sadeh, A., Gruber, R., & Raviv, A. (2003). The effects of sleep restriction and extension on school-age children: What a difference an hour makes. *Child Development, 74*, 444–455.

Sadeh, A., Lavie, P., & Scher, A. (1994). Sleep and temperament: Maternal perceptions of temperament of sleep-disturbed toddlers. *Early Education and Development, 5*, 311–322.

Sadeh, A., Raviv, A., & Gruber, R. (2000). Sleep patterns and sleep disruptions in school-age children. *Developmental Psychology, 36*, 291–301.

Sadeh, A., Sharkey, K. M., & Carskadon, M. A. (1994). Activity-based sleep-wake identification: An empirical test of methodological issues. *Sleep, 17*, 201–207.

Sadeh, A., Tikotzky, L., & Scher, A. (2010). Parenting and infant sleep. *Sleep Medicine Reviews, 14*, 89–96.

Schaefer, C. E. (1990). Night waking and temperament in early childhood. *Psychological Reports, 67*, 192–194.

Scher, A. (2005). Infant sleep at 10 months of age as a window to cognitive development. *Early Human Development, 81*, 289–292.

Scher, A., Epstein, R., Sadeh, A., Tirosh, E., & Lavie, P. (1992). Toddlers' sleep and temperament: Reporting bias or a valid link? A research note. *Journal of Child Psychology and Psychiatry, 33*, 1249–1254.

Scher, A., Epstein, R., & Tirosh, E. (2004). Stability and changes in sleep regulation: A longitudinal study from 3 months to 3 years. *International Journal of Behavioral Development, 28*, 268–274.

Scher, A., Tirosh, E., & Lavie, P. (1998). The relationship between sleep and temperament revisited: Evidence for 12-month-olds: A research note. *Journal of Child Psychology and Psychiatry, 39*, 785–788.

Scher, A., Zukerman, S., & Epstein, R. (2005). Persistent night waking and settling difficulties across the first year: Early precursors of later behavioural problems? *Journal of Reproductive and Infant Psychology, 23*, 77–88.

Shang, C. Y., Gau, S. S., & Soong, W. T. (2006). Association between childhood sleep problems and perinatal factors, parental mental distress and behavioral problems. *Journal of Sleep Research, 15*, 63–73.

Simard, V., Nielsen, T. A., Tremblay, R. E., Boivin, M., & Montplaisir, J. Y. (2008). Longitudinal study of preschool sleep disturbance: The predictive role of maladaptive parental behaviors, early sleep problems, and child/mother psychological factors. *Archives of Pediatrics and Adolescent Medicine, 162*, 360–367.

Sitnick, S. L., Goodlin-Jones, B. L., & Anders, T. F. (2008). The use of actigraphy to study sleep disorders in preschoolers: Some concerns about detection of nighttime awakenings. *Sleep, 31*, 395–401.

Smedje, H., Broman, J. E., & Hetta, J. (2001). Associations between disturbed sleep and behavioural difficulties in 635 children aged six to eight years: A study based on parents' perceptions. *European Child & Adolescent Psychiatry, 10*, 1–9.

Spilsbury, J. C., Storfer-Isser, A., Drotar, D., Rosen, C. L., Kirchner, H. L., & Redline, S. (2005). Effects of the home environment on school-aged children's sleep. *Sleep, 28*, 1419–1427.

Spruyt, K., O'Brien, L. M., Cluydts, R., Verleye, G. B., & Ferri, R. (2005). Odds, prevalence and predictors of sleep problems in school-age normal children. *Journal of Sleep Research, 14*, 163–176.

Staples, A. D., & Bates, J. E. (2009, April). The role of parenting in the continuity of sleep patterns in toddlerhood. In M. El-Sheikh, & P. S. Keller (Chairs), *Children's sleep and adjustment: Family and socio-cultural influences.* Symposium conducted at the biennial meeting of the Society for Research in Child Development, Denver, CO.

Stein, M. A., Mendelsohn, J., Obermeyer, W. H., & Amromin, J., & Benca, R. (2001). Sleep and behavior problems in school-aged children. *Pediatrics, 107*, 1–9.

Stickgold, R. (2005). Sleep-dependent memory consolidation. *Nature, 437*, 1272–1278.

Tikotzky, L., & Sadeh, A. (2001). Sleep patterns and sleep disruptions in kindergarten children. *Journal of Clinical Child Psychology, 30*, 581–591.

Touchette, E., Petit, D., Paquet, J., Boivin, M., & Japel, C., Tremblay, R. E., & Montplaisir, J. Y. (2005). Factors associated with fragmented sleep at night across early childhood. *Archives of Pediatrics & Adolescent Medicine, 159*, 242–249.

Touchette, E., Petit, D., Seguin, J. R., & Boivin, M., Tremblay, R. E., & Montplaisir, J. Y. (2007). Associations between sleep duration patterns and behavioral/cognitive functioning at school entry. *Sleep, 30*, 1213–1219.

Tryon, W. W. (2004). Issues of validity in actigraphic sleep assessment. *Sleep, 27*, 158–165.

Van Tassel, E. B. (1985). The relative influence of child and environmental characteristics on sleep disturbances in the first and second years of life. *Journal of Developmental & Behavioral Pediatrics, 6*, 81–85.

Walker, M. P., & Stickgold, R. (2006). Sleep, memory, and plasticity. *Annual Review of Psychology, 57*, 139–166.

Ward, T. M., Gay, C., Alkon, A., Anders, T. F., & Lee, K. A. (2008). Nocturnal sleep and daytime nap behaviors in relation to salivary cortisol levels and temperament in preschool-age children attending child care. *Biological Research For Nursing, 9*, 244–253.

Weissbluth, M. (1984). Sleep duration, temperament, and Conners' ratings of three-year-old children. *Journal of Developmental & Behavioral Pediatrics, 5*, 120–123.

Weissbluth, M. (1989). Sleep-loss stress and temperamental difficultness: Psychobiological processes and practical considerations. In G. A. Kohnstamm, J. E. Bates, & M. K. Rothbart (Eds.), *Temperament in Childhood*, (pp. 357–376). Chichester, England: Wiley.

Werner, H., Molinari, L., Guyer, C., & Oskar, J. G. (2008). Agreement rates between actigraphy, diary, and questionnaire for children's sleep patterns. *Archives of Pediatrics and Adolescent Medicine, 162*, 350–358.

Wolfson, A. R., & Carskadon, M. A. (2003). Understanding adolescents' sleep patterns and school performance: A critical appraisal. *Sleep Medicine Reviews, 7*, 491–506.

Zuckerman, B., Stevenson, J., & Bailey, V. (1987). Sleep problems in early childhood: Continuities, predictive factors, and behavioral correlates. *Pediatrics, 80*, 664–671.

Part II

Sleep: Socio-Cultural Influences

8

Developmental Cultural Ecology of Sleep

Carol M. Worthman

Introduction

The scientific community long has viewed sleep as a basic biological function, a behavior as natural, necessary, and universal as eating. Accordingly, sleep has been studied like other such functions, where settings and social conditions are treated as moderating factors that influence exposure to sleep constraints or disrupters such as discomfort and noise, worries, or work demands. Culture has been disregarded altogether. Only recently has it become clear that sleep, like eating, is heavily conditioned by culture, and that a great deal might be learned about the bases of sleep and sleep disorders through the study of cultural factors. This chapter builds on that insight and explores the role of culture in sleep practices, perceptions, and problems.

The discussion necessarily remains exploratory because the cross-cultural ethnographic and empirical evidence base remains thin. Such a curious omission of the most prevalent human behavior from anthropological and ethological inquiry stems partly from a view of behavior as produced by a conscious agent, and of sleep itself as absent of meaning and cultural constructions, except in dreams. Thus, we find reciprocal gaps in the literature, that of culture in sleep science and that of sleep in cross-cultural research. Together, the paucity of data plus the emerging recognition of culture's possible significance offer an exciting opportunity for sleep science, for which conceptual frameworks and hypotheses are needed to map the field of inquiry and inform systematic research that will fill a real lacuna in current understandings of sleep.

The present discussion aims to help bridge that gap from a developmental perspective, using the approaches of biocultural anthropology. Commencing with a consideration of adaptive-evolutionary constraints that have shaped the place of sleep in human development, this chapter outlines a bioecocultural model that provides a framework for integration of culture into the study of human development. This model inspired a study of the comparative developmental ecology of sleep that is then summarized in terms of initial insights into cultural patterns and variation in the physical ecology of sleep, and the recognition of sleep as a form of social behavior. The suggestive findings from this cross-cultural survey are followed by results from an empirical investigation of the role of culture in shaping sleep across the life course in a specific society, namely Egypt. Study results showed that cultural factors powerfully structured sleep, accounting for much of the variance in sleep across the life course. This example engages a number of issues regarding the impact of culture change and globalization (schooling, media, family and residential patterns, nutrition) on sleep schedules and consequently on functioning and health. The emerging global literature on these topics is briefly surveyed.

A concluding section deploys psychological anthropology to consider the role of cultural models in how sleep is conceptualized and how such models inform behavior and perception, with particular regard to parental behavior. Building on a cultural consensus analysis from our study of parenting and development of child self-regulation in American families, I delineate two key dimensions in an American cultural model of sleep, along with the resultant scripts for sleep and parenting practices. Then, based on our comparative work, contrasting elements in non-Western cultural models of sleep and their attendant scripts are proposed. A central insight from this perspective is that sleep is embedded in a moral framework that powerfully shapes not only behavior, but also evaluations of sleep as appropriate or disordered. Thus, the cultural construction of sleep across the life course can also be understood as a project that directly concerns crucial intangibles such as personhood, morality, and social relations, as well as the urgent practical ones of health, subsistence, and survival.

Adaptive and Evolutionary Background

The lingeringly mysterious adaptive foundations of sleep lie outside the scope of this chapter (see Worthman, 2008), but a consideration of adaptive constraints on human sleep patterns must be a starting point for any comparative study and raises four points. First, humans inhabit a huge range of environments, using an array of cultural and biological adaptations to flourish under widely diverse ecological conditions. Second, sociality and culture are obligatory to humans, indispensable for survival and integral to development and function. Third and consequently, culture shapes human ecology. Children are provisioned, learn language, and become competent by living in social groups structured and operating through culture. Fourth, and related to cultural dependence, developmental design anticipates reliable inputs from the expectable environments of rearing for assembling complex features such as the immune or nervous system (Worthman, 2003). Thus, culture gets under the skin.

Design implications for sleep include that it must be fitted into the daily activities necessary for survival and consequently must be malleable to the range of ecological and cultural circumstances that humans inhabit. Indeed, humans manifest prodigious capacity for adjusting sleep schedules and tolerating sleep restriction (Worthman, 2008). Furthermore, culturally prescribed sleep practices may themselves meet adaptive challenges presented by specific environments. For example, cross-cultural analysis of selected non-Western cultures has found that the practice of afternoon napping is not related to hot climates or agricultural labor, but to the presence of malaria and other parasitic and infectious diseases (Barone, 2000). Then, in line with most of humans' primate relatives, sleep should commonly occur in social groups, for safety and as an extension of group life. Co-sleeping has been widespread across societies. For instance, all reports in an ethnographic sample of 173 traditional societies identified infants as sleeping in the same bed or room as others (Barry & Paxson, 1971). Finally, dependence of development on input from rearing conditions suggests that ontogeny of sleep regulation would be shaped by sleeping practices. The developmental ecology of sleep—that is, regularities in patterning and conditions of sleep—may therefore be an important factor in the development of the systems related to its regulation.

The Ecobiocultural Perspective on Human Development

The primary role of culture in shaping rearing environments has prompted the claim that of all the things one could do to influence the development of an infant "the most important would be to decide where on earth—in what human community—that infant is going to grow up" (Weisner, 1996, p. 276). A developmental-ecological framework builds on both adaptationist and cultural ecological perspectives and provides a powerful basis for a fresh approach to sleep. The ecobiocultural approach integrates the pervasive influence of culture on living conditions and experience, with the environmental expectancy of the developing child (reviewed in Worthman, in press). Cultural beliefs, values, and cognitive-affective orientations directly inform behaviors, practices, physical conditions, materials, and settings that members of the culture produce, to yield the patterned matrix of human ecology. The actual conditions under which children grow up, or the developmental niche, thereby are society-specific products of culturally grounded views and practices for the care and rearing of the young (Super & Harkness, 1986).

The developmental niche of any society must also work with human variation and incorporate elasticity responsive to the individual child. Cultural goals and values built in to the niche (e.g., parent assessments and responses) engage with the child's endogenous or constitutional conditions including temperament, epigenetics and genetics, physical or functional features, capacities, and health to both drive and respond to her/his perceived developmental states and needs toward culturally desired results. Outcomes such as state regulation, physical function and health, and cultural competence are formed in this cultured space. Systems that regulate sleep, as well as those influenced by sleep patterns, count among these outcomes, and thus can be viewed as products of the developmental niche. Such logic argues for the possibly constitutive role of culture in sleep behavior and regulation, and provides a general framework for linking "distal" cultural factors to more proximal accounts, such as Sadeh and Anders' transactional model of infant sleep problems (Sadeh & Anders, 1993). Methodologically, it follows that ethnography should play a key role in the study of human development and sleep.

The bioecocultural model supports research design by operationalizing culture and its actions in development in terms of observable phenomena, including the behaviors, perceptions, relationships, and conditions that constitute the context of rearing. Thus, an ecobiocultural model represents a powerful tool for systematic study of sleep in other cultures in relation to human development. It draws attention to on-the-ground patterns of sleep behavior and experience as important factors in the development not only of sleep itself, but also of the other aspects of life—emotional, social, and productive—of which it forms an integral part. The next section describes a general framework for the ecology of sleep and the unexpected insights yielded from its use in an exploratory cross-cultural ethnographic study.

A Comparative Ecology of Sleep

The gap between paradigms for laboratory-based investigation of sleep and how it is practiced around the world formed the impetus for our initial study over a decade ago to begin filling this gap from the side of anthropology (Worthman, 1999). Investigation of cross-cultural patterns and variation in sleep behavior and corresponding physiology had scarcely begun at that time (Reimao, Souza, & Gaudioso, 1999; Reimao, Souza, Medeiros, & Almirao, 1998; reviewed in McKenna 1996; McKenna 2000). Although direct comparative empirical reports on sleep behavior were scant, the physical and social ecology of sleep was more accessible in ethnographic and historical accounts (Ekirch, 2005; McKenna et al., 1993). Thus, we used the ecobiocultural model to formulate an a priori descriptive framework for characterizing the developmental ecology of sleep in diverse societies, in microecological terms that determine sleeping conditions (e.g., where, when, how, and with whom), along with macroecological cultural, demographic, and climatic factors that pattern sleep behavior at any age and physical or social condition (see Table 8.1, left column). The framework was used to elicit structured ethnographic inventories from colleagues having society-specific expertise (Robert Bailey, Fredrik Barth, Magdalena Hurtado, Bruce Knauft, Mel Konner, and John Wood) concerning ten traditional cultures ranging in subsistence strategy and geographic location, from foragers in Botswana and Paraguay, to horticulturalists in New Guinea and Zaire, pastoralists in Pakistan and Kenya, and agriculturalists in Bali. This analysis revealed

TABLE 8.1 Sleep ecology and settings: elements and contrasts

Elements of sleep ecology	Characteristics of sleep settings	"non-Western" / historic	"Western" / globalizing
Microecology	**Security**		
Proximate physical ecology	risk from pathogens, predators, elements, enemies	present	absent
Bedding			
Presence of fire	**Sensory stimulation**	moderate-high	low-minimal
Sleeping place or structure	sleeping arrangements: co-sleeping	extensive	solitary/limited
Proximate social ecology	body contact	extensive	limited
Sleeping arrangements	thermal properties	heat/cold	stable
Separation of sleep-wake states	use of fire	yes	no
	noise	dynamic	silent
Biotic macro- and micro-ecology	light	dim/dark	dark/dim
	odors	present	minimal
Domestic animals	bedding	minimal	elaborate
Parasites and nighttime pests	sleep surfaces and bedding	rough	smooth, padded
Macropredators (animal, human)	**Variability of sensory properties**	variable	stable
Macroecology	regulation of thermal conditions	human, active	climate-control
Labor demands	disturbance (noise, movement, light)	episodic, erratic	absent/minimal
Social activity			
Ritual practices			
Beliefs about sleep and dreaming			
Status (social status, class, gender)			
Life history, lifespan processes			
Ecology, climate			
Demography and settlement patterns			

areas of commonality along with diversity in the proximal conditions or microecology under which people sleep, and documented the pervasive effects of social, cultural, and physical ecological factors, or macroecology, on sleep patterns (Worthman & Melby, 2002).

Unexpectedly, the comparative evidence flagged some characteristics of contemporary sleep ecology and practices as unusual (Table 8.1). Across this small non-Western sample, sleep settings were social and solitary sleep rare; bedtimes fluid and napping common; bedding minimal; fire present; conditions dim or dark and relatively noisy with people, animals, and little or no acoustic and physical barrier to ambient conditions. As such, sleep settings offered rich and dynamic sensory properties including security and comfort through social setting; fuzzy boundaries in time and space; and little climate control. Postmodern industrial societies, by contrast, appear to have relatively impoverished, stable sensory properties including solitary or low-contact sleep conditions; scheduled bedtimes and wake times with consolidated sleep; padded bed and profuse bedding; absence of fire; darkness; silence; and high acoustic as well as physical boundaries to sleep spaces. Features of these much more static "modernized" sleep conditions that may make sleep regulation more challenging include habitual solitary sleep or limited cosleep from infancy onward; a "lie down and die" model of sleep in restricted intervals with few, brief sleep-wake transitions; and sensory deprivation of physical and social cues in sleep settings. An untested question is whether distinctively "modernized" habits and settings place high, sustained burdens on the development of sleep-wake regulation systems and, in turn, contribute to contemporary sleep problems and disorders. Conversely, another hypothesis might propose that traditional settings placed high, sustained sensory loads straining sleep maintenance, fostering sleep fragmentation, and requiring more distributed and variable sleep that necessitated robust sleep-wake regulation.

Our cross-cultural survey also identified features of the developmental niche for sleep that were common across the sample but distinctive from prevailing Western practices. First is extensive co-sleeping androoming. In line with the cross-cultural evidence (Barry & Paxson, 1971), virtually all infants and most children in our sample normatively were provided with sleeping partners from birth onward, and solitary sleep was an exception rather than a rule. Second, as with adults, fixed bedtimes were absent for children: daily routines were common, but also highly flexible. As with adults, sleep commonly occurred as needed, interspersed with ongoing quotidian affairs. Thus, for example, young children listen, observe, and may doze during family food preparation and gossip, or during evening parlays or rituals. Third, and related to the absence of fixed bedtimes and the ability to accommodate individual sleep needs around the clock, we found no strong sense of specific, stage-graded developmental needs for sleep. Most societies surveyed regarded sleep not as a wholly distinct state, but as a range of attentional states situated along a spectrum graduated from here-and-now engagement, through somnolence, to light sleep, to profound "awayness." Developmental goals commonly concerned socialization for appropriate sleep intensity along an attentional spectrum for physical or spiritual safety in sleep. Fourth was the common importance of normative and moral frame-works that structure sleep. For instance, concerns for spiritual safety mandated co-sleeping and socialization for light sleep in some societies, including the Papua New Guinean Gebusi and Zairian Lese. These four features of the developmental niche for sleep reflect cultural influences grounded in shared models and schemas concerning sleep that will be discussed in later sections of this chapter.

Cultural Patterning of Sleep across the Life Course: An Egyptian Case Study

Our initial cross-cultural analysis intrigued the sleep science community (Jenni & O'Connor, 2005) and elicited cogent questions about generaliz-ability to contemporary urban populations. Our survey, too, had revealed a need for studies of sleep in the context of everyday activities and social settings. Consequently, we undertook a household-based study among Egyptian families living at two sites, Cairo or a densely settled agrarian village. Egypt holds one of the longest continuous records for urbanized, stratified, cosmopolitan living, has moderate to very high population densities, and maintains the historic circum-Mediterranean tradition of co-sleeping and bimodal sleep. Study data included one week of con-tinuous activity records by all household members, details of each sleep event, sleep history since birth, and ethnographic interviews about sleep (Worthman & Brown, 2007).

Qualitative evidence from interviews and sleep histories endorsed a strong customary preference for co-sleeping, which was regarded as expectable, protective, comforting, and integral to foundational relationships and family life (Worthman & Brown, 2007). All participants reported routine co-sleeping and breastfeeding during infancy, followed by co-sleeping in early childhood. The great majority also reported co-sleeping or co-rooming through middle and late childhood, as well as through adulthood. All reported napping routinely earlier in life, and most endorsed its virtues even if they rarely napped later on. Customary practices of providing sleep partners for persons of all ages are constrained by rules of sexual propriety that reduce the feasibility of reliably doing so for adolescents and single young adults. Hence, established patterns of co-sleeping and co-rooming were most likely to be disrupted during adolescence and unmarried young adulthood, if there was no age-and-gender-appropriate sleeping partner available.

Family activity records revealed that participants averaged 8.4 hours of sleep per day, but followed a pattern of bimodal sleep with daytime napping and habitual co-sleeping (Worthman & Brown, 2007). Cultural norms for sleep and sleeping arrangements strongly determined sleep pattern and amount across the life course, such that age, gender, likelihood of co-sleeping, and relationship to co-sleeper varied with age and gender of the sleeper. Specifically, key features of sleep behavior (onset, night sleep, arousals, and total sleep) all were strongly predicted by culturally moderated factors, most particularly bed-sharing habits, followed by age and gender. Family relationships formed the context for sleep. Hence, most nighttime sleep events and a near majority of afternoon naps involved co-sleeping. Furthermore, few sleep events (one-fifth) were solitary, without roommate or bed partner. In this setting, sleep with a partner appeared to be more regular, compact, and undisturbed: co-sleeping, but not co-rooming, was associated with earlier, less variable onset of night sleep; shorter, less variable length of nighttime sleep; less sleep disturbance represented by reported arousals; and less total sleep per day.

Co-sleeping may qualify as the most intimate behavior that can be shared by partners of all ages and genders. While sharing their sleeping hours, co-sleepers in close body contact share space, air, warmth, and time (a third of the day) during a vital chronobiological period. Such shared experience creates a context for mutual regulation that also shapes the developmental course of systems regulating arousal and affect (McKenna, Mosko, Dungy, & McAninch, 1990). Based on his experimental preclinical work, Hofer (1978) early proposed that relationships act as regulators that inform development and shape adult function. Subsequent research has borne out this prediction and revolutionized understandings of the roles of early environment and epigenetics in the process of development. Work among rodents, in particular, has detailed the impact of expectable environments of rearing and functioning, particularly maternal behavior and early postnatal conditions, on organization of arousal and affect regulation, among many other systems (Szyf, McGowan, & Meaney, 2008; Weaver, 2007). Different developmental periods thus present particular opportunities and vulnerabilities to contextual cues that drive regulation of systems closely involved in sleep (McKenna, 2000).

In line with such views, data from our family study in Egypt indicate that co-sleeping habits directly influenced sleep budgets and sleep quality, and that interruption of these habits in adolescence and young adulthood was associated with increased likelihood of sleep dysregulation and disruption in males and females, respectively. But the data do not address the logical questions of whether and how sleeping arrangements, and co-sleeping in particular, influence the development of systems that regulate sleep and arousal (Thoman, 2006). These compelling issues remain open to empirical investigation in emerging comparative research on sleep.

Culture and Sleep: Recent Directions

Research on sleep and human development in different settings is expanding in two directions, one being documentation of sleep patterns and related outcomes in increasing numbers of non-Western settings, another being the emergence of comparative cross-national cross-cultural research. The former is particularly valuable for drawing attention to divergent as well as shared issues across contexts that vary by wealth and technology, as well as other cultural factors such as lifestyle. The latter is needed to characterize relationships of sleep ecology and developmental niche to the formation of sleep-wake patterns and self regulation.

Culture, Culture Change, and Child Sleep

Globalization and the forces of rapid social change are transforming the developmental niche in many ways. These include changing daily schedules for new forms of labor, introduction of mass media and technologies, altered settlement patterns (particularly urbanization) and housing, and shifts in family and household structure. Each of these transformations likely has profound effects on sleep ecology and behavior, but research on these concerns remains an urgent need. These changes in lifestyle furthermore impose different demands on attention and emotion regulation that raise the stakes for understanding how corresponding changes in the developmental niche influences development of these systems, including sleep.

A major factor driving contemporary young people's daily schedules and activity is formal education. By 2006, the global project of universal schooling had progressed to the point that 88% of primary school–aged children and 78% of secondary school–aged youth were in school (Watkins, 2008). This phenomenon has important consequences for sleep (see also Wolfson and Richards, chapter 12 in this volume for environmental factors that pose challenges for young adolescents' sleep). Children must be present and alert during the school hours, which means that school start times determine wake times, while factors that erode alertness will impair school performance. For example, an early start (7:10 A.M.) for fifth-grade Israeli students, compared to the usual 8:00 A.M., was related to less sleep and greater daytime sleepiness, as well as increased difficulty concentrating regardless of hours slept (Epstein, Chillag, & Lavie, 1998). Schooling also makes children sedentary. Daytime inactivity has been linked to reduced sleep time and quality in British youth (Murdey, Cameron, Biddle, Marshall, & Gorely, 2004), and to degree of sleep disturbance in a multiethnic study of American adolescents (Gupta, Mueller, Chan, & Meininger, 2002). Schooling places scheduling demands on families whose ability to meet those demands vary by factors such as parent education and workloads. Thus, for instance, schoolchildren in

Riyadh, Saudi Arabia, with less educated mothers had later bedtimes and less weekday sleep, while those with working mothers had more total sleep (BaHammam, Bin Saeed, Al-Faris, & Shaikh, 2006). The same was true among Portugese schoolchildren, who also exhibited a direct relationship of physical activity with total sleep (Padez, Mourao, Moreira, & Rosado, 2009).

These and other studies document the impact of media use on children's activity and sleep budgets. Children who watch more television sleep less than those who watch less. Similarly, the spread of computer use among Brazilian adolescents has been related to sleep disruption and daytime sleepiness (Mesquita & Reimao, 2007). We observed the same phenomenon in our Egypt study (Worthman & Brown, 2007). Such effects promise to intensify as access to these media spreads worldwide. The attractions of media are not the only source of time load and schedule disruption for young people. In developing countries, children's domestic or paid labor is vital for household welfare and adds to the scheduling burden of school. Moreover, school overcrowding in many regions may prompt rotating morning and evening shifts that, together with parent labor schedules, further complicate timetables and compromise youth sleep (Radosevic-Vidacek & Koscec, 2004; Teixeira, Fischer, de Andrade, Louzada, & Nagai, 2004). Accommodation of shifting sleep schedules comes at a cost to neurobehavioral functioning in children: for instance, Sadeh and colleagues have reported that children could adjust to small reductions or extensions within the range of naturalistic variation, but showed large effects on response times and continuous performance tasks (Sadeh et al., 2003).

Combined, these sleep studies also illuminate sources for the global spread of obesity not only in adults, but increasingly in youth (Darnton-Hill, Nishida, & James, 2004). Reduced sleep has been linked firmly to greater risk for childhood obesity in diverse populations (Chen, Beydoun, & Wang, 2008; Hui, Nelson, Yu, Li, & Fok, 2003). Increased inactivity has been related to sleep reduction, and both in turn are related to schooling and media use. Thus, calls for sleeping longer to combat obesity would also need to consider schooling demands and media opportunities when both may be valued by youth as means to build vital skills and social networks.

Even as obesity spreads, malnutrition still afflicts many and directly affects brain development. Nevertheless, its relationship to sleep is rarely considered. The scant evidence on development of sleep-wake patterns suggests disruption in malnourished infants, which may reflect delayed neurological development that can be remediated by nutritional rehabilitation (Shaaban, Ei-Sayed, Nassar, Asaad, & Gomaa, 2007). Children in developing countries who participate in subsistence and domestic labor on top of schooling often are marginally nourished. A rare empirical study of nutrition, activity, and sleep tested whether sleep plays an energy-sparing role (Benefice, Garnier, & Ndiaye, 2004). Despite heavy daily workloads, sleep duration in this sample of Senegalese girls was no greater than reported for Western counterparts (Benefice et al., 2004). Activity level during the day did not predict amount of sleep, although malnourished Senegalese girls did sleep longer and more deeply than their better nourished peers. Continuing expansion of inequities in resources and nutrition enlarges the need for understanding the impact of malnutrition on sleep and its regulation.

In sum, viewed globally, schedules, activity levels, and sleep budgets of children increasingly are driven by their workloads for subsistence *plus* school and influenced by media use. The impact of widespread malnutrition on sleep remains understudied and merits attention.

Cross-cultural Studies

A new generation of empirical cross-national research is just emerging and aims to characterize sleep practices and ecology during human development. A parallel trend is the documentation of everyday sleep settings and behaviors in larger, if not yet population-based, samples within Western populations as well. These studies are valuable not only for delineating actual normative conditions and practices, but also for characterizing their within-population variability. Alliance of such research with developmental study designs will significantly accelerate identification of the predictors of key outcomes, including sleep behavior and quality, self-regulation, and sleep difficulties. Early steps in this direction include reports documenting developmental curves and variation for sleep schedule, duration, difficulties, and bed sharing in a Swiss longitudinal study of nearly 500 children ages 1 month through 10 years (Iglowstein, Jenni, Molinari, & Largo, 2003; Jenni, Fuhrer, Iglowstein, Molinari, & Largo, 2005). Population-typical age curves that include centile distributions of individual variation provide both bases for individual assessment and a "reality check" for the cultural expectations that inform parental and clinical goals and assessments.

More recent studies have begun to solicit details of sleep ecology (setting, arrangements, and parent behaviors), using the internet to recruit larger samples of parental reports on early sleep. Findings from a sample of over 5,000 parents in the United States and Canada document features of sleep ecology to age three and their relationship to sleep patterns including the emergence of sleep consolidation (Sadeh et al., 2009). They also emphasized dramatic infant variation in sleep duration during the first year. Excluding age, parent behaviors (regularity of bedtime routines, sleep interventions) were the principal factors related to night sleep duration and quality. A limitation of this approach is reliance on parent perceptions that are filtered by their access to and evaluation of the relevant information. Yet there may be advantages insofar as parent perceptions, such as are reflected in reported sleep problems, predict childcare and form the developmental niche.

The same internet measure was used to sample nearly 30,000 parents of under-3 children in 12 Asian and 5 Western Anglophone countries or regions. This new evidence shows large population differences in sleep schedules and duration, bed- or room-sharing practices, and perceived sleep problems (Mindell, Sadeh, Wiegand, How, & Goh, in press). While it lends empirical support for our earlier ethnographic analysis, more importantly this study lays the foundations for identification of population differences and similarities in sleep conditions, behaviors, and outcomes. For example, parent behaviors emerged as the strongest predictors of nighttime sleep and mediated the relationship of co-sleeping and co-rooming with reduced sleep duration and quality (Mindell, Sadeh, Kohyama, & How, in press).

In summary, new evidence about sleep ecology in infancy and toddlerhood consistently points to the impact of social actors (parents) on the development of sleep patterns and problems. Thus, the developmental niche sculpts the systems regulating sleep.

Cultural Models of Child Development, Parenting, and Sleep

Expanding cross-cultural research probing associations between sleep practices and outcomes also increases the need for inquiry into the cultural rationales and meanings that underlie differences in sleep ecology and behaviors. Cultures are distinguished by not only distinctive patterns of behavior and living conditions, but also the beliefs and values that motivate behavior and give meaning to experience. From this it follows that an account of the role of culture in the developmental ecology of sleep would be incomplete without a consideration of cultural cognition, or how culture operates in thought and emotion. The ecobiocultural approach suggests that, by systematically informing caregiver perceptions and behavior, cultural beliefs about human development and appropriate parenting are powerful determinants of both the developmental niche in which children grow up, and the assessment of outcomes as satisfactory or problematic. This section considers an approach to cultural analysis that permits linkage to human behavior, experience, and health.

Cultural Models

Culture comprises complex arrays of distributed beliefs, values, and practices, and it is organized by intersecting cognitive models or schemas that provide integrated accounts of how the world works and how one lives in it. These cognitive cultural resources have both shared and individual, experience-based properties that generate meanings, motives, and action to make sense of experience, address challenges, and pursue goals (Strauss & Quinn, 1997). Cultural models act as cognitive frameworks that organize a phenomenological domain (such as human development) as a basis for thought and action, by recruiting multiple cognitive resources to the domain mapped by the model (Shore, 1996). Schemas, in turn, are structured, experience-based sets of representations regarding a perception (child) or concept (daughter) that include both generalized propositions and specific exemplars, and embodied-affective and motivational features (Shore, 1996). Schemas also concern social phenomena from roles (father), to persons (dad), to stereotypes (dads), to self (person). Models and their informing schemas range in particularity from specific scripts (infant feeding) to foundational schemas (gender) that inform multiple domains. And they are not merely abstractions, but also automatic and visceral.

By scaffolding both behavior and interpretation of others' behavior, cultural models and schemas move out of the realm of personal experience to circulate "in the world" and become tangibly "real" (Garro, 2000). Cultural cognition also attains moral force through the internalized values that motivate scripts, and the ability to live by shared codes and do the right thing thereby become crucial to cultural competence, and even to health. For example, ability to achieve internalized cultural lifestyle goals has been associated with physical and mental health status in both Brazilians and rural African Americans (Dressler, 2004; Dressler, Balieiro, Ribeiro, & Dos Santos, 2007).

Cultural Model of Child Development, U.S.

Results from our study of middle-class Atlanta families exemplify how cultural models and scripts work, translating a large domain into the organization of daily life (DeCaro & Worthman, 2007). Parental models of young child development identified two core needs, namely that for security and safety, as well as that for opportunity and growth. The former requires stability, control, predictability, and support that create a protected space for development. The latter involves enrichment, stimulation, exploration, and spontaneity for physical and psychosocial growth. Resolution of the tension between these two fundamental needs relied on parent efforts to strike a balance between them that optimizes the specific child's development. Action schemas for parenting related to security/safety included producing a predictable, simple schedule with continuous surveillance by "good" caregivers. Those for opportunity/ growth included good schooling, extracurricular activities, and play opportunities. That for balance included tailoring to individual child needs and abilities, and subordination of parental priorities and schedules to children's needs. The moral corollary was that parent stress indexes effort and compliance with demands of this model, and thus, signals parental virtue. We found that parents of young children did enact this model and related schemas in the organization of daily family life, but that maternal and family functioning moderated markers of child emotion and arousal regulation (DeCaro & Worthman, 2008a, 2008b). These findings explored how cultural models of child development and schemas for appropriate parenting systematically structure the developmental niche and shape child psychobehavioral outcomes.

Cultural Models of Sleep, U.S.

Similarly, sleep behavior and settings are grounded in cultural accounts of sleep and schemas for appropriate sleep, and also intersect with models of development and schemas for parenting. Although not the direct target of the Atlanta family study (DeCaro & Worthman, 2008a, 2008b), sleep was integral to its round-the-clock activity monitoring and ethnographic interviews. Based on this evidence for illustrative purposes in this discussion, a rough cultural model of sleep can be delineated that includes two dimensions, restoration and regulation (see Table 8.2, left column). The restorative dimension treats sleep as a mysterious but essential and positive function, an autonomous self-maintenance behavior, an escape or withdrawal from daily care and demands, and a vulnerable state sensitive to disturbances. The dimension of regulation casts sleep as a physiologically and socially bounded state: one is either awake or asleep, and sleep should be scheduled, fitted into life demands, and consolidated into a single block in proper settings. In moral terms, sleep expresses self-regulation, autonomy, and independence: sleeping too much reflects sloth or disorganization, poor sleep reflects a failure in self-regulation, and sleep loss reflects self-control and life demands. This model of sleep relates to the notion that Western societies characteristically feature a foundational schema of the self as independent rather than interdependent (Markus & Kitayama, 1991; Oyserman, Coon, & Kemmelmeier, 2002, and comments).

The American cultural model of sleep interdigitates with schemas that shape sleep behaviors and settings (Table 8.2, middle column) (DeCaro & Worthman, 2007). Concerning restoration, sleep is treated as: 1.) essential, something of which one should "get enough" for mental and physical health (though how much is enough is uncertain); 2.) self-maintenance, permissive for demanding space to meet individual sleep

TABLE 8.2   Cultural model and schemas of sleep in the U.S.: An outline

Components of cultural model	Action schemas, scripts	Parenting schemas
Restoration		
Essential yet mysterious	"Get enough" but amount uncertain	Provide adequate protected sleep
Self maintenance	Meet individual requirements	Child sleeps alone, may "crash"
Withdrawal, escape	Seek solitary, quiet, separate setting	Provide separate sleeping space
Vulnerable, sensitive	Minimize external stimuli	Minimize stimuli, disturbance
Regulation		
Distinct, bounded	Limit to specific time, place	Establish/maintain bedtimes
Necessarily consolidated	Consolidate sleep into a block	Foster single nighttime blocks
Subordinate to life demands	Schedule, curtail as needed	Structure regular schedule
Moral frame		
Restoration: sustaining, natural, involuntary	good sleep = necessity, excusative	good sleep = good child = good parent
Regulation: self regulation, autonomy, efficiency	right sleep = self control, social "fit"	right sleep = good child = good parent
Foundational schema		
Independent self	Sleep an individual responsibility	"Tough love" to master sleep habits = learn independence

requirements; 3.) withdrawal, involving solitary, quiet, comfortable, and separate spaces; and 4.) vulnerable, requiring minimization or shielding from disruptive stimuli. The corresponding moral framework posits sleep as sustaining, natural, and involuntary. Consequently, good sleep is treated as a positive good because it is necessary, and a need for sleep can excuse taking "time out" from work and social demands.

The regulation aspect of sleep clearly stands in tension to its restorative aspect. Regulation mandates a push to sleep in a single well-timed nocturnal episode on a bed in a bedroom, to subordinate sleep to ongoing daily demands, and thus to curtail it when necessary. Moral entailments include that sleep steals time from life priorities. Sleeping right expresses good social adjustment produced by attitudes and commitment to meeting life demands combined with the self-control to regulate sleep accordingly. Thus, sleeping too much, at inappropriate times or places, or inability to sleep through the night may be viewed as failures of will or of physiology and thus, as psychological or physical dysfunction. Moreover, sleep at the "wrong" time and place or broken sleep may not count as real sleep. Demands related to the restorative aspect, such as demonstrated sleep needs, illness, or inimical conditions (e.g., living near an airport), may be invoked to excuse nonconforming behaviors or claim damages. These tensions become particularly apparent in sleep socialization and parenting.

Intersecting Models of Sleep and Child Development, U.S.

Consideration of cultural models and morals provides insight into American normative practices of sleep socialization and difficulties in infancy and childhood (Table 8.2, right column). Prevailing views of sleep directly inform parenting goals for child sleep. The young are understood to have special sleep needs and undergo a developmental curve in sleep-wake regulation; it is the parents' responsibility both to ensure that the child gets proper sleep and acquires correct sleep habits. For proper child development, parents should foster adequate safe sleep by providing a separate, specified bed and sleeping space that is buffered from disturbances (noise, light, heat/cold). And they should be indulgent of a young child's sleep dysregulation and periodic "crashes" when over-extended. Setting up and furnishing the newborn's sleeping space are crucial preparations for parenthood among Americans, who also expect to undergo a protracted period of disrupted sleep-wake schedules during the child's early years. Concurrently, parents are expected to inculcate well-regulated sleep in their child as swiftly as possible, by establishing and maintaining bedtimes and regular daily schedules that promote consolidated nighttime sleep with appropriate amounts of napping. The process may require parents to be firm, as this popular source suggested: "When a baby has repeated problems falling asleep, Mom and Dad may need to show some tough love" (Staff, 2009, p. 54). Correspondingly, a large on-line survey of North American parents found that longer, more consolidated infant night sleep at ages 0–3 years was associated with parental behaviors fostering self-soothing and independence (Sadeh et al., 2009). Variation from the "ideal" cultural model was extensive: over a third of infants sleep in their parents' room or bed.

Within a few months after birth, American parents routinely are asked: "Is she/he a good baby?" The question actually inquires whether the baby sleeps through the night, goes to sleep without a lot of fussing and crying, and is easy to soothe if she/he wakes up. The moral stakes are clearly expressed: "good" or correct sleep habits manifest good infant development that results from good parenting. The sleep habits and soothability of the child symbolize both the current quality of the parent-child relationship and the cumulative quality of care for the child's appropriate mastery of self-regulatory skills. Good babies have good parents. Given these views and the intense investments of parenting, the moral—in addition to existential—distress that goes with refractory infant crying, bedtime struggles, and sleep problems can be personal and profound (Barr, Paterson, MacMartin, Lehtonen, & Young, 2005). Notably, bedtime and sleep problems account for a 20–30% of pediatric consults (Moore, Meltzer, & Mindell, 2008).

In sum, cultural models on sleep perceptions, practices, and settings are readily tapped, as illustrated above for a well-studied population, the United States. Attention to the moral dimensions that motivate such models furthermore can yield fresh insight into social pressures and affective loading on what counts as sleep, how it should be done, and what can go wrong that influence how people behave and what sleep problems they experience.

Non-Western Cultural Models of Sleep

Our earlier survey of ethnographic accounts for the study of sleep ecology (Worthman and Melby, 2002) also provided an overview of diverse cultural cognitions and practices around sleep. Some elements of cultural models in non-Western societies overlap with those extant among Americans, but other widespread themes do not. These include dominant concerns for danger and for social integration in sleep. A corresponding foundational schema is the interdependent self, viewed in terms of relationships with others rather than of independent autonomy (Oyserman et al., 2002). From that perspective, sleep relates intimately to social integration and security.

For heuristic purposes, the prevalent (though not universal) themes of sociability and danger have been outlined (Table 8.3, left column) for contrast with the U.S. cultural model. The dimension of sociality poses the boundary of sleep-wake as rather fuzzy, graded along a continuum in alertness and social engagement. Sleep also constitutes a social behavior determined by relationships and one's place in society. Correspondingly, sleeping is opportunistic and accommodating, fitted into daily life and social priorities. Overall, an emphasis on sleep as sociable, anchored and framed by people, also counterbalances the theme of danger and risk.

TABLE 8.3   Other cultural models and schemas for sleep

Components of cultural model	Action schemas	Parenting schemas
Sociability		
Fluid, unbounded	Sleep as needed and possible	Permit sleep contingent on need
Social behavior	Sleep with proper partners	Carry, provide sleeping partners
Opportunistic, accommodating	Coordinate to life demands	Fit sleep into ongoing activities
Anchored by people	Do not sleep alone	Rapid response to fuss, cry
Danger		
Not of this world	Seek sleeping partners	Passive surveillance
Risky necessity	Observe conditions for safety	Provide social, spiritual security
Death-like, difficult to "break"	Avoid extended deep sleep	Expect sleep in high stimulus load
Moral logic		
Sociability: social life and status	right sleep = social integration = security	calm, adaptable sleep = secure child = good conditions
Danger: social or spiritual conditions	good sleep = social/ spiritual alignment = safety	untroubled sleep = safe child = good parent
Foundational schema		
The "connected" self	Sleep as social behavior	Accommodate to master fluid sleep = learn interdependence

Many societies ally sleep with altered states, unworldly or moribund, and regard it as a dangerous necessity and/or spiritual opportunity. Deep sleep risks encounters with incorporeal realms and malign or beneficent forces; as such, profound sleep may be difficult to break and require the presence of others for safe return.

Action schemas (Table 8.3, middle column) related to the sociability component emphasize avoidance of sleeping alone, sleeping with proper partners, and flexibility in time and place for sleep. Entailments from the danger component include measures for safety, finding security in sleeping partners, proper conditions, and cultivation of moderate sleep depths with avoidance of protracted deep sleep. From a moral perspective, sleeping "right" or properly expresses the social integration that generates security, while a "good" sleep expresses the social or spiritual alignment that generates safety. It is both boon and existential barometer. Priorities for parenting from such cultural views (Table 8.3, right column) include largely on-demand sleep schedules that fit into daily life, infant carrying and provision of sleeping partners, and rapid response to fussing and crying with expected rapid development of robust self-soothing. Danger is palliated through passive surveillance from presence of others, provision of social and spiritual security (proper sleep partners, amulets), and sensory loads involved in social sleep.

From this generalized "non-Western" cultural view, unfussy, adaptable sleep is a hallmark of the secure, properly adjusted child, while untroubled sleep reflects safety. Each, in turn, comes from "good" conditions mediated in part through parents (usually mothers) but also reflective of the social order. The resultant well-regulated interdependent child fits in.

This section has hazarded broad generalizations to explore the role of cultural models and their related behavioral, developmental and moral agendas in formation of the developmental niche for sleep. Methodologically, analysis of these factors can reveal the cultural roots of normal sleep or dysfunction, whether perceived or actual. With the exception of co-sleeping in infancy (McKenna, 2000), the analysis of cultural models and moral agendas has been largely absent from sleep science and medicine. But the large roles they play in determining behavior and health makes them promising targets for systematic study with real practical value.

Conclusion

This chapter has outlined conceptual approaches and surveyed first steps toward bridging gaps in sleep science and anthropology that limit current accounts of sleep function and dysfunction in the "real world." So far, results are promising. We now recognize that sleep can be construed as social, that it is heavily influenced by context, that context is largely culturally determined, and that cultural models and morals infuse sleep behavior, settings, and sensibilities. The present challenge is to empirically expand these insights and explore their implications for understanding sleep, particularly during child development. This chapter has discussed conceptual and methodological tools for that effort. Accumulating evidence from our own and others' research suggests that the contexts of sleep are important factors in sleep behavior and quality. An ecological approach has proved to be a valuable tool for studies of sleep patterns and settings, their variation within and between populations, and key variables driving sleep outcomes. The ecological perspective can be extended to life course analysis, as demonstrated in our comparative study of sleep ecology.

Recognition of the importance of context has led to another insight: culture matters for sleep. The challenge is to operationalize culture in tractable terms that can be related to outcomes such as sleep behavior, physiology, and quality. Two frameworks from anthropology address this challenge, one being the ecobiocultural model of human development and the other being cultural models and schemas that ground cultural cognition. The ecobiocultural model of human development points to key pathways by which culture influences child outcomes by shaping the developmental niche. And indeed, new cross-cultural research has identified a decisive role of parent behaviors in child sleep and sleep difficulties. Such work resonates with discovery of the social dimension of sleep, as was highlighted in our comparative study of sleep ecology and more recent family study in Egypt. How, where, and how well people sleep reflects culturally characteristic social relationships and views of the self. Equally pressing are wider issues of family and household structure, housing and settlement patterns, work and leisure activities, nutrition and inequity that influence sleep and presently are undergoing dramatic global shifts.

Sleep follows cultural models and related schemas about how to behave, how things work, and how they go wrong. As illustrated in the case of the United States, analysis of these frameworks in cultural cognition is critical for understanding sleep behavior and ecology. It also reveals the moral dimension of sleep, accounting for the distress and perceived dysfunction that erupt when behaviors or outcomes do not conform to cultural expectations. These dynamics are clearly in play in parenting and child sleep. As the generalized contrasting models from non-Western societies illustrate, there are different ways to view what sleep is, how best to do it, and how these relate to child development and parenting. Put most simply, the meanings attached to sleep can prove important for understanding sleep behavior and distress throughout the life course.

In sum, although the comparative study of sleep in human development is in its infancy, many factors converge to predict its rapid growth and capacity to yield important insights into sleep and its relationship to developmental processes. Concerns about sleep problems and their psychobehavioral sequelae alongside globalizing changes that affect sleep, lend practical urgency to a project that promises fully to engage sleep science with human diversity in everyday social life.

REFERENCES

BaHammam, A., Bin Saeed, A., Al-Faris, E., & Shaikh, S. (2006). Sleep duration and its correlates in a sample of Saudi elementary school children. *Singapore Medical Journal*, *47*, 875–881.

Barone, T. L. (2000). Is the siesta an adaptation to disease? A cross-cultural examination. *Human Nature*, *11*, 233–258.

Barr, R. G., Paterson, J. A., MacMartin, L. M., Lehtonen, L., & Young, S. N., (2005). Prolonged and unsoothable crying bouts in infants with and without colic. *Journal of Developmental and Behavioral Pediatrics*, *26*, 14–23.

Barry, H., III., & Paxson, L. M. (1971). Infancy and early childhood: Cross-cultural codes 2. *Ethnology*, *10*, 466–508.

Benefice, E., Garnier, D., & Ndiaye, G. M. (2004). Nutritional status, growth and sleep habits among Senegalese adolescent girls. *European Journal of Clinical Nutrition*, *58*, 292–301.

Chen, X., Beydoun, M. A., & Wang, Y. (2008). Is sleep duration associated with childhood obesity? A systematic review and meta-analysis. *Obesity*, *16*, 265–274.

Darnton-Hill, I., Nishida, C., & James, W. P. T. (2004). A life course approach to diet, nutrition and the prevention of chronic diseases. *Public Health Nutrition, 7*, 101–121.

DeCaro, J. A., & Worthman, C. M. (2007). Cultural models, parent behavior, and young child experience in working American families. *Parenting: Science and Practice, 7*, 177–203.

DeCaro, J. A., & Worthman, C. M. (2008a). Culture and the socialization of child cardiovascular regulation at school entry in the U.S. *American Journal of Human Biology, 20*, 572–583.

DeCaro, J. A., & Worthman, C. M. (2008b). Return to school accompanied by changing associations between family ecology and cortisol. *Developmental Psychobiology, 50*, 183–195.

Dressler, W. W. (2004). Culture and the risk of disease. *British Medical Bulletin, 69*, 21–31.

Dressler, W. W., Balieiro, M. C., Ribeiro, R. P., & Dos Santos, J. E. (2007). Cultural consonance and psychological distress: Examining the associations in multiple cultural domains. *Culture, Medicine and Psychiatry, 31*, 195–224.

Ekirch, A. R. (2005). *At day's close: Night in times past.* New York: Norton.

Epstein, R., Chillag, N., & Lavie, P. (1998). Starting times of school: Effects on daytime functioning of fifth-grade children in Israel. *Sleep, 21*, 250–256.

Garro, L. C. (2000). Remembering what one knows and the construction of the past: A comparison of cultural consensus theory and cultural schema theory. *Ethos, 3*, 275–319.

Gupta, N. K., Mueller, W. H., Chan, W., & Meininger, J. C. (2002). Is obesity associated with poor sleep quality in adolescents? *American Journal of Human Biology, 14*, 762–768.

Hofer, M. (1978). Hidden regulatory processes in early social relationships. In P. P. G. Bateson & P. J. Klopfer (Eds.), *Perspectives in ethology: Vol. 2. Social behavior* (pp. 135–166). Oxford, England: Plenum.

Hui, L. L., Nelson, E. A. S., Yu, L. M., Li, A. M., & Fok, T. F. (2003). Risk factors for childhood overweight in 6-to 7-y-old Hong Kong children. *International Journal of Obesity, 27*, 1411–1418.

Iglowstein, I., Jenni, O. G., Molinari, L., & Largo, R. H. (2003). Sleep duration from infancy to adolescence: Reference values and generational trends. *Pediatrics, 111*, 302–307.

Jenni, O. G., Fuhrer, H. Z., Iglowstein, I., Molinari, L., & Largo, R. H. (2005). A longitudinal study of bed sharing and sleep problems among Swiss children in the first 10 years of life. *Pediatrics, 115*, 233–240.

Jenni, O. G., & O'Connor, B. B. (2005). Children's sleep: An interplay between culture and biology. *Pediatrics, 115*, 204–216.

Markus, H. R., & Kitayama, S. (1991). Culture and the self: Implications for cognition, emotion, and motivation. *Psychological Review, 98*, 224–253.

McKenna, J. J. (1996). Sudden infant death syndrome in cross-cultural perspective: Is infant-parent cosleeping protective? *Annual Review of Anthropology, 25*, 201–216.

McKenna, J. J. (2000). Cultural influences on infant and childhood sleep biology, and the science that studies it: Toward a more inclusive paradigm. In G. M. Loughlin, J. L. Caroll & C. L. Marcus (Eds.), *Sleep and breathing in children: A developmental approach* (pp. 99–130). New York: Marcel Dekker.

McKenna, J. J., Mosko, S., Dungy, C., & McAninch, J. (1990). Sleep and arousal patterns of co-sleeping human mother/infant pairs: A preliminary physiological study with implications for the study of infant death syndrome (SIDS). *American Journal of Physical Anthropology, 83*, 331–347.

McKenna, J. J., Thoman, E. B., Anders, T., Sadeh, A., Schechtman, V., & Glotzbach, S. (1993). Infant-parent co-sleeping in an evolutionary perspective: Implications for understanding infant sleep development and the sudden infant death syndrome. *Sleep, 16*, 263–282.

Mesquita, G., & Reimao, R. (2007). Nightly use of computer by adolescents: Its effect on quality of sleep. *Arquivos de Neuro-Psiquiatria, 65*, 428–432.

Mindell, J. A., Sadeh, A., Kohyama, J., & How, T. H. (in press). Parental behaviors and sleep outcomes in infants and toddlers: a cross-cultural comparison. *Sleep Medicine.*

Mindell, J. A., Sadeh, A., Wiegand, B., How, T. H., & Goh, D.Y.T. (in press). Cross-cultural differences in infant and toddler sleep. *Sleep Medicine.*

Moore, M., Meltzer, L. J., & Mindell, J. A. (2008) Bedtime problems and night wakings in children. *Primary Care: Clinics in Office Practice, 35*, 569–581.

Murdey, I. D., Cameron, N., Biddle, S. J. H., Marshall, S. J., & Gorely, T. (2004). Pubertal development and sedentary behaviour during adolescence. *Annals of Human Biology, 31*, 75–86.

Oyserman, D., Coon, H. M., & Kemmelmeier, M. (2002). Rethinking individualism and collectivism: Evaluation of theoretical assumptions and meta-analyses. *Psychological Bulletin, 128*, 3–72.

Padez, C., Mourao, I., Moreira, P., & Rosado, V. (2009). Long sleep duration and childhood overweight/obesity and body fat. *American Journal of Human Biology, 21*, 371–376.

Radosevic-Vidacek, B., & Koscec, A. (2004). Shifworking families: Parents' working schedule and sleep patterns of adolescents attending school in two shifts. *Revista de Saúde Pública, 38*, 38–46.

Reimao, R., Souza, J. C., & Gaudioso, C. E. V. (1999). Sleep habits in Native Brazilian Bororo children. *Arquivos de Neuro-Psiquiatria, 57*, 14–17.

Reimao, R., Souza, J. C., Medeiros, M. M., & Almirao, R. I. (1998). Sleep habits in native Brazilian Terena children in the state of Mato Grosso do Sul, Brazil. *Arquivos de Neuro-Psiquiatria, 56*, 703–707.

Sadeh, A., & Anders, T. F. (1993). Infant sleep problems: Origins, assessment, interventions. *Infant Mental Health Journal, 14*, 17–34.

Sadeh, A., Gruber, R., & Raviv, A. (2003). The effects of sleep restriction and extension on school-age children: What a difference an hour makes. *Child Development, 74*, 444–455.

Sadeh, A., Mindell, J. A., Luedtke, K., Wiegand, B. (2009). Sleep and sleep ecology in the first 3 years: a web-based study. *Journal of Sleep Research, 18*, 60–73.

Shaaban, S. Y., Ei-Sayed, H. L., Nassar, M. F., Asaad, T., & Gomaa, S. M. (2007). Sleep-wake cycle disturbances in protein-energy malnutrition: Effect of nutritional rehabilitation. *Eastern Mediterranean Health Journal, 13*, 633–645.

Shore, B. (1996). *Culture in mind: Cognition, culture, and the problem of meaning.* New York, NY: Oxford University Press.

Staff. (2009, November). The year in health from a to z. *Time, 174*, 51–89.

Strauss, C., & Quinn, N. (1997). *A cognitive theory of cultural meaning.* Cambridge, UK: Cambridge University Press.

Super, C. M., & Harkness, S. (1986). The developmental niche: A conceptualization at the interface of child and culture. *International Journal of Behavioral Development, 9*, 545–569.

Szyf, M., McGowan, P., & Meaney, M. J. (2008). The social environment and the epigenome. *Environmental and Molecular Mutagenesis, 49*, 46–60.

Teixeira, L. R., Fischer, F. M., de Andrade, M. M. M., Louzada, F. M., & Nagai, R. (2004). Sleep patterns of day-working, evening high-schooled adolescents of Sao Paulo, Brazil. *Chronobiology International, 21*, 239–252.

Thoman, E. B. (2006). Co-sleeping, an ancient practice: Issues of the past and present, and possibilities for the future. *Sleep Medicine Reviews, 10*, 407–417.

Watkins, K. (2008). *Education for All Global Monitoring Report 2009.* Oxford: Oxford University Press and UNESCO.

Weaver, I. C. (2007). Epigenetic programming by maternal behavior and pharmacological intervention. Nature versus nurture: Let's call the whole thing off. *Epigenetics, 2*, 22–28.

Weisner, T. S. (1996). Why ethnography should be the most important method in the study of human development. In R. Jessor, A. Colby, & R. Shweder (Eds.), *Ethnography and human development: Context and meaning in social inquiry* (pp. 305–324). Chicago: The University of Chicago Press.

Worthman, C. M. (1999). Comparative ecology of human sleep. *American Journal of Physical Anthropology Suppl., 28*, 21.

Worthman, C. M. (2003). Energetics, sociality, and human reproduction: Life history theory in real life. In K. W. Wachter & R. A. Bulatao (Eds.), *Offspring: Human fertility behavior in biodemographic perspective* (pp. 289–321). Washington, DC: National Academies Press.

Worthman, C. M. (2008). After dark: the evolutionary ecology of human sleep. In W. R. Trevathan, E. O. Smith & J. J. McKenna (Eds.), *Evolutionary medicine and health: New perspectives* (pp. 291–313). New York, NY: Oxford University Press.

Worthman, C. M. (in press). The ecology of human development; evolving models for cultural psychology. *Journal of Cross-Cultural Psychology* published on-line 8 April 2010.

Worthman, C. M., & Brown, R. A. (2007). Companionable sleep: Social regulation of sleep and co-sleeping in Egyptian families. *Journal of Family Psychology, 21*, 124–135.

Worthman, C. M., & Melby, M. K. (2002). Toward a comparative developmental ecology of human sleep. In M. A. Carskadon (Ed.), *Adolescent sleep patterns: Biological, social, and psychological influences* (pp. 69–117). New York, NY: Cambridge University Press.

9

Sleep Environments of Young Children in Post-Industrial Societies

Melissa M. Burnham and Erika E. Gaylor

Introduction

The daytime and nighttime sleep environments of young children in industrialized nations have been topics of interest and investigation for slightly over four decades (e.g., Caudill & Plath, 1966). Although the term "sleep environment" suggests an easily quantifiable and definable subject, the sheer variety of sleep environments, the variability within families regarding the regularity of environments, and the variables with which they are correlated make the subject difficult to quantify at best. In this chapter, we will explicate a variety of normative sleeping environments for children in post-industrial societies[1], as well as the contextual and developmental factors associated with them. Using a developmental systems perspective, it is clear that where, with whom, and under what circumstances infants and young children sleep are based on intra-, inter-, and extra-individual variables that transact across time.

Developmental Systems Theory (DST) posits that an individual's behaviors cannot be understood without considering the contexts within which that individual is embedded (Ford & Lerner, 1992). It views the "person-in-context as the focal unit of interest" (p. 92). Thus, any given human behavior is only understood as a function of the multiple contexts within which it occurs. The contexts are viewed as embedded systems and include community, society, and culture, as well as designed and natural environments. Another essential component of DST is its propositions regarding the transactional nature of human development.

That is, "the reciprocal relation between the interrelated features of the person and his or her context are held to not merely 'interact' in the linear sense. ... Instead, person and context transact or 'dynamically interact'" (Ford & Lerner, 1992, p. 11). These two overarching propositions of DST (individuals as embedded within contexts and in transaction with these contexts) make it particularly well suited to frame a discussion of sleep environments. As will be discussed in detail later, sleep environments are influenced by culture, defined as the shared beliefs and values of a group, society, the customs and laws of people sharing a particular country or region, and community, a group of people living in a common area. Recent research also documents great intra-cultural and intra-societal variability in sleep environments. One's sleep environment (for self and family) is influenced by characteristics of the individual in transaction with his/her personal circumstances, beliefs, and values as well as those of the broader social context. As noted by Shweder, Jensen, and Goldstein (1995), "who sleeps by whom is not merely a personal or private activity. It is a social practice ... which is invested with moral and social meaning" (p. 37).

In this chapter, we will delineate the sleep environments found in industrialized nations using the DST as a framework for understanding their variability. The environments of both nighttime and daytime sleep will be discussed, and our focus will be on infants and young children (those of preschool age). We argue that sleep environments cannot be understood as unitary constructs, but rather are only understood by examining the characteristics of individuals who choose them and the society, community, and culture within which those individuals are embedded.

Nighttime Sleep

The focus of most research to date on infants' and young children's sleep environments has been placed on nighttime sleep environments within the family home. A great deal of variability in such environments has been found across industrialized nations. Both solitary and social sleeping arrangements are noted, and a wide array of contextual variables has been found to relate to families' choices of sleeping environments and arrangements.

"Co-sleeping" and "Solitary Sleeping" Arrangements

Multiple definitions of "co-sleeping" (i.e., social sleeping arrangements or those involving others) and "solitary sleeping" have been used in the extant literature. This makes comparison across studies difficult and must be kept in mind whenever examining and considering the implications of a study of sleep environments. Broad definitions of "co-sleeping" and "solitary sleeping" will be presented first, followed by a further distinction and analysis of common patterns that occur. While some authors define co-sleeping as strictly bed-sharing, others define it more broadly. And, while some authors define solitary sleeping based on where the child begins the night, others have urged the restriction of this definition based on both inter-and intra-nighttime criteria. That is, some researchers have cautioned that a child should not be categorized as a solitary sleeper if he/she regularly moves to the parents' bed/room at some point during the night (intra-nighttime criterion), and/or sleeps regularly with others (inter-nighttime criterion). Moving from within and between-night variability to a broader time frame, sleeping arrangements may well change across the years of infancy and early childhood as well, such that a "solitary sleeper" at one age may become a "co-sleeper" or vice versa, and it is probable that some children may switch back and forth several times during the childhood years. That co-sleeping rates change across the broader time frame of months and/or years has been verified by studies of children in Switzerland (Jenni, Fuhrer, Iglowstein, Molinari, & Largo, 2005), in the United States (Hauck, Signore, Fein, & Raju, 2008; Taylor, Donovan, & Leavitt, 2008), and in Australia (Buckley, Rigda, Mundy, & McMillen, 2002).

As many authors have noted, social sleeping arrangements, or sleep environments that include others, represent a broad spectrum of possibilities for co-sleeping (e.g., Ball, Hooker, & Kelly, 1999; McKenna & McDade, 2005). These possibilities include both bed-sharing and room-sharing, which then may occur with a variety of sleeping partners (most often, parent(s), sibling(s), and/or extended family members). Thus, "co-sleeping" itself cannot be thought of as a simple, universal sleeping arrangement. Solitary sleeping, on the other hand, is distinct in that it refers to young children sleeping in settings that are excluded from others (e.g., in their own room and bed). A strict definition of solitary sleep would restrict it based on time criteria as well, such that solitary sleepers would not only start the night in their own setting, but remain in that setting throughout the night regularly (barring illness or the like). Indeed, Ball, Hooker, and Kelly's (1999) research illuminates the importance of considering time as a criterion in defining different sleeping arrangements. These researchers found that, whereas only 9% of infants started the night in the parents' bed, a full 70% were moved to the parents' bed at least occasionally during the night. If they had defined the sleep environment by what occurred at the beginning of the night, as many researchers do, they would have missed this important shift to the parental bed that occurred for the majority of infants in their sample.

The reported rates of "co-sleeping" and "solitary sleeping" for children in industrialized nations vary widely, but generally suggest that solitary sleeping arrangements are much less common than are shared sleep environments. Shweder and colleagues (1995) note, "the ritualized isolation and solitude imposed on young children every night in the middle-class Anglo-American culture region are not practiced in most other regions of the world" (p. 24). In the early 1970s, for example, a characterization of 186 societies worldwide did not find a single instance of substantiated, regular nighttime solitary sleep (Barry & Paxson, 1971); see Worthman, chapter 8 in this volume for considerations of the cultural ecology of sleep. Although this sample included many nonindustrialized societies, several industrialized societies were included as well. Reporting data from the International Child Care Practices Study on three-month-old infants, Nelson and colleagues (2001) found an average prevalence rate for room-sharing of 71% among the industrialized nations studied. Notably, the United States was not included in either of these international studies. In the United States, solitary sleeping arrangements have been noted to be less common among some groups, such as young, African American mothers (e.g., McCoy et al., 2004; New & Richman, 1996; Wolf, Lozoff, Latz, & Paludetto, 1996). However, as will be discussed later, the different rates reported may be a function of how one defines a given sleep environment as much as they reflect differing cultural, societal, and familial viewpoints and characteristics in transaction with the child's own characteristics.

Room-Sharing, Bed-Sharing, and Solitary Sleeping

Sleep environments are more distinctly characterized by examining the details of the arrangements. For example, co-sleeping encompasses both room-sharing and bed-sharing arrangements, each of which may have a distinct and unique impact on young children (McKenna & McDade, 2005). Specifically, room-sharing encompasses any sleep environment in which children share the same room with another individual (specific room-sharing partners will be discussed in the next section). Within the room-sharing categorization is the more specific category of bed-sharing, which refers to the practice of young children sharing the same sleeping surface with at least one other individual. Even these fine distinctions can be muddied when one pauses to consider: (a) the traditional futon sleeping arrangements of a typical Japanese family, where the actual sleeping surface may differ but mother and child may be close enough to experience bodily contact (e.g., Wolf et al., 1996), or (b) the "side-car" crib that attaches to a typical Western bed, where again the sleeping sur-face is separate, yet bodily contact with another is possible. Some authors have suggested that proximity is a more potent variable distinguishing co-sleeping environments than is sharing a sleeping surface (e.g., Lozoff, Askew, & Wolf, 1996; McKenna & McDade, 2005). Although somewhat cumbersome, it is only with these fine-tuned distinctions that we can begin to understand the potential impact of different sleep environments on children's health, safety, and concurrent as well as future well-being. Unfortunately, definitional issues are often ignored in favor of broad categorizations, and many researchers (e.g., Carpenter, 2006; Drago & Dannenberg, 1999; Nakamura, Wind, & Danello, 1999; Kemp et al., 2000) have drawn conclusions about "co-sleeping" without sufficient detail on the nature and definition of the co-sleeping environment to warrant them.

With that caveat in mind, we will now turn to a discussion of the prevalence rates of different sleeping environments that have been reported in the literature. In general, most research has reported a higher prevalence of shared sleep environments for infants and young children in Asian industrialized nations (e.g., Japan, Hong Kong) when compared with Western nations (e.g., United States, Finland) (Caudill & Plath, 1966; Latz, Wolf, & Lozoff, 1999; Sourander, 2001; Willinger, Ko, Hoffman, Kessler, & Corwin, 2003). Some have attributed this difference to cultural propensities toward independence or interdependence, with shared sleep more common in cultures placing higher value on interdependence (e.g., Caudill & Plath, 1966; Giannotti, Cortesi, Sebastiani, & Vagnoni, 2008; Kawasaki, Nugent, Miyashita, Miyahara, & Brazelton, 1994). Indeed, many Western mothers believe that solitary sleep will promote independence in their children, and Western parenting literature often communicates this same message (Ramos & Youngclarke, 2006; Rowe, 2003). Incidentally, despite the traditional Western value of independence and the common assumption that solitary sleeping arrangements foster autonomy, recent research has not substantiated an effect of sleeping arrangements on children's relative degree of independence (Keller & Goldberg, 2004). For example, Keller and Goldberg (2004) report that the young children in their sample who had begun co-sleeping in early infancy were reportedly *more* self-reliant and exhibited greater social independence compared to other groups.

Wolf and colleagues (1996) suggest that attributing the reason for co-sleeping or solitary sleeping to the cultural values of interdependence or independence may be overly simplistic. They assert that groups that practice co-sleeping may promote independence in their children in other ways. These researchers found that regular co-sleeping (defined as parents and children sleeping in bodily contact at least three times per week for the month prior to interview) was more common in their sample of black families with children aged 6 to 48 months in the United States (57.8%) than it was in white U.S. families (19.2%). Despite this difference, both black and white families in this sample endorsed values related to their children's early independence and autonomy. Consistent with other research (e.g., Madansky & Edelbrock, 1990; McCoy et al., 2004), the percentage of black families engaging in regular co-sleeping was quite similar to the percentage of regular co-sleeping Japanese families (58.1%) even though these two groups were reported to hold different cultural values (Wolf et al., 1996). Thus, viewing variability in sleeping arrangements as due to differences in cultural values regarding independence or interdependence appears to be an oversimplification. In the words of Shweder and colleagues (1995), "the moral goods of a culture constrain but do not determine the sleeping arrangements in any particular household" (p. 27).

There is little doubt that overarching cultural values provide a context within which parental goals and behaviors regarding sleeping environments are established. This is consistent with DST, and may help to explain middle-class, white, Western parents' tendency to endorse solitary sleeping as preferable (e.g., Ball et al., 1999; Rowe, 2003). To the extent that standard parenting advice advocating solitary sleep is both common and influenced by culture (e.g., Ramos & Youngclarke, 2006; Wolf et al., 1996), and the propensity for white, American, middle-class parents to attempt to follow this advice (e.g., New & Richman, 1996), this tendency toward solitary sleeping environments may be partly explained. However, it is also clear that culture does not act alone in influencing a given family's sleeping arrangements. And, even in white samples within the United States, co-sleeping is much more prevalent than might be expected if the overarching value of independence was a primary determinant. Other, more proximal, factors have been found to relate to the prevalence of shared sleep environments. For example, in Madansky and Edelbrock's (1990) community sample of parents with two- and three-year-old children in the United States, father absence was significantly related to more frequent bed-sharing. Similarly, Weimer and colleagues (2002) reported that 88% of their largely African American sample had an infant or young child who had co-slept with the caregiver, and single parenthood was related to co-sleeping. McCoy and colleagues (2004) also reported that, in their sample of over 10,000 mothers in the United States, bed-sharing (defined as an infant sharing the same bed with another person for "most of the previous night") was more prevalent in younger, never married mothers with lower household incomes and less than a high school education (p. 142).

As mentioned above, intra-cultural variability in sleeping environments is confounded by differences in definitions of terms used to describe these environments. The reported prevalence rate of "co-sleeping," for example, is extremely high when researchers ask parents if they have ever co-slept with their child (e.g., Blair & Ball, 2004; Willinger, Ko, Hoffman,

Kessler, & Corwin, 2003). However, prevalence rates tend to decrease when frequency criteria are implemented in the definition of co-sleeping (Blair & Ball, 2004; Rigda, McMillen, & Buckley, 2000).

Further compounding the problem of identifying prevalence rates for different sleeping environments are the differences in personal parental beliefs that underlie the reasoning for sharing a sleep environment with one's child. Madansky and Edelbrock (1990), for example, suggest that some parents may co-sleep as a reaction to a child's bedtime settling or night waking difficulties ("reactive co-sleepers"), while other parents co-sleep as a practice consistent with their personal parenting goals and/or beliefs. Indeed, others have concurred that a specific subset of parents who endorse co-sleeping exists; this group has been labeled as "intentional cosleepers" (Ramos, 2003). Keller and Goldberg (2004) confirm this distinction and have taken it a step further with the finding that intentional (or "early") co-sleeping mothers had more independent preschool-aged children, as noted above, and were more supportive of their child's autonomy when compared to either solitary sleeping mothers or reactive co-sleepers. Another interesting distinction made was that mothers who intentionally co-slept did not define their child's night waking as problematic, whereas reactive co-sleeping mothers did, despite similar rates of night waking between the two co-sleeping groups.

Defining "reactive" and "intentional" co-sleepers is itself problematic; simple definitions based on timing or the presence or absence of reported sleep problems have not been sufficient to fully capture the idiosyncrasies of each group (Ramos, 2003). Clearly, more work is necessary to better define the contexts in which co-sleeping (bed-sharing and room-sharing) is more or less prevalent. In sum, it appears that different subcultures exist with different views of the appropriateness of different sleep environments, that the choice of solitary and co-sleeping arrangements may be influenced by the overarching values of one's culture, and that specific proximal variables (e.g., single parenthood) may influence families' chosen sleeping environments.

Sleep Partners

Compared with research on sleep environments themselves, even less is known about the sleep partners of co-sleeping children, although it is assumed that sleep partners make up an important part of the young child's sleep environment. Many different configurations are possible. For example, the mother, father, and child may sleep in the same room (or bed); the mother may sleep with the child in the same room (or bed) while the father sleeps in a separate room; siblings may share a room (or bed); extended family members may share a room (or bed) with older siblings while younger children sleep with their parents, etc. The number of possible configurations is not limitless, but it should be clear that, depending on the number of sleeping rooms available and the number of members of the household, the possibilities are extensive (e.g., Shweder et al., 1995). The choices of sleeping partners and configurations are, at least in part, influenced by one's cultural context and household constraints.

In general, when children in industrialized nations co-sleep, it is usually with at least one parent as a sleep partner. For example, Latz and colleagues (1999) found that 62% of their U.S. sample of infants and young children had their own room, 33% shared a room with a sibling, and 2% shared a bed with a sibling. In contrast, only 18% of Japanese children had their own room and 14% shared a room with a sibling. Most Japanese children (68%) had a bed or futon in the parents' bedroom. In 23% of Japanese families, the father slept in a separate room; this arrangement was not found in any of the families in their U.S. sample. A study conducted in New Zealand on 40 regular bed-sharing families with infants under 6 months of age found that in 48% of the cases, infants and mothers slept together, in 43% of the cases, infant, mother, and partner (usually father) shared a bed, and in 9% of the cases siblings were present in the bed as well (Baddock, Galland, Taylor, & Bolton, 2007). In only 10% of the families with a father present did the father choose not to sleep in the same bed with the mother and the infant. Interestingly, regardless of the presence of others, infants spent the majority of the night in direct contact with the mother only. This pattern of close mother contact during sleep was present in a sample of South Korean infants (Lee, 1992) and in a sample of Latino mother-infant pairs in the United States (Richard, Mosko, McKenna, & Drummond, 1996). Ball and colleagues (2000) studied 36 dual-parent households with young infants in the United Kingdom and found that both parents were bed-sharing partners with the infant in the vast majority of cases. When nighttime bed-sharing is practiced with an infant or young child, the most common bed-sharing partner appears to be at least one parent, with a triadic bed-sharing arrangement most common when fathers are present in the household.

Interestingly, despite the admonition in Western parenting literature that bed-sharing with a child may have a negative impact on the parents' relationship or the child's independence, research to date has been inconclusive. With regard to the marital relationship, while Rothrauff, Middlemiss, and Jacobson (2004) did find a positive association between marital satisfaction and solitary sleeping arrangements for toddlers in their sample of American families, no such relation was apparent in the sample of Austrian families. Given that Rothrauff and colleagues' (2004) findings were based on a retrospective study, the results are difficult to interpret without more knowledge of other contextual variables that may be contributing to marital satisfaction, or the direction of relations between variables. That is, it is not possible to determine if toddler room-sharing *led to* lower levels of satisfaction, the opposite, or if a third factor may relate to both. Ball and colleagues (2000), in their investigation of families in England, noted that it did not bother the fathers in their sample to have their infants in the marital bed. It is clear that there is not a simple answer to the question of whether or not co-sleeping contributes to relationship difficulties among parents. There are probably many contextual factors that play a role, including concordance of parental beliefs and ideologies and reasons for bed-sharing.

To summarize, with regard to co-sleeping negatively impacting children's independence, research to date has failed to confirm any negative effect. In addition to the research by Keller and Goldberg (2004) discussed above, Okami and colleagues (2002) found no later adverse consequences of parent–child bed-sharing that occurred in infancy and early childhood. Similarly, although there are stated concerns that bed-sharing may negatively impact the interparental relationship, research to date has not fully substantiated these concerns.

The Controversy on Sleep Environments

The topic of sleep environments has been ensconced in controversy in recent years. The controversy is often dichotomized into "pro" and "con" camps, neither of which fully considers the unique individual, cultural,

and other contextual influences that may make one particular sleep environment more or less desirable than another. While it seems myopic to
universally accept or prescribe any particular environment as the best for
all individuals during development, this is precisely the path that many
researchers have selected.

Several Western researchers have argued that bed-sharing in a typical
Western context is unsafe for infants, due to the risk of overlying, entrap-
ment, or related risks. Some cite epidemiological data implicating bed-
sharing as a risk factor for Sudden Infant Death Syndrome (SIDS), or
death by suffocation (e.g., Drago & Dannenberg, 1999; Nakamura et al.,
1999). In fact, Kemp and colleagues (2000) showed in their retrospective
review of death-scene and medical examiner investigation reports that
47% of infants who were diagnosed as dying from SIDS, accidental suffocation, or undetermined causes were found on a shared sleeping surface (Kemp et al., 2000). Other studies concluding that bed-sharing is
dangerous have reviewed data collected by the U.S. Consumer Product
Safety Commission (CPSC) on children's deaths. For instance, Nakamura
and colleagues (1999) reported a total of 515 deaths across an eight-year
period in the 1990s that were attributed to causes related to sleeping on
an adult bed. Drago and Dannenberg (1999) reviewed CPSC data as well,
and state that 102 cases (of 2,178 between 1980 and 1997) were reported
to involve an infant being overlain by a sleeping partner in an adult bed.
Each of these authors has cautioned against the practice of bed-sharing
due to these results. Other researchers have found that bed-sharing does
increase nighttime thermal conditions (Baddock, Galland, Beckers,
Taylor, & Bolton, 2004; Fleming, Young, & Blair, 2006) and results in a
higher risk for airway covering (Ball, 2009). However, these investigators
found no negative impact of these conditions on the typically developing infants in their samples. Infants were able to maintain a normal core
temperature despite being in warmer thermal conditions during bed-
sharing (Baddock et al., 2004; Fleming et al., 2006). Further, although
Ball (2009) found that 70% of infants spent a portion of the night with
their airways covered, there was no negative effect on oxygen saturation
or heart rate and either parent or infant movements terminated all bouts
of airway covering.

Notwithstanding the clear dangers of bed-sharing under certain
circumstances, one common problem with the above retrospective

investigations is the unknown context within which bed-sharing occurred and the understudied risk factors that may have led to the infants' deaths. Indeed, Alexander and Radisch (2005) found that a high proportion of infants dying of SIDS in their retrospective examination of autopsy reports were found co-sleeping. However, they conclude that because tobacco or drug use was not controlled among co-sleeping adults, a general recommendation cannot be made against co-sleeping. Their conclusion supports the notion that to surmise that bed-sharing itself is the cause of death from retrospective reports seems inappropriate. Nonetheless, the American Academy of Pediatrics, in their revised policy statement on SIDS risk, has recommended that parents sleep close to their infants (i.e., room-share), but avoid bed-sharing due to the potential risks discussed above (Task Force on Sudden Infant Death Syndrome, 2005).

In the aforementioned investigations, data are not presented on the sobriety of the parents or the incidence of parental smoking, both of which have been shown to increase the risk of death among bed-sharing infants (Blair et al., 1999). In their population-based case-control study conducted in England, Blair and colleagues (1999) reported that the risk of SIDS associated with being found in the parental bed was not significant for infants of parents who did not smoke, or for infants whose mothers had not recently consumed alcohol. Sharing a sofa for sleep was determined to be a high risk. In another case-control study in the United States, Klonoff-Cohen and Edelstein (1995) found no significant relationship between routine bed-sharing and SIDS risk.

Along with these epidemiological investigations of risk factors, other researchers have concluded that shared sleeping environments in the absence of the risk factors identified above may be beneficial to infants and parents for a variety of reasons. For instance, several researchers have found that bed-sharing tends to promote breastfeeding, at least among some parents who adopt a bed-sharing arrangement (Baddock et al., 2006; Ball, 2006; Blair & Ball, 2004; McCoy et al., 2004; McKenna, Mosko, & Richard, 1997). One study of a largely African American inner-city population below the poverty line, however, did not find a relation between bed-sharing and breastfeeding (Brenner et al., 2003). Furthermore, McCoy and colleagues (2004) found that bed-sharing and breastfeeding were related only for white, non-Hispanic, and Asian mothers and not for Hispanic or black mothers. Thus, again, contextual factors surrounding bed-sharing need to be considered when trying to determine the relative influence of bed-sharing environments on infants and parents. In a series of studies of bed-sharing mother-infant pairs, McKenna and colleagues have found other potential benefits of bed-sharing, including increased infant arousability and heart rate (Mosko, Richard, McKenna, & Drummond, 1996; Richard & Mosko, 2004), minimizing the prone infant sleeping position, and increasing maternal nighttime vigilance (Richard, Mosko, McKenna, & Drummond, 1996). These potential positive impacts need to be considered within the overall context of bed-sharing environments and may not be the same for all bed-sharing mother-infant pairs. However, they do suggest possible benefits of bed-sharing for at least some parents and their infants.

Another possible benefit of co-sleeping (room and/or bed-sharing) is supporting secure infant-parent attachments; this proposition has been discussed but not fully investigated. Nighttime parenting in the Western, solitary sleeping context has been viewed as a separation, thus potentially activating the attachment system (e.g., Anders, 1994). An important component of "attachment parenting" (e.g., Sears & Sears, 2001) is a shared sleep environment, which is purported to support secure attachments. Indeed, preliminary work suggests that securely attached infants tend to wake regularly during the nighttime (Scher, 2001). This pattern makes sense in terms of attachment theory when one considers that night-waking may be a proximity-seeking behavior, a hallmark of secure attachment. Whether bed-sharing influences (or is related to) the security of infant-parent attachment remains to be seen, and seems to be a ripe area for further research (see Keller, chapter 3 in this volume for relations between attachment security and sleep).

Despite the controversy over bed-sharing in the United States, it remains clear that bed-sharing occurs safely in many other industrialized nations. Some researchers have concluded that, rather than universally recommending one sleep environment or another, practitioners should try to understand the cultural, ethnic, and parenting context within which shared or solitary sleep arrangements occur, assess the risk factors associated with specific sleeping arrangements within these contexts, and make suggestions based on these characteristics (e.g., Germo, Goldberg, & Keller, 2009; Jenni & O'Connor, 2005; Morgan, Groer, & Smith, 2006;

Owens, 2002; Wailoo, Ball, Fleming, & Platt, 2004). McKenna and McDade (2005) conclude from their review that "it is highly unlikely that any one single, ... population-based, rather than family-based, recommendation either promoting bed-sharing, or recommending against it, is appropriate because outcomes appear to be context-specific" (p. 148).

Daytime Sleep

Although daytime sleep is clearly prevalent and viewed as developmentally appropriate at least through the early childhood years, investigations of daytime sleep environments for young children are curiously lacking. While some researchers have begun to examine the napping *patterns* of young children in child care (e.g., Ward, Gay, Anders, Alkon, & Lee, 2008), detailed examinations of particular nap *environments* are absent. Given that 57% of young children in the United States are enrolled in center-based early care and education programs (U.S. Department of Education, National Center for Education Statistics, 2005) and a substantial proportion are cared for in other regulated forms of care (e.g., family child-care settings), it seems reasonable to examine the environments for napping provided by such settings. Yet, with two notable exceptions that will be discussed below, such data are nonexistent. The little information that we do have comes from our personal experiences working in and with child-care centers and family child-care homes in a professional capacity, from national data on state child-care regulations regarding sleep, and from two studies of nap environments in Japan.

The Napping Context in Child-Care Settings (United States)

Generally, infants, toddlers, and preschool-aged children in child-care settings in the United States are given an opportunity to take a nap on a daily basis. State child-care regulations provide guidelines for the type of sleeping surface(s) appropriate for different age groups of children, how far apart nap mats must be placed, and sleep positioning for young infants—that is, back to sleep. Accepted practices from a well-respected national early childhood education organization are published (Copple & Bredekamp, 2009), and supply child-care providers with guidelines to follow regarding napping. For example, in order to be considered "developmentally appropriate," infants' sleeping areas must be separated from active play and eating areas, infants should have their own cribs, lights are dimmed, the sleeping area is quiet, and each infant is put down for naps by a familiar adult. Toddler-aged children should have their own cot and bedding (which may be placed in the play area if all children are expected to sleep at the same time), cots should be separated, and a nap transition routine is provided (Copple & Bredekamp, 2009). Interestingly, no specific guidelines are provided for the naps of preschool-aged children, although a significant number of three- to five-year-old children are still napping (Ward et al., 2008).

The transition to nap time in group care settings can be challenging. Often, caregivers will dim the lights, provide soft music, and may rub the backs or stroke the hair of children who have difficulty settling on their own. However, these are anecdotal observations and not substantiated by research across child-care settings. It is assumed that young children who are cared for in their own homes sleep in the same environment that they use for nighttime sleep, although this, too, is not explicitly verified by research. It is possible, for example, that some young children who typically bed-share at night sleep by themselves during the day. More research is necessary to verify such patterns.

A study of national child-care regulations regarding infant sleep environments in the United States has provided important information (Moon, Kotch, & Aird, 2006). These investigators examined state regulations regarding infant sleep position, crib safety regulations, and bedding regulations, among other such factors in child-care centers and family child-care homes. Alarmingly, Moon and colleagues found that only seven states required child-care providers to be trained in SIDS risk reduction, 26 states had a regulation regarding infant sleep position, 41 states had regulations for crib safety, and 23 states had bedding regulations that prohibited the use of soft bedding or objects. While this study details state regulations, no data are available on specific sleeping arrangements in individual child-care settings. Clearly, more research is necessary to determine the nature of the specific contexts of children's daytime sleep environments in the United States.

The Napping Context in Child Care Settings (Japan)

Two small, largely qualitative, investigations of infant, toddler, and pre-school-aged children's napping in Japanese child-care centers have been published. In the first, Ben-Ari (1996) reports on data collected primarily in one child-care center in the southwestern part of Kyoto. Ben-Ari discusses the naptime routines, which sound remarkably like those that occur in the United States, with a few notable exceptions. For example, the children begin the transition by setting up the naptime environment with their own personal nap mats, the teachers read stories and play quiet music, and the lights are dimmed. The mats are not necessarily placed in the same location each day, however, and the children change into paja-mas, two exceptions to customary practice in the United States. Ben-Ari then explains that the teachers move around to each of the children, helping individuals to fall asleep by softly patting their backs, softly strok-ing them, and lying down next to them. These practices are similar to the ways in which Japanese parents induce nighttime sleep, and are remark-ably similar to the practices we have personally observed in child-care settings in the United States.

The second study examined the daytime sleep practices of teachers and young children in a child-care center in northeast Japan (Tahhan, 2008). In this study that largely relied on participant-observations and interviews, Tahhan discusses the naptime rituals experienced in this par-ticular center and describes how teachers influence the children's falling asleep. She emphasizes the Japanese term, *soine*: "to accompany someone to sleep" (p. 39). Indeed, in this child-care center, teachers consciously and deliberately induced sleep in the children by becoming aware of and in tune with what each individual child found relaxing. This often involved direct body contact, especially with the younger age groups. Tahhan emphasizes that the teachers were not viewed as "separate from" the child in an attempt to induce sleep. Rather, they became in tune with the child through physical proximity and relaxing themselves due to a belief that only by creating security and comfort could the child settle into sleep. Again, the specific practices of lying next to the child, touch-ing him/her, and becoming in tune (e.g., through matching breathing patterns, softly stroking) are similar to some of the napping practices we have personally experienced in U.S. child-care settings, especially among "master" teachers in high quality settings.

Clearly, more work is necessary in order to more fully understand the daytime sleep context of young children in industrialized nations. It seems safe to assume that daytime sleep practices most likely conform to larger cultural goals and ideologies, although the similarities between the sleep-induction strategies of child-care teachers in Japan and the United States may not be consistent with this assumption, and deserve empirical investigation. It is likely that daytime environments, like nighttime environments, are influenced by embedded contextual factors that transact across time.

Summary

What seems clear from this review of sleeping environments in industrialized nations is that the topic is complex. When viewed from a developmental systems perspective, however, the complexity makes sense. Clearly, distal components such as culture, ethnicity, and societal values provide the overall backdrop for choice of sleeping environments for family members. From a sociological perspective, Schwartz (1970) concludes that "a person *belongs* where he sleeps; sleep establishes where the person is in social as well as spatial terms; it situates him in accordance with membership rather than mere presence and, thereby, generates an identity for him" (p. 493; emphasis in original). It is logical to conclude that the given society within which one develops will partly constrain the possible sleep environments available, thereby situating the individual within the rich set of values and ideologies seen as desirable in a given society. More proximal components, however, cannot be de-emphasized. Indeed, within any given culture, ethnic group, or society, diversity among families is apparent and should not be ignored (e.g., Jenni & O'Connor, 2005).

We have presented evidence that sleeping arrangements are partly influenced by the particular values that families deem important within a given distal context. Moving to the individual level, it is also reasonable to conclude that young children themselves play a role in where they sleep. For example, individual differences due to temperament, attachment, and sleeping characteristics (positioning, amount of movement, etc.) probably have an impact on young children's sleep environment. That a specific subset of families exists who "reactively" co-sleep provides evidence of the impact of the individual on his/her sleep environment. It is also clear that time plays an important role, not only in defining the sleep environment but also in how sleep environments change across time (whether that be within the night, between nights, or across months or years). The main components of DST (individuals developing within embedded contexts, the transactional nature of development, and change over time) are clearly illustrated when viewing the topic of sleep environments. More work examining the complexity evident in these transactions is both warranted and desirable to improve our understanding of sleep environments for children in post-industrial societies.

NOTE

1. For the purpose of this chapter, "industrialized" and "post-industrial" will reflect the definition of the United Nations using the Human Development Index (a measure that includes a country's life expectancy, knowledge and education, and standard of living; scores greater than .90 categorize a country as relatively "more developed"). Under this definition, 33 countries are included in the most recent report, encompassing most of the countries in the European Union as well as Japan, Australia, New Zealand, Israel, and the United States (United Nations Development Programme, 2008).

REFERENCES

Alexander, R. T., & Radisch, D. (2005). Sudden Infant Death Syndrome risk factors with regards to sleep position, sleep surface, and co-sleeping. *Journal of Forensic Science, 50,* 1–5.

Anders, T. F. (1994). Infant sleep, nighttime relationships, and attachment. *Psychiatry, 57,* 11–21.

Baddock, S. A., Galland, B. C., Beckers, M. G. S., Taylor, B. J., & Bolton, D. P. G. (2004). Bed-sharing and the infant's thermal environment in the home setting. *Archives of Disease in Childhood, 89,* 1111–1116.

Baddock, S. A., Galland, B. C., Bolton, D. P. G., Williams, S. M., & Taylor, B. J. (2006). Differences in infant and parent behaviors during routine bed sharing compared with cot sleeping in the home setting. *Pediatrics, 117,* 1599–1607.

Baddock, S. A., Galland, B. C., Taylor, B. J., & Bolton, D. P. G. (2007). Sleep arrangements and behavior of bed-sharing families in the home setting. *Pediatrics, 119,* e200–e207.

Ball, H. L. (2006). Bed-sharing on the postnatal ward: Breastfeeding and infant sleep safety. *Paediatrics & Child Health, 11*(Suppl A), 43A–46A.

Ball, H. L. (2009). Airway covering during bed-sharing [Electronic version]. *Child: Care, Health, & Development, 35*, 728–737. doi: 10.1111/j.1365-2214.2009.00979.x

Ball, H. L., Hooker, E., & Kelly, P. J. (1999). Where will the baby sleep? Attitudes and practices of new and experienced parents regarding cosleeping with their newborn infants. *American Anthropologist, 101*, 143–151.

Ball, H. L., Hooker, E., & Kelly, P. J. (2000). Parent-infant co-sleeping: Fathers' roles and perspectives. *Infant & Child Development, 9*, 67–74.

Barry, H., III, & Paxson, L. M. (1971). Infancy and early childhood: Cross-cultural codes 2. *Ethnology, 10*, 466–508.

Ben-Ari, E. (1996). From mothering to othering: Organization, culture, and nap time in a Japanese day-care center. *Ethos, 24*, 136–164.

Blair, P. S., & Ball, H. L. (2004). The prevalence and characteristics associated with parent-infant bed-sharing in England. *Archives of Disease in Childhood, 89*, 1106–1110.

Blair, P. S., Fleming, P. J., Smith, I. J., Platt, M. W., Young, J., Nadin, P., ... CESDI SUDI Research Group. (1999). Babies sleeping with parents: Case-control study of factors influencing the risk of the sudden infant death syndrome. *British Medical Journal, 319*, 1457–1461.

Brenner, R. A., Simons-Morton, B. G., Bhaskar, B., Revenis, M., Das, A., & Clemens, J. D. (2003). Infant-parent bed sharing in an inner-city population. *Archives of Pediatric & Adolescent Medicine, 157*, 33–39.

Buckley, P., Rigda, R. S., Mundy, L., & McMillen, I. C. (2002). Interaction between bed sharing and other sleep environments during the first six months of life. *Early Human Development, 66*, 123–132.

Carpenter, R. G. (2006). Overview of epidemiological studies on the risks of sudden infant death syndrome associated with bed sharing: Summary and conclusions. *Paediatrics & Child Health, 11*(Suppl A), 32A–33A.

Caudill, W., & Plath, D. W. (1966). Who sleeps by whom? Parent–child involvement in urban Japanese families. *Psychiatry, 29*, 344–366.

Copple, C., & Bredekamp, S. (Eds.). (2009). *Developmentally appropriate practice in early childhood programs serving children from birth through age 8* (3rd ed.). Washington, DC: NAEYC.

Drago, D. A., & Dannenberg, A. L. (1999). Infant mechanical suffocation deaths in the United States, 1980–1997. *Pediatrics, 103*(5), e59. doi: 10.1542/peds.103.5.e59

Fleming, P., Young, J., & Blair, P. (2006). The importance of mother-baby interactions in determining nighttime thermal conditions for sleeping infants: Observations from the home and the sleep laboratory. *Paediatrics & Child Health, 11*(Suppl A), 7A–10A.

Ford, D. H., & Lerner, R. M. (1992). *Developmental systems theory: An integrative approach*. Newbury Park, CA: Sage.

Germo, G. R., Goldberg, W. A., & Keller, M. A. (2009). Learning to sleep through the night: Solution or strain for mothers and young children? *Infant Mental Health Journal, 30*, 223–244.

Giannotti, F., Cortesi, F., Sebastiani, T., & Vagnoni, C. (2008). Sleep practices and habits in children across different cultures. In A. Ivanenko (Ed.), *Sleep and psychiatric disorders in children and adolescents* (pp. 37–48). New York, NY: Informa Healthcare USA Inc.

Hauck, F. R., Signore, C., Fein, S. B., & Raju, T. N. K. (2008). Infant sleeping arrangements and practices during the first year of life. *Pediatrics, 122*, S113–S120.

Jenni, O G., Fuhrer, H. Z., Iglowstein, I., Molinari, L., & Largo, R. H. (2005). A longitudinal study of bed sharing and sleep problems among Swiss children in the first 10 years of life. *Pediatrics, 115*, 233–240.

Jenni, O. G., & O'Connor, B. B. (2005). Children's sleep: An interplay between culture and biology. *Pediatrics, 115*, 204–216.

Kawasaki, C., Nugent, J. K., Miyashita, H., Miyahara, H., & Brazelton, T. B. (1994). The cultural organization of infants' sleep. *Children's Environments, 11*, 135–141.

Keller, M. A., & Goldberg, W. A. (2004). Co-sleeping: Help or hindrance for young children's independence? *Infant & Child Development, 13*, 369–388.

Kemp, J. S., Unger, B., Wilkins, D., Psara, R. M., Ledbetter, T. L., Graham, M. A., … Thach, B. T. (2000). Unsafe sleep practices and an analysis of bedsharing among infants dying suddenly and unexpectedly: Results of a four-year, population-based, death-scene investigation study of Sudden Infant Death Syndrome and related deaths. *Pediatrics, 106*(3), e41. doi: 10.1542/peds.106.3.e41

Klonoff-Cohen, H., & Edelstein, S. L. (1995). Bed sharing and the sudden infant death syndrome. *British Medical Journal, 311*, 1269–1272.

Latz, S., Wolf, A. W., & Lozoff, B. (1999). Cosleeping in context: Sleep practices and problems in young children in Japan and the United States. *Archives of Pediatric & Adolescent Medicine, 153*, 339–346.

Lee, K. (1992). Pattern of night waking and crying of Korean infants from 3 months to 2 years old and its relation with various factors. *Journal of Developmental & Behavioral Pediatrics, 13*, 326–330.

Lozoff, B., Askew, G. L., & Wolf, A. W. (1996). Cosleeping and early childhood sleep problems: Effects of ethnicity and socioeconomic status. *Journal of Developmental & Behavioral Pediatrics, 17*, 9–15.

Madansky, D., & Edelbrock, C. (1990). Cosleeping in a community sample of 2- and 3-year-old children. *Pediatrics, 86*, 197–203.

McCoy, R. C., Hunt, C. E., Lesko, S. M., Vezina, R., Corwin, M. J., Willinger, M., … Mitchell, A. A. (2004). Frequency of bed sharing and its relationship to breastfeeding. *Journal of Developmental & Behavioral Pediatrics*, *25*, 141–149.

McKenna, J. J., & McDade, T. (2005). Why babies should never sleep alone: A review of the co-sleeping controversy in relation to SIDS, bedsharing, and breast feeding. *Paediatric Respiratory Reviews*, *6*, 134–152.

McKenna, J. J., Mosko, S. S., & Richard, C. A. (1997). Bedsharing promotes breastfeeding. *Pediatrics*, *100*, 214–219.

Moon, R.Y., Kotch, L., & Aird, L. (2006). State child care regulations regarding infant sleep environment since the Healthy Child Care America-Back to Sleep Campaign. *Pediatrics*, *118*, 73–83.

Morgan, K. H., Groer, M. W., & Smith, L. J. (2006). The controversy about what constitutes safe and nurturant infant sleep environments. *JOGNN*, *35*, 684–691.

Mosko, S., Richard, C., McKenna, J., & Drummond, S. (1996). Infant sleep architecture during bedsharing and possible implications for SIDS. *Sleep*, *19*, 677–684.

Nakamura, S., Wind, M., & Danello, M. A. (1999). Review of hazards associated with children placed in adult beds. *Archives of Pediatric & Adolescent Medicine*, *153*, 1019–1023.

Nelson, E. A., Taylor, B. J., Jenik, A., Vance, J., Walmsley, K., Pollard, K., … Nepomyashchaya, V (2001). International child care practices study: Infant sleeping environment. *Early Human Development*, *62*, 43–55.

New, R. S., & Richman, A. L. (1996). Maternal beliefs and infant care practices in Italy and the United States. In S. Harkness & C. M. Super (Eds.), *Parents' cultural belief systems: Their origins, expressions, and consequences* (pp. 385–404). New York: Guilford.

Okami, P., Weisner, T., & Olmstead, R. (2002). Outcome correlates of parent–child bedsharing: An eighteen-year longitudinal study. *Journal of Developmental & Behavioral Pediatrics*, *23*, 244–253.

Owens, J. A. (2002). Cosleeping. *Journal of Developmental & Behavioral Pediatrics*, *23*, 254–255.

Ramos, K. D. (2003). Intentional versus reactive cosleeping. *Sleep Research Online*, *5*, 141–147.

Ramos, K. D., & Youngclarke, D. M. (2006). Parenting advice books about child sleep: Cosleeping and crying it out. *Sleep*, *29*, 1616–1623.

Richard, C. A., & Mosko, S. S. (2004). Mother-infant bedsharing is associated with an increase in infant heart rate. *Sleep*, *27*, 507–511.

Richard, C., Mosko, S., McKenna, J., & Drummond, S. (1996). Sleeping position, orientation, and proximity in bedsharing infants and mothers. *Sleep*, *19*, 685–690.

Rigda, R. S., McMillen, I. C., & Buckley, P. (2000). Bed sharing patterns in a cohort of Australian infants during the first six months after birth. *Journal of Paediatrics & Child Health, 36*, 117–121.

Rothrauff, T., Middlemiss, W., & Jacobson, L. (2004). Comparison of American and Austrian infants' and toddlers' sleep habits: A retrospective, exploratory study. *North American Journal of Psychology, 6*, 125–144.

Rowe, J. (2003). A room of their own: The social landscape of infant sleep. *Nursing Inquiry, 10*, 184–192.

Sears, W., & Sears, M. (2001). *The attachment parenting book: A commonsense guide to understanding and nurturing your baby*. New York: Little, Brown and Company.

Scher, A. (2001). Attachment and sleep: A study of night waking in 12-month-old infants. *Developmental Psychobiology, 38*, 274–285.

Schwartz, B. (1970). Notes on the sociology of sleep. *The Sociological Quarterly, 11*, 485–499.

Shweder, R. A., Jensen, L. A., & Goldstein, W. M. (1995). Who sleeps by whom revisited: A method for extracting the moral goods implicit in practice. In J. J. Goodnow, P. Miller, F. Kessel (Eds.). *New directions for child development # 67: Cultural practices as contexts for development* (pp. 21–39). San Francisco, CA: Jossey Bass.

Sourander, A. (2001). Emotional and behavioural problems in a sample of Finnish three-year-olds. *European Child & Adolescent Psychiatry, 10*, 98–104.

Tahhan, D. A. (2008). Depth and space in sleep: Intimacy, touch and the body in Japanese co-sleeping rituals. *Body & Society, 14*, 37–56.

Task Force on Sudden Infant Death Syndrome. (2005). The changing concept of Sudden Infant Death Syndrome: Diagnostic coding shifts, controversies regarding the sleeping environment, and new variables to consider reducing risk. *Pediatrics, 116*, 1245–1255.

Taylor, N., Donovan, W., & Leavitt, L. (2008). Consistency in infant sleeping arrangements and mother-infant interaction. *Infant Mental Health Journal, 29*, 77–94.

United Nations Development Programme. (2008). Human development index trends. Retrieved from http://hdr.undp.org/en/statistics/

U. S. Department of Education, National Center for Education Statistics (2005). Participation in education. Retrieved from: http://www.nces.ed.gov/programs/coe/2007/section1/table.asp?tableID=662.

Wailoo, M., Ball, H. L., Fleming, P. J., & Ward-Platt, M. W. (2004). Infants bed-sharing with mothers. *Archives of Disease in Childhood, 89*, 1082–1083.

Ward, T. M., Gay, C., Anders, T. F., Alkon, A., & Lee, K. A. (2008). Sleep and napping patterns in 3-to-5-year-old children attending full-day childcare centers. *Journal of Pediatric Psychology, 33*, 666–672.

Weimer, S. M., Dise, T. L., Evers, P. B., Ortiz, M. A., Welldaregay, W., & Steinmann, W. C. (2002). Prevalence, predictors, and attitudes toward cosleeping in an urban pediatric center. *Clinical Pediatrics, 41*, 433–438.

Willinger, M., Ko, C. -W, Hoffman, H. J., Kessler, R. C., & Corwin, M. J. (2003). Trends in infant bed sharing in the United States, 1993–2000. *Archives of Pediatric & Adolescent Medicine, 157*, 43–49.

Wolf, A. W., Lozoff, B., Latz, S., & Paludetto, R. (1996). Parental theories in the management of young children's sleep in Japan, Italy, and the United States. In S. Harkness & C. M. Super (Eds.), *Parents' cultural belief systems: Their origins, expressions, and consequences* (pp. 364–384). New York, NY: Guilford Press.

10

Children's Sleep in the Context of Socioeconomic Status, Race, and Ethnicity

Les A. Gellis

Introduction

As demonstrated in other chapters of this book, children's sleep can play a powerful role in the quality of life and functioning of the individual child and the entire family. Studies show that disrupted sleep is associated with serious and long-term health problems in adolescents and adults, such as risk for depression (Roane & Taylor, 2008), suicide (Bernert & Joiner, 2007; Wojnar et al., 2009), weakened immune response (Hall et al., 1998; Savard, Laroche, Simard, Ivers, & Morin, 2003), decreased functioning and quality of life (Roth, 2007), and mortality (Gallicchio & Kalesan, 2009).

Because of the negative consequences associated with sleep problems in children, and to prevent potential long-term problems in adulthood, there has been an increased interest in understanding the sleep habits of children and adolescents. It has been estimated that approximately 10% of elementary school children experience daytime sleepiness (Owens, Spirito, McGuin, & Nobile, 2000; Stein, Mendelsohn, Obermeyer, Amromin, & Benca, 2001) and 20% report having fatigue during the school day (Stein, et al., 2001). These problems increase significantly during the adolescent years, and approximately 25–42% of adolescents report excessive sleepiness during the day (Anderson, Storfer-Isser, Taylor, Rosen, & Redline, 2009; Gibson et al., 2006).

Sleep-related problems are likely due to a variety of factors, and individuals of various racial, ethnic, and socioeconomic groups may be at increased risk for sleep disturbances. For instance, negative life events and daily or ongoing stressors (Healey et al., 1981; Vahtera et al., 2007); environmental events such as loud noise, poor temperature control, and uncomfortable mattresses; behaviors such as napping, sleep schedule, and exercise (American Academy of Sleep Medicine, 2005; Stepanski & Wyatt, 2003); as well as physical health problems (Stein, Belik, Jacobi & Sareen, 2008), are among the many variables that can influence sleep. These factors appear to make individuals with fewer resources susceptible to sleep problems. For instance, adults with lower education typically have less health related knowledge (Winkleby, Jatulis, Frank, & Fortmann, 1992) and may be less aware of behaviors that affect sleep. Fewer economic resources may increase the possibility of poor temperature control (e.g., no air conditioning) or sleeping on an uncomfortable mattress, and living in a crowded urban environment may increase the chances of sleep-disrupting noise. Individuals with fewer resources are also more likely to experience greater physical and psychosocial impairment, which can affect sleep (Adler et al., 1994).

In addition to economic resources, race/ethnicity has been associated with sleep. In the United States, there are current disparities in education and economic resources among individuals of various racial/ethnic groups. Specifically, African Americans are more likely to have less education (U.S. Census Bureau, 2003) and income (U.S. Census Bureau, 2008) than European Americans. African American children, in turn, may be more susceptible to sleep problems than European American children. Further, perceived racial discrimination has been shown to be associated with increased stress and psychological problems (Williams, Neighbors, & Jackson, 2003), which can impact sleep. Finally, African American preschool children are less likely to sleep in their own room than children from other ethnic groups (Lozoff, Askew, & Wolf, 1996) even without space limitations (Milan, Snow, & Belay, 2007); this sleep behavior may be associated with sleep difficulties (Lozoff et al., 1996).

In this chapter, literature pertaining to clinical sleep disorders and nonclinical aspects of sleep patterns among children and adolescents in relation to socioeconomic status (SES) and race/ethnicity is summarized. SES is often used as a proxy for social or economic status, and this construct has traditionally been measured using assessments of education, income and/or occupation. In assessing ethnic/racial associations with sleep, the majority of studies in the United States have focused on comparisons between European and African Americans and this focus will be reflected in the review. Given the multicultural state of the United States, it is of the utmost importance to understand normative sleep patterns in children from various demographic groups. Further clarification of the relation between race/ethnicity and SES with sleep in this chapter will hopefully contribute to greater understanding of the factors and contextual conditions that may contribute to sleep disturbances in children and adolescents.

Sleep duration, quality, and/or scheduling will be compared in individuals of various SES and ethnic/racial backgrounds. First, initial epidemiologic studies assessing sleep parameters among members of these groups will be reviewed. Following this initial summary, more recent studies will be summarized, and these investigations will be separated into those conducted with participants in three age groups: young children (ages two through eight years), preadolescents (ages 8 to 13 years), and adolescents. Then, the literature comparing individuals of various SES levels and racial/ethnic backgrounds on symptoms and diagnoses of sleep disordered breathing (SDB) will be reviewed. SDB will be discussed because of the significant daytime consequences associated with this illness and because of recent studies showing disparities in SDB associated with SES and race/ethnicity. Finally, conclusions, limitations, and future directions will be highlighted.

Sleep Patterns in Children: Relations with SES, Ethnicity, and Race

The early studies that assessed the relations between sleep and either SES or ethnicity/race in children involved large scale epidemiologic investigations based in Great Britain (Gulliford, Price, Rona, & Chinn, 1990; Pollack, 1994; Rona, Li, Gulliford, & Chinn, 1998). Gulliford and colleagues (1990) investigated relations between various variables and total sleep time in 4,145 children born in England and Scotland between the ages of 5 and 11 years. SES was indicated by the education level of the mother, the father's unemployment status, and an indicator of overcrowding (the number of people in the family divided by the number of rooms

occupied excluding bathroom and kitchen). Total sleep time was estimated as the duration between the child's usual bed and wake times, as
assessed by parental report. Among other significant correlations, the
authors noted greater total sleep time in children (~ 15 minutes) of white
origin on schooldays and over the full week as compared to children of
Afro-Caribbean or Asian descent. There were no associations between
total sleep time and education attainment of the mother, overcrowding
in the home, or parental unemployment.

This initial study was followed by Pollack (1994), who assessed
predictors of night-waking in children at five years of age in over 12,000
British children born in 1970. Night-waking was assessed by the mother
who classified her child's sleep disturbance as being "no problem," "mild,"
or "severe." In this study, children of mothers born in England and the
West Indies or Africa had greater night-waking difficulties than those
from Scotland and Wales, and those from the West Indies or Africa were
particularly likely to have difficulties.

Finally, Rona, Li, Gulliford, and Chinn (1998) assessed sleep in a
random sample of 14,372 British children in primary schools in England
and Scotland, and compared these children to an English inner-city
population. The authors indicated that the sample from England and
Scotland showed social characteristics that were representative of the
country, and the inner-city population showed characteristics of "deprivation". Parents were asked whether their child had disturbed sleep
at night, excluding periods of illness, and chose one of six responses:
(1) sleep disturbed most nights—cries and needs attention; (2) sleep disturbed once or twice a week—cries and needs attention; (3) sleep disturbed occasionally—cries and needs attention; (4) sleep disturbed—wants
attention but does not cry; (5) sleeps poorly but lies quietly when awake;
or (6) usually sleeps well. Children were categorized as disturbed sleepers
if parents reported disturbed sleep at least once per week. SES was
assessed by the mother's level of education and the father's occupation
status (non-manual, skilled manual, semi-skilled, unskilled). White children from England and Scotland were compared to white children from
the inner city, Afro-Caribbean individuals, and children from the Indian
subcontinent.

Results of Rona and colleagues' (1998) study showed that children
from the Indian subcontinent and white children from the inner city

were greater than twice more likely to be disturbed sleepers as compared to white Scottish children. There were no other ethnic differences in relation to sleep quality. Children whose mothers had no education or only primary education were 2.4 times more likely to have disturbed sleep as compared to children of college graduates; children who had fathers who engaged in semi-skilled or unskilled labor were 1.4 times more likely to have disturbed sleep than those involved in non-manual labor. The results of this study were different from those of Gulliford and colleagues (1990) in that they showed significant differences in children's sleep according to the educational attainment of the mother. Rona et al. (1998) further noted that those mothers with only primary or no education and those from the Indian subcontinent were likely to be first generation immigrants into Britain. Results from this study were compared to those of Pollack (1994), and the authors noted that Afro-Caribbean children (who also reported more disturbed sleep) were also likely to be first generation immigrants. These initial findings suggested that low SES and minority ethnic status may indeed be risk factors for poor sleep in children, perhaps serving as proxy variables for the stress of cultural change and other environmental circumstances associated with recent immigration.

The relationships between race/ethnicity or SES and sleep were first assessed in the United States using data from the household component of the 1987 national medical expenditure survey (Cornelius, 1991). This study focused on a sample of 6,722 children ages 5–17 years. SES was measured by poverty status and education level of the highest wage earner in the family, and children were assessed on their average parent reported total sleep time (TST). Findings indicated that children from poor and low income families or with parents with lower education levels (< 12 years) were more likely to have TST of 7 to 8 hours. Parents of children and adolescents with education levels greater than 12 years were more likely to sleep 9 to 10 hours. With regard to race/ethnicity, African American teenagers aged 13–17 years were more likely to sleep fewer than six hours per night (6.8%) as compared to Hispanic American teenagers (4.6%) and European American teenagers (2.3%).

In summary, initial epidemiologic studies noted lower total sleep time in African American children residing in the United States and African-Caribbean children in Great Britain. These initial studies also suggested shorter sleep duration among children newly assimilated into society. After these investigations, a considerable increase in number of studies assessing sleep in relation to SES and race/ethnicity occurred in the first decade of the 21st century. In these studies, researchers began to focus on children of more narrow age groups and varied types of sleep patterns and problems. These studies are summarized below and separated by age group: young children (ages 2–8 years), preadolescents (ages 8–11 years), and adolescents (ages 13–17 years).

Sleep Patterns and Problems of Children Ages Two to Eight Years

Montgomery-Downs, Jones, Molfese, and Gozal (2003) assessed racial/ethnic differences in sleep in 3,795 preschool students up to five years of age (mean age = 4.2 years, SD = .53) enrolled in the Jefferson County Kentucky public schools Early Jump Start programs. In this low SES sample, sleep duration was estimated by the parent, who endorsed one of the following six categories reflecting the child's average total sleep time per night: 4–5 hours, 6–7 hours, 8–9 hours, 10–11 hours, and more than 11 hours. Results showed that African American children were more likely to sleep 8–9 hours, and European American children were more likely to sleep 10–11 hours.

McLaughlin Crabtree and colleagues (2005) followed up this investigation, and assessed ethnic/racial and SES differences in sleep among 3,371 children between the ages of two and seven years on a number of sleep-related measures. These children were also in the Jefferson County Kentucky public schools system where the Montgomery-Downs and colleagues' (2003) study was conducted. Parents responded to questions about various sleep behaviors in their children on a five-point scale ranging from never to almost always, and SES was assessed via the median annual income of the family zip code based on data from the 2000 U.S. Census Bureau. A composite sleep behavior score was generated, and this measure included items related to children's fear of sleeping in the dark, ease of waking in the morning, willingness to sleep, restless sleep, nighttime awakenings, sleep talking, sleepwalking, enuresis, nightmares, difficulties initiating sleep, and ease of falling sleep. Excessive daytime sleepiness was assessed using items including falling asleep watching television, falling asleep at school, and daytime sleepiness. Finally, usual total sleep time was assessed, and this measure was categorized into five groups: 4–5, 6–7, 8–9, 10–11, and >11 hours of sleep per night.

Racial/ethnic differences in nighttime sleep emerged and indicated that African American children slept significantly less than European American children, even after controlling for both median household income and age (McLaughlin Crabtree et al., 2005). Indeed, African American children were more likely to sleep 8–9 hours per night, and European Americans were more likely to sleep 10–11 hours. This shorter nighttime sleep corresponded with an increased likelihood of later bedtimes for African American children. African American children also reported significantly greater sleepiness than European American children after controlling for SES and age; however, there were no ethnic/racial differences in relation to disruptive sleep behaviors (e.g., sleeping in the dark, ease of waking in the morning, willingness to sleep, restless sleep).

Furthermore, parents with a median household income below the U.S. average were significantly more likely to report problematic sleep behaviors, excessive daytime sleepiness, and less nighttime sleep for their children, even after controlling for ethnicity/race (McLaughlin Crabtree et al., 2005). Children in the higher income group were also more likely to sleep 10–11 hours per night as compared to those in the lower income group. Finally, age moderated the relationships between SES or race/ethnicity and sleep after separating children into various age groups (two to four years and five to seven years). African American children and children in the lower SES group between the ages of five and seven had the highest level of sleep behavior problems, and the African American children and children in the lower SES group between the ages of two to four had the lowest level of sleep behavior problems.

The results described above indicate shorter nighttime sleep among African American children and those of lower SES as measured by neighborhood income. Crosby, LeBourgeois, and Harsh (2005) extended these findings to assess sleep duration over the entire 24-hour day/night including naps. This study compared total sleep time and napping of European and African American children using a large sample ($N = 1,043$) of two- to eight-year-olds recruited from three counties in southern Mississippi. Parents reported children's bedtime, wake time, and nap duration for the previous month, and total sleep time was based on total time in bed. Nap duration was estimated as the duration between nap start time and nap end time. African American children spent approximately 20 fewer minutes in bed on weekday nights than European American children. African American children, however, were significantly more likely to nap than European American children, and total sleep duration for the entire day/night was nearly identical at each age for children in both racial/ethnic groups.

To summarize, few studies have examined the role of SES or ethnicity/race in relation to young children's sleep patterns. Nevertheless, existing evidence replicated the findings from the initial epidemiologic studies that focused mostly on preadolescents. Findings stemming from research with toddlers and young children suggested that African American children slept less than European American children during the evening, and these differences in total sleep time were possibly due to the later bedtimes of the African American children as opposed to disrupted sleep continuity (McLaughlin Crabtree et al., 2005). These findings, however, need to be considered along with Crosby and colleagues' (2005) results that showed no differences in total sleep time between European and African Americans in this age group when considering the entire 24-hour day. McLaughlin Crabtree and colleagues (2005) also showed that children in lower SES groups (lower income per zip code) had greater sleepiness, problematic sleep schedules, problematic sleep behaviors, and worse nighttime sleep than their counterparts from higher SES groups. In fact, relations between sleep disturbances and either race/ethnicity or SES were significant even after controlling for each other, suggesting that both demographic variables may be independent risk factors for sleep problems. Finally, McLaughlin Crabtree and colleagues (2005) highlighted the importance of considering age when assessing sleep by SES and race/ethnicity; recall that disparities in sleep problems associated with SES or race/ethnicity became greater as age increased.

Sleep Patterns and Problems in Older Children and Preadolescents Ages 8 to 13 Years

Sadeh, Raviv, and Gruber (2000) examined the correlation between SES and sleep status in 140 children and preadolescents in second grade

(n = 50; ages 7.2–8.6 years), fourth grade (n = 37; ages 9.3–10.4 years), and sixth grade (n = 53; ages 9.9–12.7 years) living in Israel. Approximately 75% of the children were at least second-generation Israeli-born. The majority of the children were from families of mostly moderate to high education levels, as both the mothers and the fathers averaged 14.7 years of education (SD = 2.9 and 2.8 for mothers and fathers, respectively). Children completed four to five nights of actigraphy, an objective measure of sleep based on monitoring activity. In this study, poor sleep was defined as sleeping less than 90% of the time from sleep onset to morning awakening, and/or waking three or more times per night with each waking episode being five minutes or longer. Based on these criteria, 25 children (17% of the sample) were considered poor sleepers. SES was assessed using the mean education level of both parents. Despite a limited range of education levels among parents, results showed that lower education was significantly associated with increased likelihood of poor sleep among children (beta = .31).

A subsequent study involved a comprehensive assessment of race/ethnicity and sleep in children aged eight to eleven years residing in the Cleveland, Ohio, metropolitan area (Spilsbury et al., 2004). In this study, 755 children were recruited via stratified random sampling and completed seven days of sleep diaries. Outcome variables included total sleep time and variability of sleep duration, which was assessed by the coefficient of variation (CV; standard deviation of sleep duration divided by the mean sleep duration); greater CV scores reflect more night-to-night variability. Children were categorized as European American or as a minority, which included African Americans, Asian Americans, Native Americans, Hispanic Americans or biracial. The sample included 35% minorities, of whom 88% were African American. Ethnic minority children on average slept six minutes less than nonminority children (9.56 vs. 9.66 hours); however, total sleep time was moderated by age and gender as clarified next.

Minority boys ages 10 to 11 years showed significantly shorter mean sleep duration during all days (9.12 hours) as compared to minority girls and nonminority boys and girls ages 10–11; this sleep amount was 19 to 43 minutes shorter than the sleep of children in all other subgroups including all other age groups (Spilsbury et al., 2004). Minority boys and girls ages 10–11 years also reported the latest bedtimes (10:33 p.m. and

10:37 p.m., respectively), and this was approximately 20 minutes later than those of both nonminority boys and girls. There were no significant differences in average total sleep time among nonminority boys, nonminority girls and minority girls for any of the three age groups. After controlling for potential confounds such as vacation status (e.g., being on summer or holiday vacation) and chronic health conditions, minority boys slept less than children in all other gender/ethnic groups across all ages. In the entire sample, 16% of children reported total sleep time less than nine hours; however, 43% of 10–11 year old minority boys reported fewer than nine hours of sleep, in comparison to between 5% and 26% for children in all other age-sex-ethnicity subgroups. With regard to variability of sleep duration examined via the CV statistic, only 10% of the sample had a CV greater than 15%, and only 3% of the sample had a CV greater than 20%. The CV for minority boys was 19% for the nine-year-olds, and 22% for the 10–11-year olds.

In summary, studies conducted with older children and preadolescents extend previous findings by showing shorter sleep duration among children whose parents had less education and among African American boys while using more rigorous measures of sleep. First, Sadeh and colleagues (2000) showed increased disruption in the sleep of children from lower SES backgrounds using an objective measure of sleep (actigraphy). Although the study included a small sample size for an epidemiologic study, it replicated previous findings using an objective measure of sleep. Second, Spilsbury and colleagues (2004) assessed differences in children's sleep based on SES and race/ethnicity using seven days of sleep diaries. Sleep diaries not only allow for more precise estimates of sleep as compared to categorical outcomes and to global, retrospective reports, but nightly sleep diaries also provide data that are more highly associated with objective sleep data obtained through polysomnography (Carskadon et al., 1976); see Sadeh, chapter 15 in this volume for advantages and disadvantages of various sleep assessment methodologies. Using this more rigorous assessment of sleep, there were only minor overall differences in the total sleep time of minority and European American children. However, these results showed that older minority boys, of whom 88% were African American, were in fact vulnerable to reduced total sleep time, and this vulnerability appeared to be related to delayed bedtimes. In the same study, associations between reduced total sleep time and ethnicity continued to exist after controlling for potential confounds. Thus, it is likely that reduced sleep among African American boys in this age group is related to sleep-scheduling behaviors versus other sleep problems such as insomnia.

Sleep Patterns and Problems of Adolescents

Roberts, Lee, Hernandez, and Solari (2004) collected measures of insomnia symptoms, sleep quality, and total sleep time from 5,118 students in the ninth grade from four southernmost counties in Texas. Overall quality of sleep was assessed on a four-point scale ranging from very good to very bad. Problems related to insomnia were assessed with four questions related to difficulties initiating sleep (DIS), difficulties maintaining sleep (DMS), early morning awakenings (EMA), and non-restorative sleep (NRS) over the past four weeks on a four-point scale ranging from "rarely or never" to "almost every day". The frequency of waking up feeling rested was also measured on a four-point scale ranging from "rarely or never" to "almost every day." Anyone who experienced restorative sleep rarely or never in the past four weeks and who also reported experiencing at least one symptom of insomnia (DIS, DMS, or EMA) was identified as having problems with insomnia. Participants chose one of the following four income categories: (1) Very well off, (2) Living comfortably, (3) Just getting along, or (4) Nearly poor or poor. In this study, foreign-born Mexican American participants reported a decreased likelihood of insomnia (8.6%) as compared to native-born second generation Mexican American participants (15.0%), native-born first generation Mexican American participants (11.8%), and native Caucasian Americans (11.5%). Foreign-born Mexican Americans were also less likely to report non-restorative sleep, more likely to rate their sleep as very good, and less likely to report difficulties initiating or maintaining sleep. Those in the poor or nearly poor category were almost four times more likely to report having problems with insomnia even after controlling for ethnicity.

Roberts, Roberts, and Chan (2006) used data from the Teen Health 2000 study in the Houston metropolitan area. Every household with a child between 11 and 17 years and enrolled in a local health maintenance organization was eligible to participate, and 4,175 children or adolescents reported symptoms of insomnia in the past four weeks. In this study, European Americans, Mexican Americans (born in the United States or Mexico), and African Americans were compared with regard to difficulties initiating sleep (DIS), difficulties maintaining sleep (DMS), early morning awakenings (EMA), and non-restorative sleep (NRS). DMS was measured in two ways. In DMS-1, the individual had difficulty maintaining sleep and had trouble returning to sleep; in DMS-2, the individual was able to go back to sleep quickly. SES was assessed using parental income and education. Education was categorized into three groups: (1) low—less than or equal to 12 years; (2) middle—13–14 years; and (3) high—15 years or greater. Income was also separated into three groups: (1) low—less than $35,000; (2) middle—$35,000 to $64,000; and (3) high—$65,000 or greater.

Results indicated that European American respondents reported greater difficulties initiating sleep (8.3%) as compared to Mexican American (6.0%) and African American (4.7%) adolescents (Roberts et al., 2006). Respondents who were African American (4.3%) reported greater DMS-1 as compared to Mexican American (2.5%) and European American (2.8%) adolescents. Adolescents who were African American (6.7%) also reported greater DMS-2 as compared to their Mexican American (5.8%) and European American (4.1%) counterparts. These ethnic/racial differences existed after controlling for SES and age. Adolescents in the lower income group (7.6%) reported greater DMS-2 as compared to middle (5.0%) and high (3.9%) income groups. Furthermore, adolescents in the higher education group reported fewer DMS-2 (4.1%) as compared to the middle (5.2%) and low (6.3%) education groups.

In another investigation, adolescent sleep habits were assessed using a nationally representative sample in the United States (Adam, Snell, & Pendry, 2007). In this study, 1,267 adolescents of ages 12–19 years completed a diary during one weekday and one weekend day. In the diary, adolescents detailed school and recreational activities and napping behaviors during the day as well as wake time and bed time. Parents completed multiple measures of family functioning including assessments of parental warmth, family rules, family conflict, and stress. Parents were asked to rate their child's physical health on a likert scale from excellent to poor (1–5). Children's behavioral problems were also assessed by the parent using internalizing and externalizing behavioral problem indices. SES was assessed by the average number of years of parental education (mothers and fathers), and parents' income in categories of $10,000. Total sleep time was the main outcome variable, which was recorded as the difference between bed and wake times. Total sleep time was examined in relation to adolescents' race/ethnicity (African, European, Hispanic, and Asian Americans) and SES variables; these analyses controlled for potential confounds including other demographic factors, child health, and behavioral adjustment.

After controlling for potential confounds, African American adolescents had significantly later weekday bedtimes and fewer hours of sleep than their European American counterparts during the weekday (.42 hours of less sleep) and weekend (.47 hours of less sleep)(Adam et al., 2007). The difference in sleep duration between children from the two ethnic groups decreased from .59 hours to.42 hours when "time traveling to school" was not included in the model. After controlling for all other variables, education and income were unrelated to weekday and weekend total sleep time, and adolescents with parents with higher education were more likely to have later bedtimes during the week and on weekends.

Finally, using data from the Cleveland Children's Sleep and Health study, Anderson and colleagues (2009) compared sleep patterns of adolescents from various ethnic/racial and SES backgrounds. In this investigation, sleep was assessed in 236 adolescents between the ages of 13 and 16 years with a week of actigraphy. Sleepiness was assessed using the Epworth sleepiness scale (ESS; Johns, 1991), a validated measure of sleepiness, and excessive sleepiness was defined as a score of 11 or greater. Adolescents with sleep apnea and suspected narcolepsy were excluded. SES was indexed by family income using a seven-point scale from $5,000 to $50,000, and caregiver education was separated into four groups (high school drop-out, high school graduate, some college, and college degree or higher). Finally, SES was also measured via the median income of the child's neighborhood by linking the child's address to data from the 2000 U.S. Bureau of the Census. Adolescents in the excessive daytime sleepiness group (n = 62) were significantly more likely to be African American (73.6%); these adolescents were also significantly more likely to have household incomes under $20,000 (40.7%), and to live in a neighborhood of lower median income. Caregiver education level was unrelated to excessive daytime sleepiness. Adolescents with short sleep duration (< 6.5 hours; n = 26) were significantly more likely to be African American (73%), and have incomes under $20,000 (45.8%). Median neighborhood income and caregiver education were unrelated to short sleep duration. These findings thus showed that adolescents from low income families or of African American ethnicity were at increased risk for sleepiness and short sleep duration.

Taken together, African American adolescents were consistently more likely to have less total sleep time than European American adolescents, and this finding appeared to be related to sleep scheduling as opposed to problems with sleep continuity. There were no differences in the overall prevalence of insomnia symptoms among adolescents of various ethnic/racial groups (Roberts et al., 2006), and ethnic differences in total sleep time existed even after controlling for other sleep disorders (Anderson et al., 2009). Indeed, Adam and colleagues (2007) showed that the most important factors related to less total sleep time among African American adolescents were later bedtimes and the amount of time needed to travel to school. Anderson and colleagues also showed excessive daytime sleepiness among African American adolescents even after controlling for other sleep disorders, which suggests that daytime complaints due to total sleep time may not be otherwise explained by another sleep problem. Findings among adolescents also showed that foreign-born Mexican Americans were less likely to have sleep disruption as compared to Mexican Americans born in the United States and European Americans (Anderson et al., 2009). These results conflicted with previous epidemiological studies conducted in Europe and described earlier (e.g., Rona et al., 1998), which showed that recent immigration was associated with increased sleep problems.

The relationship between SES and sleep among adolescents is not clear. Lower income was associated with both an increased likelihood of insomnia symptoms even controlling for ethnicity (Roberts et al., 2004), and decreased total sleep time examined actigraphically (Anderson et al., 2009). However, Adam and colleagues (2007) showed that SES was unrelated to sleep duration after controlling for numerous potential confounds. It is possible that the SES-sleep link is better explained by other demographic and psychosocial, and/or health-related variables.

Also, even though Anderson and colleagues showed that income was associated with sleep disruption, that study suggested that caregiver education was unrelated to any adolescent sleep variable; however, the sample included few individuals who dropped out of high school, a group particularly vulnerable to sleep problems (Gellis et al., 2005). Additionally, in Anderson and colleagues' study, education was categorized into four groups. Thus, the range on the parental education variable may have been restricted and/or the study may not have had enough power to detect differences among groups.

Obstructive Sleep Apnea in Children and Adolescents: Relations with SES and Ethnicity/Race

Obstructive sleep apnea (OSA) is a condition involving repetitive episodes of discontinued breathing during sleep, which often occurs with loud snoring and daytime sleepiness. Sleep disordered breathing affects approximately 1–2% of children (Bixler et al., 2009; Rosen et al., 2003), and this disorder is associated with multiple daytime impairments (Montgomery-Downs et al., 2003). In the following section of the chapter, associations between SES and ethnicity/race in relation to a diagnosis of OSA and risk factors for the disease will be summarized. Because of multiple studies with wide age ranges, all studies will be summarized in the section below and are not separated by participants' ages.

The risk for sleep apnea was first assessed in relation to SES in a study conducted in Great Britain in which 132 boys and girls ranging in age between 4.5 to 5.5 years participated (Ali, Pitson, & Stradling, 1993). The risk for sleep apnea was identified via a questionnaire that assessed symptoms such as snoring, restless sleeping, night breathing, and the frequency of coughs and colds. SES was assessed using parental occupation, which was categorized into manual and non-manual labor groups using definitions from the Office of Population and Censuses and Surveys. The results of this study showed that children from families classified in the manual compared to the non-manual occupation category were over three times more likely to be in the high-risk group for sleep apnea.

The increased risk of OSA among children from lower SES groups was replicated by Chervin and colleagues (2003). Participants were recruited from schools in the Detroit, Michigan, metropolitan area. These authors assessed the risk of OSA using the Pediatric Sleep Questionnaire (PSQ) in 145 students in the second and fifth grades. The OSA subscale of the PSQ showed an 81% sensitivity and 87% specificity in predicting OSA. There were 16 children identified as having high risk for OSA, and 129 identified as being low risk. SES was indexed by participation in the school lunch assistance program, and children were categorized into two groups: lunch assistance versus no lunch assistance. This study included 53% African American children, who were compared to other children, the majority of whom were Asian American. Low SES was associated significantly with increased risk for OSA even after controlling for race/ethnicity. After controlling for obesity, SES was no longer related to OSA. Thus, these results not only reproduced an association between low SES and OSA, but also provided some evidence that obesity may be a mechanism in this relation. In this study race/ethnicity was not associated with OSA after controlling for SES.

While findings from Chervin and colleagues' (2003) study did not support relations between race/ethnicity and OSA, other studies have reported significant associations. The frequency of OSA in children of various ethnic/racial groups was first assessed using a series of 198 patients younger than 17 years of age seen at the University of Illinois at Chicago Center for Sleep and Ventilatory Disorders (Stepanski, Zayyad, Nigro, Lopata, & Basner, 1999). The majority of the children were referred to the clinic to rule out sleep disordered breathing, and their average age was 5.9 years (SD = 3.7). The following percentages reflect ethnic representation in the sample: 68% African American, 19% Latino, and 12% European American. Although the frequency of OSA diagnosis did not differ among children of various ethnic/racial groups, African American children had more severe levels of disturbed breathing.

Racial/ethnic differences in OSA were replicated using the Cleveland family study, which is a community based epidemiologic investigation of sleep apnea (Redline et al., 1999). In this study, children and adolescents aged 2–18 years were assessed for sleep apnea objectively using a home-based monitoring system, results from which were shown to be highly correlated with polysomnography. The sample included 399 children, and 273 participants were members of an index family (i.e., a member had lab confirmed sleep apnea). The sample included 27% African

American children, and the majority of the sample was European American. An apnea-hypopnea index (AHI) greater than or equal to 10 was used to identify OSA, and an AHI <5 was chosen as the control group criterion. The AHI indexes the total number of complete cessations in breathing (apneas) and partial cessations in breathing (hypopneas). A greater AHI equals worse pathology. In adults, mild OSA is typically defined as an AHI between 5 and 15, although this cut-off is typically lowered for children. After controlling for recruitment sources and familial correlations within the data, African American children were approximately 3.5 more likely to have OSA than European American children even after controlling for obesity, asthma, and sinus problems.

Higher prevalence of OSA in African American children was further replicated in another investigation with home-based assessments for OSA in 8–11-year-old-children also from the Cleveland metropolitan area (Rosen et al., 2003). Data were used from the Cleveland Children's Sleep Health Study (CCSHS), which is an investigation of SDB and health in 907 children randomly sampled at birth between 1988 and 1993 from three major Cleveland area hospitals. In this study, 243 children were assessed on snoring behaviors, and were categorized as "snorers" if the caregiver answered "yes" to loud snoring at least 1–2 times per week during the last month. Children were categorized as sleepy if the caregiver reported that the child had fallen asleep 3–4 times per week or 5–7 times per week while watching television, reading, eating, talking at school, or playing. OSA was defined with a cutoff point of an AHI of at least 5, at least 1 event per hour, or either. Race/ethnicity was categorized as African American, European American, and other.

Results indicated that snoring was more common among African American children (24% to 13%) as compared to all other children in the sample (Rosen et al., 2003). African American children (4.8%) compared to European American children (1%) were more likely to have an AHI of at least 5. Similarly, African American children (8.1%) as compared to European American children (1.4%) were more likely to have an AHI of at least 1 event per hour. After adjusting for BMI and preterm birth status, African American children were more likely to have an AHI of at least 5 [odds ratio (OR) = 4.9], at least one event per hour (OR = 6.3) or either category (OR = 4.3) as compared with European American children. Although the clinical significance of an AHI of 5 is unclear,

African American children were at greater risk for this mild form of sleep apnea as compared to European American children. These findings were significant even after controlling for obesity, suggesting that the mechanism underlying the link between ethnicity and AHI scores may not necessarily be increased weight.

In subsequent analyses using the same cohort from the CCSHS, OSA prevalence was assessed according to neighborhood SES variables and race/ethnicity in children ages 8–11 years (Spilsbury et al., 2006). Neighborhood SES was assessed using the 2000 U.S. Bureau of the Census tract and participants were identified as living in a severely disadvantaged neighborhood if their census tract had at least three of the following four criteria: (1) ≥ 25.1% of persons in poverty; (2) ≥ 34.3% of households headed by a single female with related children 0–17 years of age; (3) ≥ 20.7% of persons 16–19 years of age neither enrolled in or graduated from high school; and 4) ≥ 37.1% civilian, noninstitutionalized males of working age (16–64 years) either unemployed or not in the labor force. In this study, 843 of the 907 children completed assessments for OSA and had addresses that could be linked to a census tract. OSA was defined and measured as reported in the previous study (i.e., AHI of ≥ 5 OSA and/or at least one event per hour).

Findings indicated that children living in a distressed neighborhood were five times more likely to be diagnosed with OSA as compared to those not living in a severely disadvantaged neighborhood (Spilsbury et al., 2006). The association between neighborhood SES and OSA remained significant even after controlling for prematurity, race/ethnicity, and obesity. Neighborhood SES did not reduce the strength of the association between OSA and obesity, but reduced the strength of the relationship between OSA and African American ethnicity by approximately 50%.

Similarly, ethnicity/race-related effects in OSA were reported in a population-based study of 3,795 preschool students enrolled in Jefferson County Kentucky public schools (Montgomery-Downs et al., 2003). The population selected for the study consisted of Early Jump Start programs serving low SES children five years of age and younger. Snoring was examined as a measure for OSA, defined as the presence of snoring ≥ three days per week, which was rated by the parent as medium

loud, loud, very loud, or extremely loud; this sample was described earlier in the chapter. Results showed that African American preschoolers
were at risk for OSA more frequently than European Americans (OR =
1.76), even after controlling for SES.

In summary, preliminary studies showed an increased risk for OSA
among children from lower SES backgrounds or African American ethnicity. Using self report measures of OSA, children who have parents in
the manual labor group (Ali et al., 1993) and those involved in the school
lunch program (Chervin et al., 2003) demonstrated increased risk for the
disorder. These studies were replicated by Spilsbury and colleagues (2006),
who found that objectively defined OSA was related to neighborhood
disadvantage even after controlling for obesity and ethnicity/race.
Findings regarding ethnicity/race and OSA showed a greater risk for
African American than European American children as demonstrated by
increased snoring (Montgomery-Downs et al., 2003; Rosen et al., 2003)
and objectively defined OSA (Redline et al., 1999; Rosen et al., 2003).
However, it should be noted that the cut-off for OSA used in Rosen and
colleagues' study (AHI of $\geq$ 5 or an AHI of $\geq$ 1 per hour) is mild, and it
is unclear if this severity level implies any clinical long-term consequences. The association between race/ethnicity and OSA remained
after controlling for SES (Montgomery-Downs et al., 2003) and obesity
(Rosen et al., 2003).

Final Conclusions, Implications, and Future Directions

We are only beginning to understand the normative sleep patterns and
the prevalence of sleep disruptions in relation to ethnicity, SES, and race.
There are only a handful of studies that have examined the role of these
variables in relation to children's sleep. Three preliminary conclusions,
however, have emerged from these early studies. First, there are greater
sleeping problems in children from lower socioeconomic backgrounds.
The majority of all available studies show greater sleep disruptions,
increased daytime sleepiness, lower total sleep time, and an increased risk
for OSA among children from lower than higher SES backgrounds.
Second, African American children sleep less than European American

children. Studies consistently show that African American children as compared to European American children are more likely to sleep less than 6.5 hours or between 8–9 hours per night; European American children are more likely to sleep greater than 10 hours per night as compared to their African American counterparts. Third, African American children have a greater risk for OSA than European Americans. Multiple studies show an increased risk for OSA among African Americans when considering objectively defined OSA and clinical manifestations of the disorder including snoring, difficulty maintaining sleep, and daytime sleepiness.

Despite these consistent findings, a number of important questions remain regarding the role that SES and ethnicity play in influencing sleep patterns and clinically-significant sleep problems in children and adolescents. First, what is the exact nature of the sleep dysfunction among groups? Are differences between groups clinically significant? What are the causes of these sleep disturbances? Are findings consistent across different SES measures? These issues will be addressed next.

What Is the Exact Nature of Sleep Dysfunction among Children of Various SES and Ethnic/Racial Backgrounds?

The majority of the extant literature involves epidemiologic studies using large sample sizes and only a few of these investigations focus on relations between race/ethnicity or SES and sleep. Thus, many of the studies rely on global and retrospective subjective assessments of sleep disturbance and parent estimates of total sleep time based on bed and rise times. These measures are not as reliable as sleep assessed over many nights using more real time analysis, and these assessments do not elucidate the nature of the sleep pattern or problem. Particularly among children ages two to eight years, it is unclear whether reduction in total sleep time among African Americans and those from lower SES backgrounds are related to sleep scheduling or a sleep disorder such as insomnia or OSA. Future studies should assess children using various sleep methodologies (e.g., actigraphically defined sleep and sleep diaries) over multiple days to assess aspects of sleep continuity along with total sleep time; other sleep problems such as enuresis and nightmares should also be investigated and/or controlled when assessing sleep patterns.

What are Potential Causes of Sleep Problems among Individuals of Various SES and Ethnic/Racial Groups?

The current literature offers some evidence that increases our understanding of both the nature of the sleep disturbance in relation to race/ethnicity and SES and possible causes underlying these associations; the status of this knowledge base is summarized next. Multiple studies suggest later bedtimes are significant for determining shorter sleep duration among African American children (McLaughlin Crabtree et al., 2005; Spilsbury et al., 2004; Adam et al. 2007). Decreases in total sleep time among African Americans continue to exist after controlling for possible health factors (Spilsbury et al., 2004), other sleep disorders (Anderson et al., 2009), multiple health, behavioral, and family functioning variables (Adam et al., 2007), and SES (Montgomery-Downs et al., 2003). Furthermore, among younger children ages two to eight years, there are no disruptions in a global measure of sleep problems (McLaughlin Crabtree et al., 2005), and there are no differences in overall diagnoses of insomnia between African and European American adolescents (Roberts et al. 2006). It should be noted that these findings should be replicated in future investigations with rigorous assessments of nighttime sleep that include measurements of sleep continuity along with measurements of time spent in bed. Future investigations should also assess whether attributes such as co-sleeping and perceived racial discrimination contribute to sleep patterns and disruptions along with sleep scheduling factors, as well as examine factors associated with sleep scheduling behaviors in children from various backgrounds.

Studies also show an increase in the prevalence of OSA among African American than European American children even after controlling for obesity or SES. Further studies could assess whether biological differences exist between members of various racial groups that may increase susceptibility to OSA or whether other environmental, behavioral, and/or cultural practices are mechanisms of effects. Few studies have assessed racial/ethnic differences in OSA among children, and these conclusions require further testing and replication.

Finally, individuals of lower SES position report multiple sleep problems including problematic sleep behaviors, less total sleep time, and a greater risk for OSA, and it is unclear what factors are determining these differences. Later bedtime is observed among individuals from lower SES groups, which may explain less total sleep time; however, there may also be a greater risk for OSA and general sleep disruption. A number of possible explanations can account for the various problems listed above. First, those in poverty are more likely to live in a chaotic and unstable environment, which is associated with greater child distress (Evans, Gonnella, Marcynyszyn, Gentile, & Salpekar, 2005), and such unstable environments may be associated with less consistent and regulated bedtimes. Impoverished and chaotic environments may also be associated with family disruption, which has been associated with sleep disturbances in children (El-Sheikh, Buckhalt, Keller, Cummings, and Acebo 2007). These explanations are consistent with Adam and colleagues' (2007) results, which showed that after controlling for various family functioning variables and child behavioral problems, SES was not significantly related to total sleep time. Future studies should also assess whether the SES-sleep association is related to children's physical and mental health.

Assessments of Clinical Significance

Whether there are meaningful differences in total sleep time between African American and European American children or between children of various SES backgrounds remains unclear. When sleep is measured using sleep diaries, there are minimal overall differences in sleep based on race/ethnicity (Spilsbury et al., 2004). More rigorous assessments of sleep and variables associated with SES and race/ethnicity are needed to address the significance of differences in sleep parameters among children of various backgrounds.

It is also uncertain whether group differences in total sleep time are related to functional impairment. Although African American individuals and those of lower SES backgrounds reported greater daytime sleepiness that corresponded with less total sleep time, only one of these studies also controlled for other sleep disorders. Thus, it is unclear whether less total sleep time or other sleep disorders are the cause of increased daytime sleepiness in African American children or those from lower SES backgrounds. It would be important for future studies to assess whether functioning complaints are indeed related to this decreased total sleep time, and to measure children's sleep throughout the entire day.

Are Sleep Differences Consistent across Different SES Measures?

Different measures are used as proxies for SES including parental education, parental income, unemployment, occupation, and median income per zip code. When assessing the univariate relationship between income or poverty status and sleep disruption, studies consistently show worse sleep among those in the lowest income group. The majority of studies also show that less parental education is related to poor sleep among children. Two studies show that those living in a poor neighborhood are more likely to have sleep problems (Anderson et al., 2009; McLaughlin Crabtree et al., 2005). This neighborhood-level analysis of SES may capture variables such as crime, pollution, and disturbing noise (Krieger, Williams, & Moss, 1997). Thus, it is possible that environment-related disturbances are a cause of sleep problems in individuals from lower SES backgrounds. Assessing neighborhood-based measures of SES, in addition to familial SES measures, when examining relations between SES and sleep is likely to enhance understanding of why SES is associated with sleep.

In summary, it is premature to conclude definitively that there are differences in sleep problems among individuals of different racial/ethnic or SES backgrounds. However, existing evidence suggests decreased total sleep time and an increased risk of OSA among African American children and increased overall vulnerability in children from the lowest SES backgrounds. Future studies would benefit from using more rigorous measures of sleep and SES, and attempting to explicate variables associated with either SES or race/ethnicity that may impact children's sleep.

REFERENCES

Adam, E. K., Snell, E. K., & Pendry, P. (2007). Sleep timing and quantity in ecological and family context: A nationally representative time-diary study. *Journal of Family Psychology*, 21, 4–19.

Adler, N. E., Boyce, T., Chesney, M. A., Cohen, S., Folkman, S., Kahn, R. L., & Syme, S. L. (1994). Socioeconomic status and health: The challenge of the gradient. *American Psychologist*, 49, 15–24.

Ali, N. J., Pitson, D. J., & Stradling, J. R. (1993). Snoring, sleep disturbance, and behavior in 4-5 year olds. *Archives of Disease in Childhood*, 68, 360–366.

American Academy of Sleep Medicine. (2005). *International classification of sleep disorders: Diagnostic and coding manual* 2nd *edition*. Westchester, IL: Author.

Anderson, B., Storfer-Isser, A., Taylor, H. G., Rosen, C. L., & Redline, S. (2009). Associations of executive function with sleepiness and sleep duration in adolescents. *Pediatrics*, 123, e701–e707.

Bernert, R. A., & Joiner, T. E. (2007). Sleep disturbances and suicide risk: A review of the literature. *Neuropsychiatric Disease and Treatment*, 3, 735–743.

Bixler, E. O., Vgontzas, A. N., Lin, H. M., Liao, D., Calhoun, S., Vela-Bueno, A., ... Graff, G. (2009). Sleep disordered breathing in children in a general population sample: Prevalence and risk factors. *Sleep*, 32, 731–736.

Carskadon, M. A., Dement, W. C., Mitler, M. M., Guilleminault, C. Zarcone, V. P. & Spiegel, R. (1976). Self-reports versus sleep laboratory findings in 122 drug-free subjects with complaints of chronic insomnia. *The American Journal of Psychiatry*, 133, 1382–1388.

Chervin, R. D., Clarke, D. F. Huffman, J. L., Szymanski, E., Ruzicka, D. L., Miller, V., ... Giordani, B. J. (2003). School performance, race, and other correlates of sleep-disordered breathing in children. *Sleep Medicine*, 4, 21–27.

Cornelius, L. J. (1991). Health habits of school-age children. *Journal of Health Care for the Poor and Underserved*, 2, 374–395.

Crosby, B., LeBourgeois, M. K., & Harsh, J. (2005). Racial differences in reported napping and nocturnal sleep in 2- to 8-year-old children. *Pediatrics*, 115, 225–232.

El-Sheikh, M., Buckhalt, J. A., Keller, P. S., Cummings, E. M., & Acebo, C. (2007). Child emotional insecurity and academic achievement: The role of sleep disruptions. *Journal of Family Psychology*, 21, 29–38.

Evans, G. W., Gonnella, C. A., Marcynyszyn, L. A., Gentile, L. E., & Salpekar, N. A. (2005). The role of chaos in poverty and children's socioemotional adjustment. *Psychological Science: A Journal of the American Psychological Society/APS*, 16, 560–565.

Gallicchio, L., & Kalesan, B. (2009). Sleep duration and mortality: A systematic review and meta-analysis. *Journal of Sleep Research*, 18, 148–158.

Gellis, L. A., Lichstein, K. L., Scarinci, I. C., Durrence, H. H., Taylor, D. J., Bush, A. J. & Riedel, B. W. (2005). Socioeconomic status and insomnia. *Journal of Abnormal Psychology*, 114, 111–118.

Gibson, E. S., Powles, A. C. P., Thabane, L., O'Brien, S., Molnar, D. S., Trajanovic, N., ... Chilcott-Tanser, L. (2006). "Sleepiness" is serious in adolescence: Two surveys of 3235 Canadian students. *BMC Public Health*, 6, 116. doi:10.1186/1471-2458-6-116

Gulliford, M. C., Price, C. E., Rona, R. J. & Chinn, S. (1990). Sleep habits and height at ages 5 to 11. *Archives of Disease in Childhood*, 65, 119–122.

Hall, M., Baum, A., Buysse, D. J., Prigerson, H. G., Kupfer, D. J., & Reynolds 3rd, C. F. (1998). Sleep as a mediator of the stress-immune relationship. *Psychosomatic Medicine*, 60, 48–51.

Healey, E. S., Kales, A., Monroe, L. J., Bixler, E. O., Chamberlin, K. & Soldatos, C. R. (1981). Onset of insomnia: Role of life-stress events. *Psychosomatic Medicine*, 43, 439–451.

Johns, M. W. (1991). A new method for measuring daytime sleepiness: The Epworth sleepiness scale. *Sleep*, 14, 540–545.

Krieger, N., Williams, D. R., & Moss, N. E. (1997). Measuring social class in US public health research: Concepts, methodologies, and guidelines. *Annual Review of Public Health*, 18, 341–378.

Lozoff, B., Askew, G. L., & Wolf, A. W. (1996). Cosleeping and early childhood sleep problems: Effects of ethnicity and socioeconomic status. *Journal of Developmental and Behavioral Pediatrics: JDBP*, 17, 9–15.

McLaughlin Crabtree, V., Beal Korhonen, J., Montgomery-Downs, H. E., Faye Jones, V., O'Brien, L. M., & Gozal, D. (2005). Cultural influences on the bedtime behaviors of young children. *Sleep Medicine*, 6, 319–324.

Milan, S., Snow, S., & Belay, S. (2007). The context of preschool children's sleep: Racial/ethnic differences in sleep locations, routines, and concerns. *Journal of Family Psychology: JFP: Journal of the Division of Family Psychology of the American Psychological Association (Division 43)*, 21, 20–28.

Montgomery-Downs, H. E., Jones, V. F., Molfese, V. J., Gozal, D. (2003). Snoring in preschoolers: Associations with sleepiness, ethnicity, and learning. *Clinical Pediatrics*, 42, 719–726.

Owens, J. A., Spirito, A., McGuinn, M., & Nobile, C. (2000). Sleep habits and sleep disturbance in elementary school-aged children. *Journal of Developmental and Behavioral Pediatrics*, 21, 27–36.

Pollock, J. I. (1994). Night-waking at five years of age: Predictors and prognosis. *Journal of Child Psychology and Psychiatry and Allied Disciplines*, 35, 699–708.

Redline, S., Tishler, P. V., Schluchter, M., Aylor, J., Clark, K. & Graham, G. (1999). Risk factors for sleep-disordered breathing in children: Associations with obesity, race, and respiratory problems. *American Journal of Respiratory and Critical Care Medicine*, 159, 1527–1532.

Roane, B. M., & Taylor, D. J. (2008). Adolescent insomnia as a risk factor for early adult depression and substance abuse. *Sleep*, 31, 1351–1356.

Roberts, R. E., Lee, E. S., Hernandez, M., & Solari, A. C. (2004). Symptoms of insomnia among adolescents in the lower Rio Grande valley of Texas. *Sleep*, 27, 751–760.

Roberts, R. E., Roberts, C. R., & Chan, W. (2006). Ethnic differences in symptoms of insomnia among adolescents. *Sleep*, 29, 359–365.

Rona, R. J., Li, L., Gulliford, M. C., & Chinn, S. (1998). Disturbed sleep: Effects of sociocultural factors and illness. *Archives of Disease in Childhood*, 78, 20–25.

Rosen, C. L., Larkin, E. K., Kirchner, H. L., Emancipator, J. L., Bivins, S. F., Surovec, S. A.,... Redline, S. (2003). Prevalence and risk factors for sleep-disordered breathing in 8- to 11-year-old children: Association with race and prematurity. *The Journal of Pediatrics*, 142, 383–389.

Roth, T. (2007). Insomnia: Definition, prevalence, etiology, and consequences. *Journal of Clinical Sleep Medicine: JCSM: Official Publication of the American Academy of Sleep Medicine*, 3(5 Suppl), S7–S10.

Sadeh, A., Raviv, A. & Gruber, R. (2000). Sleep patterns and sleep disruptions in school-age children. *Developmental Psychology*, 36, 291–301.

Savard, J., Laroche, L., Simard, S., Ivers, H. & Morin, C. M. (2003). Chronic insomnia and immune functioning. *Psychosomatic Medicine*, 65, 211–221.

Spilsbury, J. C., Storfer-Isser, A., Drotar, D., Rosen, C. L., Kirchner, L. H. Benham, H. & Redline, S. (2004). Sleep behavior in an urban US sample of school-aged children. *Archives of Pediatrics & Adolescent Medicine*, 158, 988–994.

Stein, M. B. Belik, S., Jacobi, F., & Sareen, J. (2008). Impairment associated with sleep problems in the community: Relationship to physical and mental health comorbidity. *Psychosomatic Medicine*, 70, 913–919.

Stein, M. A., Mendelsohn, J., Obermeyer, W. H., Amromin, J. & Benca, R. (2001). Sleep and behavior problems in school-aged children. *Pediatrics*, 107, E60. Retrieved from http://www.pediatrics.org/cgi/content/full/107/4/e60

Stepanski, E., Zayyad, A., Nigro, C., Lopata, M., & Basner, R. (1999). Sleep-disordered breathing in a predominantly african-american pediatric population. *Journal of Sleep Research*, 8, 65–70.

Stepanski, E. J., & Wyatt, J. K. (2003). Use of sleep hygiene in the treatment of insomnia. *Sleep Medicine Reviews*, 7, 215–225.

U.S. Bureau of the Census, U.S. Department of Commerce Economics, and Statistics Administration. (2003). *Educational attainment in the United States: 2003.* Retrieved from http://www.census.gov/prod/2004pubs/p20-550.pdf

U.S. Bureau of the Census. (2008). *Current Population Reports, P60-P235.* Retrieved from http://www.census.gov/compendia/statab/2010/tables/10s0679.pdf

Vahtera, J., Kivimaki, M., Hublin, C., Korkeila, K., Suominen, S., Paunio, T., & Koskenvuo, M. (2007). Liability to anxiety and severe life events as predictors of new-onset sleep disturbances. *Sleep*, 30, 1537–1546.

Williams, D. R., Neighbors, H. W., & Jackson, J. S. (2003). Racial/ethnic discrimination and health: Findings from community studies. *American Journal of Public Health*, 93, 200–208.

Winkleby, M. A., Jatulis, D. E., Frank, E., & Fortmann, S. P. (1992). Socioeconomic status and health: How education, income, and occupation contribute to risk factors for cardiovascular disease. *American Journal of Public Health*, 82, 816–820.

Wojnar, M., Ilgen, M. A., Wojnar, J., McCammon, R. J., Valenstein, M., & Brower, K. J. (2009). Sleep problems and suicidality in the national comorbidity survey replication. *Journal of Psychiatric Research*, 43, 526–531.

I I

Children's Sleep, Cognition, and Academic Performance in the Context of Socioeconomic Status and Ethnicity

Joseph A. Buckhalt and Lori E. Staton

Introduction

Parents have long consulted medical professionals for help with children's sleep, especially in infancy, and considerable attention has been paid to clinical sleep disorders that manifest later in childhood. More recently, relations between sleep parameters and numerous aspects of well-being in typically developing school-age children have been investigated.

The greater health risks affecting families in the United States with fewer economic and social resources have long been topics of considerable concern. Although the importance of sleep for fostering good health has been known anecdotally for centuries, scientific understanding of the mechanisms is in an emergent stage. Sleep research has become increasingly international, with much attention on aspects that generalize across countries and cultures. Even in the United States, variations in race, ethnicity, and socioeconomic status (SES) have rarely been a primary area of interest in sleep research. Thus, in most studies examining sleep, participants have been homogeneous, SES and race/ethnicity have been confounded, or analyses examining relations between sleep and SES or race/ethnicity have not been conducted or reported.

In addition to health risks, children from lower SES families are at greater risk for problems in school, including underachievement, behavioral maladjustment, and early dropout. These problems have been the focus of intense attention by researchers and educators, and the proposed explanations and interventions have been many. The purpose of this chapter is to make the case for a connection between sleep and school performance in children from socioeconomically disadvantaged as well as ethnic minority families that may enrich explanatory theory and in turn guide prevention and remedial interventions. Research relevant to this topic has been conducted with children who have no known clinical sleep disorders, with children who do have disorders such as sleep apnea, and with children who have diagnosed learning and behavior problems; all of which will be reviewed in this chapter. School performance is defined as academic achievement and behavioral adjustment necessary for that achievement. Academic achievement is also presumed to relate to cognitive functioning, defined generally as the ability to acquire and retain information.

The SES Achievement Gap

Socioeconomic status has important implications for families' quality of life, including substandard housing, family turmoil, and community violence (Evans & English, 2002). The effects of SES are also manifested in numerous domains, including nutrition (Wang & Zhang, 2006), health (Adler & Newman, 2002), attainment of material resources (Bradley & Corwyn, 2002), and longevity (Jokela, Elovainio, Singh-Manoux, & Kivimaki, 2009). Income, material resources, occupation, and education are all used in estimating SES level, and the highest level of education reached by family members (often termed "educational attainment"), is regarded by some scholars as the best single index of SES (Winkelby, Jatulius, Frank, & Fortman, 1992). Of all the indicators of SES, low educational attainment by parents may be a major factor relating to the difficulties children experience at school including (a) low academic achievement in the form of lower classroom grades, lower standardized test scores, and lower level of grade completion (Sirin, 2005); and (b) problem behaviors that are not congruent with expectations and rules of the teachers and the school environment often resulting in disciplinary actions, which in turn impair achievement. Lower SES children also are referred for special education services more frequently than their higher SES counterparts (Blair & Scott, 2002).

Considerable intellectual and financial resources have been devoted during the past half-century to searching for causes and solutions for disparities in academic achievement between children of differing SES levels (and racial/ethnic identities) in the United States (Harris & Herrington, 2006; Ladson-Billings, 2006). Every year brings new studies, continued analysis and interpretation, and renewed commitment to initiatives to narrow or close what has been called the achievement gap (U.S. Department of Education, 2008). But unfortunately, in the words of Michael Nettles of the Educational Testing Service, "Despite a long-running national focus on closing gaps in academic achievement among America's students, by race/ethnicity and by socio-economic status, they remain wide and persistent" (Educational Testing Service, ETS, 2009, p. 2).

Worries about children's low school achievement are not new, and in a number of historical periods those concerns have prompted action by legislative, judicial, and executive branches of federal and state governments. Over the period between 1852 and 1918, all U.S. states enacted compulsory school attendance laws. Rationales for these laws were based partly on concern about exploitative child labor. Another rationale was that the country needed a more educated workforce as it moved from a predominantly agrarian economy into one driven more by industry and manufacturing (Lleras-Muny, 2002). Even after compulsory education laws were passed, few Americans attended school long enough to attain a high school diploma. In 1940, when the U.S. census began collecting data about education, only 24.5% of adults over the age of 25 reported high school graduation. By 1970, this number had risen only to 52.3%. In the Deep South, where incomes were low relative to the United States, graduation rates were even lower. In Alabama, for example, 15.9% of census respondents had high school degrees in 1940 and 41.3% in 1970 (Stoop, 2009).

Concern about the achievement gap continues to the present, and the amount of commentary in the public media and academic journals is substantial (e.g., Fiscella & Kitzman, 2009; Schemo, 2006). The discourse has societal implications beyond rhetoric, as public policy and considerable expenditures of public funds are at stake. The estimated federal expenditures for the No Child Left Behind Act of 2001 (see U.S. Department of Education, 2005) is in the billions of dollars, and the question of whether the bill has been effective has fueled much heated public debate (Finn, 2008) and serious scholarly inquiry (Mathis, 2005). More importantly, the implications of low academic achievement for millions of American children from impoverished homes are profound.

Speculation and research about possible reasons for the achievement gap and its resistance to elimination or even narrowing have been important continuing aspects of the general debate. The Moynihan Report (1965) placed the cause on dysfunctional families and consequent inadequate parenting. But critics quickly assailed the report as "blaming the victim" (Ryan, 1971). Following on its heels was the Coleman Report (1966), which took an empirical approach to argue that unequal opportunities were the root cause. When Lyndon Johnson became president in 1963, he established an "unconditional war on poverty" that ultimately led to the creation of massive government programs in the areas of health and education during the mid-1960s (Goodwin, 1976). One such program was Project Head Start, begun in 1965 with the expectation that providing disadvantaged children a quality early educational experience would prove beneficial for their later academic progress. Many scholars argued that all children were equally capable of learning and any failure to learn was the fault of uninspired and uninformed teaching (see Gottfredson, 2005). For over 40 years, no consensus has been reached either about the cause for the gap or the solution.

Two books illustrate the fact that divisions are as wide and deeply entrenched as ever. Charles Murray, well known for *The Bell Curve* (Herrnstein & Murray, 1994), makes the case in *Real Education: Four Simple Truths for Bringing America's Schools Back to Reality* (2008) that schools have ignored the fact that abilities are normally distributed, and that those differences result in inevitable lower educational attainment for a sizeable percentage of children. At the other end of the spectrum, Richard Nisbett, in *Intelligence and How to Get It: Why Schools and Culture Count* (2009) advances the sanguine view that intelligence and achievement can be increased substantially for all children, including those from lower-class families. He argues that doing so requires that effective educational methods are implemented, and that the number of families in poverty is markedly reduced. Although the rhetoric has been impassioned for decades, few empirical studies have shed light on the dilemma, and few original ideas for explaining or changing the achievement gap have appeared in quite some time (Educational Testing Service, 2009).

Sleep, Cognitive Functioning, and Academic Performance

Attention, cognition, and memory are significantly impaired after total or partial sleep deprivation. Comprehensive reviews (Durmer & Dinges, 2005; Pilcher & Huffcut, 1996) have documented this robust effect in adults, and evidence continues to accumulate. Ratcliff and Van Dongen (2009) provide evidence that sleep deprivation in adults affects multiple aspects of cognitive processing, from reduced arousal and attention to diminished central processing. Recently, research incorporating imaging techniques has revealed some primary neurological mechanisms underlying relations between sleep and learning (Chee & Chuah, 2008). Sleep following attempts to learn seems to play a role in the consolidation and strengthening of memory, especially declarative memory (Gais et al., 2007; Walker & Stickgold, 2006; Wilhelm, Dieklemann, & Born, 2008). There is evidence that sleep deprivation following a learning task is related to impairment of communication between the hippocampus and the prefrontal cortex that ordinarily occurs during sleep, resulting in poorer memory (Van Der Werf et al., 2009). Moreover, some evidence suggests a particularly important role for slow wave sleep (SWS) in memory consolidation (Born, Rasch, & Gais, 2006; Diekelmann, Wilhelm, & Born, 2009; Rasch, Buchel, Gais, & Born, 2007). Insufficient amounts of SWS, even in the context of typical length of overall sleep, may be detrimental for memory.

The preponderance of sleep research, and nearly all of the experimental studies, have been conducted with human adults and nonhuman animals. For developing children, learning new information and skills is a primary daily occupation, especially in the early years when the basic building blocks of knowledge are forming. It has long been known that younger children sleep longer than older children, and all typically sleep more than adults. Sleep may play a different or a more important role in children than in adults in relation to short and long term cognitive functioning.

Only in recent years has sleep been related to children's cognitive functioning and their academic performance. Reviews of this literature (Buckhalt, Wolfson, & El-Sheikh, 2009; Curcio, Ferrara, & De Gennaro, 2006; Mitru, Millrood, & Mateika, 2002; Sadeh, 2007; Wolfson & Carskadon, 2003) indicate that a number of sleep parameters, including short sleep time, inconsistent sleep/wake schedules, late bedtimes and rise times, and poor sleep quality are all related to a variety of cognitive and academic outcomes. Such outcomes include lower teacher ratings and grades, as well as worse scores on individual and group achievement tests, narrow tests of neurocognitive functioning, and comprehensive intelligence tests. More than 30 such studies have been reported (e.g. Anderson, Storfer-Isser, Taylor, Rosen, & Redline, 2009; Buckhalt, El-Sheikh, & Keller, 2007; Meijer, 2008; Sadeh, Gruber, & Raviv, 2002), of which the majority have used cross-sectional designs and correlational statistics.

At least one longitudinal study examining links between children's sleep and their cognitive functioning and academic performance has been conducted using structural equation modeling. Results show that nonclinical sleep problems have directional effects on cognitive performance and academic achievement two years later (Buckhalt, El-Sheikh, Keller, & Kelly, 2009). Crucial for validation of direction of effects, a few experimental studies with children have shown diminished cognitive performance after sleep is restricted by as little as one hour per night (Fallone, Acebo, Seifer, & Carskadon, 2005; Randazzo, Muehlbach, Schweitzer, & Walsh, 1998; Sadeh, Gruber, & Raviv, 2003).

Thus far, the studies mentioned here are those done with samples of typically developing children. Importantly, studies have shown that children with clinical sleep disorders have cognitive impairments compared to healthy controls. Over 50 child clinical studies have been reported since 2000, and sleep-disordered children have been discovered to have a variety of cognitive and academic problems (Beebe, 2006; Blunden & Beebe, 2006; Blunden, Lushington, Lorenzen, Martin, & Kennedy, 2005; Halbower & Mahone, 2006; Owens, 2009). For example, there appears to be a dose-dependent relation between obstructive sleep apnea in children and numerous neurobehavioral outcomes; this association is postulated to be a function of episodic hypoxia and associated sleep fragmentation (Kheirandish & Gozal, 2006). Some evidence shows that when certain sleep disorders are treated, cognitive performance and behavior improve (Garetz, 2008). In a study of children with sleep disordered breathing, Chervin et al. (2006) reported that adenotonsil-lectomy resulted in one year post-surgery improvements in attention and cognition. Wei et al. (2009) found that behavioral improvements were maintained two years after surgery.

Children whose primary diagnosis is one that has been related to impaired learning and academic achievement experience more sleep problems than typically developing children. Children with ADHD have atypical sleep in many instances (Cohen-Zion & Ancoli-Israel, 2004; Cortese, Farone, Konofal, & Lecendreux, 2009), and it is probable that some portion of children diagnosed with ADHD have undiagnosed sleep disorders. Likewise, children with mental retardation, autism spectrum disorders, and other developmental disorders have high rates of sleep problems (Ming, Sun, Nachajon, Brimacombe, & Walters, 2009; Richdale & Schreck, 2009; Stores & Wiggs, 2001; Williams, Sears, & Allard, 2004).

Longitudinal research to determine whether sleep problems in early childhood have lasting effects on cognitive performance and school achievement is only beginning, but our own results have shown that deleterious effects of poor sleep may endure. We found that poorer sleep of eight-year-old children was related to lower scores on the Woodcock-Johnson Tests of Cognitive Ability (Woodcock, McGrew, & Mather, 2001) and the Stanford Achievement Test (2005) two years later (Buckhalt, El-Sheikh et al., 2009). Replications are needed, and casual connections are difficult to confirm, but it is likely that problems related to sleep may become cumulative since much school material must be well learned to attain advanced skills in succeeding years.

Sleep, Behavior Problems at School, and Achievement

Success at school is dependent on more than cognitive functioning. In fact, an equally important determinant of doing well in school is having the ability and motivation to behave well, including compliance with the expectations of the teachers within the constraints of the typical school environment. Behavior problems can have immediate

(Bub, McCartney, & Willett, 2007) and long-lasting (Breslau et al., 2009) effects on academic achievement. Children from lower SES families are more likely to engage in behaviors that parents and teachers consider disruptive (Dodge, Pettit, & Bates, 1994; Huaqing Qi & Kaiser, 2003). The precise mechanisms involved in the relationship have been the subject of much inquiry, with most of the speculation involving deficient parenting practices. Parents of lower SES are subject to a greater number of (as well as higher intensity) stressors, which are believed to impair their ability to care well for their children (Barry, Dunlap, Cotton, Lochman, & Wells, 2005), and family disorganization and low expectations have been noted (Taylor & Lopez, 2005). In the school setting, lower SES children receive more disciplinary sanctions, and are referred for special education (behavior disorders) more frequently than their higher SES counterparts (Blair & Scott, 2002; Nelson, Gonzalez, Epstein, & Benner, 2003).

The ability to behave according to expectations and avoid conflict with other children and with teachers has been linked to emotion regulation. Children who exhibit poor regulation of emotions have been observed to have lower achievement (Eisenberg, Sadovsky, & Spinard, 2005; Graziano, Reavis, Keane, & Calkins, 2007). While the issues and interpretations are complex (Raver, 2004), poor regulation of emotions is shown by many children from lower SES families. The chaotic living conditions associated with lower SES households, including more residential noise, family instability, and overcrowding, have been linked to poorer self-regulatory functioning in children (Evans, Gonnella, Marcynyszyn, Gentile, & Salpekar, 2005). The relations between sleep, mood, and manifested behavior have been well established with adults (Bonnet, 1985), but research in this area conducted with children has been limited. Furthermore, designs in research with children have been correlational, with no longitudinal or experimental studies to confirm the suspected direction of effects. However, the available evidence indicates that when children do not get sufficient, good quality sleep, they are tired, irritable, emotionally labile, unable to concentrate, and unmotivated to carry out daily tasks (Dahl & Harvey, 2007; Meijer, Habekothe, & van den Wittenboer, 2000). Recent evidence with kindergarteners links poor sleep, altered hypothalamic-pituitary-adrenocortical (HPA) axis processes, and behavioral and emotional problems, suggestive of a possible underlying biobehavioral mechanism (Hatzinger et al., 2009).

Disrupted sleep has been associated with numerous problematic conditions in children, including internalizing problems such as depression and anxiety, and externalizing problems such as conduct disorders (e.g., Aronen, Paavonen, Fjallberg, Soininen, & Torronen, 2000; Dahl & Lewin, 2002; Gregory & Eley, 2005; Wolfson & Carskadon, 1998). Reid, Hong, and Wade (2009) provide evidence that the relationship between sleep and emotional/behavioral problems is independent of other commonly identified risk factors for psychopathology. Additional research has shown that children exposed to higher levels of marital conflict and children who show poorer emotional security in the family relationships have poorer sleep (El-Sheikh, Buckhalt, Keller, Cummings, & Acebo, 2007; El-Sheikh, Buckhalt, Mize, & Acebo, 2006; Kelly, Hinnant, & El-Sheikh, 2009); see El-Sheikh and Kelly, chapter 1 in this volume. Further, vagal regulation and emotional intensity, both associated with emotion regulation, have been related to children's sleep (El-Sheikh & Buckhalt, 2005). Although it is not surprising that children who periodically do not sleep well due to a variety of putative problems may show compromised functioning from time to time, children with chronic sleep problems due to exposure to chronic stressors may suffer poor behavioral adjustment and concomitant poor academic achievement over longer periods of time.

Sleep and SES

As documented by Gellis, chapter 10 in this volume, significant differences in sleep dimensions have been discovered when group comparisons by SES and race/ethnicity have been made. In a review of 30 studies, Durrence and Lichstein (2006) reported that African American adults had rates of sleep-disordered breathing twice that of European Americans. Stamatakis, Kaplan, and Roberts (2007) reported that African American and Hispanic adults, and those with less income and education, were more likely than any other American groups to sleep less than seven hours per night. Using data from the 2004–2007 National Health Interview Survey, Krueger and Friedman (2009) show that being non-Hispanic black, attaining a low education level, working long hours, and having low financial resources were all risks for short sleep duration. In another survey, individuals with lower incomes reported more trouble sleeping, and African American adults reported more frequent naps, perhaps an indirect indication of insufficient nighttime sleep (Pew Research Center, 2009). As for children, African American children and children from low-income families have been found to have higher rates of sleep disordered breathing, shorter sleep times, poorer sleep quality, and more frequent weekend napping (Crosby, LeBourgeois, & Harsh, 2005; Redline et al., 1999; Rosen et al., 2003; Stepanski, Zayyad, Nigro, Lopata, & Basner, 1999) in comparison to their European American and middle- to high-income counterparts. Furthermore, one study found that even after controlling for maternal education, family structure, and household composition, African American children had later bedtimes and were less likely to have regular bedtimes or bedtime routines than European American children (Hale, Berger, LeBourgeois, & Brooks-Gunn, 2009).

Brown and Low (2008) discovered that chaotic living conditions of economically disadvantaged preschool children predicted hopelessness and helplessness of children's responses to an independently administered academic challenge. In addition, chaotic living conditions significantly affected mothers' reports of their preschoolers' subjective sleep problems. Overall, the findings indicate that sleep mediates partially the relation between SES and academic indices, suggesting that sleep problems may be a mechanism through which SES impacts academic challenges. Importantly, the early exposure to economic stressors may undermine children's ability to deal with challenges, which may in turn impact their academic success later in life (Evans et al., 2005).

In our lab, we have addressed relations between sleep, cognitive functioning, and academic achievement in the context of varying SES and race/ethnicity (African American and European American families). To unconfound these variables, we have recruited participants from the two racial/ethnic groups across a wide range of SES. Specifically, the sample consisted of 166 school-aged children (31% African American), with comparable numbers of European American and African American children classified across the various SES categories (Hollingshead, 1975). The sample was comprised of 27% low SES, 41% middle SES, and 32% high SES families. Sleep was assessed with seven consecutive nights of actigraphy and sleep diaries, as well as child subjective reports. Cognitive performance was measured with the Woodcock-Johnson Tests of Cognitive Ability III (Woodcock et al., 2001) and via a reaction time task. In addition, academic achievement was examined using standardized scores on the Stanford Achievement Test- 10 (2005). In a report from the first wave of a longitudinal study (Buckhalt et al., 2007), a primary finding was that SES moderated the relationship between sleep and cognitive performance. When sleep schedules were less variable and sleep quality was high, children from lower and higher SES families performed similarly on cognitive tasks. But when sleep problems were evident, children from lower SES families performed more poorly on cognitive tests. In a two-year follow-up (Buckhalt, El-Sheikh et al., 2009), moderation effects were again found for SES, and were particularly strong for parent education. Findings illustrated that longitudinal links between sleep problems and cognitive functioning were especially evident for children with less educated parents. Our conclusion is that parental education is a proxy variable that reflects a wide range of conditions that act to amplify or dampen the effects of poor sleep on cognitive functioning and academic performance.

We have presented evidence that SES functions as a moderator of the relationship between sleep and important outcomes for children. It is likely that the impact of sleep problems are not uniform for all children and the relationships may be affected by individual differences, as well as by differences in membership in SES and racial/ethnic groups. One helpful framework is the health disparities view (Carter-Pokras & Baquet, 2002), which proposes that certain populations, including lower SES and racial/ethnic minorities, may have a higher burden of adverse conditions that negatively affect health. In the presence of multiple stressors on the system, sleep problems may have a more deleterious effect than when stressors are relatively low and psychosocial supports are relatively strong.

Sleep and the Achievement Gap: Implications for Research and Public Policy

We have presented the basis for proposing a new hypothesis: Differences in various sleep parameters (amount, quality, schedule) among children from different levels of SES may explain some portion of the achievement gap. Sleep appears to function as a mediator between learning and retention in all children, and that relationship is moderated by SES, such that children from lower SES families may fare worse than their higher SES counterparts when sleep is either insufficient or of poorer quality. This hypothesis does not imply that sleep is *the* answer to the achievement gap problem. In fact, it is likely only part of the explanation. But even if it can be shown to account for any significant part of relations between SES and cognitive functioning/academic performance, it has implications for enriching theory and formulating interventions.

Much remains to be investigated about the relations between children's sleep and cognitive and academic performance. More studies that attempt to disentangle SES and racial/ethnic differences would assist in delineating the role of these characteristics in the link between sleep and cognitive functioning. Moreover, the examination of multiple aspects of sleep (subjective and objective), as well as a wide range of cognitive and academic outcomes (e.g., narrow neurocognitive tasks, broad cognitive ability tests, standardized achievement tests, and grades) would allow for more specification of what aspects of sleep are related to particular cognitive and academic measures. Furthermore, experimental studies would be beneficial, even though they are difficult to conduct with children. Large-scale longitudinal studies across ages from infancy to adulthood are needed to examine how sleep is related to different developmental trajectories, to test hypotheses about accumulation of problems with chronically insufficient sleep, and to examine long-term effects of periodic and chronic sleep problems. More knowledge is needed about generalized, normative patterns of child sleep, and also about clinical and nonclinical individual differences. Sleep intervention studies must be conducted first on a small scale with individuals and small groups, and then with increasingly large groups. At this time, there is scant knowledge about the degree to which sleep improvement is related to improvements in learning (Buckhalt, Wolfson, & El-Sheikh, 2009), and virtually no knowledge about whether sleep improvement may provide a differential increase in academic performance among lower functioning children.

While lower SES has been related to sleep problems, little is available regarding which particular aspects of low SES are the operative ones. Material, biomedical, and psychosocial factors have been shown to relate to sleep, and many of these covary with SES. In the material domain, homes of lower SES families are relatively small for family size, with fewer bedrooms and more crowding. They have less than ideal heating, cooling, and ventilation systems, high levels of allergens, and lower quality/older bedding. Biomedical problems such as asthma and obesity, linked to sleep problems in children (Fagnano et al., 2009; Owens, Mehlenbeck, Lee, & King, 2008), are more prevalent in individuals with lower SES (Chen et al., 2006). In the psychosocial domain, they are apt to have more chaotic and inconsistent schedules (Brown & Low, 2008) and have more family stressors and insufficient parental monitoring (Pettit, Laird, Dodge, Bates, & Criss, 2001). Furthermore, these domains interact. To give but one example of interaction, adult smoking, which is more prevalent among individuals from lower SES backgrounds (Barbeau, Krieger, & Soobader, 2004), exposes children to second-hand smoke. A smaller, poorly ventilated house or apartment increases the likelihood and intensity of exposure. Asthma, as noted above, is associated with sleep-disordered breathing and is also more prevalent among lower SES ethnic minority individuals.

Once the critical factors are identified, and ways the factors interact to create problems are better understood, intervention studies are needed to determine if improvements in these domains can be accomplished, and if those changes ultimately result in improved learning and educational attainment. Improving the conditions that impair sleep will not be easy. Material resource changes will require financial solutions as well as education about how to make wise choices in purchasing. Biomedical interventions will be costly, and medical/pharmacological education is challenging. Finally, changing psychosocial factors that may lead to better sleep habits may be as difficult as changing nutrition and exercise habits.

REFERENCES

Adler, N. E., & Newman, K. (2002). Socioeconomic disparities in health: Pathways and policies. *Health Affairs*, *21*, 60–76.

Anderson, B., Storfer-Isser, Taylor, G., Rosen, C. L., & Redline, S. (2009). Associations of executive functioning with sleepiness and sleep duration in adolescents. *Pediatrics*, *123*, e701–e707.

Aronen, E. T., Paavonen, E. J., Fjallberg, M., Soininen, M., & Torronen, J. (2000). Sleep and psychiatric symptoms in school-age children. *Journal of the American Academy of Child and Adolescent Psychiatry, 39*, 502–508.

Barbeau, E. M., Krieger, N., & Soobader, M. (2004). Working class matters: Socioeconomic disadvantage, race/ethnicity, gender, and smoking in NHIS 2000. *American Journal of Public Health, 94*, 269–278.

Barry, T. D., Dunlap, S. A., Cotton, J., Lochman, J. E., & Wells, K. S. (2005). The influence of maternal stress and distress on disruptive behavior problems in boys. *Journal of the American Academy of Child & Adolescent Psychiatry, 44*, 265–273.

Beebe, D. W. (2006). Neurobehavioral morbidity associated with disordered breathing during sleep in children: A comprehensive review. *Sleep, 29*, 1115–1134.

Blair, C., & Scott, K. G. (2002). Proportion of LD placements associated with low socioeconomic status: Evidence for a gradient? *Journal of Special Education, 36*, 14–22.

Blunden, S. L., & Beebe, D. W. (2006). The contribution of intermittent hypoxia, sleep debt and sleep disruption to daytime performance deficits in children: Consideration of respiratory and nonrespiratory problems. *Sleep Medicine Reviews, 10*, 109–118.

Blunden, S. L., Lushington, K., Lorenzen, B., Martin, J., & Kennedy, D. (2005). Neuropsychological and psychosocial function in children with a history of snoring or behavioral sleep problems. *Journal of Pediatrics, 144*, 780–786.

Bonnet, M. (1985). Effect of sleep disruption on sleep, performance, and mood. *Sleep, 8*, 11–19.

Born, J., Rasch, B., & Gais, S. (2006). Sleep to remember. *The Neuroscientist, 12*, 410–424.

Bradley, R. H., & Corwyn, R. F. (2002). Socioeconomic status and child development. *Annual Review of Psychology, 53*, 371–399.

Breslau, J., Miller, E., Breslau, N., Bohnert, K., Lucia, V., & Schweitzer, J. (2009). The impact of early behavior disturbances on academic achievement in high school. *Pediatrics, 123*, 1472–1476.

Brown, E. D. & Low, C. M. (2008). Chaotic living conditions and sleep problems associated with children's responses to academic challenge. *Journal of Family Psychology, 22*, 920–923.

Bub, K. L., McCartney, K., & Willett, J. B. (2007). Behavior problem trajectories and first-grade cognitive ability and achievement skills: A latent growth curve analysis. *Journal of Educational Psychology, 99*, 653–670.

Buckhalt, J. A., El-Sheikh, M., & Keller, P. S. (2007). Children's sleep and cognitive functioning: Race and socioeconomic status as moderators of effects. *Child Development, 78*, 213–231.

Buckhalt, J. A., El-Sheikh, M., Keller, P., & Kelly, R. J. (2009). Concurrent and longitudinal relationships between children's sleep and cognitive functioning: The moderating role of parent education. *Child Development, 80*, 875–892.

Buckhalt, J. A., Wolfson, A., & El-Sheikh, M. (2009). Children's sleep and school psychology practice. *School Psychology Quarterly, 24*, 60–69.

Carter-Pokras, O., & Baquet, C. (2002). What is "health disparity"? *Public Health Reports, 117*, 426–434.

Chee, M. W. L., & Chuah, L. Y. M. (2008). Functional neuroimaging insights into how sleep and sleep deprivation affect memory and cognition. *Current Opinion in Neurology, 21*, 417–423.

Chen, E., Hanson, M., Paterson, L. Q., Griffin, M. J., Walker, H. A., & Miller, G. E. (2006). Socioeconomic status and inflammatory processes in childhood asthma: The role of psychological stress. *Journal of Allergy and Clinical Immunology, 117*, 1014–1020.

Chervin, R. D., Ruzicka, D. L., Giordan, B. J., Weatherly, R. A., Dillon, J. E., Hodges, E. K., … Guire, K. E. (2006). Sleep-disordered breathing, behavior, and cognition in children before and after adenotonsillectomy. *Pediatrics, 117*, e769–e778.

Cohen-Zion, M., & Ancoli-Israel, S. (2004). Sleep in children with attention-deficit hyperactivity disorder (ADHD): A review of naturalistic and stimulant intervention studies. *Sleep Medicine Reviews, 8*, 379–402.

Coleman, J. S. (1966). *Equality of educational opportunity.* Washington, D.C.: U.S. Department of Health, Education, and Welfare.

Cortese, S., Farone, S. V., Konofal, E., & Lecendreux, M. (2009). Sleep in children with attention-deficit/hyperactivity disorder: Meta-analysis of subjective and objective studies. *Journal of the American Academy of Child & Adolescent Psychiatry, 48*, 894–908.

Crosby, B., LeBourgeois, M., & Harsh, J. (2005). Racial differences in reported napping and nocturnal sleep in 2- to 8-year old children. *Pediatrics, 115*, 225–232.

Curcio, G., Ferrara, M., & De Gennaro, L. (2006). Sleep loss, learning capacity, and academic performance. *Sleep Medicine Reviews, 10*, 323–337.

Dahl, R. E., & Harvey, A. G. (2007). Sleep in children and adolescents with behavioral and emotional disorders. *Sleep Medicine Reviews, 2*, 501–511.

Dahl, R. E., & Lewin, D. S. (2002). Pathways to adolescent health: Sleep regulation and behavior. *Journal of Adolescent Health, 31*, 175–184.

Diekelmann, A., Wilhelm, I., & Born, J. (2009). The whats and when of sleep-dependent memory consolidation. *Sleep Medicine Reviews, 13*, 309–321.

Dodge, K. A., Pettit, G. S., & Bates, J. E. (1994). Socialization mediators of the relation between socioeconomic status and child conduct problems. *Child Development, 65*, 649–655.

Durmer, J. S. & Dinges, D. F. (2005). Neurocognitive consequences of sleep deprivation. *Seminars in Neurology, 25*, 117–129.

Durrence, H. H., & Lichstein, K. L. (2006). The sleep of African-Americans: A comparative review. *Behavioral Sleep Medicine, 4,* 29–44.

Educational Testing Service (2009). *Parsing the Achievement Gap II.* Policy Information Report. Princeton, NJ: ETS. Retrieved from http://www.ets. org/Media/Research/pdf/PICPARSINGII.pdf

Eisenberg, N., Sadovsky, A., & Spinard. T. L. (2005). Associations of emotion-related regulation with language skills, emotion knowledge, and academic outcomes. *New Directions in Child and Adolescent Development, 109,* 109–118.

El-Sheikh, M., & Buckhalt, J. A. (2005). Vagal regulation and emotional intensity predict children's sleep problems. *Developmental Psychobiology, 46,* 307–317.

El-Sheikh, M., Buckhalt, J. A., Keller, P. S., Cummings, E. M., & Acebo, C. (2007). Child emotional security and academic achievement: The role of sleep disruptions. *Journal of Family Psychology, 21,* 29–38.

El-Sheikh, M., Buckhalt, J. A., Mize, J., & Acebo, C. (2006). Marital conflict and disruption of children's sleep. *Child Development, 77,* 31–43.

Evans, G. W. & English, K. (2002). The environment of poverty: Multiple stressor exposure psychophysiological stress, and socioemotional adjustment. *Child Development, 73,* 1238–1248.

Evans, G. W., Gonnella, C., Marcynyszyn, L. A., Gentile, L., & Salpekar, N. (2005). The role of chaos in poverty and children's socioemotional adjustment. *Psychological Science, 16,* 560–565.

Fagnano, M., van Wijngaarden, E., Connolly, H. V., Carno, M. A., Forbes-Jones, E., & Halterman, J. S. (2009). Sleep-disordered breathing and behaviors of inner-city children with asthma. *Pediatrics, 124,* 218–225.

Fallone, G., Acebo, C., Seifer, R. & Carskadon, M. A. (2005). Experimental restriction of sleep opportunity in children: Effects on teacher ratings. *Sleep, 28,* 1561–1567.

Finn, C. (2008). *Five myths about No Child Left Behind.* Retrieved from http://www.washingtonpost.com/wpdyn/content/article/2008/03/28/ AR2008032802976.html

Fiscella, K. & Kitzman, H. (2009). Disparities in academic achievement and health: The intersection of child education and health policy. *Pediatrics, 123,* 1073–1080.

Gais, S., Albouy, G., Boly, M., Dang-Vu, T. T., Darsaud, A., Desseilles, M., ... Peigneux, P. (2007). Sleep transforms the cerebral trace of declarative memories. *Proceedings of the National Academy of Sciences, 104,* 18778–18783.

Garetz, S. L. (2008). Behavior, cognition, and quality of life after adenotonsillectomy for pediatric sleep-disordered breathing: Summary of the literature. *Otolaryngology-Head and Neck Surgery, 138,* S19–S26.

Goodwin, D. K. (1976). *Lyndon Johnson and the American dream.* New York: Harper & Row.

Gottfredson, L. S. (2005). Suppressing intelligence research: Hurting those we intend to help. In R. H. Wright & N. A. Cummings (Eds.), *Destructive trends in mental health: The well intentioned road to hell.* New York: Routledge.

Graziano, P. A., Reavis, R. D., Keane, S. P., & Calkins, S. D. (2007). The role of emotion regulation in children's early academic success. *Journal of School Psychology*, *45*, 3–19.

Gregory, A. M., & Eley, T. C. (2005). Sleep problems, anxiety and cognitive style in school-aged children. *Infant and Child Development*, *14*, 435–444.

Halbower, A. C., & Mahone, E. M. (2006). Neuropsychological morbidity linked to childhood sleep disordered breathing. *Sleep Medicine Reviews*, *10*, 97–107.

Hale, L., Berger, L. M., LeBourgeois, M. K., & Brooks-Gunn, J. (2009). Social and demographic predictors of preschoolers' bedtime routines. *Journal of Developmental & Behavioral Pediatrics*. Advance online publication. doi:10.1097/DBP.ob013e3181ba0e64

Harris, D. N., & Herrington, C. D. (2006). Accountability, standards, and the growing achievement gap: Lessons from the past half-century. *American Journal of Education*, *112*, 209–238.

Hatzinger, M., Brand, S., Perren, S., Stadelmann, S., von Wyl, A., von Klitzing, K., & Holsboer-Trachsler, E. (2009). Sleep actigraphy pattern and behavioral/emotional difficulties in Kindergarten children: Association with hypotha-lamic-pituitary-Adrenocortical (HPA) activity. *Journal of Psychiatric Research*. Advance online publication doi:10.1016/j.jpsychires.2009.08.012

Herrnstein, R. J., & Murray, C. (1994). *The bell curve: Intelligence and class structure in American life*. New York: Simon & Schuster.

Hollingshead, A. B. (1975). *Four factor index of social status*. Unpublished manuscript.

Huaqing Qi, C., & Kaiser, A. P. (2003). Behavior problems of preschool children from low-income families: Review of the literature. *Topics in Early Childhood Special Education*, *23*, 188–216.

Jokela, M., Elovainio, M., Singh-Manoux, A., & Kivimaki, M. (2009). IQ, socio-economic status and early death: The US National Longitudinal Survey of Youth. *Psychosomatic Medicine*, *71*, 322–328.

Kelly, R. J., Hinnant, B., & El-Sheikh, M. (2009, April). Parenting, children's sleep, and academic functioning: A mediated relationship. Poster session presented at the Biennial Meeting of the Society for Research in Child Development, Denver, CO.

Kheirandish, L., & Gozal, D. (2006). Neurocognitive dysfunction in children with sleep disorders. *Developmental Science*, *9*, 388–399.

Krueger, P. M., & Friedman, E. M. (2009). Sleep duration in the United States: A population-based study. *American Journal of Epidemiology*, *169*(9). Advance online publication. doi:10.1093/aje/kwp023

Ladson-Billings, G. (2006). From the achievement gap to the education debt: Understanding achievement in U.S. schools. *Educational Researcher*, *35*, 3–12.

Lleras-Muny, A. (2002). Were compulsory attendance and child labor laws effective? An analysis from 1915 to 1939. *The Journal of Law and Economics*, *45*, 401–435.

Mathis, W. J. (2005). The cost of implementing the federal No Child Left Behind act: Different assumptions, different answers. *Peabody Journal of Education, 80,* 90–119.

Meijer, A. M. (2008). Chronic sleep reduction, functioning at school and school achievement in preadolescents. *Journal of Sleep Research, 17,* 395–405.

Meijer, A. M., Habekothe, R. T., & van den Wittenboer, G. L. H. (2000). Time in bed, quality of sleep and school functioning of children. *Journal of Sleep Research, 9,* 145–153.

Ming, X., Sun, Y-M., Nachajon, R. V., Brimacombe, M., & Walters, A.S. (2009). Prevalence of parasomnia in autistic children with sleep disorders. *Clinical Medicine: Pediatrics, 3,* 1–10.

Mitru, G., Millrood, J. L., & Mateika, H. (2002). The impact of sleep on behavior and learning of adolescents. *Teacher's College Record, 104,* 704–726.

Moynihan, D. P. (1965). *The Negro family: A case for national action.* Retrieved from U.S. Department of Labor website: http://www.dol.gov/oasam/programs/history/webid-meynihan.htm

Murray, C. (2008). Real education: Four simple truths for bringing America's schools back to reality. New York: Crown Forum.

Nelson, J. R., Gonzalez, J. E., Epstein, M. H., & Benner, G. J. (2003). Administrative discipline contacts: A review of the literature. *Behavioral Disorders, 28,* 249–281.

Nisbett, R. (2009). Intelligence and how to get it. Why schools and culture count. New York: Norton.

Owens, J.A. (2009). Neurocognitive and behavioral impact of sleep disordered breathing in children. *Pediatric Pulmonology, 44,* 417–422.

Owens, J. A., Mehlenbeck, R. Lee, J., & King, M. M. (2008). Effect of weight, sleep duration, and comorbid sleep disorders on behavioral outcomes of children with sleep-disordered breathing. *Archives of Pediatric and Adolescent Medicine, 162,* 313–321.

Pettit, G. S., Laird, R. D., Dodge, K. A., Bates, J. E., & Criss, M. M. (2001). Antecedents and behavior-problem outcomes of parental monitoring and psychological control in early adolescence. *Child Development, 72,* 583–598.

Pew Research Center (2009). *Nap time.* Pew Research Center, Social and Demographic Trends. Retrieved from http://pewsocialtrends.org/pubs/737/americans-napping-habits#en2

Pilcher, J. J., & Huffcut, A. I. (1996). Effects of sleep deprivation on performance: A meta-analysis. *Sleep, 19,* 318–326.

Randazzo, A. C., Muehlbach, M. J., Schweitzer, P. K., & Walsh, J. K. (1998). Cognitive function following acute sleep restriction in children ages 10–14. *Sleep, 21,* 861–868.

Rasch, B., Buchel, C., Gais, S., & Born, J. (2007). Odor cues during slow-wave sleep prompt declarative memory consolidation. *Science, 315,* 1426–1429.

Ratcliff, R., & Van Dongen, H. P. A. (2009). Sleep deprivation affects multiple distinct cognitive processes. *Psychonomic Bulletin and Review, 16*, 742–751.

Raver, C. C. (2004). Placing emotional regulation in sociocultural and socioeconomic contexts. *Child Development, 76*, 345–353.

Redline, S. S., Tishler, P. V., Schluchter, M., Aylor, J., Clark, K., & Graham, G. (1999). Risk factors for sleep-disordered breathing in children: Associations with obesity, race, and respiratory problems. *American Journal of Respiratory Critical Care, 159*, 1527–1532.

Reid, G. J., Hong, R. Y., & Wade, T. J. (2009). The relation between common sleep problems and emotional and behavioral problems among 2- and 3-year-olds in the context of known risk factors for psychopathology. *Journal of Sleep Research, 18*, 49–59.

Richdale, A. L., & Schreck, K. A. (2009). Sleep problems in autism spectrum disorders: Prevalence, nature, and possible biopsychosocial aetiologies. *Sleep Medicine Reviews.* Advance online publication. doi: 10.1016/j. smrv.2009.02.003

Rosen, C. L., Larkin, E. K., Kirchner, H. L., Emancipatro, J. L., Bivins, S. F., Surovec, S. A., … Redline, S. (2003). Prevalence and risk factors for sleep-disordered breathing in 8- to 11-year-old children: Association with race and prematurity. *The Journal of Pediatrics, 142*, 383–390.

Ryan, W. (1971). *Blaming the victim.* New York: Pantheon.

Sadeh, A. (2007). Consequences of sleep loss or sleep disruption in children. *Sleep Medicine Reviews, 2*, 513–520.

Sadeh, A., Gruber, R., & Raviv, A. (2002). Sleep, neurobehavioral functioning, and behavior problems in school-age children. *Child Development, 73*, 405–417.

Sadeh, A., Gruber, R., & Raviv, A. (2003). The effects of sleep restriction and extension on school-age children: What a difference an hour makes. *Child Development, 74*, 444–455.

Schemo, D. J. (2006, August 9). It takes more than schools to close the achievement gap. *The New York Times.* Retrieved from http://www.nytimes.com

Sirin, S. R. (2005). Socioeconomic Status and academic achievement: A meta-analytic review of research. *Review of Educational Research, 75*, 417–453

Stamatakis, K. A., Kaplan, G. A., & Roberts, R. E. (2007). Short sleep duration across income, education, and race/ethnic group: Population prevalence and growing disparities during 34 years of follow-up. *Annals of Epidemiology, 17*, 948–955.

Stanford Achievement Test (2005). *Stanford Achievement Test series (10th ed.).* San Antonio, TX: Harcourt.

Stepanski, E., Zayyad, A., Nigro, C., Lopata, M., & Basner, R. (1999). Sleep-disordered breathing in a predominantly African-American pediatric population. *Journal of Sleep Research, 8*, 65–70.

Stoop, N. (2009). A half century of learning: Historical census statistics on educational attainment in the United States, 1940 to 200. Retrieved from http://www.census.gov/population/www/socdemo/education/intro-phct41.html

Stores, G., & Wiggs, L. (Eds.). (2001). *Sleep disturbance in children and adolescents with disorders of development*: Its significance and management. Oxford, United Kingdom: MacKeith.

Taylor, R. D., & Lopez, E. I. (2005). Family management practice, school achievement, and problem behavior in African American adolescents: Mediating processes. *Applied Developmental Psychology, 26,* 39–49.

U.S. Department of Education (2008). *Mapping America's Educational Progress.* Retrieved from http://www.ed.gov/nclb/accountability/results/progress/nation.pdf

U.S. Department of Education (2005). *How No Child Left Behind benefits African Americans.* Retrieved from http://www.ed.gov/nclb/accountability/achieve/nclb-aa.html

Van Der Werf, Y. D., Altena, E., Schoonheim, M. M., Sanz-Arigita, E. J., Vis, J. C., De Rijke, W., & Van Someren, E. J. W. (2009). Sleep benefits subsequent hippocampal functioning. *Nature Neuroscience, 12,* 122–123.

Walker, M. P., & Stickgold, R. (2006). Sleep, memory, and plasticity. *Annual Review of Psychology, 10,* 139–166.

Wang, Y., & Zhang, Q. (2006). Are American children and adolescents of low socioeconomic status at increased risk of obesity? Changes in the association between overweight and family income between 1971 and 2002. *American Journal of Clinical Nutrition, 84,* 707–716.

Wei, J. L., Bond, J., Mayo, M. S., Smith, H. J., Reese, M., & Weatherly, R. A. (2009). Improved behavior and sleep after adenotonsillectomy in children with sleep-disordered breathing: Long-term follow-up. *Archives of Otolaryngology-Head & Neck Surgery, 135,* 642–646.

Wilhem, I., Diekelmann, S., & Born, J. (2008). Sleep in children improves memory performance on declarative but not procedural tasks. *Learning and Memory, 15,* 373–377.

Williams, P. G., Sears, L. L., & Allard, A. (2004). Sleep problems in children with autism. *Journal of Sleep Research, 13,* 265–268.

Winkelby, M. A., Jatulius, D. E., Frank, E., & Fortman, S. P. (1992). Socioeconomic status and health: How education, income, and occupation contribute to risk factors for cardiovascular disease. *American Journal of Public Health, 82,* 816–820.

Wolfson, A. R., & Carskadon, M. A. (1998). Sleep schedules and daytime functioning in adolescents. *Child Development, 69,* 875–887.

Wolfson, A. R., & Carskadon, M. A. (2003). Understanding adolescents' sleep patterns and school performance: A critical appraisal. *Sleep Medicine Reviews, 7,* 491–506.

Woodcock, R. W., McGrew, K. S., & Mather, N. (2001). *Woodcock-Johnson Tests of Cognitive Abilities.* Itasca, IL: Riverside.

12

Young Adolescents

Struggles with Insufficient Sleep

Amy R. Wolfson and Melissa Richards

Introduction

Early adolescence, generally defined as ages 10 to 15 years or 5th through 9th grade, is an evolving stage when individuals experience rapid and intense changes in their lives while transitioning from elementary to middle school (Caissy, 1994; Larson & Richards, 1989; Wigfield, Byrne, & Eccles, 2006). Despite ongoing physiological and cognitive change during this developmental phase, health habits and behaviors become increasingly more established. Throughout this period, young adolescents develop competencies, independence, and responsibility for their own health behaviors. The majority of adolescents manage this time in their lives successfully without encountering significant psychological, academic, social, and/or health difficulties. Yet, it is still important to monitor and acknowledge the wide variety of influences—family, culture, media, school, etc.— that affect adolescents' health behaviors. Likewise, when examining young adolescent behavior, one must recognize the intertwined nature of cognitive, physiological, social, and emotional development.

One significant and historically ignored area of functioning and development for the young adolescent is sleep. The consequences of inadequate and erratic sleep patterns for the young adolescent can have implications for multiple areas in his or her life. In this chapter, we discuss the myriad of factors that influence developmental changes in sleep timing and quantity for 10-15-year-old, early adolescents. We begin by outlining how sleep duration, patterns, and circadian timing change over the course of early adolescence. Second, we present data that indicates that early adolescents today have insufficient and erratic sleep-wake patterns. Third, we discuss the collection of factors present in adolescents' microenvironment that challenge young adolescents' sleep, including school start times, television and computer use, and caffeine consumption. Finally, we put forward some of the significant consequences such as academic difficulties and struggles with depressed mood that arise when sleep is compromised over the early adolescent years and offer recommendations for improvements.

Sleep and Circadian Timing

Over the last 25 years, researchers, educators, and health care providers have recognized early adolescence as a developmental time that is unique and distinct from late childhood and later adolescence (Urdan & Klein, 1998). Instead of viewing early adolescence as one of *storm and stress* (Hall, 1904), scholars and practitioners now see this period as one of remarkable change that is accompanied by both multiple stressors and new avenues for growth (Arnett, 1999; Eccles et al., 1993; Steinberg & Levine, 1997). In particular, a more nuanced understanding of adolescents' sleep requirements, schedules, and bioregulatory processes has emerged (Carskadon & Acebo, 2002; Carskadon, Acebo, & Jenni, 2004; Carskadon, Wolfson, Acebo, Tzischinsky, & Seifer, 1998; Crowley, Acebo, & Carskadon, 2007; Jenni, Achermann, & Carskadon, 2005; Jenni & Carskadon, 2004; Taylor, Jenni, Acebo, & Carskadon, 2005). Findings from longitudinal and cross-sectional designs as well as from laboratory and field-based studies indicate that sleep requirements do not change from ages 10 to 17 years; if anything, older adolescents require more sleep and fall asleep later in the evening (Carskadon, 1982; Carskadon & Acebo, 2002; Carskadon et al., 1980).

In a groundbreaking study at a summer sleep camp at Stanford University during the 1970s, boys and girls aged 10–12 years were monitored annually for five or six years (Carskadon et al., 1980). While researchers hypothesized that older children would need less sleep during the 10-hour nocturnal window they were given (i.e., 10:00 P.M. to 8:00 A.M.), they found that regardless of age, sex, or Tanner stage of pubertal development, the early adolescents all slept about 9.2 of the 10 hours. As they moved through adolescence, they continued to get the same amount of sleep, but they no longer woke spontaneously before the end of the sleep window at 8:00 A.M. In addition, the Multiple Sleep Latency Test (MSLT) revealed that the youngsters showed greater alertness at 8:00 P.M. than earlier in the day and even greater alertness at 10:00 P.M.

In contrast, young adolescents' real world sleep patterns indicate that many adolescents from a range of countries report sleeping from one to two (or more) hours less each night than nine hours, particularly on school nights (e.g., Carskadon & Acebo, 2002; Thorleifsdottir, Björnsson, Benediktsdottir, Gislason, & Kristbjarnarson, 2002; Tynjala, Kannas & Levalahti, 1993; Wolfson & Carskadon, 1998). Similarly, the 2006 National Sleep Foundation Sleep in America Poll (National Sleep Foundation [NSF], 2006) indicated that 21% of middle school students get an insufficient amount of sleep on school nights (less than eight hours) and only 35% obtain an optimal amount (nine or more hours).

Our own data across five studies demonstrates that middle school–aged adolescents fail to obtain their requisite amounts of sleep (Azuaje et al., 2009; Marco, Wolfson, Rabidou, Wilkey, & LeChasseur, 2002; Rossi, Campbell, Vo, Marco, & Wolfson, 2002; Vo, LeChasseur, Wolfson, & Marco, 2003). Remarkably consistent results were found, despite the fact that the data were collected from five different samples in three different states, over about an eight-year time span, using different methodologies (i.e., survey, diary, and actigraph). On school nights, average sleep onset (i.e., time sleep commenced) for adolescents in the five samples was approximately 10:15 P.M. Average wake time was also consistent at approximately 6:15 A.M. with a later wake time for the seventh graders attending two later starting middle schools (mean wake time: 7:12 A.M.; school start time: 8:37 a.m.). The average school-night sleep duration of all the participants was about 8.2 hours with students at the latest starting middle schools obtaining more sleep. It is noteworthy that the students' school and weekend night sleep durations were significantly less than their self-reported ideal amount of approximately 9 hours of sleep (Marco et al., 2002).

In addition to ongoing insufficient sleep over the course of adolescence, teenagers frequently experience a great discrepancy between school and weekend-night sleep schedules (Fredrikson, Rhodes, Reddy, & Way, 2004; Iglowstein, Jenni, Molinari, & Largo, 2003; Laberge et al., 2001; NSF, 2006; Strauch & Meier, 1988; Thorleifsdottir, et al., 2002; Wolfson, Acebo, Fallone, & Carskadon, 2003; Wolfson, Carskadon, et al., 2003; Wolfson, Spaulding, Dandrow, & Baroni, 2007). One major contributing factor to this inconsistency is that school-night sleep length declines markedly over the adolescent years, whereas weekend and summer sleep schedules change less. As early as middle school, adolescents also report significantly delayed bedtimes and wake times, particularly on weekends (Azuaje et al., 2009; Carskadon & Acebo, 2002; Carskadon, Vieira, & Acebo, 1993; Carskadon et al., 1998; NSF, 2006). The data across the five samples discussed above (Azuaje et al., 2009; Marco et al., 2002; Rossi et al., 2002; Vo et al., 2007) revealed that on weekends, students went to sleep over an hour later and awoke two hours later than on school days. Average weekend sleep onset was approximately 11:30 P.M., nearly an hour later than during the week. Average wake time was relatively consistent across samples at approximately 8:24 A.M., about two hours later than during the week. Similarly, in our most recent sample of seventh graders, their average actigraphically estimated school-night midsleep time (midpoint between start of sleep and wake time) was 2:54 A.M. (SD =:42) and on weekends it was 4:24 A.M. (SD=:70) (Marco, Wolfson, Sparling, & Azuaje, manuscript in preparation). As addressed later in the chapter, this weekend oversleep is widely considered to be indirect evidence of a sleep debt build up during the week and can be associated with less optimal outcomes.

Although the underlying biological process is not well understood, the onset of puberty appears to be associated with a delay in the timing of young adolescents' sleep-wake schedules (Carskadon & Acebo, 2002; Laberge et al., 2001). Sadeh, Dahl, Shahar, & Rosenblat-Stein's (2009) recent longitudinal study of 9 to 11-year-olds provides the first insight into the timing of puberty and these sleep schedule changes. Utilizing actigraphy and self-reported pubertal status, the investigators demonstrated that adolescent changes in sleep (delayed sleep phase and disrupted sleep patterns) are evident prior to the bodily changes associated with puberty (Sadeh et al., 2009). The role of puberty in understanding sleep and circadian changes during early adolescence is delineated further below. Certainly, adolescents tend to stay up later at night and sleep until later hours in the morning. This delay of the sleep period is most obvious on weekend and vacation nights, whereas the timing of sleep on school days is largely determined by school start time schedules (Carskadon et al., 1998; Epstein, Chillag, & Lavie, 1998; Szymczak, Jasińka, Pawlak, & Zwierzykowska, 1993).

In one hallmark study attempting to investigate the association between sleep patterns and school start time, Carskadon and colleagues (1998) evaluated the impact of a 65-minute advance (earlier) of school start time for approximately 40 students across the transition from grade 9 (junior high start time: 8:25 A.M.) to grade 10 (senior high start time: 7:20 A.M.). Objectively documented sleep records demonstrated that only 62% of the students in 9th grade, and fewer than 50% of the students in 10th grade obtained an average of seven hours or more of sleep on school nights. As expected, students woke significantly earlier on school days in 10th grade than in 9th grade. In 10th grade, students also displayed atypical sleep patterns on a laboratory nap test of sleepiness (Multiple Sleep Latency Test, MSLT). These young adolescents fell asleep faster in 10th than in 9th grade (particularly on an 8:30 A.M. assessment), and just about half of 10th grade participants' experienced at least one rapid eye movement (REM) sleep episode on the MSLT. Furthermore, the onset time of melatonin secretion delayed significantly in 10th grade. As discussed in the original study, this unusual pattern is disturbing because it mimics the clinical findings of patients with narcolepsy—a major sleep disorder (Carskadon et al., 1998; Guilleminault & Pelayo, 2000). These findings have been attributed to a combination of too little sleep occurring at a time mismatched to circadian rhythms (Carskadon et al., 1998). In other words, these 10th graders were expected to function in school at a time when their bodies were meant to sleep.

Research from Carskadon's laboratory has demonstrated that several identifiable changes in the circadian process affect this phase delay. Specifically, delay of intrinsic circadian phase, delay in timing of melatonin secretion, lengthening of the intrinsic period of the circadian clock, heightened sensitivity to evening light, or decreased sensitivity to morning light may contribute to the pubertal phase delay (Carskadon & Acebo, 2002; Carskadon, Acebo, Richardson, Tate, & Seifer, 1997;

Carskadon et al., 1998; Carskadon et al., 2004). Likewise, recent studies on sleep homeostasis in adolescents have demonstrated that the rise rate of sleep need during the day is slower in mature adolescents in comparison to early pubertal adolescents, contributing to the delay in the timing of sleep over the course of puberty (Jenni et al., 2005; Jenni & Carskadon, 2004). This indicates that less mature, younger adolescents may be more sensitive to extended wakefulness and live with more sleep pressure at bedtime than older, more mature adolescents. In particular, Taylor and colleagues (2005) found that after being awake for 14.5, 16.5, and 18.5 hours, sleep tendency (assessed by the time participants fell asleep) was significantly higher in prepubertal than postpubertal adolescents.

These developmental changes in sleep homeostasis and circadian timing may decrease older adolescents' sensitivity to sleep loss and increase tolerance for sleep pressure, making it easier to function in adult culture. Although the typical teenager's delayed sleep onset may make it easier to participate in evening activities, it increases their vulnerability to sleep-wake difficulties such as delayed sleep phase syndrome (i.e., circadian rhythm disorder in which the sleep period is chronically delayed with respect to clock time by two or more hours) and other physical, emotional, and cognitive consequences. In contrast, early adolescents tend to have considerable difficulty functioning in this 24/7, technology-intensive culture. For example, middle school and older elementary school–age youth tend to have far more difficulty functioning (e.g., completing homework, managing mood and behavior) following a weekend sleepover. Similarly, young adolescents may exhibit more daytime sleepiness, grumpiness, irritable behaviors, poor academic performance, and greater inability to keep their eyes open in school when they are not able to obtain an adequate amount of sleep (Chervin, Dillon, Archbold, & Ruzicka, 2003; Drake et al., 2003; Fuligni & Harway, 2006; Wolfson & Carskadon, 1998).

Culture and Socioeconomic Status

Sleep duration and schedules have been found to be strikingly comparable across different countries. A growing number of studies have queried adolescents in a range of different countries regarding their sleep. Research examining adolescents' self-reported sleep-wake patterns in Iran, China, India, Greece, and several European countries all demonstrate that teens report decreased total sleep, increasingly later bed times, and growing discrepancies between school and weekend-night sleep/wake schedules over the adolescent years (Ghanizadeh et al., 2008; Gupta et al., 2008; Liu et al., 2008; Loessl et al., 2008; Paraskakis et al., 2008). Similar to U.S. samples, a study of 7th versus 10th graders in Hong Kong revealed that 7th graders slept an average of one hour more than 10th graders, and that insufficient school night sleep was attributable to the early rise times required by school schedules (Liu et al., 2008). Likewise, German adolescents (ages 12–18 years) reported, on average, sleeping less than nine hours on school nights with the latest bedtimes on Friday and Saturday nights (Loessl et al., 2008).

However, despite the seemingly universal nature of the findings above, culture and environment inevitably have an enormous influence on early adolescents' sleep-wake patterns. Few conclusions can be drawn regarding the cultural influences on adolescents' sleep as the research approaches are varied in terms of study design, questions posed, sample sizes and settings (e.g., Liu, Zhao, Jia, & Buysse, 2008; Loessl et al., 2008; Paraskakis et al., 2008; Thorleifsdottir, et al., 2002; Tynjala, et al., 1993). Findings suggest that sleep hygiene (e.g., behavioral practices, environmental conditions, and other factors that are assumed to influence the quality and quantity of sleep) (Stepanski & Wyatt, 2003) nonetheless varies to some extent between countries and cultures (e.g., LeBourgeois, Giannotti, Cortesi, Wolfson, & Harsh, 2005; Liu, et al., 2008; Randler, 2008). For example, Italian adolescents (ages 12–17 years) report better sleep hygiene than their American peers (LeBourgeois et al., 2005), and teens residing in Greece who report taking a regularly scheduled nap or siesta (mean length 1.5 hours; 43% of sample) experience significantly less daytime sleepiness than non-nappers (Paraskakis et al., 2008).

In addition to cross-cultural comparisons, a small number of studies have addressed intracultural differences by considering factors such as socioeconomic status (SES). Currie and Lin (2007) found that poor youth are almost 20% less likely than non-poor youth to be rated in very good or excellent health during their adolescent years. Low SES has also been associated with poorer physical, emotional, and behavioral health over the course of childhood and adolescence (Chen, Martin, & Matthews, 2006; Dodge, Pettit, & Bates, 1994; Felner et al., 1995; McLoyd et al., 2009). In the same way that SES is an important factor in determining health, research is beginning to suggest that youth and adults from lower socioeconomic groups have a higher probability of exposure to adverse, unstable conditions that may potentially affect sleep (Buckhalt, El-Sheikh, & Keller, 2007; Hale, 2005; Moore, Adler, Williams, & Jackson, 2002; Steptoe, O'Donnell, Marmot, & Wardle, 2008). Buckhalt and colleagues (2007) found that SES is a moderator of effects in the association between children's sleep problems and their cognitive outcomes; relations between sleep and cognitive functioning were more pronounced for children from lower SES backgrounds. In Owens, Stahl, Patton, Reddy, and Crouch's (2006) sample of low SES fifth through ninth graders, early adolescents with later bedtimes and less than optimal amounts of sleep reported more daytime sleepiness. Further, in a study with predominantly low income preschoolers, greater variability in sleep schedules was associated with worse school adjustment (Bates, Viken, Alexander, Beyers, & Stockton, 2002). Similarly, in a sample of more than 3,000 preschoolers, children from disadvantaged households were less likely to have consistent bedtime routines (Hale, Berger, LeBougeois, & Brooks-Gunn, 2009).

In our study of seventh graders' actigraphically estimated sleep (34% of households with incomes below $30,000), school and weekend-night sleep were associated with SES, household income, neighborhood condition, and the number of single family homes in the neighborhood (Apollon et al., 2008; Marco et al., manuscript in preparation; Sparling, Azuaje, Marco, & Wolfson, 2009). Results revealed that young adolescents from lower SES households fell asleep later, had shorter sleep durations, and had less consistent school-weekend-night sleep schedules than those from higher SES households. Similarly, seventh graders living in neighborhoods with more single family homes and poor external neighborhood conditions (e.g., litter, fewer trees) obtained less sleep and had less consistent sleep schedules than their peers (Marco et al., manuscript in preparation; Sparling et al., 2009). SES is a complex construct having social, economic, environmental, and behavioral components; see Gellis, chapter 10 in this volume, for a more thorough discussion of relations between SES and sleep. Studies reviewed here indicate, however, that further research is needed to explore how social class impacts the external home environment and ultimately impacts sleep for children and adolescents.

Young Teens' Environment

Cultural setting and SES are large-scale, contextual factors that are generally not under young teens' control. Other factors such as school start times, screen use (e.g., televisions, video games, computers, and cell phones), and caffeine consumption are a part of the adolescents' microenvironment and are more controllable—at least by someone. These external factors can be detrimental to adolescents' sleep schedules and requirements (Carskadon et al., 1980; Carskadon et al., 1998; Johnson, Cohen, Kasen, First, & Brook, 2004; Mesquita & Reimão, 2007; Söderqvist, Carberg, & Hardell, 2008; Van den Bulck, 2003; Wolfson, 2002; Wolfson & Carskadon, 1998; Wolfson et al., 2007). In the section below, associations between school start times, screen use, and caffeine consumption on early adolescents' sleep are examined.

School Schedules

A slowly increasing number of school districts have responded to research reports regarding the prevalence of inadequate sleep among middle and high school students with a systematic countermeasure—delaying school start times. However, other districts continue to debate fiercely whether or not to delay school start times for this age group. Well over a decade ago, Wahlstrom assessed over 18,000 high school students in the Minneapolis School District before and after the district's school start time changed from 7:15 A.M. in the 1996–1997 school year to 8:40 A.M. beginning with the 1997–1998 school year (Wahlstrom, 2002a; 2002b). The following significant findings were reported: (1) attendance rates for students in grades 9 through 11 improved; (2) the percentage of high school students continuously enrolled in the district or the same school also increased; (3) grades showed a slight but not statistically significant improvement; and (4) high school students reported bedtimes similar to students in schools that did not change start times, obtaining nearly an hour more of sleep on school nights during the 1999–2000 school year (Wahlstrom, 2002a; 2002b). Strikingly similar findings were reported in a study conducted in our lab for young adolescent-age students in an urban, New England school district. Seventh and eighth graders at a later starting middle school (8:37 A.M.) reported less tardiness, less daytime sleepiness, better academic performance (especially the eighth graders), more school night total sleep, and later rise times in comparison to middle school students at an earlier starting school (7:15 A.M.) (Wolfson et al., 2007). Similarly, a pilot study of 116 fifth and sixth graders attending early (7:45 A.M.) versus late (8:25 A.M.) starting elementary schools from the same large, urban New England district mentioned above found that students attending the later starting school reported waking up later, obtaining more sleep, and less daytime sleepiness (particularly on school nights) than their preadolescent peers at the earlier starting school (Spaulding, Butler, Daigle, Dandrow, & Wolfson, 2005). Similar results were reported by Epstein and colleagues (1998) who surveyed 811 10–12 year olds from 18 Israeli schools with starting times that ranged from 7:10 to 8:30 A.M. The investigators compared schools that started at least two days per week at 7:15 A.M. or earlier with schools that started regularly at 8:00 A.M. Based on self-report data, the mean total sleep times of the children attending the schools with early start times were significantly shorter than those of the students at the later starting schools (8.7 versus 9.1 hours). The former group expressed more frequent complaints of daytime sleepiness, a greater tendency to doze off in class, feeling most sleepy during their first period classes, and attention/concentration difficulties (Epstein et al., 1998). Clearly, young adolescents, similar to their older, high school age peers, benefit from starting school at later times in the morning.

Although focused on older adolescents, Wolfson and Carskadon (2005) surveyed 345 public high school personnel about high school start times, factors influencing school start times, and decision making around school schedules. Most respondents had not contemplated changing or changed their school start times. Of those schools in which changes were contemplated, 32% noted concerns about teenagers' sleep needs, and about 50% of the respondents endorsed possible positive outcomes, such as lower tardiness and absenteeism rates. Perceived barriers to changing school schedules commonly endorsed included sports practices, after-school activities, and the transportation system (Wolfson & Carskadon, 2005).

Since the late 1990s, the independent nonprofit National Sleep Foundation has done some tracking of school start time changes as a part of their ongoing focus on educating the public about adolescents' sleep needs. In 2000, they established the Sleep and Teens Task Force made up of researchers and clinicians in the field. The task force published a report, *Adolescent Sleep Needs and Patterns*, documenting existing research about sleep-related issues affecting adolescents and, later, the NSF developed a tool kit to assist school professionals, parents, and teens advocating for later school start times (NSF, 2000, 2005). Unfortunately, there is no reporting mechanism through professional education organizations; however in 2007, NSF estimated that close to 80 U.S. school districts had delayed the start of their high schools and decision makers in over 140 districts were contemplating a change (as cited in Wolfson, 2007). The districts range from large, urban school districts, such as Denver and Minneapolis, to smaller, suburban districts or towns, such as Wilton, Connecticut, and West Des Moines, Iowa. The focus has been primarily on high schools, so it is difficult to estimate what percentage of these changes included middle schools. Moreover, a delay might be as short as 7:15 to 7:30 A.M. versus 8:00 to 9:00 A.M. In addition, the 2006 NSF poll reported that for most sixth to eighth graders, school starts at 8:00 A.M. or later (69%); however, just over half of the high school students reported that their high schools start before 8:00 A.M. (52%) (NSF, 2006). An empirically based reporting and monitoring system is needed to evaluate and track school start time changes and related sleep education recommendations.

Furthermore, it is recommended that future research explores other countermeasures and interventions that may positively impact adolescents' sleep habits and daytime behaviors either independently or combined with school start time and schedule changes. In our 2007 study (Wolfson et al., 2007), twice as many students at the later start time middle school obtained the recommended nine hours of sleep on school nights in comparison to students attending the earlier start time school. Even with a delayed school start time, however, only about one-third of the students obtained this standard of nine hours. Unquestionably, other factors that contribute to inadequate sleep in adolescents need to be assessed and targeted. School start time changes are a large-scale, environmental countermeasure. Interventions and assessments at the individual level such as sleep hygiene preventive programs and sleep education classes for adolescents, parents, and school professionals may positively affect sleep quantity and quality (Cortesi, Giannotti, Sebastiani, Bruni, & Ottaviano, 2004; de Sousa, Araujo, & de Azevedo, 2007; Vo et al., 2003).

Media: Television, Video Games, and Cell Phones

A prominent and controllable contextual factor related to young adolescents' sleep is media use. With the popularity of television (TV), computers, home video game systems, Digital Video Disk (DVD) players, and more accessible cell phone and text messaging plans, young adolescents devote a great amount of their time to screen use (Gentile, Lynch, Linder, & Walsh, 2004; Martin & Oppenheim, 2007; Rideout, Foehr, & Roberts, 2010; Van den Bulck, 2004; Van den Bulck, 2007). During a typical day, young adolescents aged 11–14 are exposed to nearly 12 hours of screen media, audio media, print media, computers, and video games—with over a quarter of that time devoted to using more than one technological outlet at once, also known as media multitasking (Rideout et al., 2010). Furthermore, in the past five years, young people's daily media exposure has increased by over two hours (Rideout et al., 2010).

Studies that have gathered specific data on television viewing have reported that young adolescents watch between 21 and 25 hours of television a week (Van den Bulck, 2004) and five hours of television each day (Rideout et al., 2010) despite the American Academy of Pediatrics' (AAP) recommendation that children and adolescents over the age of two not watch more than two hours of television daily (AAP, 2001). Given the prevalence of TV use, a growing number of psychology and communications researchers have focused their work on television's implications for adolescents' behavior and development. In recent years, television viewing has been linked to various aspects of child and adolescent health, with studies demonstrating an association between excessive television viewing and a range of negative consequences, including inactivity and risk of being overweight (Dennison, Erb, & Jenkins, 2002; DuRant, Baranowksi, Johnson, & Thompson, 1994; Gortmaker et al. 1996; Robinson, 2001), attention difficulties (Christakis, Zimmerman,

DiGiuseppe, & McCarty, 2004), behavioral problems, (Johnson, Cohen, Smailes, Kasen, & Brook, 2002; Singer, Slovak, Frierson, & York, 1998), and academic difficulties (Sharif & Sargent, 2006).

Furthermore, adolescents from a range of socioeconomic backgrounds report that they have televisions in their bedrooms (Christakis, Ebel, Rivara, & Zimmerman, 2004; Marco et al., manuscript in preparation; Owens et al, 1999; Rideout et al., 2010; Taveras, Hohman, Price, Gortmaker, & Sonneville, 2009). Approximately 71% of U.S. 8–18 year olds (Rideout et al., 2010) and 62% of low SES seventh graders (Marco et al., manuscript in preparation) report having a TV set in their bedrooms. Given this widespread phenomenon, research has focused on the impact of television viewing on sleep patterns. Among young adolescents (fifth to ninth graders), duration of television viewing is associated with prolonged sleep onset latency (SOL) (Alexandru et al., 2006), sleep difficulty and anxiety (Owens et al., 1999), and shorter sleep duration (Adam, Snell, & Pendry, 2007). In a study with school-age children, passive TV exposure was especially related to sleep disruption, even when socioeconomic status, family income, father's work schedule, family conflicts, and child's psychiatric symptoms were controlled (Paavnonen, Pennonen, Roine, Valkonen, & Lahikainen, 2006). Although these studies demonstrate moderate effects, the greatest evidence for a *causal* relationship between television and sleep problems is demonstrated in Johnson and colleagues' (2004) longitudinal study. Results revealed that adolescents who watched three or more hours of television each day during early (mean age 14) and middle (mean age 16) adolescence were at risk for more sleep problems during emerging adulthood, even after controlling for age, earlier sleep problems, sex, psychiatric disorders, education of parents, and income level. Furthermore, adolescents who reduced television viewing from over one hour to less than an hour a day showed reduced risk for sleep problems as emerging adults at age 22 (Johnson et al., 2004).

Television, however, is not the only form of media that dominates the lives of young adolescents. Video and computer games have become increasingly popular, with nearly 81% of 8–18 year olds reporting that they play video games at least once a month (Martin & Oppenheim, 2007). Furthermore, studies specifically assessing young adolescents found that they use video games nine hours a week (Gentile et al., 2004) and over one hour on a typical day (Rideout et al., 2010). In addition, the rise in popularity of home computers has provided adolescents with another outlet for playing digital games and spending leisure time. Eleven to fourteen year olds typically spend just under two hours each day using the computer for recreational purposes, a substantial increase in the past five years (Rideout et al., 2010).

Despite the large percentage of computers and digital game players in adolescents' bedrooms (Rideout et al., 2010), few studies have investigated the relationship between video game playing and young adolescents' sleep. Nonetheless, research with adults suggests that computer games are associated with higher levels of arousal, shorter sleep duration, less REM sleep, and poorer sleep quality (Higuchi, Motohasi, Liu, & Maeda, 2005). With children aged 5 to 13 years in particular, computer games and internet use for recreational reasons negatively affects sleep-wake parameters such as daytime sleepiness, bedtimes, and total sleep (Oka, Suzuki, & Inoue, 2008; Van den Bulck, 2004). Although the relationship between sleep and digital game use may appear to be one-dimensional, it can be significantly affected by the young adolescent's reasons for playing the games. According to Wallenius, Rimpelä, Punamäki, and Lintonen (2009), adolescents with instrumental motives and interest in learning and developing skills from playing digital games had earlier bedtimes and better sleep habits than those with ritualized motives focused on relaxing and forgetting worries.

In addition to television and computer use, another screen that dominates adolescents' free time is the cellular (cell) phone. National surveys aimed at profiling the preferences and habits of young people's technology use have revealed that the number of youth (ages 8–18) that report owning a mobile phone has increased by nearly 30% in the past five years (Rideout et al., 2010). More specifically, young adolescents (ages 11–14) spent 36 minutes talking on their cell phones each day (Rideout et al., 2010). However, among young cell phone users today, making calls is not the only reason for using mobile devices. Text messaging has become incredibly popular, with adolescents frequently citing the technology as an essential aspect of their social lives (Harris Interactive & CTIA—The Wireless Association, 2008). Forty-six percent of young people send text messages, and adolescents in 7th–12th grade report spending approximately an hour and a half text messaging on a typical day (Rideout et al., 2010).

Furthermore, text messaging and talking on the cell phone seems to negatively impact young adolescents' sleep patterns. Research aimed directly at elucidating the relationship between cell phone use and sleep has demonstrated that after 9:00 P.M., 34% of high school students text messaged and 44% engaged in phone conversations (Calamaro, Mason, & Ratcliffe, 2009). Another study surveying 13- and 16-year-old Belgian adolescents revealed that over 50% of the participants sent text messages and 42% received phone calls at least once a month at bedtime (Van den Bulck, 2007). Nighttime cell phone use, in particular, negatively affects sleep patterns. For example, those who engaged in mobile phone use after lights out were more than two times more likely to be classified as very tired (Van den Bulck, 2007). Likewise, 13- and 16-year-olds who reported being awakened by text messages experienced higher levels of daytime sleepiness (Van den Bulck, 2007). Moreover, night-time disruptions may get more frequent as adolescents get older. Forty percent of 16-year-olds reported that they are awakened at least once a month during the night by a text message, significantly more often than 13-year-olds (Van den Bulck, 2003).

Various theories have attempted to explain why media negatively affects sleep. One hypothesis suggests that media displaces the hours in an adolescent's day usually allotted for sleep and exercise. Because most media activities do not have a defined start and end time to limit their use, adolescents find themselves devoting a great amount of time to screen use and cutting back on sleep (Owens et al., 1999; Zimmerman, 2008). Likewise, it has also been proposed that the time that is spent watching television and/or playing video games replaces the time that could be used for activities such as athletics, which are known to promote good sleep (Nixon et al., 2009; Youngstedt, 2005). For example, Nixon and colleagues' (2009) study with school age children found that more daytime physical activity was associated with a decrease in sleep latency. Despite these indicative results, others have not found a relationship between reduced television viewing and school age children's physical activity (Robinson, 1999).

Furthermore, circadian researchers have suggested that bright lights present in screens may delay an individual's melatonin secretion at night (Higuchi, Motohashi, Liu, Ahara, & Kaneko, 2003; Higuchi, Motohashi, Maeda, & Ishibashi, 2005; Kubota et al. 2002). This hypothesis, however, is controversial, as the light emitted from a computer screen alone

(45 lux) does not seem to affect sleep latency (Higuchi, Motohashi, Liu et al., 2005). With adolescents' escalating use of multiple screens, future research needs to better understand the impact of light from television and computer monitors along with cell phones and laptop computers on the timing of sleep and wakefulness.

Finally, others have suggested that media exposure might negatively affect sleep due to content. Certainly, the relationship between television and children's fears is well documented; in the past few decades, television programs' content has been criticized for being anxiety provoking and overly stimulating, making it difficult for viewers to fall asleep (Cantor, 1994; Harrison & Cantor, 1999). Perhaps what is most worrisome about this relationship between early adolescents' sleep and media use is that many parents believe that television and other technology can have calming effects suitable to incorporate into a bedtime routine. Of the 7th and 10th graders surveyed by Eggermont & Van den Bulck (2006), nearly 37% admitted to using the television as a sleep aid, while 22% use computer games, and 60% use music. None of these media venues, however, had advantageous effects on sleep, as those who reported using television, music, and/or computer games as aids reported less total sleep and more daytime sleepiness (Eggermont & Van den Bulck, 2006). Going forward, studies should focus on studying sleep and interactive and social media tools such as instant messaging and social networking websites that are becoming increasingly popular among youth.

Substance Use: Caffeine

Caffeine use among young people has become extremely popular, despite its possibly negative effects on health and sleep in particular. Previous research has demonstrated that caffeine has a significant effect on adults' sleep (for review see Snel, 1993). Specifically, caffeine negatively affects sleep duration (Smith, 2002), quality (Hindmarch et al., 2000), onset (Penetar et al., 1993), efficiency (Drapeau et al., 2006), and some studies have demonstrated that caffeine reduces REM and slow-wave sleep (Carrier et al., 2009; Smith, 2002).

Considerably less research, however, has examined early adolescents' sleep patterns and caffeine intake. Caffeine use in the form of soft drinks, coffee, tea, energy drinks, chocolate, and caffeine pills appears to be common for middle and high school age adolescents (Bernstein, Carroll, Thuras, Cosgrove, & Roth, 2002; Ludden & Wolfson, 2010; Oberstar, Bernstein, & Thuras, 2002; Pollak & Bright, 2003), with a recent survey of 155 seventh graders revealing that nearly 84% of the respondents drank caffeinated soft drinks at least one or two times a week (Wolfson, unpublished data). Soft drinks are undoubtedly the most common way for adolescents to consume caffeine—among high school students who use caffeine, 60.5% use caffeinated soft drinks, 19.3% use coffee, 6.1% use energy drinks, and 8.8% use other caffeinated products (Ludden & Wolfson, 2010).

The reasons behind caffeine use among adolescents differ. High schoolers often use caffeine with the expectation that caffeine will help them get through the day (Ludden & Wolfson, 2010), enhance their energy levels (O'Dea, 2003), and increase endurance and performance during exercise (Reissig, Strain, & Griffiths, 2009), thus providing evidence for emerging dependency—like behaviors for a subset of teens. Yet, youth may be misinformed, as research suggests that adolescents (particularly of high school age) consuming high levels of caffeine have more sleep disturbances, daytime sleepiness, nighttime awakenings, and earlier wake times than those consuming low levels of caffeine (Lee, McEnany, & Weekes, 1999; Ludden & Wolfson, 2010; Orbeta, Overpeck, Ramcharran, Kogan, & Ledsky, 2006). In addition, weekend caffeine use is associated with negative mood, decreased alertness, and school absenteeism in seventh graders (Canton et al., 2007).

Despite these striking findings, few studies have focused particularly on young adolescents and preadolescents. Pollak and Bright's study (2003) is important to highlight with its specific focus on middle schoolers and the use of a prospective methodology—sleep diaries. Pollak and Bright found that the majority of their seventh- and eighth-grade participants (mean age 12.7 years) consumed caffeine through soft drinks, with boys using significantly more than girls. In addition, the young adolescents with a higher caffeine intake had longer sleep onset times, longer bouts of daytime sleep, shorter nocturnal sleep durations, and more nights of interrupted sleep. Finally, a weekly cycle of caffeine use was observed, with most caffeine use increasing after Wednesday. The authors suggest that caffeine was consumed to offset the sleepiness that was brought on by school-night sleep deprivation (Pollak & Bright, 2003).

Although these studies have added substantially to understanding caffeine use and sleep, new research should examine the possible confounding variables that may influence the relationship between sleep and caffeine in young adolescents, including mental health, family stresses, inadequate parental monitoring, socioeconomic status, and other forms of substance use/abuse. For example, depressed mood is associated with disrupted sleep (Wolfson & Armitage, 2009; Wolfson & Carskadon, 1998) and adolescents with depressive symptoms report greater caffeine use than their peers (Fulkerson, Sherwood, Perry, Neumark-Sztainer, & Story, 2004; Whalen et al., 2008). Therefore, it is possible that mood and/or mental health may be a mediating or a confounding variable in the relationship between caffeine and sleep.

Struggles with Insufficient Sleep: Academics and Emotional Well-Being

As middle schoolers negotiate the early years of adolescence they may be particularly vulnerable to the consequences of insufficient and irregular sleep, including poor academic performance, depressed mood, externalizing behaviors, and other health problems (Chervin et al., 2003; Drake et al., 2003; Gibson et al., 2006; Wolfson & Armitage, 2009; Wolfson & Carskadon, 2003). In the sections that follow, we discuss the work that has been done on conceptualizing and understanding the consequences of inconsistent and inadequate sleep on young teens' school work and emotional well-being.

Academic Performance and Behavior

Current research allows us to draw conclusions about the relationship between sleep patterns and academic performance. A number of experimental studies have connected inadequate sleep with significant decreases in cognitive, working memory, and psychomotor performance (Fallone, Owens, & Deane, 2002; Menna-Baretto & Wey, 2008; Sadeh, Gruber, & Raviv, 2002; Steenari et al., 2003). Further, researchers have examined the association between sleep habits and schedules and academic performance in adolescents and preadolescents over the middle, high school, and college years (see reviews: Curcio, Ferrara, & De Gennaro, 2006; Mitru, Millrood, & Mateika, 2002; Sadeh, 2007; Wolfson & Carskadon, 2003). Below, we examine the studies that focused on young adolescents' sleep and educational performance and behavior in real world settings.

Since the 1980s, over 30 studies of sleep habits and some aspect of academic performance have been published as abstracts and peer-reviewed articles (e.g., Curcio et al., 2006; Fredriksen et al., 2004; Meijer, 2008; Pagel, Forister, & Kwiatkowski, 2007; Wahlstrom, 2002a, 2002b; Wolfson & Carskadon, 1998; Wolfson & Carskadon, 2003); however, only a handful of the studies focus on early adolescents. As discussed in Wolfson and Carskadon's review (2003), these studies were based almost entirely on self-report for grades and sleep habits with sample sizes ranging from approximately 100 to 6,000 participants. The majority of these studies operationally defined academic performance as self-reported Grade Point Average (GPA); however, a few researchers looked at other aspects of school performance, such as concentration/attention, achievement, motivation, and attendance/tardiness. While most of the studies focused on self-reported sleep/wake habits, such as bedtime, rise time, and total sleep, others relied on self-reported sleep quality. The studies that were reviewed by Wolfson and Carskadon (2003) demonstrated that self-reported shortened total sleep time, irregular sleep/wake schedules, late bed and rise times, and poor sleep quality are associated with poor academic performance for preadolescents and adolescents from middle school through the college years.

More recent projects have assessed early adolescents. As discussed previously, we found that seventh and eighth graders attending an early starting middle school (reporting 50 minutes less school-night sleep) had four times more tardiness and poorer academic performance than their peers at a later starting school (Wolfson et al., 2007). Fredriksen and colleagues (2004) followed 2,259 students over the middle school years and concluded that young adolescents who obtained less sleep in sixth grade exhibited lower self esteem, increased depressed mood, and lower grades. Yet, the middle schoolers who reported decreased sleep over time continued to report higher levels of depressive symptoms and worse self-esteem, but no longer demonstrated poorer academic performance (Fredriksen et al., 2004). In a smaller study of 450 sixth to eighth graders, middle schoolers who reported more daytime sleepiness obtained less sleep and experienced lower school achievement, more negative views of school, increased absenteeism, and more frequent illnesses (Drake et al., 2003). Similarly, controlling for age and income, Pagel and colleagues (2007) found that symptoms of sleep disorders, daytime sleepiness, and difficulty concentrating were associated with lower GPAs in 6th though 11th graders.

In summary, the implications of the studies reviewed here are convincing. Schools, parents, and health care providers need to focus on the role of sleep and sleep disturbances in relation to academic grades, test scores, school attendance, emotional difficulties, and other aspects of school behavior and adolescent development. Likewise, just as sleep researchers need to consider other factors besides sleep in relation to school performance, behavioral scientists in other fields focused on adolescent development and school achievement need to incorporate adolescents' sleep into their studies.

Emotional Well-Being

Mental health difficulties are a significant problem for today's adolescents. At any point in time, one in every 10 children and adolescents is affected by serious emotional disturbances with about half of all disorders referenced in the *Diagnostic and Statistical Manual of Mental Disorders* (*DSM-IV*) starting at about age 14 and three-quarters by age 24 (American Psychiatric Association [*DSM-IV-TR*], 2000; Kessler, Chiu, Demler, & Walters, 2005). Using a range of different approaches and measures, researchers have examined the complex relationship between adolescents' sleep patterns and emotional well-being. Studies have reported cross-sectional associations between sleep problems, depressed mood, and other behavioral difficulties in school age children and teens (Blunden & Chervin, 2007; Kirmil-Gray, Eagleston, Gibson, & Thoresen, 1984; Morrison, McGee, & Stanton, 1992; Roberts, Lewinsohn, & Seeley, 1995; Saarenpaa-Heikkila, Laippala, & Koivikko; 2001; Wolfson & Carskadon, 1998). For example, in their retrospective survey of high school students, Wolfson and Carskadon (1998) found that adolescents with more adequate sleep habits (defined as longer total sleep times and more regular sleep schedules across the week) reported lower levels of depressed mood, fewer complaints of daytime sleepiness, and fewer sleep-wake behavior problems in comparison to students with inadequate sleep habits. Utilizing another research approach, early adolescents were characterized as sleepy or as poor sleepers. This research design indicated that poor sleepers had more problematic coping behaviors (e.g., more difficulty recognizing, appraising, and adapting to stressful situations), displayed more behavior problems, and/or reported higher levels of anxious and/or depressed mood (Fallone et al., 2002; Morrison et al., 1992; Sadeh et al., 2002; Wolfson et al., 1995).

Other investigators have utilized methodologies such as sleep diaries and actigraphy to examine adolescents' sleep time, activities, and psychological well-being (e.g., Aronen, Paavonen, Fjallberg, Soininen, & Torronen, 2000; Hardway & Fuligni, 2006; Paavonen et al., 2002). Using diaries in a sample of 14- and 15-year-olds, Hardway and Fuligni (2006) found that adolescents who spent less time sleeping each night tended to report more negative and less positive daily moods than those who obtained more sleep. In particular, adolescents with more inconsistent nightly sleep reported more depressed mood, anxiety, and fatigue. Likewise, using actigraphic estimates of sleep in a younger adolescent sample, Aronen and colleagues found that shorter sleep was significantly associated with both externalizing and internalizing symptoms (Aronen et al., 2000). Other longitudinal studies have documented that mental health disturbances such as depressive symptoms and substance abuse are significantly associated with the development and persistence of sleep problems in young adolescents (Kaneita et al., 2009; Patten, Choi, Gillin, & Pierce, 2000).

Taken together, studies strongly suggest that young adolescents with inadequate sleep, irregular sleep/wake schedules, and/or sleep disturbances struggle and cope less effectively with emotional/behavior difficulties. The direction, possible longitudinal nature, and the quality of the relationship between sleep quantity and schedules and emotional well-being, however, remains unclear. The quantity, quality, and timing of sleep seem to be associated with both internalizing emotional difficulties (e.g., depression) as well as externalizing difficulties (e.g., attention, conduct problems). It is essential to highlight the overlap between sleep regulation and behavioral/emotional problems in children and adolescents.

There is clearly a two-way interaction between these two systems. Studies have shown that sleep loss may limit the ability to control mood and behavior; therefore insufficient sleep may contribute to the development or exacerbation of behavioral and emotional problems (Dahl, 1999). Likewise, the development, regulation, and timing of sleep can be altered by behavioral/emotional disorders (Dahl et al., 1996).

Conclusions and Recommendations

In sum, irregular and insufficient sleep can have a plethora of effects on a young adolescent's life. This chapter illustrates this fact by examining the ways that sleep patterns change over the course of early adolescence, discussing the myriad of environmental factors that are detrimental to young adolescents' sleep, and outlining the consequences that arise when sleep is compromised. Dryfoos (2000) formulated the notion of "safe passage" to represent what we all wish for adolescents—that they will not be too severely affected by the risk factors lodged in all of the opportunities they will encounter passing from childhood to adolescence to adulthood. Good quality, sufficient, and consistent sleep clearly help to ensure such safe passage.

Although an increasing number of studies have advanced our understanding of sleep and well-being in children and adolescents, more research should focus specifically on early adolescents and preadolescents aged 10–15 years. Discerning ways of improving sleep for early adolescents is crucial, as the habits that are established during this time will undoubtedly serve as a foundation for healthy behaviors in the future. In addition to focusing on 10–15 year-olds, future research should take into account the mediating and moderating variables that may be present in any study that focuses on health and sleep. To elucidate these connections, young adolescents should be studied longitudinally. Longitudinal approaches (e.g., Aronen, et al., 2000; Buckhalt, El-Sheikh, Keller, & Kelly, 2009; Johnson et al., 2004; Marco et al., manuscript in preparation) are beginning to provide clear evidence for the causal relationships between contextual factors (e.g., socioeconomic status, culture, early adversity, emotional well being, media use, substance abuse) and sleep over early adolescence. Such studies are instrumental in helping to suggest environments that are advantageous to adolescents' sleep and daytime functioning.

Looking back over the last decade or so, researchers and clinicians certainly know far more about the development of sleep-wake patterns over adolescence and the negative ramifications of insufficient and erratic sleep for young people. Likewise, there has been fairly consistent media and public attention to the sleep needs of adolescents. There is a school start-time movement, which has been stimulated and supported by school communities, private foundations, governmental organizations, parents, and health care providers. Additionally, there is a recognized and developing focus on sleep education and preventive efforts for adolescents in the education and medical communities.

In striking contrast to these efforts, a significant number of early adolescents continue to get far less sleep than they need, have poor sleep hygiene, and experience serious consequences such as substance abuse, school absenteeism, diminished academic performance, and emotional difficulties. At this juncture, then, what is needed? The following recommendations are certainly not exclusive, but are crucial steps in improving the sleeping and waking lives of adolescents.

(1) Model adequate sleep habits for adults in teenagers' lives.
(2) Pursue delaying start times of middle and high schools with an improved system for tracking changes.
(3) Limit the amount of caffeine consumed by adolescents through education programs and policies that recommend removing caffeinated drinks from school vending machines.
(4) Develop guidelines to reduce electronic media use in the evening hours with particular attention to the location of televisions, computers, and cell phones.
(5) Increase community-research partnerships that focus on adolescents' sleep needs.
(6) Promote legislation on adolescent work hours, driver education, and drowsy driving.
(7) Develop and evaluate preventive interventions and sleep education programs.
(8) Increase governmental and private funding of initiatives, basic and applied research, and education programs focused on child/adolescent sleep needs, and related behavioral outcomes.

NOTE

Some of the work discussed in this chapter was made possible through a grant from NIH, NICHD, 5 R01 HD047928-05.

REFERENCES

Adam, E. K., Snell, E. K., & Pendry, P. (2007). Sleep timing and quantity in ecological and family context: A nationally representative time-diary study. *Journal of Family Psychology, 21*, 4–19.

Alexandru, G., Michikazu, S., Shimako, H., Xiaoli, C., Hitomi, K., Takashi, Y., … Sadanobu, K. (2006). Epidemiological aspects of self-reported sleep onset latency in Japanese junior high school children. *Journal of Sleep Research, 15*, 266–275.

American Academy of Pediatrics [AAP]. (2001). Children, adolescents, and television. *Pediatrics, 107*, 423–426.

American Psychiatric Association (2000). *Diagnostic and statistical manual of mental disorders* (Revised 4th ed.). Washington, DC: Author.

Apollon, S., Azuaje, A., Sparling, M., Nadig, N., Marco, C., & Wolfson, A.R. (2008). Late starting city middle schools: Role of family income and health care on 7th graders' sleep patterns. *Sleep (Supplement), 31*, A68.

Arnett, J. J. (1999). Adolescent storm and stress, reconsidered. *American Psychologist, 54*, 317–326.

Aronen, E. T., Paavonen, E. J., Fjallberg, M., Soininen, M., & Torronen, J. (2000). Sleep and psychiatric symptoms in school-age children. *Journal of the American Academy of Child & Adolescent Psychiatry, 39*, 502–508.

Azuaje, A., Sparling, M., Nadig, N., Spiro, K., Zujkowski, M., Marco, C. A., et al. (2009). Young adolescents' sleep patterns across different neighborhood environments. *Sleep (Supplement), 32*, A86.

Bates, J. E., Viken, R. J., Alexander, D. B., Beyers, J., & Stockton, L. (2002). Sleep and adjustment in preschool children: Sleep diary reports by mothers relate to behavior reports by teachers. *Child Development, 73*, 62–74.

Bernstein, G. A., Carroll, M. E., Thuras, P. D., Cosgrove, K. P., & Roth, M. E. (2002). Caffeine dependence in teenagers. *Drug and Alcohol Dependence, 66*, 1–6.

Blunden, S. L., & Chervin, R. D. (2007). Sleep problems are associated with poor outcomes in remedial teaching programmes: A preliminary study. *Journal of Paediatrics and Child Health, 44*, 237–242.

Buckhalt, J. A., El-Sheikh, M., & Keller, P. (2007). Children's sleep and cognitive functioning: Race and socioeconomic status as moderators of effects. *Child Development, 78*, 213–231.

Buckhalt, J. A., El-Sheikh, M., Keller, P. S., & Kelly, R. J. (2009). Concurrent and longitudinal relationships between children's sleep and cognitive functioning: The moderating role of parent education. *Child Development, 80,* 875–892.

Caissy, G.A. (1994). *Early adolescence: Understanding the 10 to 15 year old.* NewYork, NY: Perseus Publishing.

Calamaro, C.J., Mason, T.B., & Ratcliffe, S.J. (2009). Adolescents living the 24/7 lifestyle: Effects of caffeine and technology on sleep duration and daytime functioning. *Pediatrics, 123,* 1005–1010.

Canton, B., Patel, B., Quinn, A., Barry, K., Naku, K., Marco, C., et al. (2007). Wired or tired: Caffeine use, expectancies, and sleep patterns in adolescents-Two pilot studies. *Sleep (Supplement), 30,* A68.

Cantor, J. (1994). Fright reactions to mass media. In J. Bryant & D. Zillmann (Eds.), *Media effects: Advances in theory and research* (2nd ed., pp.169–197). Mahwah, NJ; Lawrence Erlbaum Associates.

Carrier, J., Paquet, J., Fernandez-Bolanos, M., Girouard, L., Roy, J., Selmaoui, B., & Filipini, D. (2009). Effects of caffeine on daytime recovery sleep: A double challenge to the sleep - wake cycle in aging. *Sleep Medicine, 10,* 1016–1024.

Carskadon, M. A. (1982). The second decade. In C. Guilleminault (Ed.), *Sleeping and waking disorders: Indications and techniques* (pp. 99–125). Menlo Park, CA: Addison-Wesley.

Carskadon, M. A., & Acebo, C. (2002). Regulation of sleepiness in adolescents: Update, insights, and speculation. *Sleep, 25,* 606–614.

Carskadon, M. A., Acebo, C., & Jenni, O. G. (2004). Regulation of adolescent sleep: Implications for behavior. *Annals of the New York Academy of Sciences, 1021,* 276–291.

Carskadon, M.A., Acebo, C., Richardson, G.S., Tate, B.A., & Seifer, R. (1997). An approach to studying circadian rhythms of adolescent humans. *Journal of Biological Rhythms, 12,* 278–289.

Carskadon, M. A., Harvey, K., Duke, P., Anders, T. F., Litt, I. F., & Dement, W. C. (1980). Pubertal changes in daytime sleepiness. *Sleep, 2,* 453–460.

Carskadon, M. A., Vieira, C., & Acebo, C. (1993). Association between puberty and delayed phase preference. *Sleep, 16,* 258–262.

Carskadon, M. A., Wolfson, A. R., Acebo, C., Tzischinsky, O., & Seifer, R. (1998). Adolescent sleep patterns, circadian timing, and sleepiness at a transition to early school days. *Sleep, 21,* 871–881.

Chen, E., Martin, A. D., & Matthews, K. A. (2006). Socioeconomic status and health: Do gradients differ within childhood and adolescence? *Social Science & Medicine, 62,* 2161–2170.

Chervin, R. D., Dillon, J. E., Archbold, K. H. & Ruzicka, D. L. (2003). Conduct problems and symptoms of sleep disorders in children. *Journal of American Academy of Child & Adolescent Psychiatry, 42,* 201–208.

Christakis, D. A., Ebel, B. E., Rivara, F. P., & Zimmerman, F. J. (2004). Television, video, and computer game usage in children under 11 years of age. *The Journal of Pediatrics, 145,* 652–656.

Christakis, D. A., Zimmerman, F. J., DiGiuseppe, D. L., & McCarty, C. A. (2004). Early television exposure and subsequent attentional problems in children. *Pediatrics, 113,* 708–713.

Crowley, S. J., Acebo, C., & Carskadon, M. A. (2007). Sleep, circadian rhythms, and delayed phase in adolescence. *Sleep Medicine, 8,* 602–612.

Cortesi, F., Giannotti, F., Sebastiani, T., Bruni, O., & Ottaviano, S. (2004). Knowledge of sleep in Italian high school students: Pilot-test of a school-based sleep educational program. *Journal of Adolescent Health, 34,* 344–351.

Curcio, G., Ferrara, M., & De Gennaro, L. (2006). Sleep loss, learning capacity and academic performance. *Sleep Medicine Reviews, 10,* 323–337.

Currie, J., & Lin, W. (2007). Chipping away at health: More on the relationship between income and child health. *Health Affairs, 26,* 331–344.

Dahl, R. E. (1999). The consequences of insufficient sleep for adolescents: Links between sleep and emotional regulation. *Phi Delta Kappan, 80,* 354–359.

Dahl, R. E., Ryan, N. D., Matty, M. K., Birmaher, B., Al-Shabbout, M., Williamson, D. E., & Kupfer, D. J. (1996). Sleep onset abnormalities in depressed adolescents. *Biological Psychiatry, 39,* 400–410.

Dennison, B. A., Erb, T. A., & Jenkins, P. L. (2002). Television viewing and television in bedroom associated with overweight risk among low-income preschool children. *Pediatrics, 109,* 1028–1035.

de Sousa, I. C., Araujo, J. F., & de Azevedo, C. V. M. (2007). The effect of a sleep hygiene education program on the sleep-wake cycle of Brazilian adolescent students. *Sleep and Biological Rhythms, 5,* 251–258.

Dodge, K. A., Pettit, G. S., & Bates, J. E. (1994). Socialization mediators of the relation between socioeconomic status and child conduct problems. *Child Development, 65,* 649–665.

Drake, C., Nickel, C., Burduvali, E., Roth, T., Jefferson, C., & Badia, P. (2003). The Pediatric Daytime Sleepiness Scale (PDSS): Sleep habits and school outcomes in middle-school children. *Sleep, 26,* 455–458.

Drapeau, C., Hamel-Hebert, I., Robillard, R., Selmaoui, B., Filipini, D., & Carrier, J. (2006). Challenging sleep in aging: The effects of 200 mg of caffeine during the evening in young and middle-aged moderate caffeine consumers. *Journal of Sleep Research, 15,* 133–141.

Dryfoos, J. G. (2000). *Safe passage: Making it through adolescence in a risky society: What parents, schools, and communities can do.* New York, NY: Oxford University Press.

DuRant, R. H., Baranowski, T., Johnson, M., & Thompson, W. O. (1994). The relationship among television watching, physical activity, and body composition of young children. *Pediatrics, 94,* 449–455.

Eccles, J. S., Midgley, C., Wigfield, A., Buchanan, C. M., Reuman, D., Flanagan, C., & Iver, D. M. (1993). Development during adolescence: The impact of stage-environment fit on young adolescents' experiences in schools and in families. *American Psychologist, 48*, 90–101.

Eggermont, S., & Van den Bulck, J. (2006). Nodding off or switching off? The use of popular media as a sleep aid in secondary-school children. *Journal of Paediatrics and Child Health, 42*, 428–433.

Epstein, R., Chillag, N., & Lavie, P. (1998). Starting times of school: Effects on daytime functioning of fifth-grade children in Israel. *Sleep, 21*, 250–256.

Fallone, G., Owens, J. A., & Deane, J. (2002). Sleepiness in children and adolescents: Clinical implications. *Sleep Medicine Reviews, 6*, 287–306.

Felner, R. D., Brand, S., DuBois, D. L., Adan, A. M., Mulhall, P. F., & Evans, E. G. (1995). Socioeconomic disadvantage, proximal environmental experiences, and socioemotional and academic adjustment in early adolescence: Investigation of a mediated effects model. *Child Development, 66*, 774–792.

Fredriksen, K., Rhodes, J., Reddy, R., & Way, N. (2004). Sleepless in Chicago: Tracking the effects of adolescent sleep loss during the middle school years. *Child Development, 75*, 84–95.

Fuligni, A. J., & Harway, C. (2006). Daily variation in adolescents' sleep, activities, and psychological well-being. *Journal of Research on Adolescence, 16*, 353–378.

Fulkerson, J. A., Sherwood, N. E., Perry, C. L., Neumark-Sztainer, D., & Story, M. (2004). Depressive symptoms and adolescent eating and health behaviors: A multifaceted view in a population-based sample. *Preventive Medicine, 38*, 865–875.

Gentile, D. A., Lynch, P. J., Linder, J. R., & Walsh, D. A. (2004). The effects of violent video game habits on adolescent hostility, aggressive behaviors, and school performance. *Journal of Adolescence, 27*, 5–22.

Ghanizadeh, A., Kianpoor, M., Rezaei, M., Rezaei, H., Moini, R., Aghakhani, K., ... Moeini, S. R. (2008). Sleep patterns and habits in high school students in Iran. *Annals of General Psychiatry, 7*, E5.

Gibson, E. S., Powles, A. C. P., Thabane, L., O'Brien, S., Molnar, D. S., Trajanovic, N., ... Chilcott-Tanser, L. (2006). "Sleepiness" is serious in adolescence: Two surveys of 3235 Canadian students. *BMC Public Health, 6*, 116.

Gortmaker, S. L., Must, A., Sobol, A. M., Peterson, K., Colditz, G. A., & Dietz, W. H. (1996). Television viewing as a cause of increasing obesity among children in the United States, 1986–1990. *Archives of Pediatric and Adolescent Medicine, 150*, 356–362.

Guilleminault, C., & Pelayo, R. (2000). Narcolepsy in children: A practical guide to its diagnosis, treatment and follow-up. *Pediatric Drugs, 2*, 1–9.

Gupta, R., Bhatia, M. S., Chhabra, V., Sharma, S., Dahiya, D., Semalti, K., ... Dua, R. S. (2008). Sleep patterns of urban school-going adolescents. *Indian Pediatrics, 45*, 183–189.

Hale, L. (2005). Who has time to sleep? *Journal of Public Health, 27*, 205–211.

Hale, L., Berger, L. M., LeBourgeois, M. K., & Brooks-Gunn, J. (2009). Social and demographic predictors of preschoolers' bedtime routines. *Journal of Developmental and Behavioral Pediatrics, 30*, 394–402.

Hall, G. S. (1904). *Adolescence: Its psychology and its relations to physiology, anthropology, sociology, sex, crime, religion, and education (Vols. I & II)*. New York, NY: Appleton.

Hardway, C., & Fuligni, A. J. (2006). Dimensions of family connectedness among adolescents with Mexican, Chinese and European backgrounds. *Developmental Psychology, 42*, 1246–1258.

Harris Interactive & CTIA- The Wireless Association. (2008, September 12). *Research Report- Teenagers: A generation unplugged*. Retrieved January 17, 2010, from http://www.ctia.org/advocacy/research/index.cfm/AID/11483.

Harrison, K., & Cantor, J. (1999). Tales from the screen: Enduring fright reactions to scary media. *Media Psychology, 1*, 97–116.

Higuchi, S., Motohashi, Y., Liu, Y., Ahara, M., & Kaneko, Y. (2003). Effects of VDT tasks with a bright display at night on melatonin, core temperature, heart rate, and sleepiness. *Journal of Applied Physiology, 94*, 1773–1776.

Higuchi, S., Motohashi, Y., Maeda, T., & Ishibashi, K. (2005). Relationship between individual difference in melatonin suppression by light and habitual bedtime. *Journal of Physiological Anthropology, 24*(4), 419–423.

Higuchi, S., Motohashi, Y., Liu, Y., & Maeda, A. (2005). Effects of playing a computer game using a bright display on presleep physiological variables, sleep latency, slow wave sleep and REM sleep. *Journal of Sleep Research, 14*, 267–273.

Hindmarch, I., Rigney, U., Stanley, N., Quinlan, P., Rycroft, J. & Lane, J. (2000). A naturalistic investigation of the effects of day-long consumption of tea, coffee and water on alertness, sleep onset and sleep quality. *Psychopharmacology, 149*, 203–216.

Iglowstein, I., Jenni, O. G., Molinari, L., & Largo, R. H. (2003). Sleep duration from infancy to adolescence: Reference values and generational trends. *Pediatrics, 111*, 302–307.

Jenni, O. G., Achermann, P., & Carskadon, M. A. (2005). Homeostatic sleep regulation in adolescents. *Sleep, 28*, 1446–1454.

Jenni, O. G., & Carskadon, M. A. (2004). Spectral analysis of the sleep electroencephalogram during adolescence. *Sleep, 27*, 774–783.

Johnson, J. G., Cohen, P., Kasen, S., First, M. B., & Brook, J. S. (2004). Association between television viewing and sleep problems during adolescence and early adulthood. *Archives of Pediatrics and Adolescent Medicine, 158*, 562–568.

Johnson, J. G., Cohen, P., Smailes, E. M., Kasen, S., & Brook, J. S. (2002). Television viewing and aggressive behavior during adolescence and adulthood. *Science, 295*, 2468–2471.

Kaneita, Y., Yokoyama, E., Harano, S., Tamaki, T., Suzuki, H., Munezawa, T., ... Ohida, T. (2009). Associations between sleep disturbance and mental health status: A longitudinal study of Japanese junior high school students. *Sleep Medicine, 10*, 780–786.

Kessler, R. C., Chiu, W. T., Demler, O., & Walters, E. E. (2005). Prevalence, severity, and comorbidity of 12-month DSM-IV disorders in the National Comorbidity Survey Replication. *Archives of General Psychiatry, 62*, 617–627.

Kirmil-Gray, K., Eagleston, J. R., Gibson, E., & Thoresen, C. E. (1984). Sleep disturbance in adolescents: Sleep quality, sleep habits, beliefs about sleep, and daytime functioning. *Journal of Youth and Adolescence, 13*, 375–384.

Kubota, T., Uchiyama, M., Suzuki, H., Shibui, K., Kim, K., Tan, X., ... Inoue, S. (2002). Effects of nocturnal bright light on saliva melatonin, core body temperature and sleep propensity rhythms in human subjects. *Neuroscience Research, 42*, 115–122.

Laberge, L., Petit, D., Simard, C., Vitaro, F., Tremblay, R. E., & Montplaisir, J. (2001). Development of sleep patterns in early adolescence. *Journal of Sleep Research, 10*, 59–67.

Larson, R., & Richards, M.H. (1989). Introduction: The changing life space of early adolescence. *Journal of Youth and Adolescence, 18*, 501–509.

LeBourgeois, M. K., Giannotti, F., Cortesi, F., Wolfson, A. R., & Harsh, J. (2005). The relationship between reported sleep quality and sleep hygiene in Italian and American adolescents. *Pediatrics, 115*, 257–265.

Lee, K., McEnany, G., & Weekes, D. (1999). Gender differences in sleep patterns for early adolescents. *Journal of Adolescent Health, 24*, 16–20.

Liu, X., Zhao, Z., Jia, C., & Buysse, D. J. (2008). Sleep patterns and problems among Chinese adolescents. *Pediatrics, 121*, 1165–1173.

Loessl, B., Valerius, G., Kopasz, M., Hornyak, M., Riemann, D., & Voderholzer, U. (2008). Are adolescents chronically sleep-deprived? An investigation of sleep habits of adolescents in the southwest of Germany. *Child: Care, Health and Development, 34*, 549–556.

Ludden, A. B., & Wolfson, A. R. (2010). Understanding adolescent caffeine use: Connecting use patterns with expectancies, reasons, and sleep. *Health Education and Behavior, 37*(3), 330–342.

Marco, C. A., Wolfson, A. R., Rabidou, J., Wilkey, S., & LeChasseur, K. (2002). School and weekend night sleep patterns in middle school students: A pilot study. *Sleep (Supplement), 25*, A428.

Marco, C. A., Wolfson, A. R., Sparling, M., & Azuaje, A. (manuscript in preparation). Socioeconomic disparities in young adolescents' actigraph-measured sleep patterns.

Martin, S., & Oppenheim, K. (2007). Video gaming: General and pathological use. *Trends & Tudes, 6*(3), 1–7.

McLoyd, V. C., Kaplan, R., Purtell, K. M., Bagley, E. J., Hardaway, C. R., & Smalls, C. (2009) Poverty and socioeconomic disadvantage in adolescence. In L. Steinberg & R. M. Lerner (Eds.), *Handbook of adolescent psychology* (3rd ed., pp. 444–491). New York, NY: Wiley.

Meijer, A. M. (2008). Chronic sleep reduction, functioning at school and school achievement in preadolescents. *Journal of Sleep Research, 17,* 395–405.

Menna-Baretto, L., & Wey, D. (2008). Time constraints in the school environment: What does a sleepy student tell us? *Mind, Brain and Education, 2,* 24–28.

Mesquita, G., & Reimão, R. (2007). Nightly use of computer by adolescents: Its effect on quality of sleep. *Arquivos de Neuro-Psiquiatria, 65,* 428–432.

Mitru, G., Millrood, D. L., & Mateika, J. H. (2002). The impact of sleep on learning and behavior in adolescents. *Teachers College Record, 104,* 704–726.

Moore, P. J., Adler, N. E., Williams, D. R., & Jackson, J. S. (2002). Socioeconomic status and health: The role of sleep. *Psychosomatic Medicine, 64,* 337–344.

Morrison, D. N., McGee, R., & Stanton, W. R. (1992). Sleep problems in adolescence. *Journal of the American Academy of Child and Adolescent Psychiatry, 31,* 94–99.

National Sleep Foundation (2000). *Adolescent sleep needs and patterns: Research report and resource guide.* Washington, DC: Author.

National Sleep Foundation. (2005). *School start times tool kit.* Washington, DC: Author.

National Sleep Foundation. (2006). *Sleep in America poll.* Washington, DC: Author.

Nixon, G. M., Thompson, J. M., Han, D.Y., Becroft, D. M., Clark, P. M., Robinson, E., ... Mitchell, E.A. (2009). Falling asleep: The determinants of sleep latency. *Archives of Disease in Childhood, 94,* 686–689.

Oberstar, J.V., Bernstein, G.A., & Thuras, P.D. (2002). Caffeine use and dependence in adolescents: One-year follow-up. *Journal of Child and Adolescent Psychopharmacology, 12,* 127–135.

O'Dea, J.A. (2003). Consumption of nutritional supplements among adolescents: Usage and perceived benefits. *Health Education Research, 18,* 98–107.

Oka, Y., Suzuki, S., & Inoue, Y. (2008). Bedtime activities, sleep environment, and sleep/wake patterns of Japanese elementary school children. *Behavioral Sleep Medicine, 6,* 220–233.

Orbeta, R., Overpeck, M., Ramcharran, D., Kogan, M., & Ledsky, R. (2006). High caffeine intake in adolescents: Associations with difficulty sleeping and feeling tired in the morning. *Journal of Adolescent Health, 38,* 451–453.

Owens, J., Maxim, R., McGuinn, M., Nobile, C., Msall, M. & Alario, A. (1999). Television-viewing habits and sleep disturbance in schoolchildren. *Pediatrics, 104,* e27.

Owens, J.A., Stahl, J., Patton, A., Reddy, U., & Crouch, M. (2006). Sleep practices, attitudes, and beliefs in inner city middle school children: A mixed-methods study. *Behavioral Sleep Medicine, 4,* 114–134.

Paavonen, E. J., Almqvist, F., Tamminen, T., Moilanen, I., Piha, J., Rasanen, E., Aronen, E. T. (2002). Poor sleep and psychiatric symptoms at school: An epidemiological study. *European Child and Adolescent Psychiatry, 11*, 10–17.

Paavnonen, E. J., Pennonen, M., Roine, M., Valkonen, S., & Lahikainen, A. R. (2006). TV exposure associated with sleep disturbances in 5- and 6- year old children. *Journal of Sleep Research, 15*, 154–161.

Pagel, J. F., Forister, N., & Kwiatkowski, C. (2007). Adolescent sleep disturbance and school performance: The confounding variable of socioeconomics. *Journal of Clinical Sleep Medicine, 3*, 19–23.

Paraskakis, E., Ntouros, T., Ntokos, M., Siavana, O., Bitsori, M., & Galanakis, E. (2008). Siesta and sleep patterns in a sample of adolescents in Greece. *Pediatrics International, 50*, 690–693.

Patten, C. A., Choi, W. S., Gillin, J. C., & Pierce, J. P. (2000). Depressive symptoms and cigarette smoking predict development and persistence of sleep problems in US adolescents. *Pediatrics, 106*, e23.

Penetar, D., McCann, U., Thorne, D., Kamimori, G., Galinski, C., Sing, H., … Belenky, G. (1993). Caffeine reversal of sleep deprivation effects on alertness and mood. *Psychopharmacology, 112*, 359–365.

Pollak, C. P., & Bright, D. (2003). Caffeine consumption and weekly sleep patterns in US seventh- eighth-, and ninth-graders. *Pediatrics, 111*, 42–46.

Randler, C. (2008). Differences in sleep and circadian preference between Eastern and Western German Adolescents. *Chronobiology International, 25*, 565–575.

Reissig, C. J., Strain, E. C., & Griffiths, R. R. (2009). Caffeinated energy drinks—A growing problem. *Drug and Alcohol Dependence, 99*, 1–10.

Rideout, V. J., Foehr, U. G., & Roberts, D. F. (2010). *Generation M²: Media in the lives of 8–18 year olds.* Menlo Park, CA: Henry J. Kaiser Family Foundation.

Roberts, R. E., Lewinsohn, P. M., & Seeley, J. R. (1995). Symptoms of DSM-III-R major depression in adolescence: Evidence from an epidemiological survey. *Journal of the American Academy of Child & Adolescent Psychiatry, 34*, 1608–1617.

Robinson, T. N. (1999). Reducing children's television to prevent obesity: A randomized controlled trial. *JAMA: The Journal of the American Medical Association, 282*, 1561–1567.

Robinson, T. N. (2001). Television viewing and childhood obesity. *The Pediatric Clinics of North America, 48*, 1017–1025.

Rossi, C. M., Campbell, A. L., Vo, O. T., Marco, C. A., & Wolfson, A. R. (2002). Middle school sleep-smart program: A pilot evaluation. *Sleep (Supplement), 25*, A279.

Saarenpaa-Heikkila, O., Laippala, P., & Koivikko, M. (2001). Subjective daytime sleepiness and its predictors in Finnish adolescents in an interview study. *Acta Pædiatrica, 90*, 552–557.

Sadeh, A. (2007). Consequences of sleep loss or sleep disruption in children. *Sleep Medicine Clinics, 2*, 513–520.

Sadeh, A., Dahl, R.E., Shahar, G., & Rosenblat- Stein, S. (2009). Sleep and the transition to adolescence: A longitudinal study. *Sleep, 32,* 1602–1609.

Sadeh, A., Gruber, R. & Raviv, A. (2002). Sleep, neurobehavioral functioning, and behavior problems in school-age children. *Child Development, 73,* 405–417.

Sharif, I., & Sargent, J.D. (2006). Association between television, movie, and video game exposure and school performance. *Pediatrics, 118,* 1061–1070.

Singer, M. I., Slovak, K., Frierson, T., & York, P. (1998). Viewing preferences, symptoms of psychological trauma, and violent behaviors among children who watch television. *Journal of the American Academy of Child and Adolescent Psychiatry, 37,* 1041–1048.

Smith, A. (2002). Effects of caffeine on human behavior. *Food and Chemical Toxicology, 40,* 1243–1255.

Snel, J. (1993). Coffee and caffeine: Sleep and wakefulness. In S. Garattini (Ed.), Caffeine, Coffee and Health (pp. 255–290). New York, NY: Raven Press.

Söderqvist, F., Carlberg, M., & Hardell, L. (2008). Use of wireless telephones and self-reported health symptoms: A population-based study among Swedish adolescents aged 15–19 years. *Environmental Health, 7,* 1–10.

Sparling, M., Azuaje, A., Marco, C. & Wolfson, A. R. (2009, April). *Socioeconomic factors in young adolescents' sleep disparities.* Poster session presented at the biennial meeting of the Society for Research in Child Development, Denver, CO.

Spaulding, N., Butler, E., Daigle, A., Dandrow, C., & Wolfson, A. R. (2005). Sleep habits and daytime sleepiness in students attending early versus late starting elementary schools. *Sleep (Supplement), 28,* A78.

Steenari, M. R., Vuontela, V., Paavonen, E. J., Carlson, S., Fjallberg, M., & Aronen, E. (2003). Working memory and sleep in 6- to 13-year-old schoolchildren. *Journal of the American Academy of Child & Adolescent Psychiatry, 42,* 85–92.

Steinberg, L., & Levine, A. (1997). *You and your adolescent: A parents' guide for ages 10–20.* Dunmore, PA: HarperCollins.

Stepanski, E.J., & Wyatt, J.K. (2003). Use of sleep hygiene in the treatment of insomnia. *Sleep Medicine Reviews, 7,* 215–225.

Steptoe, A., O'Donnell, K., Marmot, M. & Wardle, J. (2008). Positive affect, psychological well-being, and good sleep. *Journal of Psychosomatic Research, 64,* 409–415.

Strauch, I., & Meier, B. (1988). Sleep need in adolescents: A longitudinal approach. *Sleep, 11,* 378–386.

Szymczak, J.T., Jasi ska, M., Pawlak, E., & Zwierzykowska, M. (1993). Annual and weekly changes in the sleep-wake rhythm of school children. *Sleep, 16,* 433–435.

Taveras, E. M., Hohman, K. H., Price, S., Gortmaker, S. L., Sonneville, K. (2009). Televisions in the bedrooms of racial/ethnic minority children: How did they get there and how do we get them out? *Clinical Pediatrics, 48,* 715–719.

Taylor, D. J., Jenni, O. G., Acebo, C., & Carskadon, M. A. (2005). Sleep tendency during extended wakefulness: Insights into adolescent sleep regulation and behavior. *Journal of Sleep Research, 14,* 239–244.

Thorleifsdottir, B., Björnsson, J. K., Benediktsdottir, B., Gislason, T., & Kristbjarnarson, H. (2002). Sleep and sleep habits from childhood to young adulthood over a 10-year period. *Journal of Psychosomatic Research, 53,* 529–537.

Tynjala, J., Kannas, L., & Levalahti, E. (1997). Perceived tiredness among adolescents and its association with sleep habits and use of psychoactive substances. *Journal of Sleep Research, 6,* 189–198.

Urdan, T., & Klein, S. (1998). *Early Adolescence: A review of the literature.* Paper prepared for the U.S. Department of Education, Office of Educational Research and Improvement: Washington, DC.

Van den Bulck, J. (2003). Text messaging as a cause of sleep interruption in adolescents, evidence from a cross-sectional study. *Journal of Sleep Research, 12,* 263.

Van den Bulck, J. (2004). Television viewing, computer game playing, and Internet use and self-reported time to bed and time out of bed in secondary-school children. *Sleep, 27,* 101–104.

Van den Bulck, J. (2007). Adolescent use of mobile phones for calling and for sending text messages after lights out: Results from a prospective cohort study with a one-year follow-up. *Sleep, 30,* 1220–1223.

Vo, O. T., LeChasseur, K., Wolfson, A., & Marco, C. (2003). Sleepy pre-teens: Second pilot of Sleep-Smart Program in 7th graders. *Sleep (Supplement), 26,* A411.

Wahlstrom, K. L. (2002a). Accommodating the sleep patterns of adolescents within current educational structures: An uncharted path. In M. Carskadon (ed.), *Adolescent sleep patterns: Biological, social, and psychological influences* (pp. 172–197). Cambridge, UK: Cambridge University Press.

Wahlstrom, K. L. (2002b). Changing times: Findings from the first longitudinal study of later high school start times. *NASSP Bulletin, 86,* 3–21.

Wallenius, M., Rimpelä, A., Punamäki, R., & Lintonen, T. (2009). Digital game playing motives among adolescents: Relations to parent-child communication, school performance, sleeping habits, and perceived health. *Journal of Applied Developmental Psychology, 30,* 463–474.

Wigfield, A., Byrnes, J. P., & Eccles, J. S. (2006). Development during early and middle adolescence. In P.A. Alexander & P.H. Winne (Eds.), *Handbook of educational psychology* (2nd ed.) (pp. 87–114). Mahwah, NJ: Lawrence Earlbaum Associates.

Whalen, D. J., Silk, J. S., Semel, M., Forbes, E. E., Ryan, N. D., Axelson, D.A., ... Dahl, R.E. (2008). Caffeine consumption, sleep, and affect in the natural environments of depressed youth and healthy controls. *Journal of Pediatric Psychology, 33,* 358–367.

Wolfson, A. R. (2009). [Survey and actigraphically measured middle-school sleep patterns]. Unpublished raw data.

Wolfson, A. R. (2002). Bridging the gap between research and practice: What will adolescents' sleep-wake patterns look like in the 21st century? In M.A. Carskadon (Ed.), *Adolescent sleep patterns: Biological, social, and psychological influences* (pp. 198–219). New York, NY: Cambridge University Press.

Wolfson, A. R., Acebo, C., Fallone, G., & Carskadon, M.A. (2003). Actigraphically-estimated sleep patterns of middle school students. *Sleep (Supplement) 26*, G0313.

Wolfson, A. R. (2007). Adolescent sleep update: Narrowing the gap between research and practice. *Sleep Review: The Journal for Sleep Specialists*, 8, 28–32.

Wolfson, A. R., & Armitage, R. (2009). Sleep and its relation to adolescent depression. In S. Nolen-Hoeksema (Ed.) *Handbook of depression in adolescents* (pp. 279–301). New York, NY: Routledge.

Wolfson, A. R., & Carskadon, M. A. (1998). Sleep schedules and daytime functioning in adolescents. *Child Development, 69*, 875–887.

Wolfson, A. R., & Carskadon, M. C. (2003). Understanding adolescents' sleep patterns and school performance: A critical appraisal. *Sleep Medicine Reviews*, 7, 491–506.

Wolfson, A. R., & Carskadon, M. A. (2005). A survey of factors influencing high school start times. *NASSP Bulletin, 89*, 47–64.

Wolfson, A. R., Spaulding, N. L., Dandrow, C., & Baroni, E. M. (2007). Middle school start times: The importance of a good night's sleep for young adolescents. *Behavioral Sleep Medicine, 5*, 194–209.

Wolfson, A. R., Tzischinsky, O., Brown, C., Darley, C., Acebo, C. & Carskadon, M. A. (1995). Sleep, behavior, and stress at the transition to senior high school. *Sleep Research, 24*, 115.

Youngstedt, S. D. (2005). Effects of exercise on sleep. *Clinics in Sports Medicine, 24*, 355–365.

Zimmerman, F. J. (2008) *Children's media use and sleep problems: Issues and unanswered questions*. Menlo Park, CA: Kaiser Family Foundation.

Part III

Assessment of Sleep, Family Functioning, and the Ecology of Economic Disadvantage

13

The Ecology of Economic Disadvantage and Children's Sleep

Brian P. Ackerman and Eleanor D. Brown

Introduction

Children's sleep patterns and problems are complex biopsychosocial phenomena that are affected by income poverty and poverty-related stressors through a variety of mechanisms. Most centrally, children's sleep is both an outcome of and a contributor to proximal parenting processes, and sleep functioning is influenced by income strains and associated stressors indirectly through adult-child interactions. Additionally, however, children's sleep may be influenced directly by family-level stressors associated with income poverty that affect all individuals and aspects of family functioning, such as poor housing quality, maternal relationship conflict and disruptions, and residential instability. Similarly, aspects of settings external to impoverished families, like exposure to neighborhood violence, environmental toxins, and school failures, may influence children directly. All of these factors within and outside the family contribute to the ecology of economic disadvantage as experienced by children, and all pose risks for normative development.

This chapter describes recent approaches to conceptualizing the ecology of disadvantage in relation to children's sleep. We treat sleep as an indicator and outcome of environmental adversity. Four salient trends in the research literature organize the chapter. The first is the change from the predominant use of socioeconomic status (SES) to represent environmental adversity for poor children to a focus on income poverty and the effects of chronic economic strain on family functioning, and on child physical health and psychosocial adjustment. The second concerns identification and representations of poverty-related stressors that reflect and affect parent and child functioning independently of economic resources, and thus help explain diversity in the outcomes of poor children. Poverty-related stressors often are represented as multifactorial aggregates (i.e., cumulative risk indexes) based on recognition of the natural co-variation of risk factors for disadvantaged families.

The third is identification of indirect and direct mechanisms linking environmental stressors and child functioning, and moderators of those links. The indirect pathways are represented by family stress models (Conger & Dogan, 2006). An emergent focus for conceptualizing both indirect and direct effects concerns physiological models of how chronic stressors get "under the skin" (Repetti, Taylor, & Seeman, 2002). The moderators reflect findings that the links occasionally differ with race/ ethnicity and gender. The fourth is consideration of developmental effects involving the timing, duration/chronicity, and dynamic changes in income poverty and poverty-related stressors, and the differential sensitivity of younger and older children and adolescents.

The chapter has several sections. We begin with a discussion of conceptual issues and stress models that frame interpretation of class and poverty effects. The next section briefly considers the strengths and weaknesses of low SES as a representation of the ecology of disadvantage. The following sections are discussions of income poverty and representations of poverty-related stressors.

Conceptual Issues and Stress Models

Interpretations of poverty effects in relation to family functioning and children's sleep implicitly privilege social factors as the primary causes of physical and psychological distress, and focus on stress and stress reactions as the proximal mechanisms of disruption and disorganization. The assumption about social causation raises several issues common to all representations of the ecology of disadvantage. We discuss these issues in this initial section to prepare evaluations of those representations and to avoid repetition. We focus on causal models and inference problems, moderators of effects, key measurement problems, and stress mechanisms. The reduction of poverty-related risks to stress mechanisms reflects our focus on children's sleep, and the need to identify specific factors linking income poverty and poverty correlates with sleep patterns and disruptions.

Causal Models and Inferences

Most uses of social class and income poverty as explanatory constructs reflect the assumption that adverse social and environmental factors are powerful causes of the behavior problems of children and adults. The social gradient of health, for example, refers to the well-documented positive relation between economic resources and physical and psychological health (Adler et al., 1994; Chen, Matthews, & Boyce, 2002). The causal assumption is that socioeconomic disadvantage is a proxy for increased exposure to a toxic physical environment and social stratification processes (Massey, 2007) that are physically and psychologically debilitating. Similarly, most explanations of the negative correlations between family income and child problem behaviors assume that income poverty degrades family functioning.

The challenges to these assumptions are well-known. One challenge is that many of the relations could reflect personal characteristics that place individuals in adverse environments. Social selection factors focusing on lifestyle and health-related behaviors (e.g., smoking, alcohol use, lack of exercise), for instance, could contribute to the social gradient of health. Lack of academic and employment skills of parents could explain family residence in risky neighborhoods. Genetic factors could constrain the cognitive competence and self-regulation of both children and parents that result in poor academic skills and that limit the ability to take advantage of opportunities to escape poverty. In these and other ways, behavioral outcomes that seem to reflect stress reactions could instead reflect stress generation associated with problematic personal characteristics.

Another challenge is the need to distinguish income poverty and poverty-related stressors in relation to child outcomes. Many studies treat social class and income poverty as singular and categorical representations of the ecology of disadvantage (i.e., poor/non-poor). This treatment

obscures diversity among poor families and ignores possible contributions of omitted variables.

A third challenge concerns examination of direct relations between
contextual adversity and child behavior. Indirect pathways are well-
documented, showing that economic stress and strain is communicated
to children through marital discord, maternal mood, and disrupted and
negative parenting processes. Less attention has been devoted to family-
level variables, which affect and reflect all aspects of family and individual
functioning, and are sources of more direct effects. Most treatments,
for example, represent economic disadvantages as a distal variable that is
external to dyadic interactions. It also may function more proximally,
however. Factors such as the physical characteristics of the home,
interpersonal and residential instability, and the lack of predictable and
organized agendas and routines, are family-level factors associated with
poverty that are likely to have proximal and direct effects on child
functioning, including sleep.

A final challenge for poverty models is the frequent confound of
race/ethnicity and class. Given that African American and Latino families
are disproportionately poor in the United States, some adaptations and
effects associated with poverty could reflect either racial/ethnic minority
culture or social class. Similarly, the confound encourages a "deficit"
model (Coll et al., 1996), in which any observed differences for minority
families and children in comparison to the majority group are interpreted
as poverty-related deficits.

Moderators of Effects

Considerable research has shown that the strength of the associations
between environmental adversity and family and child functioning often
differ for the groups comprising sociodemographic variables like race/
ethnicity, child gender, and SES. In this situation, the sociodemographic
variable moderates the relation between adversity and functioning. First,
relations may differ with class and poverty status. A good example is that
the beneficial effects of authoritative parental styles that foster independence and autonomy among young adolescents are more apparent for
low-risk families and in low-risk neighborhoods than for impoverished
families (McElhaney & Allen, 2001; Simons et al., 2002). Indeed, stronger

control and "no-nonsense" parenting may be more adaptive for disadvantaged families in that they protect children from neighborhood risks. Similarly, the relation between risk factors and outcomes usually is decreased by "democratic" decision-making in white families but may be increased for African American families (Gutman, Sameroff, & Eccles, 2002). Another example with particular relevance is that relations between children's sleep activity and cognitive/academic functioning varies with SES and parental education (Buckhalt, El-Sheikh, & Keller, 2007; Buckhalt, El-Sheikh, Keller, & Kelly, 2009; see El-Sheikh & Kelly, chapter 1 in this volume).

Second, poverty effects may differ with race/ethnicity, age, gender, and other variables. Black families are more likely than white families to live in neighborhoods characterized by high levels of family poverty ("concentrated" poverty) and to be poor for more years (Wilson & Gates, 2009), for example, which suggests that the experiences of economic disadvantage may differ for black and white families. Similarly, the risk and normativeness of single and adolescent parenthood may differ for black and white children (Wilson & Gates, 2009). Developmental variations arise because young children have less direct exposure than adolescents to neighborhood variables.

Measurement Issues

We briefly note four issues that challenge poverty researchers. The first is that family income estimates are notoriously problematic, especially for impoverished informants. Such estimates often are retrospective and vary with adult informant. The estimates also vary depending on the income source (e.g., employment or all sources), and they often reflect a snapshot view of economic resources that obscures dynamic variations. Mean estimates across several assessments may be more reliable (Conger & Dogan, 2006), though they too are insensitive to income variations. The second is the source variance problem concerning the use of a single informant to report about aspects of the ecology of disadvantage, family and adult variables, and child functioning. The problem is particularly acute for impoverished families, given the association between income poverty and single parent families.

The third is that the applicability of measures of parenting and family functioning sometimes is questionable for lower income or ethnic minority families (Coll et al., 1996). Many measures reflect the practices and values of middle income parents, and application to lower income families raises the problem of a deficit model in which difference is cast as deficiency. Subcultural adaptations to a high-risk environment and subsistence economy may be viewed as maladaptive from the perspective of majority culture. Extending the point to a stress perspective, practices that are considered nonnormative and a product of stressful and disruptive circumstances for more affluent families may be normative for lower income families. Fourth, many risk factors related to child outcomes have stronger effects for poor children than for other children. Linear models, dominant in poverty research, often are insensitive to these nonlinear effects.

Stress Models

Class and poverty models of child and family functioning, which work through stress mechanisms, require some understanding of how environmental adversity gets "under the (child's) skin" (Repetti et al., 2002). Two models focus on individual differences in stress reactivity. Both relate to children's sleep to the extent that sleep reflects the biological calibration of stress-response systems and that these systems are sensitive to the social surround. The BSC model describes individual differences in biological sensitivity to context (BSC) rooted primarily in temperament and endogeneous variables (Belsky, Bakermans-Kranenburg, & van IJzendoorn, 2007; Boyce & Ellis, 2005), but not rooted specifically in the ecology of disadvantage. Boyce and Ellis (2005) for instance, distinguish between "orchid" and "dandelion" children. The "orchid" children are acutely sensitive to both negative and positive contexts, and accordingly tend both to wilt and thrive respectively more (or more quickly) than the relatively insensitive "dandelion" children. Belsky and Pluess (2009) extend the model by arguing that differential susceptibility to environmental context may also be rooted in early nurturing experiences (e.g., "fetal programming") associated with the ecology of disadvantage.

The early experience model in contrast, is rooted in the ecology of disadvantage in terms of the higher likelihood of highly stressful negative experiences for impoverished mothers and young children. One argument is that these experiences calibrate (i.e., "scar") neuroendocrine systems that mediate stress responses early in brain development so that the systems are "set" to be more sensitive and reactive to current environmental stressors. This perspective focuses on vulnerability to current stressors (i.e., "reactivity") and does not require maladjustment in the absence of environmental adversity. Kaffman and Meaney (2007) provide examples by showing that stressing pregnant rats and handling infant rats results in long-term differences in offspring stress reactivity. Another early experience version focuses on critical or sensitive developmental periods in which exposure or lack of exposure to some environmental ingredient changes biological mechanisms in development.

The third model concerns the cumulative impact of stress, with "cumulative" referencing the accumulation of a high number of risk factors over time. The simplest variant focuses on dose–response relations. The cumulative model is a strong poverty model because environmental stressors covary with income poverty, which generates a subset of families and children experiencing high levels of environmental adversity, and because income poverty endures over time for a substantial subset of poor families, including many of those experiencing highly adverse environments at any one time. The mechanism is repeated mobilization of the multiple physiological systems that respond to stress, with "allostatic load" marking the associated wear and tear on the body (Evans, 2003). Continual activation and deactivation of stress response systems results in high allostatic load as measured by resting blood pressure, cortisol levels, and other physiological indicators.

A fourth model concerns stress pathways over time, and is nonspecific regarding physiological processes that may accompany stress. The idea is to link negative events, circumstances, and practices that degrade family and child functioning over time in an effort to explain continuity in high levels of environmental adversity for economically disadvantaged families. The events form chains of risk in which one event increases the likelihood of a subsequent negative event. From a stress perspective, the links reflect relations between stressful circumstances and reactions by family members, which then generate more stressful circumstances. Cultural aspects of the ecology of disadvantage discussed by Wilson and Gates (2009) fit this stress reaction/stress generation cycle over time, in that cultural practices that are adaptations to family and neighborhood poverty take on momentum over time and constrain escapes from poverty.

Low Socioeconomic Status

This section and the two that follow evaluate representations of the ecology of disadvantage. We begin with low socioeconomic status (LSES) because of the historical primacy of class designations as representing environmental adversity, and because of the broad agreement among social scientists that social class broadly shapes the life chances of individuals in American society in terms of physical health and mortality, academic attainment, psychosocial adjustment, and antisocial behavior (Lareau, 2009). We discuss definition and some of the associations with health and behavioral outcomes, and then limitations of the SES construct.

Definition

Socioeconomic status (SES) refers to social position relative to others in stratified and hierarchical social systems, and is interchangeable with the construct of social class for most purposes. Though there has been considerable debate about how to define relative position, most definitions center on three indicators involving income, education, and occupational prestige. One well-known measure is the Hollingshead Index of Social Status (Hollingshead, 1975), which is based on the education and occupation of each employed adult in the home. The advantage of a multidimensional over a unidimensional indicator of disadvantage (i.e., like income) is the enhanced stability and reliability of status estimates. It is a common practice, however, to use only one indicator as a proxy for SES, most frequently adult educational attainment (Ensminger & Fothergill, 2003).

SES typically is a categorical measure (e.g., low SES vs. middle SES) partitioning families and individuals into groups. It can be assessed at an individual, family, or neighborhood level (Kohen, Leventhal, Dahinten, & McIntosh, 2008). The construct has common sense value, at the least, in that American adult informants easily and accurately locate their own relative social position, and apparently use that position in an explanatory fashion (Hout, 2008). The broadness of the categories is problematic for many theorists, however, in that groups of individuals sharing common class positions have substantially different life experiences (Lareau, 2009). The construct, then, is insensitive to the diversity among families and individuals nominally in the same social status.

Health and Psychosocial Correlates of SES

SES is used widely to describe and understand the social patterning of physical and mental health (Adler et al., 1994). Indeed, for physical health, almost all the literature we reviewed used SES as the marker of social disparities. In general, SES relates negatively to morbidity and mortality with the gradient steepest for LSES, and relates to mortality from all causes as well as specific health outcomes such as cardiovascular disease, diabetes, and cancer (Gallo & Matthews, 2003). Individual factors that select risky environments (health behaviors, residence and neighborhood "choices") account for only a small percentage of the variance in the gradient (House, 2001), whereas psychosocial characteristics associated with environmental stress (anger and hostility, depression and hopelessness, personal control) contribute substantially to the gradient (Gallo & Matthews, 2003; Mirowsky & Ross, 2003). The social gradient of health has endured across dramatic health-related advances in the last century, including food adequacy, health care access for the poor, and elimination and management of diseases. The persistence of the gradient has led Link and Phelan (Carpiano, Link, & Phelan, 2008; Link & Phelan, 1995) to argue that SES is a "fundamental cause" of health outcomes, though mechanisms change over time.

Models of the social gradient of health for children and adolescents usually have three components involving strong associations between (a) SES and exposure to environmental risks, (b) environmental risk exposure and child health, and (c) SES and child health. For component (c), many reviewers have documented strong relations between SES and several aspects of children's health (Bradley & Corwyn, 2002; Chen, Matthews & Boyce, 2002; McLoyd, 1998), including aspects related to children's sleep like low birthweight, perinatal complications, and asthma, and their cognitive and neural functioning. Thus the social gradient of health generally is applicable to children.

For component (a), House (2001) argues that SES (and race/ethnicity) shapes exposure to almost all the psychosocial, environmental, and biomedical risk factors that contribute to the social disparities in health. In House's model, these factors include five kinds of psychosocial risks: (1) health behaviors (smoking, drinking, exercise, etc.), (2) social relationships and supports, (3) acute and chronic stress, (4) psychological dispositions (e.g., temperament, anger, hostility), and (5) social roles and productive activities. Exposure to these factors probably is developmentally graded in this rubric, in that young children's exposure is largely mediated by parenting processes (Bradley & Corwyn, 2002), and adolescents' exposure is more direct and contingent on social variables (McLoyd et al., 2009). Similarly, Evans and Kantrowitz (2002) detail relations between SES and many physical risk factors for family settings (but not school or work settings), including exposure to environmental toxins and wastes, ambient and indoor air and noise pollution, residential crowding and housing quality, etc.

For component (b), abundant evidence documents relations between ecological risk factors and children's health (Evans & Kantrowitz, 2002; Taylor & Repetti, 1997; Repetti et al., 2002). Research suggests that the links may be strongest between physical hazards and physical health and between psychosocial risks and mental health and behavioral adjustment (Schwartz, 2002). Considerable evidence with adults, however, also documents relations between psychosocial risks and physical health (cardiovascular functioning, etc.) mediated through negative emotions and neuroendocrine systems involved in stress reactivity (Gallo & Matthews, 2003).

These three components (a, b, and c) are the foundation for a model in which the ecological risks mediate the association between SES and children's health. Evans and Kantrowitz (2002) argue that the model has been tested only rarely and to date has little supporting evidence.

What also is missing is a treatment of proximal processes that communicate the risks associated with SES to children, and especially to psychosocial adjustment.

Limitations of SES

SES is a static measure of relative social position. Problems in applying SES in developmental research are well-described by many theorists, including McLoyd (1998), Duncan and Magnuson (2003), and Conger and Dogan (2006). One problem is that SES does not function as a coherent whole. The income indicator, for example, is more volatile than the education and occupation indicators, and each indicator tends to relate somewhat differently to child adaptation and family functioning (Duncan & Magnuson, 2003).

The differential volatility raises a more general second problem, which is that SES is static, not dynamic, and typically is used as a snapshot indicator of social adversity. The dynamic aspects that are missing include income volatility over short periods of time for low income families in particular, the cumulative effects of adversity over time, and exposure to status inequities, including the longer-term changes in income inequality, which relate to perceptions of adversity and hopelessness. In this latter respect, SES misrepresents the changing structure of inequality in American society. Wilkinson (2005), Marmot (2004), and others (Carpiano et al., 2008), for instance, distinguish between absolute and relative deprivation, and argue that the relative income gap between the affluent and the poor has consequences for physical and mental health. This gap reflects but does not reduce to social position.

A third and related general criticism is that SES is too superficial in representing environmental adversity and the ecology of disadvantage. That is, the construct has weak explanatory value for developmental researchers. Social position, for instance, provides little information about social stresses and strains, or about the economic demands families face in the context of available resources. Indeed, the categorical nature of SES discourages quantification or estimation of environmental stress or risk factors faced by family members.

Thus, SES adds little to the "stress paradigm" useful in explaining class-associated disparities in physical and mental health (Mirowsky &

Ross, 2003; Pearlin, 1989). There is more value in considering each of the three core components separately (Mirowsky & Ross, 2003), and focusing uniquely on a variable that can represent stress, like income poverty. Similarly, if SES is associated with most of the risk factors related to social disparities in physical and mental health (House, 2001), there is something to be gained by focusing on more direct representations of the risk factors and on direct experiences of stress and risk in exploring mechanisms of effects (Evans & Kantrowitz, 2002) rather than one proxy representation like SES.

Income Poverty

The second dominant representation of the ecology of disadvantage is income poverty, described as either a categorical (poor/not-poor) or a continuous variable (i.e., family income). Income poverty solves core limitations of the SES construct in that it is dynamic over time, and it has clear links to stress variables (i.e., perceived income strain, economic hardship) and is linked through well-defined family mechanisms to child functioning (i.e., family stress models). Other advantages are that focusing on income allows precise measurement of economic well-being at family and neighborhood levels (e.g., concentrated neighborhood poverty) and thus goes some of the way toward explaining diverse experiences among LSES families and individuals. We discuss measurement first, applications next, and limitations last.

Definition and Measurement

According to the National Center for Children in Poverty (2009) among the 73 million children in the United States in 2007, 18% lived in poor families defined as having total income below the federal poverty line specified for family size. Another 21% lived in families that were "near poor" in that family incomes were between 100% and 200% of the poverty line. All told, then, about 39% of children lived in families that were low income/economically disadvantaged, with disadvantage defined as family income ≤ 200% of the poverty line. The numbers undoubtedly increased with the profound economic recession starting in the last half of 2008. The numbers varied by age, and children under age six lived in low income families (about 45% in 2007) more frequently than adolescents (35%). The numbers also varied by race and ethnicity, and about 60% of black and Latino children lived in poor families in 2007 versus 26% of white children.

As an absolute standard, the federal poverty line reflects the total family income deemed necessary to meet basic family needs involving food, clothing, and shelter. In 2009, the amount for the 48 contiguous states was $22,050 for a family of four and $29,530 for a family of six. Total family income includes pre-tax employment earnings, interest and dividend income, social security, and cash assistance (i.e., from Public Assistance programs), but does not include federal Earned Income Tax Credit or in-kind benefits, such as food stamps and housing and child care assistance. For researchers, a well-accepted description of continuous position relative to the poverty line is the family's income-to-needs ratio, computed by dividing family income per capita by the federal poverty standard per capita (e.g., $5,512.50 and $4,921.67 for families sized four and six, respectively). Thus, a family of four with total income of $17,632 ($4,408.12 per capita) would have an income-to-needs ratio of 0.8. Researchers without access to family income information frequently use participation in a program for disadvantaged families and children (i.e., Head Start) as a categorical measure of income poverty.

The logic of the poverty line measure reflects 1960s conceptions of minimal basic needs based on assumptions about what constitutes a reasonable food budget and that food costs consume about one-third of a poor family's total budget. Frequent criticisms of the measure are that the food budget is low and nutritionally inadequate, that food costs vary by national region and rural/urban settings, that food realistically constitutes one-sixth to one-seventh of poor family budgets (post 1970s), and that the poverty threshold does not take into account important economic and social changes since the 1960s, like the dramatic increase in the number of working mothers with children age three and younger, and the attendant needs for child care and transportation, etc. Many theorists argue that a figure double the poverty line is more adequate in meeting minimal basic needs, and that a relative measure is more appropriate than an absolute measure, such as one-half the median income in the United States for the same sized family.

Income-to-needs ratios convert a categorical measure of poverty (below/above the poverty line) into a continuous measure reflecting the degree of poverty (i.e., position relative to the federal standard) that is sensitive to some aspects of the diversity among disadvantaged families. The "far" poor, for example, have ratios ≤ one-half the poverty line (.50 and below) and experience a considerable "poverty gap." The "near poor" have ratios between 1.0 and 2.0. The ratios are dynamic to the extent that total incomes often fluctuate substantially for many poor families from year to year, as parents gain and lose employment and gain and lose residential partners, and dynamic in the sense that the poverty standard rises with inflation but does not rise with increasing income inequality. Thus the ratios of affluent families have risen much faster than those of disadvantaged families in recent years.

Applications of Income Poverty

Many recent reviews document relations between income poverty and the likelihood of family problems and adverse child outcomes (Duncan & Brooks-Gunn, 2000; Magnuson & Duncan, 2002; McLoyd, 1998). Income poverty, for example, threatens normative development across every domain of functioning, including birth weight and physical health, cognitive competence and academic achievement, and problem behaviors. The relations are similar to but more specific than those for LSES. In this part we describe some applications of income measures that advance understanding of the relations between the ecology of disadvantage and family and child functioning beyond the typical use of SES representations. We focus on dynamic aspects of income poverty, articulation of mechanisms of effects in family stress models, and neighborhood effects.

Dynamic Effects

Income poverty status and income-to-needs ratios show substantial volatility over time for many disadvantaged families. Magnuson and Duncan (2002) recite statistics showing, for example, that about 25% of the families that are below the poverty line in one year are above that line the next year, that less than 50% of poor families show persistence over several years, and that the poverty status of about 60% of families is less than three years and short-term. The statistics also show, however, that the poverty status of about 14% of families is eight years or longer and long-term, and that persistent poverty is far more likely to character-ize black families than white families. In our own longitudinal work with a disadvantaged sample of mostly African American families (Ackerman & Brown, 2006), we found that about 20% of families showed increases and 20% showed decreases in total family income of about $20,000 over two-year intervals. Years of maternal education and occu-pational prestige (other indicators of SES) changed little.

Considerable evidence suggests that the volatility in family income matters for children's outcomes. Dearing, McCartney and Taylor (2006), for instance, have shown that child adjustment varies in relation to changes in income over time within families. Others have found similar results, supporting a general argument that income increases matter for family and child functioning and more so for poor children than for non-poor children. The reverse effect also is well-documented in that child cognitive and internalizing behavior problems are greater for fami-lies enduring persistent poverty over years relative to those showing intermittent or short-term poverty (Ackerman, Brown, & Izard, 2004b; Duncan & Brooks-Gunn, 2000).

Interpretation is muddied, however, by several factors. First, some effects are developmentally-and function-specific. For cognitive compe-tence, for instance, poverty persistence matters greatly in the preschool years, but less so thereafter (Duncan & Brooks-Gunn, 1997), though the effect may depend on the measure of competence (Aikens & Barbarin, 2008). For externalizing behaviors, current poverty matters but perhaps not poverty history (Ackerman, Brown, & Izard, 2004a). Second, persis-tence/volatility often is confounded with extent of poverty. "Far poor" families, for instance, are more likely to show persistent poverty than other poor families. Third, how volatility per se maps onto disruption of family relations and practices is unclear.

Family Stress Models

One advantage of income measures of disadvantage is that the dose of adversity is easily operationalized in perceived (and objective) economic stress/strain and material hardship. A second advantage is that the pathways communicating stress indirectly to the child are clear and well detailed, and are relevant for conceptualizing child sleep as a social phenomenon. As shown in family stress models, the pathways often and variously involve sequential links between economic stress and marital conflict and maternal distressed mood, between these variables and disrupted and negative parenting, and between parenting and child behavioral functioning. As summarized by Conger and Dogan (2006), the family stress model is replicable and robust across acute and chronic (i.e., poverty) economic stress, American and non-American samples, predominately black and white samples, and younger and older children, and the model does well in explaining both concurrent behavior and longitudinal change in child behavior over time, and hence in minimizing selection effects. A third advantage is specificity in that family stress models relate primarily to behavioral adjustment. Other models focusing on family investments do better in describing cognitive and academic achievements.

Three characteristics of family stress models are especially noteworthy in anticipating later points in this chapter. First, the mediators typically concern units of analysis and processes at the dyadic and individual level. Family-level functioning is not focal, although economic strain clearly affects all aspects of family functioning. Second, the mechanisms describe indirect pathways of influence. Third, little attention is paid to poverty cofactors (family structure, residential instability, etc.).

Neighborhood Poverty

Income measures also encourage precise estimates of the proportion of poor families in neighborhoods, and thus the effects of neighborhood poverty on family and child functioning. The effects seem to be threshold-related in terms of living in a community showing concentrated poverty in which $\geq 40\%$ of the families are poor (we have also seen 30% as the cut). As established in several detailed reviews (e.g. Leventhal, Dupere, & Brooks-Gunn, 2009), most effects are indirect and mediated through family processes, with direct effects more common for adolescents than younger children, and most effects are small but robust across estimates of selection effects. In addition, neighborhood poverty effects usually are associated with but independent of the effects of other characteristics of impoverished communities, including cohesion and aspects of social control.

Limitations of Income Representations

One limitation is that income estimates often are unreliable. A second limitation is that categorical representations (poor/non-poor) are insensitive to the diversity of disadvantaged families and diversity of outcomes for poor children. In addition, categorical measures obscure effects for risky environmental factors associated with income poverty. Collinearity in prediction often means that analyzing for poverty estimates the impact of poverty combined with cofactor effects.

Third, using poverty status as a summary representation of the ecology of disadvantage often sacrifices examination of poverty-related stressors. These include associated risk factors like residential instability and parent maladjustment, aspects of the physical environment like crowding, noise, and substandard housing, and other economic associates of income poverty, like wealth (Yeung & Conley, 2008) and material hardship (Gershoff, Aber, Raver, & Lennon, 2007) that may explain income effects. The singular focus sacrifices the ability to represent the cumulative dose of environmental adversity experienced by disadvantaged children. Fourth, few poverty studies focus on family-level difficulties associated with impoverished economic resources, like disruptions of family routines and agendas generated by atypical and variable work schedules and long commutes, or the physical illness of a primary caregiver.

Poverty-Related Stressors

A final set of representations of the ecology of disadvantage concern proximal experiences by family members of life events and circumstances that destabilize and disrupt family functioning. These experiences constitute risk factors that cut across family income levels but are strongly associated with income poverty, and hence may explain specific effects associated with social class and income poverty. These factors also help explain diversity among disadvantaged families and child outcomes.

We briefly describe representations reflecting cumulative risk, family instability, and chaotic family systems.

The representations have several features in common for our purposes. First, they directly reflect aspects of the ecology that stress caregivers and children, and in this sense bear proximal relations to functioning not available in ecological proxies, like class and income poverty. The representations, however, vary in specifying proximal mechanisms of effects, and in describing physical as well as psychosocial aspects of environmental adversity. Second, in aggregate forms (i.e., "cumulative" risk), they represent the "dose" of environmental adversity families experience, which is critical in describing stress responses and which is missing in categorical representations (LSES/Middle SES, poor/non-poor). Third, they uniquely describe functioning at a family level of analysis, rather than at dyadic or individual levels, in that the events and circumstances both reflect and affect all aspects of family functioning and family members. These family-wide influences mean that effects on children often are direct, as well as mediated through parent–child relationships. Fourth, in general, relations to child outcomes often reflect concurrent experiences, and they mostly concern behavior problems and regulation rather than cognitive limitations. The exception could concern individual differences in stress reactivity formed by adverse circumstances early in life. Fifth, the representations are vulnerable to social selection hypotheses, in that effects reflect caregiver variables.

Cumulative Risk

Cumulative risk indexes represent the quantity or "dose" of environmental adversity a family and child experiences by adding the number of environmental risks on selected variables at any one time. Continuous variables convert to categorical indicators of risk (present/absent) by means of statistical criteria (a mean, a standard deviation, etc.). Comparisons of indexes across time provide a view of enduring adversity and dynamic factors influencing change in family and child functioning. The adversity reflects discrete events and circumstances of the family, like single parent families, maternal relationship transitions, residential moves, aspects of parent maladjustment (i.e., criminality, substance use/abuse, psychiatric morbidity), maternal education, adolescent parenthood, family size, and the physical environment (substandard housing, noise, etc.), though the number of variables typically selected for inclusion in indexes varies widely. Indexes often include an economic indicator for poverty/disadvantage and indicators of risky family processes like harsh parenting.

The empirical motivation of cumulative risk representations includes arguments that single environmental risks rarely relate significantly to family and child functioning, that multivariate representations often account for substantial amounts of variance in functioning, and that aggregate representations (i.e., reducing several variables to one) are both efficient in preserving statistical power and sometimes account for unique variance beyond that associated with models that add single factors. The theoretical motivation includes arguments that there is natural covariation in environmental risk factors, that a single index is useful in representing environmental adversity as a whole in a way not captured by single variables, and that the quantity of environmental adversity/stress matters more than the quality or discrete nature of any particular stressor. A recurrent debate concerns the linearity of effects on child functioning (Gerard & Buehler, 2004), with many accounts showing degraded functioning only at a level of three or four risk factors (depending on the factors in the model) and small but consistent increments in maladjustment with each additional risk factor up to six or seven. Other issues concern the unique effects for and relations between cumulative representations of multiple domains of adversity concerning the individual, the family, the neighborhood, and the school (Deater-Deckard, Dodge, Bates, & Pettit, 1998; Gerard & Buehler, 2004), and developmental differences in the impact of risk factors (Appleyard, Egeland, van Dulmen, & Sroufe, 2005).

Research by Evans provides an excellent recent example of the relations between cumulative risk models of the ecology of disadvantage and child functioning that might have implications for children's sleep. Evans (2003) is a seminal study in describing relations between an index composed of nine physical (e.g., crowding, noise), psychosocial (child separation), and personal (poverty, single parenthood) risk factors, cardiovascular and neuroendocrine markers of stress physiology indexing "allostatic load," and the self-regulatory behavior of economically disadvantaged nine-year olds. Allostatic load reflects the cumulative wear and tear on the body caused by responses to environmental adversity over time. The study is unique in its focus on physical factors and relations between the "dose" of environmental stress and stress physiology. Later studies with the same sample extended the findings longitudinally and developmentally. Evans, Kim, Ting, Tesher, and Shannis (2007) found that cumulative risk was associated with changes in allostatic load over time (four years), with the effect moderated by maternal responsiveness. Evans and Kim (2007) found that poverty exposure since birth also predicted the stress physiology of 13-year olds, but that the effects were largely explained by cumulative risk exposure during childhood.

Limitations of cumulative risk representations are well-known. One problem concerns the wide variation in the numbers and kinds of risk factors included in cumulative indexes. Another concerns the theoretical focus of the mix of risk factors. For instance, including factors from different domains (family, person-based, neighborhood) blurs the focus, mixing structural and process (e.g., parent-child) factors constrains examination of mediators and moderators of effects (Trentacosta et al., 2008), and mixing income poverty and poverty cofactors limits specificity in predicting child behavior. A third problem is that some risk factors in an index, like maternal relationship transitions (Ackerman, Brown, Schoff D'Eramo, & Izard, 2002), may relate more strongly than others to child behavior, and so may drive the effect for the risk index. This problem relates to a second representation of poverty-related stressors focusing on family instability and transitions.

Family Instability

Family instability reflects dynamic events that threaten the continuity and coherence of family-level processes and agendas (Ackerman, Kogos, Youngstrom, Schoff, & Izard, 1999), centrally including marital separation/divorce, more general maternal relationship transitions (Ackerman, et al., 2002), parent-child separations, and residential moves (Adam, 2004). Other destabilizing life events (i.e., job loss, parent illness/death) also fit the construct. The construct loosely requires an aggregation of the number of destabilizing factors at one time, as in a cumulative instability index, or the number of a particular event (e.g., relationship transitions, household moves) over a period of time, or both. Otherwise, the construct reduces to a single factor (i.e., divorce) and loses distinctiveness as a family-level variable. Relations to child outcomes, including children's sleep, are likely to be both direct because of the disruption of family emotional climate, routines, and agendas, and indirect through disrupted parenting processes. As described in other chapters in this book (see El-Sheikh & Kelly, chapter 1 in this volume), possible mediators involve the child's emotional security (Forman & Davies, 2003).

The construct is rooted in the extensive literature on family structure, generally showing differences in child adjustment for married and single parent families (McLanahan, 1999). Such differences are difficult to interpret for many reasons, but one core problem historically is the association between family structure and income poverty: impoverished families are more likely than others to be single parent households and to show multiple transitions in maternal intimate relationships in the form of serial cohabitation. Systematic attempts to tease apart family income and structure shows specificity in effects in that income but not structure uniquely predicts children's cognitive ability, and structure uniquely predicts behavior problems (Duncan & Brooks-Gunn, 1997, 2000). Other research shows that the number of relationship transitions does well in predicting the behavior problems of disadvantaged elementary school children, and mostly explains effects for family structure (Ackerman et al., 2002). This effect for transitions promotes dynamic instability as a mechanism rather than a factor associated with family structure, like father absence.

Family Chaos

Chaos is a family-level variable focusing on social and physical disorganization in the home and a lack of predictable and controllable home environment. Chaotic families are lacking in structure and routine, and often are marked by high levels of noise and crowding, and by psychosocial factors contributing to turmoil. These factors include aspects of family instability. At a variable level, family chaos often is measured with the chaos scale (Matheny, Wachs, Ludwig, & Phillips, 1995) focusing on family confusion, "hubbub," and order, sometimes augmented with measures of family rituals and routines (Evans, Gonnella, Marcynyszyn, Gentile, & Salpekar, 2005). Family chaos is associated with economic disadvantage, though affluent families can also be chaotic, and chaos seems to function as a mediator linking family income to children's socioemotional adjustment (Evans et al., 2005). A recent book edited by Evans and Wachs (2009) represents the first systematic exploration of the chaos construct and relations to family and child functioning in a variety of sociodemographic settings.

Family chaos relates theoretically to children's sleep through the disruption and unpredictability of family routines, like bedtime routines, and perhaps through effects on children's ability to self-regulate. Brown and Low (2008) provide evidence for these ideas in showing links between chaotic living conditions of disadvantaged families and pre-school children's sleep problems, and that sleep problems partially mediate relations between chaotic conditions and children's responses to challenge. The findings suggest the need for much more research on relations between chaotic conditions in the home and children's sleep.

Summary

We explored the uses and some weaknesses of representations of the ecology of economic disadvantage, including low socioeconomic status, income poverty, and ones focusing on poverty-related stressors. The representations differ in explaining diversity among disadvantaged families and children, in focusing on indirect or direct relations between environmental adversity and child outcomes, and in capturing dynamic qualities of the functioning of impoverished families over time. Most importantly, the representations differ in describing proximal aspects of the home environment that potentially affect children's stress physiology and sleep processes.

Our review has at least five implications for future research. First, it is critically important to use a continuous measure of family economic resources, and preferably in multiple assessments over time. Poverty status (e.g., poor/not poor) alone cannot capture the impact of chronic economic stress on family and child functioning. Second, family income should be distinguished from family structure and parent factors correlated with poverty. The reason is that income and poverty cofactors tend to relate uniquely to specific child outcomes in the context of controls.

Third, possible mechanisms of poverty effects at a family level are an emerging area of research. A good example is the recent focus on chaos in family agendas, organization, and physical circumstances. Fourth, apart from Evan's recent work (Evans & Kim, 2007), bioecological models of poverty effects on children have done little to flesh out biological markers of ecological adversity. Conceptualizing poverty stressors will require more attention to stress physiology for both parents and children. Fifth, single factors alone usually explain little variance in children's behavior. Multivariate and aggregate representations do better.

REFERENCES

Ackerman, B. P., & Brown, E. D. (2006). Income poverty, poverty co-factors, and the adjustment of children in elementary school. In R. V. Kail (Ed.), *Advances in child development and behavior* (pp. 91–129). New York: Academic Press.

Ackerman, B. P., Brown, E. D., & Izard, C. E. (2004a). The relations between contextual risk, earned income, and the school adjustment of children from economically disadvantaged families. *Developmental Psychology, 40,* 204–216.

Ackerman, B. P., Brown, E. D., & Izard, C. E. (2004b). The relations between persistent poverty and contextual risk and children's behavior in elementary school. *Developmental Psychology, 40,* 367–377.

Ackerman, B. P., Brown, E. D., Schoff D'Eramo, K., & Izard, C. E. (2002). Maternal relationship instability and the school behavior of children from disadvantaged families. *Developmental Psychology, 38,* 694–704.

Ackerman, B. P., Kogos, J., Youngstrom, E., Schoff, K., & Izard, C. (1999). Family instability and the problem behaviors of children from economically disadvantaged families. *Developmental Psychology, 35,* 258–268.

Adam, E. K. (2004). Beyond quality: Parental and residential stability and children's adjustment. *Current Directions in Psychological Science, 13,* 210–213.

Adler, N. E., Boyce, T., Chesney, M. A., Cohen, S., Folkman, S., Kahn, R. L., & Syme, S. L. (1994). Socioeconomic status and health: The challenge of the gradient. *American Psychologist, 49,* 15–24.

Aikens, N. L., & Barbarin, O. (2008). Socioeconomic differences in reading trajectories: The contribution of family, neighborhood, and school contexts. *Journal of Educational Psychology, 100,* 235–251.

Appleyard, K., Egeland, B., van Dulmen, M. H. M., & Sroufe, L. A. (2005). When more is not better: The role of cumulative risk in child behavior outcomes. *Journal of Child Psychology and Psychiatry, 46,* 235–245.

Belsky, J., Bakermans-Kranenburg, M. J., & van IJzendoorn, M. H. (2007). For better and for worse: Differential susceptibility to environmental influences. *Current Directions in Psychological Science, 16,* 300–304.

Belsky, J., & Pluess, M. (2009). The nature (and nurture?) of plasticity in early human development. *Perspectives on Psychological Science, 4*, 345–351.

Boyce, W. T., & Ellis, B. J. (2005). Biological sensitivity to context: I. An evolutionary-developmental theory of the origins and functions of stress reactivity. *Development and Psychopathology, 17*, 271–301.

Bradley, R. H., & Corwyn, R. F. (2002). Socioeconomic status and child development. *Annual Review of Psychology, 53*, 371–399.

Brown, E. D., & Low, C. M. (2008). Chaotic living conditions and sleep problems associated with children's responses to academic challenge. *Journal of Family Psychology, 22*, 920–923.

Buckhalt, J. A., El-Sheikh, M., & Keller, P. S. (2007). Children's sleep and cognitive functioning: Race and socioeconomic status as moderators of effects. *Child Development, 78*, 213–231.

Buckhalt, J. A., El-Sheikh, M., Keller, P. S., & Kelly, R. J. (2009). Concurrent and longitudinal relations between children's sleep and cognitive functioning: The moderating role of parent education. *Child Development, 80*, 875–892.

Carpiano, R. M., Link, B. G., & Phelan, J. C. (2008). Social inequality and health: Future directions for the fundamental cause explanation. In A. Lareau & D. Conley (Eds.), *Social class: How does it work?* (pp. 232–263). New York: Russell Sage.

Chen, E., Matthews, K. A., & Boyce, W. T. (2002). Socioeconomic differences in children's health: How and why do these relationships change with age? *Psychological Bulletin, 128*, 295–329.

Coll, C. G., Crnic, K., Lamberty, G., Wasik, B. H., Jenkins, R., Garcia, H. V., & McAdoo, H. P. (1996). An integrative model for the study of developmental competencies in minority children. *Child Development, 67*, 1891–1914.

Conger, R. D., & Dogan, S. J. (2006). Social class and socialization in families. In J. Grusec & P. D. Hastings (Eds.), *Handbook of socialization: Theory and research* (pp. 433–460). New York: Guilford Press.

Dearing, E., McCartney, K., & Taylor, B. A. (2006). Within-child associations between family income and externalizing and internalizing problems. *Developmental Psychology, 42*, 237–252.

Deater-Deckard, K., Dodge, K. A., Bates, J. E., & Pettit, G. S. (1998). Multiple risk factors in the development of externalizing behavior problems: Group and individual differences. *Development and Psychopathology, 10*, 469–493.

Duncan, G. J., & Brooks-Gunn, J. (Eds.). (1997). *Consequences of growing up poor.* New York: Sage.

Duncan, G. J., & Brooks-Gunn, J. (2000). Family poverty, welfare reform, and child development. *Child Development, 71*, 188–196.

Duncan, G. J. & Magnuson, K. A. (2003). Off with Hollingshead: Socioeconomic resources, parenting, and child development. In M. H. Bornstein & R. H. Bradley (Eds.), *Socioeconomic status, parenting, and child development* (pp. 83–106). Mahwah, NJ: Lawrence Erlbaum.

Ensminger, M. E., & Fothergill, K. (2003). A decade of measuring SES: What it tells us and where to go from here. In M. H. Bornstein & R. H. Bradley (Eds.), *Socioeconomic status, parenting, and child development* (pp. 13–28). Mahwah, NJ: Lawrence Erlbaum.

Evans, G. W. (2003). A multimethodological analysis of cumulative risk and allostatic load among rural children. *Developmental Psychology, 39*, 924–933.

Evans, G. W., Gonnella, C., Marcynyszyn, L. A., Gentile, L., & Salpekar, N. (2005). The role of chaos in poverty and children's socioemotional adjustment. *Psychological Science, 16*, 560–565.

Evans, G. W., & Kantrowitz, E. (2002). Socioeconomic status and health: The potential role of environmental risk exposure. *Annual Review of Public Health, 23*, 303–331.

Evans, G. W., & Kim, P. (2007). Childhood poverty and health: Cumulative risk exposure and stress dysregulation. *Psychological Science, 18*, 953–957.

Evans, G. W., Kim, P., Ting, A. H., Tesher, H. B., & Shannis, D. (2007). Cumulative risk, maternal responsiveness, and allostatic load among young adolescents. *Developmental Psychology, 43*, 341–351.

Evans, G. W., & Wachs, T. D. (Eds.). (2009). *Chaos and its influence on children's development: An ecological perspective.* Washington: American Psychological Association.

Forman, E. M., & Davies, P. T. (2003). Family instability and young adolescent maladjustment: The mediating effects of parenting quality and adolescent appraisals of family security. *Journal of Clinical Child and Adolescent Psychology, 32*, 94–105.

Gallo, L. C., & Matthews, K. A. (2003). Understanding the association between socioeconomic status and physical health: Do negative emotions play a role? *Psychological Bulletin, 129*, 10–51.

Gerard, J. M., & Buehler, C. (2004). Cumulative environmental risk and youth maladjustment: The role of youth attributes. *Child Development, 75*, 1832–1849.

Gershoff, E. T., Aber, J. L., Raver, C. C., & Lennon, M. C. (2007). Income is not enough: Incorporating material hardship into models of income associations with parenting and child development. *Child Development, 78*, 70–95.

Gutman, L. M., Sameroff, A. J., & Eccles, J. S. (2002). The academic achievement of African American students during early adolescence: An examination of multiple risk, promotive, and protective factors. *American Journal of Community Psychology, 30*, 367–399.

Hollingshead, A. B. (1975). *Four-factor index of social status.* Unpublished manuscript, Yale University, New Haven, CT.

House, J. S. (2001). Understanding social factors and inequalities in health: 20th century progress and 21st century prospects. *Journal of Health and Social Behavior, 43*, 125–142.

Hout, M. (2008). How class works: Objective and subjective aspects of class since the 1970s. In A. Lareau & D. Conley (Eds.), *Social class: How does it work?* (pp. 25–64). New York: Russell Sage.

Kaffman, A., & Meaney, M. J. (2007). Neurodevelopmental sequelae of postnatal maternal care in rodents: Clinical and research implications of molecular insights. *Journal of Child Psychology and Psychiatry, 48,* 224–244.

Kohen, D. E., Leventhal, T., Dahinten, V. S., & McIntosh, C. N. (2008). Neighborhood disadvantage: Pathways of effects for young children. *Child Development, 79,* 156–169.

Lareau, A. (2009). Introduction: Taking stock of class. In A. Lareau & D. Conley (Eds.), *Social class: How does it work?* (pp. 3–24). New York: Russell Sage.

Leventhal, T., Dupere, V., & Brooks-Gunn, J. (2009). Neighborhood influences on adolescent development. In R. M. Lerner & L. Steinberg (Eds.), *Handbook of adolescent development* (pp. 411–443). Hoboken, NJ: John Wiley & Sons.

Link, B. G., & Phelan, J. (1995). Social conditions as fundamental causes of disease [Special issue]. *Journal of Health and Social Behavior, 35,* 80–94.

Magnuson, K. A., & Duncan, G. J. (2002). Parents in poverty. In M. Bornstein (Ed.), *Handbook of parenting: Social conditions and applied parenting* (2nd ed., Vol. 4, pp. 95–121). Mahwah, NJ: Lawrence Erlbaum.

Marmot, M. (2004). *The status syndrome.* New York: Henry Holt.

Massey, D. S. (2007). *Categorically unequal.* New York: Russell Sage.

Matheny, A. P., Wachs, T. D., Ludwig, J. L., & Phillips, K. (1995). Bringing order out of chaos: Psychometric characteristics of the Confusion, Hubbub, and Order scale. *Journal of Applied Developmental Psychology, 16,* 429–444.

McElhaney, K. B., & Allen, J. P. (2001). Autonomy and adolescent social functioning: The moderating effect of risk. *Child Development, 72,* 220–235.

McLanahan, S. S. (1999). Father absence and the welfare of children. In E. M. Hetherington (Ed.), *Coping with divorce, single parenting, and remarriage: A risk and resiliency perspective* (pp. 117–145). Mahwah, NJ: Erlbaum.

McLoyd, V. C., (1998). Socioeconomic disadvantage and child development. *American Psychologist, 53,* 185–204.

McLoyd, V. C., Kaplan, R., Purtell, K. M., Bagley, E., Hardaway, C. R., & Smalls, C. (2009). Poverty and socioeconomic disadvantage in adolescence. In R. M. Lerner & L. Steinberg (Eds.), *Handbook of adolescent development* (pp. 444–491). Hoboken, NJ: John Wiley & Sons.

Mirowsky, J., & Ross, C. E. (2003). *Social causes of psychological distress* (2nd ed.). Hawthorne, NY: Aldine de Gruyter.

National Center for Children in Poverty, Mailman School of Public Health, Columbia University. (2009). *Fact sheets.* Retrieved from http://www.nccp.org/publications/fact_sheets.php

Pearlin, L. I. (1989). The sociological study of stress. *Journal of Health and Social Behavior, 30,* 241–256.

Repetti, R. L., Taylor, S. E., & Seeman, T. E. (2002). Risky families: Family social environments and the mental and physical health of offspring. *Psychological Bulletin, 128*, 330–366.

Schwartz, S. (2002). Outcomes for the sociology of mental health: Are we meeting our goals? *Journal of Health and Social Behavior, 43*, 223–235.

Simons, R. L., Lin, K. H., Gordon, L. C., Brody, G. H., Murry, V., & Conger, R. D. (2002). Community differences in the association between parenting practices and child conduct problems. *Journal of Marriage and Family, 64*, 331–345.

Taylor, S. E., & Repetti, R. L. (1997). Health psychology: What is an unhealthy environment and how does it get under the skin? *Annual Review of Psychology, 48*, 411–447.

Trentacosta, C. J., Hyde, L. W., Shaw, D. S., Dishion, T. J., Gardner, F., & Wilson, M. (2008). The relations among cumulative risk, parenting, and behavior problems during early childhood. *Journal of Child Psychology and Psychiatry, 49*, 1211–1219.

Wilkinson, R. G. (2005). *The impact of inequality: How to make sick societies healthier.* New York: The New Press.

Wilson, W. J., & Gates, H. L., Jr. (2009). *More than just race: Being black and poor in the inner city.* New York: W. W. Norton.

Yeung, W. J., & Conley, D. (2008). Black-white achievement gap and family wealth. *Child Development, 79*, 303–324.

14

Assessment of Family Functioning

E. Mark Cummings, Kalsea J. Koss, and Kathleen N. Bergman

Introduction

Best practices in research on sleep, family functioning, and child development require an integration of multiple methodologies and approaches.
At the same time, given the advanced expertise required, it is unlikely
that any one investigator, or even any one research team, will possess
sufficient expertise in all of the pertinent methodologies to optimally
advance the study of these issues. For example, child development
researchers may have limited understanding of methods for assessing
sleep and related biological processes, but may be highly familiar with
observational and other approaches to the assessment of child adjustment
and family functioning. On the other hand, pediatric and sleep medicine
researchers may be expert in sleep and pertinent biological assessments,
but possess much less knowledge about the pros and cons of potential
ways to assess family and child adjustment.

These challenges have direct implications for the quality of science
that can be conducted in the investigation of sleep deprivation, and
disrupted sleep quality and schedule, as problems for American children.
Thus, focusing on pediatric research, some studies may reflect advanced
measurement of biological processes and sleep in clinical or medical
settings but include very weak assessments of family processes. The result
may be work that is superb in some regards but markedly deficient in
others, thereby limiting the quality of the contribution. Given the potential of medical and pediatric research to capture highly sophisticated

biological and sleep parameters, it is regrettable if a major research investigation is ultimately a lesser contribution because it is fundamentally lacking with regard to the measurement or assessment of family processes.

The purpose of this chapter is to advance information toward addressing one part of this equation: the development of optimal research designs for studying family processes in sleep research. That is, the goal is to present state-of-the-art information about choices to be considered in selecting behavioral and psychological assessments of family functioning when examining child development. Specifically, in this chapter we seek to inform those engaged in pediatric and sleep medicine research about assessment approaches related to the inclusion of family factors. In chapter 15 in this volume, Avi Sadeh provides an overview of assessment approaches toward the optimal employment of sleep methodology for the sake of informing behavioral and psychological researchers interested in incorporating sleep assessments in their studies.

Thus, the aim is to outline the pros and cons of various methodologies to aid in the selection of specific approaches for the assessment of family functioning as it relates to child development. Our discussion will include notions of family systems that merit study, approaches to measurement and assessment, and analysis strategies for including relatively complex family processes in sleep research. Our intention is not to provide recommendations on specific procedures that should be used but rather to outline various options for researchers interested in the assessment of family functioning and processes.

Multiple Family Relationships

Assessment of Families in Research

The family is a relatively complex social system; a first challenge is to identify conceptualizations of family relationships that merit possible study for sleep researchers. At the outset, influences within the family merit consideration as possible points for assessment of relations between family functioning and sleep. Families are comprised of individuals, each with their own roles, as well as dyadic and triadic relationships placed within the larger dynamic family system. As evident in other chapters in this volume, family researchers have examined different components of the family system, examining the functioning of individuals, smaller subsystems, and the larger family unit. Viewed from the perspective of the larger family unit, the family is composed of individuals and dyadic relationships between (a) parents and children, (b) parents, and (c) siblings. In addition to the study of individuals and specific relationships within the family, it is acknowledged that individuals and relationships are both affected by broader aspects of the family context including culture and society.

Figure 14.1 presents a framework for possible assessment of family influences in terms of a family research model. This figure depicts the different levels of analyses that are distinguished in family research, including a framework for conceptualizing their interrelationships. Consistent with various approaches to conceptualizing family influences (e.g., family systems theory), this framework also sheds light on the transactional, multidirectional, and interdependent nature of family processes. Thus, according to this view, functioning in one system of the family is likely to ultimately affect other systems, underscoring the importance of assessment among multiple family systems (Minuchin, 1974).

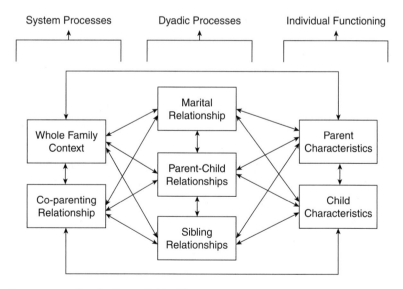

FIGURE 14.1   Family Research Model

Furthermore, it is important to recognize that the various dyadic relationships within the family do not exist in isolation; interrelations between systems and the larger context of the family is important to consider in understanding the functioning of these relationships. Thus, a key theme in family research is the need to consider the interdependence of various relationships within the family. In addition to addressing the impact of individual relationships within the family, recent research has begun to move beyond the dyadic level of analysis to examining the dynamic relationship between systems within the family, including how these dyadic relationships may interact with one another. For example, researchers have called for the examination of the association between the parent-child and the marital relationship, as well as the mother-child and father-child relationship (Cox & Paley, 1997). Another example in the context of family research is the movement to study notions of co-parenting, reflecting the degree to which mothers' and fathers' parenting processes interrelate in affecting the child (Gable, Crnic, & Belsky, 1994). Moving beyond isolating relationships within the family for study, examining the interrelationship between dyadic systems within the broader family may also advance assessment of a more contextualized understanding of family processes.

Individual Functioning in the Context of the Family

One important direction for study is to consider how the individual functions in relation to sleep and the family context. The individual functioning of both children and parents is frequently examined in the context of family research (see Figure 14.1). The functioning of children and parents is both an outcome and an influence on family processes. Child adjustment measures may assess a variety of aspects of children's adaptation including cognitive, emotional, social, physiological, and psychological constructs. Research on child characteristics in the context of family research has examined constructs such as temperament (Whiteside-Mansell, Bradley, Casey, Fussell, & Connors-Burrow, 2009), psychopathology (Burke, Pardini, & Loeber, 2008), physiological reactivity (Davies, Sturge-Apple, Cicchetti, & Cummings, 2008), and academic success (Harold, Aitken, & Shelton, 2007). Family research on child development has also studied the impact of parental characteristics such as personality and psychopathology on child and family functioning.

Parent–Child Relationships

Within the family, parent-child relationships include both mother and child and father and child relationships (see Figure 14.1). Historically, the mother-child relationship has been the most commonly researched relationship in the family pertinent to child development. However, greater attention has been placed on the importance of understanding the father-child relationship in recent years (Cummings, Davies, & Campbell, 2000). Important elements of the socialization of children occur within the context of the parent-child relationship. Research on the parent-child relationship is multidimensional and encompasses numerous aspects of this relationship, including the attachment relationship (Bowlby, 1969), parenting styles (Baumrind, 1967), parent-child conflict and communication (Maccoby & Martin, 1983), and parental warmth and responsiveness (Davidov & Grusec, 2006). Associations between parenting and sleep thus constitute an important direction for study (see Erath and Tu, chapter 2 in this volume for a review of relations between parenting practices and children's sleep).

The Marital Relationship

Traditionally, family research has focused on the effects of the parent-child relationship on child functioning and adjustment. In recent years, however, increasing attention has been paid to the effects of the marital relationship on child development (see Figure 14.1). Accumulating evidence supports the proposition that the marital relationship has a salient and influential effect on children's adjustment (Cummings et al., 2000) including effects on children's sleep (El-Sheikh, Buckhalt, Mize, & Acebo, 2006). Research on the marital relationship has advanced the significance of distinctions between constructive and destructive marital conflict, communication, and marital satisfaction, both to the quality of marital functioning and as influences on child functioning and adjustment (Cummings & Davies, 1994; Emery, 1982; Grych & Fincham, 1990).

Study of marital functioning in the context of family research has provided evidence for the active and interactive role of the child within the marital relationship (Schermerhorn, Cummings, DeCarlo, & Davies, 2007); for example, involvement or triangulation of the child in interparental conflict has been shown to affect the functioning of the marital relationship (Kerig, 1995). Moreover, recent research has demonstrated relations between marital functioning, children's emotional security toward the parental marital relationship, and children's sleep (El-Sheikh, Buckhalt, Cummings, & Keller, 2007; El-Sheikh, Buckhalt, Keller, Cummings, & Acebo, 2007; see El-Sheikh & Kelly, chapter 1 in this volume for a review of relations between emotional insecurity in the marital relationship and children's sleep).

Sibling Relationships

Childhood sibling relationships also contribute to family functioning and child development, and thus may merit consideration in sleep research (Figure 14.1). Among the key constructs examined in research on the sibling relationship are conflict, closeness, and differential treatment (Dunn, 2005). Highlighting their relative salience, sibling relationships are typically longer lasting and more significant to children's functioning than peer relationships. Interactions between siblings may be highly frequent in occurrence, and act as significant contributors to family contexts, often on a daily basis. At the same time, despite the salience and frequency of sibling interactions in families, sibling relationships are an understudied topic of study within family research (Kramer & Bank, 2005).

Assessment of Whole Family Contexts

In addition to the study of individuals and dyads within the family, family researchers have examined the nature and characteristics of whole family functioning (see Figure 14.1). For example, putting this construct in a theoretical context, family systems theory posits that the whole is greater than the sum of the parts with regard to family influences (Minuchin, 1974). This perspective signifies the importance of moving beyond understanding family process in terms of individual functioning and dyadic relationships to also consider the system as a whole context in which these specific influences occur (Cox & Paley, 1997). Research at the whole family level examines constructs such as conflict and instability (Davies, Harold, Goeke-Morey, & Cummings, 2002), cohesion (Barber & Buehler, 1996), and family structure (Kerig, 1995). One benefit of studying the whole family, beyond dyadic relationships, is the ability to study and compare diverse sets of families (e.g., two-parent families, single parent families, step families).

Families are complex systems that are constantly changing and adapting over time. Thus, measurement of family functioning in sleep research ideally captures this dynamic nature, which requires longitudinal research designs. Family research has moved beyond general description to understanding the processes by which family functioning leads to child adjustment and maladjustment. Longitudinal research designs, which assess the same families over a period of time with the use of multiple assessments, allow for the examination of the changing nature of family processes over time, and can untangle the mechanisms through which these changes relate to child development. Toward shedding light on processes of development in the context of research on sleep and families, longitudinal designs capture intraindividual change (e.g., understanding the nature of child or family change) as well as interindividual differences between children and families. While cross-sectional research designs provide a snapshot of families at one point in time, longitudinal research is essential for demonstrating the transactional processes and cyclical changes that often characterize the fundamental nature of family processes. Prospective studies, as opposed to retrospective research designs, capture the development of child and family functioning as unfolding processes, thereby providing a richer understanding of how development occurs. In contrast, retrospective research designs often bias the relationships investigated.

Multiple Methodologies

An important issue to consider for the sleep researcher interested in the integration of family variables relates to the methodology utilized in the assessment of family functioning and child development.

Each methodological approach has its own advantages and disadvantages, which we will consider below. Ideally, understanding of the dynamic nature of families is advanced by researchers employing multiple methodological techniques to capture family life. A multiple methods approach to research designs reduces the likelihood that findings reflect a mono-method bias and can provide a larger picture and deeper understanding of family processes. No single study can incorporate all methodological tools for the assessment of family processes, thus consideration must be given to the advantages and disadvantages of each as well as the appropriateness of the level of assessment inherent in different techniques. In the sections that follow, different methods for the assessment of family functioning at the individual, dyadic, and whole family level are described along with the advantages and disadvantages inherent in each methodological approach. In addition to the use of multiple methods, when self-report approaches are employed, multiple reporters should be utilized to examine unique contributions from different viewpoints within the family and reduce the effects of reporter biases.

Questionnaire Measures

Questionnaire measures that are well-designed and effectively utilized are a quick, inexpensive, and efficient way to gather information from a large group of people. Questionnaires gathered from parent-report of family functioning and child behavior allow for parents to use their broad knowledge and experience about their child and family to report on specific behaviors and events across many settings that may not be evident in other methodological tools, such as observational research (Cummings et al., 2000).

Questionnaires require a relatively minimal amount of effort on the part of the researcher in terms of collecting and compiling data and are minimally demanding on participants to complete. Questionnaires allow for comparisons across reporters, groups, and studies. Participants have the opportunity to think carefully about their answers without the implicit pressure to answer that one might feel during a face-to-face or phone interview. On the other hand, in the absence of a researcher dictating the pace and focus of an interview, participants may bore of the questions or be tempted to skip ahead in the sequence of questions without providing a thoughtful response (Bowling, 2005). Use of reverse-scored items aids in the ability to determine if participants carefully read and answered questions. Questionnaires also tend to be retrospective in nature, relying primarily on participants' memories of events, experiences, and feelings, which may not be accurate in hindsight (Bowling, 2005). Notably, some questionnaires have been designed to assess concurrent functioning by asking participants to report on feelings and behaviors within a specific time frame (e.g., the last two weeks).

Questionnaire responses may also reflect self-enhancing traits rather than objective measures of behaviors (Tourangeau & Smith, 1996); social desirability scales may help to screen out participants who are not providing an accurate view of themselves. Because questionnaires are often administered individually and completed by the participant, these methods do not allow researchers to probe for in-depth answers. Questionnaires are also particularly vulnerable to the effects of poorly worded or leading questions. Another limitation of questionnaire measures is that they require literacy of participants, making the use of questionnaires ineffective for certain demographic groups that may be of particular interest to the researcher (Bowling, 2005).

Questionnaire measures utilize a variety of approaches for quantifying behaviors; questions can consist of a series of open-ended or forced choice questions, or a combination of the two (Boynton & Greenhalgh, 2004). Forced-choice questions can be employed in a variety of formats, including dichotomous answers, Likert scales, and multiple-choice. Dichotomous formats require respondents to reply affirmatively or negatively, whereas multiple choice formats require participants to choose from a small variety of answers. Additionally, answer options that force a choice but allow for a range of responses on a number or Likert-type scale, such as answers ranging from strongly agree to strongly disagree, allow for quantifying answers while also providing answer options, which allow participants to generate the response that is most appropriate to their experience (Boynton & Greenhalgh, 2004). Researchers concerned with ceiling and floor effects, due to social desirability, for example, can utilize a Q-sort methodology in which participants are asked to select traits that are most and least like them with specific numbers of traits allowed for each response category (Waters & Deane, 1985). This technique allows participants to choose fewer answers that are most descriptive. Questionnaires may also be presented in formats that allow for more flexibility in participants' answers, such as fill-in-the-blank or short answer. Researchers who plan to use questionnaire measures should carefully consider how their data will be used and the type of information that will be instrumental in the analysis phase of their study.

Questionnaires sometimes need to be developed to measure and quantify previously untested phenomena. For example, in accordance with Emotional Security Theory (Davies & Cummings, 1994), the Security in the Interparental Subsystem scale (SIS) and Security in the Marital Subsystem scale (SIMS; Davies, Forman, Rasi, & Stevens, 2002) were developed by Patrick Davies and colleagues to assess child- and parent-report of children's emotional security about the marital relationship. Emotional Security Theory posits that children have a set-goal or desired level of emotional security about the marital relationship that they constantly monitor and seek to maintain. Thus, when the set-goal is threatened or violated by exposure to destructive marital conflict, children may become emotionally and/or behaviorally dysregulated as a result of the distress induced by the violation of the set-goal. This distress may motivate them to try to regain their desired level of emotional security, for example, through regulatory processes, such as mediating in marital conflict (Cummings & Davies, 2010). Over time, children's sense of emotional insecurity about the interparental relationship may contribute to pathways of the development of adjustment problems (Cummings, Schermerhorn, Davies, Goeke-Morey, & Cummings, 2006), whereas children's confidence and security about the marital relationship may contribute to children's social competencies (McCoy, Cummings, & Davies, 2009).

The SIS and SIMS specifically measure children's emotional security about the marital relationship; emotional security measured in this way has been shown to mediate relations between marital conflict, sleep, and children's adjustment (El-Sheikh, Buckhalt, Cummings, et al., 2007; El-Sheikh, Buckhalt, Keller, et al., 2007). The Security in the Family System scale (SIFS; Forman & Davies, 2005) examines these processes at the whole family level, allowing for examination across a wider variety of families. Referring back to Figure 14.1, children's security about the marital relationship provides an example of the effects of dyadic processes (e.g., the marital relationship) on individual child functioning, whereas children's security about the family system may be related to the effects of whole family functioning on individual functioning.

Interview Measures

Interview methodology provides opportunities for in-depth discussion of salient constructs and experiences. Like questionnaires, interviews can be utilized to gather multiple family members' perspectives on family functioning. Conducted either face-to-face or via some form of interactive media (Bowling, 2005), interviews can range from being highly structured to unrestricted, depending on the information and constructs of interest (Cummings et al., 2000).

Structured interviews can be standardized in their administration to allow for higher reliability, although semi-structured interviews that are less rigid in their question format and sequencing may provide the most opportunities to uncover informative patterns that emerge in the data (Cummings et al., 2000). Interview methods have greater flexibility than questionnaires because they allow the interviewer to gain more information about complex processes by asking participants for further explanation or examples, and probing as needed to elucidate responses. A less structured interview may include guidelines by which experimenters determine the adequacy of responses and the direction in which to probe participants' answers so as to obtain useful information without leading respondents to a certain type of response.

Interviews can be valuable for assessing various aspects of family functioning. The McMaster Structured Interview of Family Functioning (McSIFF), for example, would be useful at the systems process level, depicted in Figure 14.1. This measure contains developmentally appropriate questions of all family members, the answers to which are used to establish scores of overall family functioning as well as scores on six more specific dimensions of family functioning, which include problem-solving, communication, roles, affective responsiveness, affective involvement, and behavioral control (for more information concerning the McSIFF interview see Akister & Stevenson-Hinde, 1991).

In addition to interviews assessing family functioning, structured and semi-structured interviews also allow for assessing diagnostic criteria for children's problem behaviors. The Children's Interview for Psychiatric

Syndromes (ChIPS; Weller, Weller, Fristad, Rooney, & Schecter, 2000) is a highly structured interview designed to screen for behaviors based on the criteria in the *Diagnostic and Statistical Manual of Mental Disorders* (American Psychiatric Association, 1994). The ChIPS is useful for children between the ages of 6 and 18 years and includes child and parent versions. The ChIPS interview would be of particular utility for researchers interested in assessments at the individual functioning level described in Figure 14.1, but its results could also be indicative of the outcomes of broader family processes.

Interviews, furthermore, make it possible to gain in-depth insight into the experiences of members of demographic groups for which questionnaires are impractical or impossible. Depth, however, comes at the expense of time on the part of the interviewer and participant. Interview data can be difficult and time-consuming to code given the broad range of possible responses. Interview measures are also sensitive to possible difficulties with consistent administration of interview protocol across interviewers. Researchers might opt to use a more structured interview format if data is to be collected by many interviewers. Despite these limitations, interviewing allows for the investigation of the meaning of family experiences. Interviews can also be structured and administered in a way that allows for clear guidelines for administration and standardization across participants.

Physiological Measures

Physiological reactivity and regulation can be assessed through the collection of diagnostic fluids such as saliva or blood, or through the use of sensors and imaging devices that measure indicators of physiological responses like heart rate, blood pressure, and brain wave activity (Cummings et al., 2000). Although the relevance of physiological assessments is most recognizable at the individual level (Booth, Carver, & Granger, 2004), physiological assessments can be collected from both members of a dyad in the context of an interaction; researchers may then be able to assess reactivity in conjunction with the behaviors and emotions occurring between individuals.

Physiological measures may provide insight into the biological mechanisms by which the family environment affects its members, and may reveal responses to situations or environments that participants are either unable or unwilling to articulate or display through their behavior. Physiological measures are limited in that they can be expensive and time-consuming, not only in their collection but also in their analysis (Granger et al., 2007). Assessment of physiological responsivity often requires specialized training, equipment and supplies, or external contracts to properly assay samples. Meaningful results may also be hard to obtain or interpret. Certain physiological indicators are particularly sensitive to the context in which they are collected, and evidence of reactivity in properly collected samples can still be hard to interpret in terms of its relation to the constructs of interest. Finally, participants may be reluctant to participate in projects that include physiological measures, due to the perceived intrusive nature of these assessments, depending on the method of collection, and the kind of physiological information gathered. Fortunately, there is a large range of response domains to examine and collection techniques to utilize, and valuable information can be gained from physiological assessment methods including those that are minimally invasive (Booth et al., 2004).

Physiological measures ideally are integrated into family research in meaningful ways, and such integration should be theory driven (Granger & Kivlighan, 2003). Stress reactivity should be induced and assessed in ways that allow for the interpretation of reactivity in conjunction with salient family stressors. Reactivity is context dependent (e.g., Watamura, Donzella, Alwin, & Gunnar, 2003) and should be elicited in ecologically valid settings, such as common family events. Studies of family functioning have measured, for example, cortisol responses to a variety of situations including events such as conflictual discussions between family members, which can provide insight into physiological reactivity to the event while maintaining a minimal level of invasiveness (Davies et al., 2008).

Researchers should attempt to balance the risk of losing participants with the benefits of the knowledge to be gained when making decisions about the level of invasiveness to which they are willing to subject their participants. Although physiological responses are informative in nature, these methods, in conjunction with family processes, are best utilized in a multi-method assessment (Granger & Kivlighan, 2003). Physiological responses ideally are combined with measures of behavioral and emotional responses to increase the interpretability of these findings.

Observational Measures

Observational measures are employed to examine complex interactions between family members in order to capture the dynamic interplay between dyads and triads within the family. These methods can be high in external validity and rich in descriptions of naturally occurring phenomena. Naturalistic observational measures have often been lauded for the removal of the self-reflective aspect in questionnaire and interview methods; however, design and coding of observations depend on researchers' notions and theories of family processes (Cummings et al., 2000).

Observational measures can be conducted in various settings; two types of observational techniques include laboratory observations and naturalistic observations (Cummings et al., 2000). Commonly, family researchers conduct laboratory observations in which family members are asked to engage in a specific task designed to elicit behaviors of interest. Laboratory observations allow for a higher degree of control than observations in naturalistic settings, and allow for the research task to increase the likelihood of specific behaviors and interactions being detected. For example, family researchers interested in understanding the nature of conflict in parent-adolescent relationships may ask families to engage in a discussion centered on a current conflictual topic.

In contrast, naturalistic observational measures are captured in the setting in which they occur. For example, researchers may observe family interactions in the home in order to understand the nature of families' daily lives. While naturalistic observation methods are especially high in external validity, it may be more difficult to observe behaviors in their natural setting. Further, compared to laboratory methods adapted to increase the likelihood of specific behaviors, observing behavior in natural settings may not enhance the probability of capturing the specific behaviors of interest (Cummings et al., 2000).

Family interactions are coded to identify and quantify specific behaviors and constructs of interest to the investigator. Numerous coding schemes have been developed to capture marital, parent-child, and whole family interactions. Interactions may be coded based on observational records or coded in the field as the interactions unfold. Coding systems focus on specific constructs of interest and may assess behaviors at either the micro- or macro-analytic levels (Kerig & Lindahl, 2001). Micro-analytic systems examine behaviors in small segments of time (e.g., 5 or 10 second intervals). Use of micro-analytic systems allows for data analyses techniques that may capture dynamic relationships within interactions and sequences of interactions over time. Macro-analytic systems allow for capturing coherence of interactions and themes that emerge, which may be lost in analysis of small time intervals. Reliability of coders is an issue of concern in both macro- and micro-analytic systems of coding (for more information on specific coding systems available for family research see Kerig & Lindahl, 2001).

For example, the Conflict in the Interparental System (CIS) Observational Coding System assesses couples' use of a variety of conflict tactics while engaging in a discussion of a problematic topic (Cummings & Davies, 2010). The CIS is a micro-coding system for assessing destructive and constructive conflict tactics for both husbands and wives in thirty second time intervals. This micro-system approach allows for study of unique research questions on the transactional nature of partner-self use of conflict tactics.

While observational measures may have high external validity, these approaches allow for less control over the situation observed and the behaviors that emerge in an interaction. Researchers cannot ensure that the behavior of interest will occur during the time frame of observation nor with the frequency required for data analysis. Additionally, these observations tend to be costly and labor-intensive in comparison to other methodological approaches. Nonetheless, these data can provide a wealth of insight into interpersonal relational patterns not often captured through other methodological approaches.

Analogue Measures

Analogue measures expose participants to hypothetical family situations and measure their responses to these scenarios. Family scenarios can be depicted in a variety of methods; the most common methods include audiotape, videotape, and written depictions of events. These methods allow for the systematic variation of a given construct and provide more control over conditions than naturalistic observational measures (Cook & Rumrill, 2005). Analogue measures can ensure that all participants are exposed to similar conditions and permit examination of differences in responses to relatively slight variations in a construct. Further, analogue measures allow for the simplification of dynamic family processes to examine specific components of family functioning. For example, children have been exposed to video clips of marital conflict that vary in the specific conflict tactics depicted as well as the degree of resolution (Goeke-Morey, Cummings, & Papp, 2007). This systematic variation provides the opportunity to examine reactions to well-defined components of conflict as opposed to viewing observations of conflict that may contain multiple and complex varieties of conflict tactics. Goeke-Morey and colleagues (2007) found, through the use of analogue measures of specific conflict tactics, that compromise between marital partners after conflict was linked to improved child functioning. Analogue measures are sometimes viewed as lower in external validity due to the use of artificial scenarios. Nonetheless, these methods allow for experimental manipulations of constructs of interest and can provide systematic investigation of complex family processes (for examples of analogue measures used in family research see Rathus & Feindler, 2004).

Diary Measures

Diary methodologies allow for the study of family processes within the natural setting, such as the home, work place, or school. Diary methods can be employed in many different ways; the most common collection techniques include the use of paper and pencil diaries or electronic devices that store participants' diary entries. Commonly used research designs include event-contingent, interval-contingent, and signal-contingent methods. Event-contingent methods ask participants to complete a diary entry upon the occurrence of specific events (e.g., at the completion of each family conflict episode). In contrast, interval-contingent methods require participants to complete diary assessments at a specified time (e.g., before bed, upon waking, etc.), including the occurrence of events over the course of the entire day as opposed to the occurrence of single events, which is captured with the event-contingent methods. Lastly, signal-contingent methods require participants to complete a diary entry in response to a signal from the research team. Participants may be signaled through the use of a beeper or an electronic device. For example, signal-contingent designs may investigate a random sampling of daily events (for a review of diary methods in family research see Laurenceau & Bolger, 2005).

Diary data can be used as a tool to examine change over the course of a specific time frame or to assess the effectiveness of family prevention work. Our research team is utilizing the interval-contingent diary assessments during a four week psycho-educational prevention program aimed at increasing the use of constructive conflict; families complete daily assessments of the use of constructive and destructive tactics that occurred during conflict in the marital and parent-child relationships. These diary assessments thus assess the efficacy of the program in producing change in behaviors in family relationships.

The use of daily diaries may enhance the external validity of laboratory findings. Daily diary assessments provide a sequence of rich data for investigating the transactional and cyclical nature of family processes. Researchers need to select a sampling period that is representative of the behaviors of interest, although there is a trade off between length of assessment period and the demands on participants' time. Owing to the fact that data are not collected in a laboratory setting, missing data and the integrity of the data are problematic in diary methods. Researchers cannot be sure that pencil and paper diary measures are being completed during the time frame requested of the participants; however, the use of electronic devices has reduced this problem.

Qualitative Methodology

Qualitative and quantitative methods can complement one another and serve to inform inquires about family processes (Plano Clark, Huddleston-Casas, Churchill, O'Neil Green, & Garrett, 2008). Qualitative methodology provides an in-depth understanding of family processes that serves to identify the meaning of complex family functioning. Qualitative analyses focus on describing phenomena, as opposed to the quantifying of behaviors or statements inherent in quantitative methodologies. Commonly used qualitative methods include ethnographies, focus groups, participant observation, and narrative accounts (for an introduction to qualitative research see Denzin & Lincoln, 2000). Inclusion of qualitative methods helps to inform and guide quantitative research designs; together these methods can better help researchers to understand the complex nature of family processes.

An example of the inclusion of qualitative measures in quantitative research designs relates to the use of focus groups in the creation of new questionnaire measures. In an effort to extend the notion of security processes beyond the family system, our research team has developed the Security in the Community Scale (SIC; Cummings, Goeke-Morey, Schermerhorn, Merrilees, & Cairns, 2009) to assess the construct of emotional security at the community level. Based on information gained through the focus groups, the SIC measures security processes in the community and cultural context with items reflecting the tenets of Emotional Security Theory. Thus, similar to the conceptualization of children's emotional security about the marital relationship, the notion is that children have a set-goal or desired level of emotional security about the community. When this set-goal is violated as a result of community violence or antisocial behavior, children may become emotionally or behaviorally dysregulated, motivating them to take action to regain their sense of emotional security, for example, by becoming involved in sectarian efforts to increase security within their own communities. Moreover, children's emotional insecurity about their community may contribute to their risk for the development of adjustment problems (Cummings et al., 2010).

Multiple Analytic Approaches

Choice of data analytic and statistical approaches for assessing relations among family functioning, sleep, and child outcomes is another essential piece of the research process in this area. Various statistical models hold promise for capturing the complex nature of families and untangling relations between family processes, explanatory mechanisms, and child outcomes.

Analytical Approaches to Family Data

Structural Equation Modeling

Structural equation modeling (SEM) is a general framework that allows for the examination of the "goodness-of-fit" between a proposed model, driven by theoretical tenets, and the sample data provided by participants (Bollen, 1989). SEM can be utilized for a variety of statistical methods, including regression analyses, linear growth modeling, factor analysis, path analysis, and multigroup analyses. SEM allows for modeling both structural and measurement models; the structural portion of the model reflects regression-like analyses demonstrating the relationships between variables, whereas the measurement portion of the model fit is to assess the relationship between latent and manifest variables. Manifest variables are observable, measurable variables such as child-report of parental warmth or observer ratings of marital aggression. Latent variables are unobserved variables that are estimated indirectly through the use of multiple, presumably related, manifest variables, which tap into the larger, unobservable, underlying construct, such as marital conflict or parenting.

Sample sizes optimal for SEM depend on the number of parameters specified in a given model, thus models that are more complex may require many families. Discrepancies among different reporters are common in developmental and family research (Achenbach, 2009); structural equation modeling allows for constructing latent variables that utilize these different reporters of family functioning (e.g., mother, father, child) to capture a more accurate picture of the underlying family processes. SEM can be utilized for testing the fit of transactional or reciprocal models as well as mediator or moderator models.

Multilevel Modeling

Multilevel modeling (or hierarchical linear modeling, HLM; Raudenbush & Bryk, 2002) has a number of advantages for use with family data. Multilevel modeling captures both within-person change and between-person differences in change, allowing for the modeling of both intraindividual change (e.g., level 1 model) and interindividual difference in intraindividual change (e.g., level 2 model). This analytical technique examines within-person change, assessing growth trajectories in longitudinal data, and identifies what and how processes are changing over time. Assessing interindividual differences in intraindividual change allows for examining correlates of change by assessing which behaviors or family processes predict different change trajectories. Referring back to Figure 14.1, HLM can be used to assess changes over time in individual functioning and determine whether these changes are the result of functioning at the dyadic level. For example, HLM can be used to answer the question of how children's academic functioning changes over time and whether those patterns of change vary by attachment classifications.

In addition to the ability to assess individual growth trajectories and correlates of growth trajectories, multilevel modeling allows for the analyses of nested data. Participants in family research rarely provide independent data, rather family research often includes data from multiple family members including mothers, fathers, and children. Thus, participants are inevitably non-independent and nested within families, and multilevel modeling allows for analyzing this nested data. Additionally, multilevel modeling can be integrated into the SEM framework, making these analysis approaches complimentary to one another (for an introduction to multilevel modeling see Nezlek, 2008).

Growth Mixture Modeling

Person-centered approaches to analyzing data focus on classifying individuals into different unobserved groups based on a subset of selected variables such as behavior or affective responses. In contrast, variable-centered approaches seek to identify the links between a given set of variables. Analytic techniques for person-centered approaches include cluster analysis, latent class analysis, and growth mixture modeling.

An advantage of growth mixture modeling is the use of both person-centered and variable-centered approaches. Growth mixture modeling allows for identifying unobserved groups or clusters of people dependent on differences in their individual growth trajectories (Muthén, 2004). Growth mixture modeling is a subset of latent class analysis that allows for within-class variation around the group mean growth trajectory; latent class analysis does not allow for within-group variation. In addition to using antecedent variables as profiles of class membership, growth mixture modeling allows for modeling subsequent behavior predicted by class membership. These techniques can be used to answer research questions such as "Do different aspects of family functioning, such as family cohesion, predict membership in different subpopulations of internalizing and externalizing problems across childhood?" Questions can also be addressed about how an individual's group membership, as determined by these different trajectories, relates to children's pathways of development over time. Person-centered approaches to data analysis provide additional flexibility to identify and understand how family processes may vary for different types of families (for an introduction on these techniques see Jung & Wickrama, 2008).

Processes Included in Analyses

Two different types of statistical models tap into different processes commonly involved in the relation between an antecedent and an outcome variable: mediator and moderator analyses. These elements are important conceptualizations for advanced process-oriented understanding of relations between family functioning, sleep, and child adjustment.

Mediator Analyses

Mediator models seek to answer questions of "how" and "why" two variables are related through the role of a third, intermediate variable. In these models, the third variable of interest captures the mechanism through which the antecedent variable relates to the outcome variable. Research questions in family research related to mediator models include questions such as "By what process is marital conflict related to child adjustment?" For example, sleep has been identified as a mediator of the relation between children's emotional insecurity in the interparental marital relationship and their adjustment (El-Sheikh, Buckhalt, Cummings, et al., 2007). Mediators play an explanatory role in the causal chain of family processes. Various analytical techniques exist to test for mediator variables (for a review on current directions in mediation analyses see MacKinnon & Fairchild, 2009).

Moderator Analyses

In contrast, moderator variables examine the possibility of an interaction between the antecedent variable and the moderator on the outcome variable, such that the strength and/or the direction of the relationship between the antecedent and outcome variable may differ depending on the level of the moderator variable. These models answer the question of "for whom," "when," and "under which conditions" does the antecedent variable relate to the outcome variable. For example, in testing moderation effects, the researcher may investigate if the relationship between two variables differs depending on child or parent gender, family structure, or socioeconomic status (for more information on mediation and moderation see Frazier, Tix, & Barron, 2004).

In addition to mediator and moderator models, recent efforts have combined these models to examine both moderated mediation and mediated moderation (Preacher, Rucker, & Hayes, 2007). Moderated mediation analyses answer the question of "for whom" does a given mechanism or process explain the relationship between the antecedent and the outcome variables (e.g., does the role of the mediator differ depending on the levels of the moderator variable?). When moderation occurs, mediated moderation analyses can examine the explanatory mechanisms through which these differences operate. Both of these analytical approaches allow for unraveling the complex processes inherent in family research.

Conclusion

In this chapter, we have outlined various assessment approaches, for the sake of researchers, including pediatric and sleep medicine investigators, interested in studying family processes and how they relate to child psychological functioning and sleep. In particular, the pros and cons for selecting specific approaches to the assessment of family functioning as it relates to child development have been considered, including notions of family systems that merit study, approaches to measurement and assessment, and key issues for analysis for advancing relatively sophisticated and process-oriented models of relations between family processes, sleep, and children's functioning. Inevitably, the investigator or investigative team must make the many critical decisions on how to proceed, shifting among the many possible alternatives. We are hopeful that our review and presentation of these issues and choice points will be helpful in this decision-making process.

REFERENCES

Achenbach, T. M. (2009). Some needed changes in DSM-V: But what about children? *Clinical Psychology: Science and Practice, 16*, 50–53.

Akister, J., & Stevenson-Hinde, J. (1991). Identifying families at risk: Exploring the potential of the McMaster Family Assessment Device. *Journal of Family Therapy, 13*, 411–421.

American Psychiatric Association. (1994). *Diagnostic and statistical manual of mental disorders* (4th ed.). Washington, DC: Author.

Barber, B. K., & Buehler, C. (1996). Family cohesion and enmeshment: Different constructs, different effects. *Journal of Marriage and Family, 58*, 433–441.

Baumrind, D. (1967). Child care practices anteceding three patterns of preschool behavior. *Genetic Psychology Monographs, 75*, 43–88.

Bollen, K. A. (1989). *Structural equations with latent variables*. New York: Wiley-Interscience Publication.

Booth, A., Carver, K., & Granger, D. A. (2004). Biosocial perspectives on the family. *Journal of Marriage and the Family, 62*, 1018–1034.

Bowlby, J. (1969). *Attachment and loss, vol. 1: Attachment*. New York, NY: Basic Books.

Bowling, A. (2005). Mode of questionnaire administration can have serious effects on data quality. *Journal of Public Health, 27*, 281–291.

Boynton, P. M., & Greenhalgh, T. (2004). Selecting, designing, and developing your questionnaire. *British Medical Journal, 328*, 1312–1315.

Burke, J. D., Pardini, D. A., & Loeber, R. (2008). Reciprocal relationships between parenting behavior and disruptive psychopathology from childhood through adolescence. *Journal of Abnormal Child Psychology, 36*, 679–692.

Cook, B. G., & Rumrill, P. D., Jr. (2005). Using and interpreting analogue designs. *Work, 24*, 93–97.

Cox, M. J., & Paley, B. (1997). Families as systems. *Annual Review of Psychology, 48*, 243–267.

Cummings, E. M., & Davies, P. T. (1994). *Children and marital conflict: The impact of family dispute and resolution*. New York, NY: The Guilford Press.

Cummings, E. M., & Davies, P. T. (2010). *Marital conflict and children: An emotional security perspective*. New York, NY: The Guilford Press.

Cummings, E. M., Davies, P. T., & Campbell, S. B. (2000). *Developmental psychopathology and family process: Theory, research, and clinical implications*. New York, NY: The Guilford Press.

Cummings, E. M., Goeke-Morey, M. C., Schermerhorn, A. C., Merrilees, C. E., & Cairns, E. (2009). Children and political violence from a social ecological perspective: Implications from research on children and families in Northern Ireland. *Clinical Child and Family Psychology Review, 12*, 16–38.

Cummings, E. M., Merrilees, C. M., Schermerhorn, A. C., Goeke-Morey, M. C., Shirlow, P., & Cairns, E. (2010). Testing a social ecological model for relations between political violence and child adjustment in Northern Ireland. *Development and Psychopathology, 22*, 405–418.

Cummings, E.M., Schermerhorn, A. C., Davies, P. T., Goeke-Morey, M. C. & Cummings, J. S. (2006). Interparental discord and child adjustment: Prospective investigations of emotional security as an explanatory mechanism. *Child Development, 77*, 132–152.

Davidov, M., & Grusec, J. E. (2006). Untangling the links of parental responsiveness to distress and warmth to child outcomes. *Child Development, 77*, 44–58.

Davies, P. T., & Cummings, E. M. (1994). Marital conflict and child adjustment: An emotional security hypothesis. *Psychological Bulletin, 116*, 387–411.

Davies, P.T., Forman, E. M., Rasi, J. A., & Stevens, K. I. (2002). Assessing children's emotional security in the interparental relationship: The security in the interparental subsystem scales. *Child Development, 73*, 544–562.

Davies, P. T., Harold, G. T., Goeke-Morey, M. C., & Cummings, E. M. (2002). Child emotional security and interparental conflict. *Monographs of the Society for Research in Child Development, 67*, 1–131.

Davies, P. T., Sturge-Apple, M. L., Cicchetti, D., & Cummings, E. M. (2008). Adrenocortical underpinnings of children's psychological reactivity to interparental conflict. *Child Development, 79*, 1693–1706.

Denzin, N. K., & Lincoln, Y. S. (2000). *Handbook of Qualitative Research* (2nd ed.). Thousand Oaks, CA: Sage Publications, Inc.

Dunn, J. (2005). Commentary: Siblings in their families. *Journal of Family Psychology, 19*, 654–657.

El-Sheikh, M., Buckhalt, J. A., Cummings, E. M., & Keller, P. S. (2007). Sleep disruptions and emotional insecurity are pathways of risk for children. *Journal of Child Psychology and Psychiatry, 48*, 88–96.

El-Sheikh, M., Buckhalt, J. A., Keller, P. S., Cummings, E. M., & Acebo, C. (2007). Child emotional insecurity and academic achievement: The role of sleep disruptions. *Journal of Family Psychology, 21*, 29–38.

El-Sheikh, M., Buckhalt, J. A., Mize, J., & Acebo, C. (2006). Marital conflict and disruptions in children's sleep. *Child Development, 77*, 31–43.

Emery, R. E. (1982). Interparental conflict and the children of discord and divorce. *Psychological Bulletin, 92*, 310–330.

Forman, E. M., & Davies, P.T. (2005). Assessing children's appraisals of security in the family system: The development of the Security in the Family System (SIFS) scales. *Journal of Child Psychology and Psychiatry, 46*, 900–916.

Frazier, P. A., Tix, A. P., & Barron, K. E. (2004). Testing moderator and mediator effects in counseling psychology research. *Journal of Counseling Psychology, 51*, 115–134.

Gable, S., Crnic, K., & Belsky, J. (1994). Coparenting within the family system: Influences on children's development. *Family Relations, 43*, 380–386.

Goeke-Morey, M. C., Cummings, E. M., & Papp, L. M. (2007). Children and marital conflict resolution: Implications for emotional security and adjustment. *Journal of Family Psychology, 21*, 744–753.

Granger, D. A., & Kivlighan, K. T. (2003). Integrating biological, behavioral, and social levels of analysis in early child development: Progress, problems, and prospects. *Child Development, 74*, 1058–1063.

Granger, D. A., Kivlighan, K. T., Fortunato, C., Harmon, A. G., Hibel, L. C., Schwartz, E. B., & Whembolua, G. L. (2007). Integration of salivary biomarkers into developmental and behaviorally-oriented research: Problems and solutions for collecting specimens. *Physiology & Behavior, 92*, 583–590.

Grych, J. H., & Fincham, F. D. (1990). Marital conflict and children's adjustment: A cognitive-contextual framework. *Psychological Bulletin, 108*, 267–290.

Harold, G. T., Aitken, J. J., & Shelton, K. H. (2007). Inter-parental conflict and children's academic attainment: A longitudinal analysis. *Journal of Child Psychology and Psychiatry, 48*, 1223–1232.

Jung, T., & Wickrama, K. A. S. (2008). An introduction to latent class growth analysis and growth mixture modeling. *Social and Personality Psychology Compass, 2*, 302–317.

Kerig, P. K. (1995). Triangles in the family circle: Effects of family structure on marriage, parenting, and child adjustment. *Journal of Family Psychology, 9*, 28–43.

Kerig, P. K., & Lindahl, K. M. (2001). *Family observational coding systems: Resources for systemic research.* Mahwah, NJ: Lawrence Erlbaum Associates.

Kramer, L., & Bank, L. (2005). Sibling relationship contributions to individual and family well-being: Introduction to the special issue. *Journal of Family Psychology, 19*, 483–485.

Laurenceau, J. P., & Bolger, N. (2005). Using diary methods to study marital and family processes. *Journal of Family Psychology, 19*, 86–97.

Maccoby, E. E., & Martin, J. A. (1983). Socialization in the context of the family: Parent-child interaction. In P. H. Mussen (Ed.), *Handbook of child psychology: Vol. 4. Socialization, personality, and social development* (4th ed., pp. 1–101). New York, NY: John Wiley & Sons.

MacKinnon, D. P., & Fairchild, A. J. (2009). Current directions in mediation analysis. *Current Directions in Psychological Science, 18*, 16–20.

McCoy, K., Cummings, E. M., & Davies, P. T. (2009). Constructive and destructive marital conflict, emotional security and children's prosocial behavior. *Journal of Child Psychology and Psychiatry, 50*, 270–279.

Minuchin, S. (1974). *Families & family therapy.* Cambridge, MA: Harvard University Press.

Muthén, B. (2004). Latent variable analysis: Growth mixture modeling and related techniques for longitudinal data. In D. Kaplan (Ed.), *Handbook of quantitative methodology for the social sciences* (pp. 345–368). Newbury Park, CA: Sage Publications.

Nezlek, J. B. (2008). An introduction to multilevel modeling for social and personality psychology. *Social and Personality Psychology Compass, 2*, 842–860.

Plano Clark, V. L., Huddleston-Casas, C. A., Churchill, S. L., O'Neil Green, D., & Garrett, A. L. (2008). Mixed methods approaches in family science research. *Journal of Family Issues, 29*, 1543–1566.

Preacher, K. J., Rucker, D. D., & Hayes, A. F. (2007). Addressing moderated mediation hypotheses: Theory, methods, and prescriptions. *Multivariate Behavioral Research, 42*, 185–227.

Rathus, J. H., & Feindler, E. L. (2004). *Assessment of partner violence: A handbook for researchers and practitioners*. Washington, DC: American Psychological Association.

Raudenbush, S. W., & Bryk, A. S. (2002). Hierarchical linear models: Applications and data analysis methods (2nd ed.). Thousand Oaks, CA: Sage.

Schermerhorn, A. C., Cummings, E. M., DeCarlo, C. A., & Davies, P. T. (2007). Children's influence in the marital relationship. *Journal of Family Psychology, 21*, 259–269.

Tourangeau, R., & Smith, T. W. (1996). Asking sensitive questions: The impact of data collection mode, question format, and question context. *The Public Opinion Quarterly, 60*, 275–304.

Watamura, S. E., Donzella, B., Alwin, J., & Gunnar, M. R. (2003). Morning-to-afternoon increases in cortisol concentrations for infants and toddlers at child care: Age differences and behavioral correlates. *Child Development, 74*, 1006–1020.

Waters, E., & Deane, K. E. (1985). Defining and assessing individual differences in attachment relationships: Q-methodology and the organization of behavior in infancy and early child hood. *Monographs of the Society for Research in Child Development, 50*, 41–65.

Weller, E. B., Weller, R. A., Fristad, M. A., Rooney, M. T., & Schecter, J. (2000). Children's Interview for Psychiatric Syndromes (ChIPS). *Journal of the American Academy of Child & Adolescent Psychiatry, 39*, 76–84.

Whiteside-Mansell, L., Bradley, R. H., Casey, P. H., Fussell, J. J., & Connors-Burrow, N. A. (2009). Triple risk: Do difficult temperament and family conflict increase the likelihood of behavioral maladjustment in children born low birth weight and preterm? *Journal of Pediatric Psychology, 34*, 396–405.

15

Sleep Assessment Methods

Avi Sadeh

Introduction

Assessing sleep in infants and children is a challenging task and there are different methods to accomplish this undertaking. Each method has its advantages and limitations and the choice of methodology depends on: (a) specific assessment goals or questions, (b) the age of the child, and (c) the availability of the equipment and knowledge required. In this chapter, the main sleep assessment methods are presented: polysomnography, videosomnography, actigraphy, direct behavioral observations, sleep diaries, and questionnaires. In presenting the various sleep assessment methodologies, special emphasis is given to their advantages and limitations. Sleep assessment methodologies that require equipment are discussed with no reference to specific brand names or companies. At the end of the chapter, some discussion of how to choose the appropriate sleep assessment method will be presented.

Polysomnography

Polysomnography (PSG) is considered the gold-standard of sleep assessment. PSG is based on laboratory or ambulatory monitoring that usually includes electrical brain activity (EEG), muscle activation (EMG), eye movements (EOG), breathing efforts and flow, oxygen saturation sensors (oximetry), video recording, and additional channels according to study requirements. Studies with infants and young children are usually conducted in sleep laboratories (because of a variety of technical and safety issues). The electrodes and sensors are attached to the child prior to bedtime and the child is required to tolerate these attachments throughout the study. These PSG studies are usually conducted for one or two nights.

PSG provides detailed information including electrical tracings of brain activity, sleep architecture, sleep stages, sleep quality, arousals, breathing patterns, oxygen saturation, eye movements, and leg movements during sleep. This information is very rich and enables clinical research and diagnosis of a variety of sleep disorders including sleep apnea, periodic movements in sleep, parasomnias, seizures, REM sleep disorders, and insomnia.

Standard methods have been developed for scoring PSG data of infants, children and adults (Anders, Emde, & Parmelee, 1971; Iber, Ancoli-Israel, Chesson, & Quan, 2007; Rechtschaffen & Kales, 1968). Additional rules and guidelines have been developed for scoring specific phenomena such as arousals (The ASDA Task Force, 1992) or leg movements (The ASDA Task Force, 1993). Standardized guidelines also include indications for the use of PSG in clinical practice of sleep medicine (Kushida et al., 2005; Littner et al., 2003a).

In the last two decades, studies in normal pediatric populations provided reference values (or norms) for sleep and sleep-related breathing measures (Acebo, Millman, Rosenberg, Cavallo, & Carskadon, 1996; Coble, Kupfer, Taska, & Kane, 1984; Montgomery-Downs, O'Brien, Gulliver, & Gozal, 2006; Moss et al., 2005; Quan et al., 2003; Tapia et al., 2008; Traeger, Schultz, Pollock, Mason, Marcus, & Arens, 2005; Uliel, Tauman, Greenfeld, & Sivan, 2004; Verhulst, Schrauwen, Haentjens, Van Gaal, De Backer, & Desager, 2007). These reference values are very important for clinical and developmental research as they reflect developmental changes that are very crucial in assessing sleep in infants and young children.

Another important use of PSG is for determination of daytime sleepiness. The multiple sleep latency test (MSLT) has been developed for this purpose (Carskadon & Dement, 1982, 1992; Carskadon, Dement, Mitler, Roth, Westbrook, & Keenan, 1986; Littner et al., 2005; Richardson,

Carskadon, Flagg, Van den Hoed, Dement, & Mitler, 1978). The MSLT is based on giving individuals a few opportunities to fall asleep at different times of the day and measuring the latency to sleep onset using PSG. The underlying rationale is that given the opportunity to sleep, sleepy individuals would fall asleep faster than non-sleepy individuals.

Another PSG-based test developed to assess daytime sleepiness is the Maintenance of Wakefulness Test (MWT), which is based on similar principles as those of the MSLT. However, the MWT procedures request that tested individuals maintain their wakefulness while they are lying in bed with an opportunity to fall asleep (Littner et al., 2005; Mitler, Doghramji, & Shapiro, 2000; Mitler, Gujavarty, & Browman, 1982).

Advantages

- PSG provides the most detailed set of data on the sleep process including information that is very crucial for brain research and sleep medicine. Diagnosis of a variety of sleep disorders cannot be accomplished without specific information derived from PSG.
- When PSG is performed in a laboratory, there is a full control and supervision on the tested individual under standardized conditions.
- PSG can be used to assess objectively daytime sleepiness with procedures such as the MSLT or the MWT.

Limitations

- PSG requires infants and children to sleep under unique conditions that require tolerance to an unnatural sleep environment (laboratory) and attached electrodes and sensors. It requires some adjustment in adults (first night effect) and it is certainly more challenging for infants and young children. Therefore, derived measures can be unrepresentative of natural sleep of specific children.
- Analyzing and scoring the data is a time-consuming process.
- Because of the costs and demands of PSG, it is often done for one or two nights only, which further compromises the representativeness of the data.

- Infants and young children often spend a significant amount of time sleeping during daytime hours. Therefore, capturing all natural sleep episodes with PSG is practically impossible.
- Although ambulatory PSG is optional, there are safety issues associated with home PSG as well as insufficient information on its reliability and validity.

Videosomnography

Videosomnography is based on video recordings of sleep that can be done in the natural sleep environment of the child (Anders, 1979; Anders, Halpern, & Hua, 1992; Anders & Sostek, 1976; Burnham, Goodlin-Jones, Gaylor, & Anders, 2002a; Sostek, Anders, & Sostek, 1976). With one or more video cameras in the child's room, it is possible to record and later to identify sleep patterns (that includes active and quiet sleep periods in infants) as well as to document parental interventions and children's behavior during nighttime waking episodes. Video-based studies have documented the development of self-soothing skills in young children and the differences between infants waking up with or without signaling to their parents by fussing or crying (Anders et al., 1992; Anders & Keener, 1985; Burnham et al., 2002a; Burnham, Goodlin-Jones, Gaylor, & Anders, 2002b; Goodlin-Jones, Burnham, Gaylor, & Anders, 2001).

In addition to the standard videosomnography described above, home videos can be used to document different episodes reported by parents for clinical evaluation. For instance, it has been shown that video recordings can be used to screen sleep apnea in children (Sivan, Kornecki, & Schonfeld, 1996). It can also be used to obtain direct impression of events such as night terrors, rhythmic behaviors, REM behavior disorders, and other parasomnias.

Advantages

- Direct assessment of sleep in the natural sleep environment of the child.
- Detailed information on child nighttime behaviors and parental interventions.

Limitations

- Requires home installation and visual scoring of data, which is time consuming.
- Positions of the video camera and child in bed can interfere with the ability to accurately score sleep-wake states.
- Some parents may feel that their privacy is compromised with nocturnal video recordings.

Direct Behavioral Observation

Direct behavioral observation is a sleep assessment method that has mostly been used to assess sleep in young infants. The method utilizes trained observers who complete real time scoring of sleep and wakefulness states over a designated period of time at the infant's home or other nursery settings. The method is very labor intensive and is limited by available human resources and usually not done overnight (Thoman, 1975; Thoman, 1990; Thoman & Acebo, 1995). Simultaneous recording of respiration (with a pressure sensitive sensor pad placed under the infant) is a recommended complementary tool. Derived states include: (a) alert; (b) non-alert waking; (c) fuss or cry; (d) drowse, daze, or sleep-wake transition; (e) active sleep; (f) quiet sleep; (g) active-quiet transition sleep. Good inter-rater reliability has been reported for sleep-wake state scoring in infants and young children. Measures derived from direct observations have demonstrated scientific validity in predicting developmental outcomes including developmental disabilities and neurobehavioral functioning (Thoman, 1975; Thoman, 1990; Thoman, Denenberg, Sievel, Zeidner, & Becker, 1981).

Advantages

- Can be done at home or other normal sleep settings of the infant.
- Provides rich information on sleep and wakefulness states as well as related behaviors that tap into neurobehavioral organization and predict later development.

Limitations

- Labor intensive and usually limited to a few hours during daytime hours.
- Suitable mostly for infants and very young children.
- Having an observer at home may interfere with family routines and sense of privacy.

Actigraphy

Actigraphy, or activity-based monitoring, utilizes a wristwatch-like device that continuously monitors body movements and can provide information on sleep-wake patterns for extended periods in the natural environment of the child. The idea that infant sleep can be documented from body movement was introduced in the early 1950s when crib movements were recorded and used for this purpose (Kleitman & Engelmann, 1953). Advances in technology have led to the development of stand alone miniature units that can be easily attached to the wrist of the child (or the ankle in infants and toddlers) and collect activity data for extended periods. Raw activity data can be translated to validated sleep measures. Validation studies against PSG and other methods have demonstrated high validity for minute-by-minute sleep-wake scoring (Ancoli-Israel, Cole, Alessi, Chambers, Moorcroft, & Pollak, 2003; Sadeh & Acebo, 2002; Sadeh, Hauri, Kripke, & Lavie, 1995). In infants, it has been shown that active and quiet sleep can also be identified with reasonable validity through actigraphy (Sadeh, Acebo, Seifer, Aytur, & Carskadon, 1995).

The value of actigraphy for clinical research with pediatric populations has been demonstrated in studies showing that: (a) actigraphy can distinguish between sleep-disturbed and control infants (Sadeh, Lavie, Scher, Tirosh, & Epstein, 1991); (b) there are significant gaps between parental reports and actigraphy on night-wakings in infants and children (Sadeh, 1996; Sadeh, Flint-Ofir, Tirosh, & Tikotzky, 2007; Tikotzky & Sadeh, 2001); and (c) actigraphy can be used to assess the efficacy of behavioral interventions for infant sleep problems (Sadeh, 1994).

Standard of practice guidelines have been developed for the use of actigraphy in sleep medicine (Littner et al., 2003b; Morgenthaler et al., 2007; Thorpy et al., 1995). The unique characteristics of actigraphy that enable continuous and extended cost-effective sleep monitoring make it a valuable tool in the assessment of sleep schedule disorders, and as a complementary method to assess insomnia and treatment response. Actigraphy is also recommended for obtaining sleep data in individuals when subjective or parental reports are not available or are unreliable.

Because actigraphy measures movements, it is vulnerable to many artifacts related to externally induced movements (e.g., a child sleeping in a moving vehicle or in a rocking crib or stroller, Sadeh, Sharkey, & Carskadon, 1994). Therefore, careful monitoring and removal of such potential artifacts is a crucial component of actigraphy. It has been demonstrated that at least five days of actigraphy are needed to obtain optimal measurement validity (Acebo, Sadeh, Seifer, Tzischinsky, Wolfson, Hafer, & Carskadon, 1999). A related issue is potential movement artifacts that may be problematic in children with movement or other neurologic disorders.

Reference values for actigraphy-based sleep measures are available from studies in typically developing infants, children, and adolescents (Acebo, Sadeh, Seifer, Tzischinsky, & Carskadon, 2000; Sadeh, Raviv, & Gruber, 2000; Tikotzky & Sadeh, 2001, 2009; Wolfson, Carskadon, Acebo, Seifer, Fallone, Labyak, & Martin, 2003).

Another potential application of actigraphy is monitoring sleep during naturalistic studies of sleep restriction and other imposed demands on children (Fallone, Seifer, Acebo, & Carskadon, 2002; Sadeh, Gruber, & Raviv, 2003). For instance, it has been shown that actigraphy can validate compliance of children during a sleep restriction/extension home study (Sadeh et al., 2003). This capacity opens new opportunities for scientists interested in studies involving sleep manipulation in natural settings. However, it should be noted, that because of the nature of this assessment method, deception (e.g., attaching the actigraph to an active friend's wrist while taking a forbidden nap) is an option, if individuals are motivated to do so.

Advantages

- Cost-effective assessment method that enables continuous monitoring for extended periods in natural settings.
- Enables 24-hour monitoring for documenting nighttime as well as daytime sleep episodes.
- Extended periods of monitoring enable intervention follow-up and assessment of sleep schedule disorders.

Limitations

- Measures activity and therefore vulnerable to movement artifacts.
- Does not provide information on sleep stages or bedtime behavior and interactions. When poor quality is detected, activity data does not provide information on the source of the disruption.

Sleep Diary

Sleep diary is a very common tool for sleep research in infants and children. Older children can complete their own sleep diary, but in younger children the parents usually complete the diaries. The diaries usually provide information on sleep schedule, night wakings and related topics. It has been shown that parents are usually good reporters on sleep schedule measures (e.g., sleep onset, morning rise time) but their reliability as reporters drops when sleep quality measures (e.g., night wakings) are estimated (Sadeh, 1996, 2004; Tikotzky & Sadeh, 2001). Older children (high school age) were found to be good reporters on sleep schedule (Gaina, Sekine, Chen, Hamanishi, & Kagamimori, 2004).

Sleep diaries are often used in clinical research on interventions for night-waking problems. In such studies, parents are requested to document their child's sleep for extended periods of baseline and intervention weeks. It has been shown that parental exhaustion from this process may lead to progressive neglect to document each night waking, which may produce or inflate treatment effects, when reduced number of night wakings is the expected result of the intervention (Sadeh, 1994).

Advantages

- Cost-effective assessment method that enables continuous monitoring for extended periods in natural settings.
- Requires no equipment.
- More accurate than general questionnaires.

Limitations

- Sensitive to reporting biases and reporter's motivation.
- Self and parental reports on sleep quality measures are usually not very accurate.

Sleep Questionnaire

Sleep questionnaires are very popular as a cost-effective way to gather extensive information on sleep patterns, sleep problems, sleep context, and sleep-related behaviors. Many studies have developed tailored questionnaires that do not permit easy comparisons between studies and populations. However, some questionnaires have been validated and established in the field.

The Sleep Disturbance Scale for Children (SDSC) is a validated and established questionnaire for assessing sleep problems in children (Bruni et al., 2006; Bruni, Ottaviano, Guidetti, Romoli, Innocenzi, Cortesi, & Giannotti, 1996; Ferreira, Carvalho, Ruotolo, de Morais, Prado, & Prado, 2009). The SDSC includes 26 items that yield 6 factors: difficulty in initiating and maintaining sleep, sleep breathing disorders, arousal disorders, sleep–wake transition disorders, disorders of excessive somnolence, and sleep hyperhydrosis (sweating). The SDSC has demonstrated good psychometric properties and discriminative validity between clinical and control samples.

Another popular questionnaire is the Children's Sleep Habit Questionnaire (CSHQ), which provides a total score as well as scores on 8 specific domains (Owens, Spirito, & McGuinn, 2000). Specific domains include: (1) bedtime resistance; (2) sleep onset delay; (3) sleep duration;

(4) sleep anxiety; (5) night wakings; (6) parasomnia; (7) sleep disordered breathing; and (8) daytime sleepiness. The CSHQ has demonstrated good psychometrics and discriminative validity between clinical and control samples. A version for younger children (toddlers and preschool age) has been developed and validated (Goodlin-Jones, Sitnick, Tang, Liu, & Anders, 2008).

Another validated questionnaire is the Sleep Habits Survey (SHS) tailored for adolescents (Wolfson & Carskadon, 1998; Wolfson et al., 2003). High correlations have been reported between reported sleep schedule measures and equivalent measures derived from actigraphy (Wolfson et al., 2003).

Luginbuehl, Bradley-Klug, Ferron, Anderson, and Benbadis (2008) developed a questionnaire suitable for children and adolescents across a very broad age range (2–18 years). This questionnaire has shown good internal consistency and test-retest reliability as well as good validity in comparison to PSG and sleep expert diagnoses.

The Brief Infant Sleep Questionnaire (BISQ) has been developed and validated as a screening tool for younger children (0–3 years) and for online (internet) administration (Sadeh, 2004). Good psychometric properties have been demonstrated including discriminative validity between clinical and control samples (Sadeh, 2004). The questionnaire has been expanded and translated to other languages and recent cross-cultural studies provided reference data from many countries (Mindell, Sadeh, Kohyama, & How, in press; Mindell, Sadeh, Wiegand, How, & Goh, in press; Sadeh, Mindell, Luedtke, & Wiegand, 2009).

Advantages

- Enables coverage of many issues including sleep patterns, sleep disorders, sleep settings, child and parental bedtime behaviors.
- Requires no equipment.
- Availability of comparative data against which to compare any one child or group of children. Some questionnaires are normed, so standard scores can be derived.

Limitations

- Sensitive to reporting biases and reporter's motivation.
- General questionnaires are less accurate in describing specific sleep measures (e.g., sleep onset time) than sleep diaries when compared to other objective sleep measures.
- Many instruments are not normed on representative large samples that are stratified by age, gender, ethnicity, country, etc.

How to Choose the Appropriate Sleep Assessment Method

Choosing the appropriate sleep assessment tool may turn out to be a challenging task considering all the alternatives and the pros and cons of each method. This task requires special considerations of: (a) the research question, (b) the target population, and (c) the available means. For instance, a brain scientist interested in processes related to REM sleep is almost forced to choose PSG (or other related methods that document REM sleep). However, if this scientist is interested in REM (or active sleep) in young infants, other options such as direct observations or videosomnography are also available. If sleep disordered breathing is the topic of interest, then available methods vary between a questionnaire (focused on snoring, apneas, sleep with open mouth, etc.), actigraphy (that may show increased activity or sleep fragmentation related to breathing difficulties), videosomnography (that can show snoring and breathing efforts and apnea), or PSG that would be the most informative and provide all the information needed for full diagnosis of potential problems and their severity. In this case, however, although actigraphy may show altered sleeping patterns in individuals with sleep disordered breathing, it would be impossible to causally link these altered sleep patterns to the breathing difficulties. In many cases the use of complementary methods enables assessing a broader picture and show the overlap and discrepancies between knowledge derived from these methods. Examples of a mismatch between research questions and methods would be to use PSG for assessing sleep schedule disorders, questionnaires for individuals with language difficulties, PSG for common night-waking problems, and actigraphy for individuals with motor disorders.

There are many questionnaires, different actigraph devices, PSG, and video systems to choose from. After choosing the optimal (or practical) method for sleep assessment, there is still a need to choose the appropriate specific tool. To accomplish this task, a review of the reliability and validity data for each specific tool for the target population is required. For instance, concluding from the literature that actigraphy is a reliable method and then choosing a specific device while paying no attention to the available reliability and validity properties of this specific device with the specific target populations (adults, infants, etc.) is a problematic practice. Similarly it is not enough to select a questionnaire without examining available reliability and validity data, unless there is a special interest in exploring these issues in the planned study. Unfortunately, there are no published reviews comparing the performance and validity of different devices.

REFERENCES

Acebo, C., Millman, R. P., Rosenberg, C., Cavallo, A., & Carskadon, M. A. (1996). Sleep, breathing, and cephalometrics in older children and young adults. Part i—normative values. *Chest, 109,* 664–672.

Acebo, C., Sadeh, A., Seifer, R., Tzischinsky, O., & Carskadon, M. A. (2000). Sleep/wake patterns in one to five year old children from activity monitoring and maternal reports. *Sleep, 23,* A30–A31.

Acebo, C., Sadeh, A., Seifer, R., Tzischinsky, O., Wolfson, A. R., Hafer, A., et al. (1999). Estimating sleep patterns with activity monitoring in children and adolescents: How many nights are necessary for reliable measures? *Sleep, 22,* 95–103.

Ancoli-Israel, S., Cole, R., Alessi, C., Chambers, M., Moorcroft, W., & Pollak, C. P. (2003). The role of actigraphy in the study of sleep and circadian rhythms. *Sleep, 26,* 342–392.

Anders, T. F. (1979). Night-waking in infants during the first year of life. *Pediatrics, 63,* 860–864.

Anders, T. F., Emde, R. N., & Parmelee, A. A. (1971). *A manual of standardized terminology, techiques and criteria for the scoring of states of sleep and wakefulness in newborn infants.* Los Angeles: UCLA Brain information Service.

Anders, T. F., Halpern, L. F., & Hua, J. (1992). Sleeping through the night: A developmental perspective. *Pediatrics, 90,* 554–560.

Anders, T. F., & Keener, M. (1985). Developmental course of nighttime sleep-wake patterns in full-term and premature infants during the first year of life. I. *Sleep, 8,* 173–192.

Anders, T. F., & Sostek, A. M. (1976). The use of time lapse video recording of sleep-wake behavior in human infants. *Psychophysiology, 13,* 155–158.

Bruni, O., Ferini-Strambi, L., Russo, P. M., Antignani, M., Innocenzi, M., Ottaviano, P., et al. (2006). Sleep disturbances and teacher ratings of school achievement and temperament in children. *Sleep Medicine, 7,* 43–48.

Bruni, O., Ottaviano, S., Guidetti, V., Romoli, M., Innocenzi, M., Cortesi, F., et al. (1996). The sleep disturbance scale for children (sdsc). Construction and validation of an instrument to evaluate sleep disturbances in childhood and adolescence. *Journal of Sleep Research, 5,* 251–261.

Burnham, M. M., Goodlin-Jones, B. L., Gaylor, E. E., & Anders, T. F. (2002a). Nighttime sleep-wake patterns and self-soothing from birth to one year of age: A longitudinal intervention study. *Journal of Child Psychology and Psychiatry and Allied Disciplines, 43,* 713–725.

Burnham, M. M., Goodlin-Jones, B. L., Gaylor, E. E., & Anders, T. F. (2002b). Use of sleep aids during the first year of life. *Pediatrics, 109,* 594–601.

Carskadon, M. A., & Dement, W. C. (1982). The multiple sleep latency test: What does it measure? *Sleep, 5 SUPPL 2,* S67–72.

Carskadon, M. A., & Dement, W. C. (1992). Multiple sleep latency tests during the constant routine. *Sleep, 15,* 396–399.

Carskadon, M. A., Dement, W. C., Mitler, M. M., Roth, T., Westbrook, P. R., & Keenan, S. (1986). Guidelines for the multiple sleep latency test (mslt): A standard measure of sleepiness. *Sleep, 9,* 519–524.

Coble, P. A., Kupfer, D. J., Taska, L. S., & Kane, J. (1984). Eeg sleep of normal healthy children. Part i: Findings using standard measurement methods. *Sleep, 7,* 289–303.

Fallone, G., Seifer, R., Acebo, C., & Carskadon, M. A. (2002). How well do school-aged children comply with imposed sleep schedules at home? *Sleep, 25,* 739–745.

Ferreira, V. R., Carvalho, L. B., Ruotolo, F., de Morais, J. F., Prado, L. B., & Prado, G. F. (2009). Sleep disturbance scale for children: Translation, cultural adaptation, and validation. *Sleep Medicine, 10,* 457–463.

Gaina, A., Sekine, M., Chen, X. L., Hamanishi, S., & Kagamimori, S. (2004). Validity of child sleep diary questionnaire among junior high school children. *Journal of Epidemiology, 14,* 1–4.

Goodlin-Jones, B. L., Burnham, M. M., Gaylor, E. E., & Anders, T. F. (2001). Night waking, sleep-wake organization, and self-soothing in the first year of life. *Journal of Developmental and Behavioral Pediatrics, 22,* 226–233.

Goodlin-Jones, B. L., Sitnick, S. L., Tang, K., Liu, J., & Anders, T. F. (2008). The children's sleep habits questionnaire in toddlers and preschool children. *Journal of Developmental and Behavioral Pediatrics, 29,* 82–88.

Iber, S., Ancoli-Israel, S., Chesson, A., & Quan, S. F. (2007). *The aasm manual for the scoring of sleep and associated events: Rules, terminology and technical specifications* Westchester, IL: American Academy of Sleep Medicine.

Kleitman, N., & Engelmann, T. G. (1953). Sleep characteristics of infants. *Journal of Applied Physiology, 6,* 269–282.

Kushida, C. A., Littner, M. R., Morgenthaler, T., Alessi, C. A., Bailey, D., Coleman, J., Jr., et al. (2005). Practice parameters for the indications for polysomnography and related procedures: An update for 2005. *Sleep, 28,* 499–521.

Littner, M., Hirshkowitz, M., Kramer, M., Kapen, S., Anderson, W. M., Bailey, D., et al. (2003a). Practice parameters for using polysomnography to evaluate insomnia: An update. *Sleep, 26,* 754–760.

Littner, M., Kushida, C. A., Anderson, W. M., Bailey, D., Berry, R. B., Davila, D. G., et al. (2003b). Practice parameters for the role of actigraphy in the study of sleep and circadian rhythms: An update for 2002. *Sleep, 26,* 337–341.

Littner, M. R., Kushida, C., Wise, M., Davila, D. G., Morgenthaler, T., Lee-Chiong, T., et al. (2005). Practice parameters for clinical use of the multiple sleep latency test and the maintenance of wakefulness test. *Sleep, 28,* 113–121.

Luginbuehl, M., Bradley-Klug, K. L., Ferron, J., Anderson, W. M., & Benbadis, S. R. (2008). Pediatric sleep disorders: Validation of the Sleep Disorders Inventory for Students. *School Psychology Review, 37,* 409–431.

Mindell, J., Sadeh, A., Kohyama, J., & How, T. W. (in press). Parental behaviors and sleep outcomes in infants and toddlers: A cross-cultural comparison. *Sleep Medicine.*

Mindell, J., Sadeh, A., Wiegand, B., How, T. W., & Goh, D. Y. (in press). Cross-cultural differences in infant, toddler sleep. *Sleep Medicine.*

Mitler, M. M., Doghramji, K., & Shapiro, C. (2000). The maintenance of wakefulness test: Normative data by age. *Journal of Psychosomatic Research, 49,* 363–365.

Mitler, M. M., Gujavarty, K. S., & Browman, C. P. (1982). Maintenance of wakefulness test: A polysomnographic technique for evaluation treatment efficacy in patients with excessive somnolence. *Electroencephalography and Clinical Neurophysiology 53,* 658–661.

Montgomery-Downs, H. E., O'Brien, L. M., Gulliver, T. E., & Gozal, D. (2006). Polysomnographic characteristics in normal preschool and early school-aged children. *Pediatrics, 117,* 741–753.

Morgenthaler, T., Alessi, C., Friedman, L., Owens, J., Kapur, V., Boehlecke, B., et al. (2007). Practice parameters for the use of actigraphy in the assessment of sleep and sleep disorders: An update for 2007. *Sleep, 30,* 519–529.

Moss, D., Urschitz, M. S., von Bodman, A., Eitner, S., Noehren, A., Urschitz-Duprat, P. M., et al. (2005). Reference values for nocturnal home polysomnography in primary schoolchildren. *Pediatric Research, 58,* 958–965.

Owens, J. A., Spirito, A., & McGuinn, M. (2000). The children's sleep habits questionnaire (cshq): Psychometric properties of a survey instrument for school-aged children. *Sleep, 23*, 1043–1051.

Quan, S. F., Goodwin, J. L., Babar, S. I., Kaemingk, K. L., Enright, P. L., Rosen, G. M., et al. (2003). Sleep architecture in normal caucasian and hispanic children aged 6-11 years recorded during unattended home polysomnography: Experience from the tucson children's assessment of sleep apnea study (tucasa). *Sleep Medicine, 4*, 13–19.

Rechtschaffen, A., & Kales, A. (Eds.). (1968). *A manual of standardized terminology: Techniques and scoring system for sleep stages of human subjects.* Los Angeles: University of California at Los Angeles. Brain Information Service/Brain Research Institute.

Richardson, G. S., Carskadon, M. A., Flagg, W., Van den Hoed, J., Dement, W. C., & Mitler, M. M. (1978). Excessive daytime sleepiness in man: Multiple sleep latency measurement in narcoleptic and control subjects. *Electroencephalography and Clinical Neurophysiology 45*, 621–627.

Sadeh, A. (1994). Assessment of intervention for infant night waking: Parental reports and activity-based home monitoring. *Journal of Consulting and Clinical Psychology, 62*, 63–68.

Sadeh, A. (1996). Evaluating night wakings in sleep-disturbed infants: A methodological study of parental reports and actigraphy. *Sleep, 19*, 757–762.

Sadeh, A. (2004). A brief screening questionnaire for infant sleep problems: Validation and findings for an internet sample. *Pediatrics, 113*, E570–E577.

Sadeh, A., & Acebo, C. (2002). The role of actigraphy in sleep medicine. *Sleep Medicine Reviews, 6*, 113–124.

Sadeh, A., Acebo, C., Seifer, R., Aytur, S., & Carskadon, M. A. (1995). Activity-based assessment of sleep-wake patterns during the 1st year of life. *Infant Behavior and Development, 18*, 329–337.

Sadeh, A., Flint-Ofir, E., Tirosh, T., & Tikotzky, L. (2007). Infant sleep and parental sleep-related cognitions. *Journal of Family Psychology, 21*, 74–87.

Sadeh, A., Gruber, R., & Raviv, A. (2003). The effects of sleep restriction and extension on school-age children: What a difference an hour makes. *Child Development, 74*, 444–455.

Sadeh, A., Hauri, P. J., Kripke, D. F., & Lavie, P. (1995). The role of actigraphy in the evaluation of sleep disorders. *Sleep, 18*, 288–302.

Sadeh, A., Lavie, P., Scher, A., Tirosh, E., & Epstein, R. (1991). Actigraphic home-monitoring sleep-disturbed and control infants and young children: A new method for pediatric assessment of sleep-wake patterns. *Pediatrics, 87*, 494–499.

Sadeh, A., Mindell, J. A., Luedtke, K., & Wiegand, B. (2009). Sleep and sleep ecology in the first 3 years: A web-based study. *Journal of Sleep Research, 18*, 60–73.

Sadeh, A., Raviv, A., & Gruber, R. (2000). Sleep patterns and sleep disruptions in school-age children. *Developmental Psychology, 36*, 291–301.

Sadeh, A., Sharkey, K. M., & Carskadon, M. A. (1994). Activity-based sleep-wake identification: An empirical test of methodological issues. *Sleep, 17*, 201–207.

Sivan, Y., Kornecki, A., & Schonfeld, T. (1996). Screening obstructive sleep apnoea syndrome by home videotape recording in children. *European Respiratory Journal, 9*, 2127–2131.

Sostek, A. M., Anders, T. F., & Sostek, A. J. (1976). Diuranal rhythms in 2- and 8-week-old infants: Sleep-waking state organization as a function of age and stress. *Psychosomatic Medicine, 38*, 250–256.

Tapia, I. E., Karamessinis, L., Bandla, P., Huang, J., Kelly, A., Pepe, M., et al. (2008). Polysomnographic values in children undergoing puberty: Pediatric vs. adult respiratory rules in adolescents. *Sleep, 31*, 1737–1744.

The ASDA Task Force. (1992). Eeg arousals: Scoring rules and examples: A preliminary report from the sleep disorders atlas task force of the American sleep disorders association. *Sleep, 15*, 173–184.

The ASDA Task Force. (1993). Recording and scoring leg movements. *Sleep, 16*, 748–759.

Thoman, E. B. (1975). Sleep and wake behaviors in neonates: Consistencies and consequences. *Merrill Palmer Quarterly, 21*, 295–314.

Thoman, E. B. (1990). Sleeping and waking states in infants: A functional perspective. *Neuroscience and Biobehavioral Reviews, 14*, 93–107.

Thoman, E. B., & Acebo, C. (1995). Monitoring of sleep in neonates and young children. In R. Ferber & M. Kryger (Eds.), *Principles and practice of sleep medicine in the child* (pp. 55–68). Philadelphia, PA: W. B. Saunders.

Thoman, E. B., Denenberg, V. H., Sievel, J., Zeidner, L. P., & Becker, P. (1981). State organization in neonates: Developmental inconsistency indicates risk for developmental dysfunction. *Neuropediatrics, 12*, 45–54.

Thorpy, M., Chesson, A., Derderian, S., Kader, G., Potolicchio, S., Rosen, G., et al. (1995). Practice parameters for the use of actigraphy in the clinical assessment of sleep disorders. *Sleep, 18*, 285–287.

Tikotzky, L., & Sadeh, A. (2001). Sleep patterns and sleep disruptions in kindergarten children. *Journal of Clinical Child Psychology, 30*, 579–589.

Tikotzky, L., & Sadeh, A. (2009). Maternal sleep-related cognitions and infant sleep: A longitudinal study from pregnancy through the first year. *Child Development, 80*, 860–874.

Traeger, N., Schultz, B., Pollock, A. N., Mason, T., Marcus, C. L., & Arens, R. (2005). Polysomnographic values in children 2-9 years old: Additional data and review of the literature. *Pediatric Pulmonology, 40*, 22–30.

Uliel, S., Tauman, R., Greenfeld, M., & Sivan, Y. (2004). Normal polysomnographic respiratory values in children and adolescents. *Chest, 125*, 872–878.

Verhulst, S. L., Schrauwen, N., Haentjens, D., Van Gaal, L., De Backer, W. A., & Desager, K. N. (2007). Reference values for sleep-related respiratory variables in asymptomatic European children and adolescents. *Pediatric Pulmonology, 42*, 159–167.

Wolfson, A. R., & Carskadon, M. A. (1998). Sleep schedules and daytime functioning in adolescents. *Child Development, 69*, 875–887.

Wolfson, A. R., Carskadon, M. A., Acebo, C., Seifer, R., Fallone, G., Labyak, S. E., et al. (2003). Evidence for the validity of a sleep habits survey for adolescents. *Sleep, 26*, 213–216.

Part IV

Intervention for Sleep Problems

16

Family-Based Interventions for Sleep Problems of Infants and Children

Courtney Johnson and Jodi A. Mindell

Introduction

Sleep problems are remarkably common in children of all ages, with 20–40% of children affected (Owens, Sheldon, Ferber, & Kryger, 2005). This chapter is dedicated to the presentation of behaviorally based sleep problems in infants, children, and adolescents, as well as their treatment. Behavioral sleep problems include such issues as bedtime resistance, problematic night wakings, nighttime fears, and insufficient sleep (see below for further descriptions and definitions). The chapter is organized by developmental age groups. For each age group discussed, we present normative data on sleep habits, developmental issues, common sleep problems, and age-appropriate treatments, with family considerations discussed.

Overall Considerations

It is first important, however, to understand that behavioral sleep problems often involve predisposing, precipitating, and perpetuating factors (Morin et al. 1999). For example a young child may be predisposed to bedtime resistance and problematic night wakings by a delay or regression in behavioral correlates of neurodevelopmental processes involved in sleep consolidation and sleep regulation. Furthermore, sleep problems must be understood within the context in which they occur, including developmental stage, child and parent characteristics, and family environment. These factors can be thought of as the precipitating and perpetuating factors.

Developmental factors are crucial to the understanding of childhood sleep problems, including physical, cognitive, and emotional development (Mindell & Owens 2009). Child-specific factors include temperament and behavioral style, circadian preference, and chronic and acute health issues, as well as acute and chronic stressors. Parental factors also play a role in the development and maintenance of sleep problems in children and adolescents, as delineated by Sadeh and Anders (1993) in their transactional model of sleep disturbances. For example, parenting style and expectations about sleep influence whether sleep behaviors are perceived as problematic. Education level and knowledge of child development, including what are age-appropriate behaviors, influence sleep and sleep behaviors. Family stress and mental health issues, especially parental depression, have been implicated in the development of sleep problems, as are parents' sleep and fatigue, which can influence parental response to child sleep problems at bedtime and throughout the night (Chang, Pien, Duntley, & Macones 2009). Finally, the family environment is a context that needs to be considered. Family composition, from having extended family all living in one household to a child being a multiple (e.g., twin, triplet), can impact parents' ability to set limits and be involved in the development of healthy sleep habits. Cultural considerations and family values, especially around the issues of cosleeping and limit-setting, are additional considerations (Jenni & O'Connor, 2005).

Research suggests that when left untreated, sleep disturbances in young children persist (Kataria, Swanson, & Trevathan, 1987; Zuckerman, Stevenson, & Bailey, 1987). Poor sleep and/or insufficient sleep have negative consequences for children across all developmental age groups and across multiple domains. Inadequate sleep has been linked to mood and behavior problems, health problems including obesity, substance use, and poor quality of life (Mindell & Owens, 2009). In addition, inadequate sleep can disrupt cognitive functioning, making it difficult for a child to attend and learn. Early identification and treatment of sleep problems is therefore vitally important for all aspects of well-being.

Infants

Normative Sleep Patterns in Early Infancy (0 to 2 Months)

Infancy is a stage of highly variable sleep patterns, occurring within the context of an active period of neurodevelopment. During the first two months of life, infants have no clear circadian pattern, with development of nocturnal and diurnal rhythms occurring by 8 to 12 weeks of age. Sleep may take place at any time and without any clear pattern, which can be difficult on families. Parents often report chronic partial sleep deprivation during this period, with an increased risk for postpartum depression due to sleep loss (D rheim, Bondevik, Eberhard-Gran, & Bjorvatn, 2009). In general, newborns sleep 13 to 14.5 hours per 24 hours; however, there is a wide range of normative sleep duration in this age group with 10 to 18 hours considered normal (Armstrong, Quinn, & Dadds, 1994; Iglowstein, Jenni, Molinari, & Largo 2003; Sadeh, Mindell, Luedtke, & Wiegand, 2009). Sleep-wake patterns are driven primarily by hunger and satiety, rather than circadian rhythms and environmental cues (Burnham, Goodlin-Jones, Gaylor, & Anders, 2002; Anders & Keener, 1985). Early infant sleep episodes typically last between two and five hours in bottle-fed infants and one to three hours in breastfed infants. Sleep episodes are separated by one to two hours awake (Quillin & Glenn, 2004).

Normative Sleep Patterns in Older Infancy (2 to 12 months)

Within the first six months of life, infants usually achieve two important developmental milestones related to sleep, sleep consolidation and sleep regulation. Sleep consolidation is generally defined as an infant's ability to sleep for a continuous period of time, with the majority of sleep occurring at night (Mindell & Owens, 2009). Sleep regulation, on the other hand, involves an infant's ability to control internal states of arousal (e.g., "self-soothe") in order to both fall asleep at bedtime without parental intervention or assistance, and to fall back asleep following normal brief arousals during the night (Mindell & Owens, 2009). Most infants begin to achieve these milestones between two and four months of age

(Sadeh et al., 2009). However, parental behaviors around sleep are key factors affecting these milestones. For example, increased parental involvement around sleep can delay sleep regulation (Sadeh & Anders, 1993). These older infants (2 to 12 months old) sleep approximately 9 to 10 hours during the night and 3 to 4 hours during the day. As they get older, their daytime naps also consolidate from four short naps to two long naps (Weissbluth, 1995).

Developmental Considerations

As previously mentioned, it is important to examine sleep and sleep problems within their developmental context. Sleep is highly sensitive and even small changes in environment or development can have a significant impact. For example, studies have shown that acquisition of gross motor milestones such as rolling-over, crawling, pulling to stand, and walking can temporarily disrupt sleep (Scher & Cohen, 2005). Sleep may also be disrupted with the achievement of cognitive and social-emotional milestones. In the second half of the first year of life, with the development of object permanence, separation anxiety may lead to increased bedtime resistance and night wakings (DeLeon & Karraker, 2007). Attachment may also play an important role in sleep during the first year of life. Insecurely attached infants are known to have more sleep problems than securely attached infants; however, it should not be inferred that sleep problems themselves are an indication of insecure attachment (see Keller, chapter 3 in this volume, for relations between attachment security and sleep in infants and children). In fact, securely attached infants who are more socially engaged with their caregivers may be more reluctant to interrupt social interactions for sleep.

Common Sleep Problems

Some "sleep problems" in infants are related to a mismatch between parental expectations and normal infant sleep (Gaylor, Goodlin-Jones, & Anders, 2001). For example, a mother who is worried about her one-month-old child who only sleeps for an hour to two at a time may have unrealistic expectations for her child's developmental age, as regular and longer sleep periods generally emerge between two and three months of age. Another common parental concern during early infancy is day/night reversal in which infants sleep more during the day than at night. This can be quite common in the first few weeks of life before an infant has developed a natural circadian rhythm. Promoting bright light exposure in the morning and limiting light in the evening may help to alleviate these issues.

Sleep consolidation begins to develop between eight weeks and three months of age. By nine months of age, 50–80% of infants will be sleeping through the night, during most nights (Gaylor, Burnham, Goodlin-Jones, & Anders, 2005). "Self-soothing" (sleep regulation) is a related skill that begins to develop around 12 weeks of life (Burnham et al., 2002), and refers to an infant's ability to independently negotiate the sleep/wake transition, both at sleep onset and during arousals throughout the night. An infant who has not developed the ability to self-soothe will require parental assistance to fall asleep and return to sleep throughout the night. Many times, this problem is exacerbated by parental presence at the time of sleep onset. Most parents do not mind, and may even enjoy rocking, feeding, or otherwise soothing their infant to sleep at bedtime, but do not enjoy having to do this repeatedly throughout the night. This is one of the most common sleep problems during infancy, and is formally referred to as Behavioral Insomnia of Childhood, Sleep Onset Association Type (American Academy of Sleep Medicine, 2005). In order to meet diagnostic criteria for sleep onset association type, a child must have (1) prolonged sleep onset latency, which occurs in the context of special conditions (such as nursing, rocking, parental presence); (2) sleep-onset associations, which are highly problematic or demanding; (3) delayed sleep onset or sleep disruption when sleep associations are not present; and (4) nighttime awakenings, which require caregiver intervention for the child to return to sleep (American Academy of Sleep Medicine, 2005). It is important to note that all infants and children wake periodically throughout the night as they cycle through different phases of sleep (Sadeh, 1994); however, children who have not learned to fall asleep independently will need parental assistance to return to sleep during these normal night wakings.

Infants who are prone to alerting their parents (usually through crying) during normal night wakings are commonly referred to as "signalers." These infants are more likely to require parental intervention to return to sleep than non-signaling infants. Parents also have differences in their natural proclivity to respond to an infant's signals during the night. Some parents avoid responding, at least initially, to an infant's crying, while other parents respond immediately. After responding, parents also differ in how they choose to soothe their infant back to sleep. Infants whose parents respond immediately to crying or signaling and engage in activities that are reinforcing to their infant, may become "trained night criers." The most common example of this phenomenon is night feedings. Most infants do not require night feedings after the sixth month of life. In addition, feeding during the night does not improve the quantity or quality of sleep and may, in fact, disrupt sleep. As discussed above, infants who are put to sleep while feeding (breast-feeding or bottle-feeding) will likely require additional feedings to return to sleep throughout the night. These feedings are not only disruptive to the parent's sleep, but may also result in prolonged night wakings, bladder distention, and discomfort from soaked diapers, and for bottle-fed infants, dental caries and otitis media (Mindell, Meltzer, Carskadon, & Chervin, 2009; Mindell & Owens, 2009).

Prevalence of Sleep Problems

Overall, 25–50% of 6- to 12-month-old infants and 30% of 1-year-old children have problematic night wakings (Burnham et al., 2002; Gaylor et al., 2005; Goodlin-Jones, Burnham, Gaylor, & Anders, 2001; Mindell, Owens, & Carskadon, 1999). Approximately 50% have sleep onset or set-tling difficulties at 12 months of age. The most common sleep disorder in this age group is Behavioral Insomnia of Childhood, Sleep Onset Association Type (American Academy of Sleep Medicine, 2005), which as discussed above involves sleep onset associations, such as feeding or rocking to sleep, that lead to problematic night wakings requiring care-giver intervention to return to sleep.

Treatment of Infant Sleep Problems

In general, the best treatment for behaviorally based sleep problems in this age group is prevention. Studies have shown that early parental education leads to improved infant sleep and decreases the prevalence of sleep problems (Adachi et al., 2009; Kerr, Jowett, & Smith, 1996; Pinilla & Birch 1993; Reid, Walter, & O'Leary, 1999; St.James-Roberts, Sleep, Morris, Owen, & Gillham, 2001; Wolfson, Lacks & Futterman, 1992). In fact, prenatal and postnatal parental education is considered a standard treatment for this age group according to the standards of practice developed by the American Academy of Sleep Medicine (Morgenthaler et al., 2006).

Early parental education is vitally important to the development of healthy sleep habits in infants. Studies have shown that sleep at three months of age predicts future sleep habits (Mindell & Owens, 2009). Infants who fell asleep independently at three months have fewer night wakings at 6 and 12-month follow-ups than infants who fell asleep with their parents present. Therefore, it is important to counsel parents early to begin to put their child to bed drowsy but awake.

As infants are still in the process of developing the physiological (e.g., circadian rhythms) and behavioral (e.g., self-soothing) skills necessary for independent consolidated sleep, most sleep issues are not considered problematic until six months of age or later (Gaylor et al., 2001). However, many parents are concerned about their infants' sleep before six months of age, which may be due to the wide range of normal sleep habits occurring in infants of this age group (Sadeh et al., 2009). Parents naturally make peer-to-peer comparisons, which may be problematic due to individual variations in sleep patterns. In addition, parenting books often provide narrow estimates of "normal" sleep habits, which may cause undue concern for inexperienced or first-time parents. Finally, when infants do not sleep, parents do not sleep. Prolonged sleep deprivation can take a significant toll on new parents and may even perpetuate sleep problems in infants as parents struggle to set limits and remain consistent when "giving in" usually results in more sleep in the short term. Initial studies also indicate that sleep disturbances are related to postpartum depression (D rheim et al., 2009); see Meltzer and Westin, chapter 6 in this volume, for relations between infants' and children's sleep and parents' well-being.

As mentioned, the first year of life is the ideal time for parents to develop healthy sleep habits for their child. One of the easiest and most effective interventions is a bedtime routine. Having a short bedtime routine that occurs in the same way each night has been shown to significantly improve sleep in young children (Mindell, Telofski, Wiegand, & Kurtz, 2009). Bedtime routines should always end with the child being placed in the crib "drowsy but awake." This simple habit allows infants to develop self-soothing skills and avoids problematic sleep associations. Transitional objects such as a pacifier or mother's shirt (knotted up for safety) may help an infant to develop self-soothing skills and feel more secure in the absence of his/her parents (Burnham et al., 2002). In order to maximize sleep at night, parents may want to take advantage of natural circadian cues such as light and dark. Infants should have a consistent sleep schedule with natural light exposure in the morning and dim lighting in the evening.

As discussed above, night feedings are a common sleep-related problem for older infants. Night feedings are usually not necessary for healthy infants six months of age or older; however, night feedings can easily become a learned behavior and often persist long after six months of age. Learned feeding behavior is usually characterized by short night feedings with little intake (e.g. 1–2 ounces or 1–3 minutes of nursing). This behavior can be changed by stopping night feedings all at once, or more gradually by slowly reducing the volume or duration of feeding. Before six months of age (or after if still taking a significant volume) parents may want to institute a dream feed at their (parents) typical bedtime to reduce later night wakings due to hunger. If an infant is particularly fussy or hard to soothe, parents should consider the possibility of an underlying medical condition, such as colic, reflux, or food allergy, and seek appropriate medical attention.

Sleep safety is critically important in infancy in order to reduce the risk of SIDS. Infants should always be placed on their "back to sleep" with their "feet to foot" (of the bed) (Task Force on Sudden Infant Death, 2005). These positional guidelines help to ensure that infants have a safe breathing environment during sleep. Parents should also avoid overheating their infant during sleep. The bedroom should be kept at a comfortable temperature. Finally, infants should only sleep in a crib or other surface that is specifically designed for sleep (see Burnham & Gaylor, chapter 9 in this volume, for sleep environments of children in industrialized societies).

Toddlers (12 Months to 3 Years)

Normative Sleep Patterns

Toddlers typically sleep between 9.5 and 10.5 hours at night and 2–3 hours during the day for a total of 11–13 hours of sleep per 24 hours (Iglowstein et al., 2003). During toddlerhood, naps usually decrease from two naps per day to one around 18 months of age (Mindell, Meltzer, et al., 2009). In fact, studies have shown that 100% of one-year-olds nap, 81% of two-year-olds nap, and just over half of three-year-olds nap (Mindell, Meltzer, et al., 2009).

Developmental Considerations

Toddlerhood is the age of exploration and increased locomotion skills often leading to increased limit testing, especially at bedtime. As toddlers gain increasing language abilities and motoric independence, they often engage in bedtime resistance activities such as "curtain calls" (e.g., "one more hug," "one more potty trip") or climbing out of their crib or bed. These behaviors are not unique to bedtime and can also result in children coming into their parents' room and/or bed in the middle of the night or early in the morning.

Toddlerhood is also a period of rapid cognitive development. Children at this age have a natural drive to learn and explore, which may make settling at bedtime and naptime difficult. In addition, toddlers are beginning to develop an appreciation for cause and effect. This new understanding can have positive or negative consequences for sleep. Understanding cause and effect enables a child to respond quickly to simple behavioral interventions from parents; however, it also enables a child to take advantage of passive parenting or poor limit-setting.

Imagination also begins to develop in toddlerhood and may lead to increased nighttime fears (Gordon, King, Gullone, Muris, & Ollendick, 2007). As language development lags behind cognitive development, toddlers may have difficulty verbalizing their nighttime fears, worries, or frustrations. Nighttime fears often lead to bedtime resistance and/or refusal to sleep independently. Toddlers may respond particularly well to transitional objects such as a blanket or stuffed animal, as they are developing an understanding of the symbolic meaning of objects.

Social and emotional development at this age leads to a natural desire for independence and autonomy, which may also lead to bedtime struggles and resistance. At the same time, separation anxiety common in toddlerhood may lead to difficulty at bedtime, as well as problematic night wakings (Jenni, Fuhrer, Iglowstein, Molinari, & Largo, 2005). Finally, when toddlers are stressed, they often regress behaviorally, which may lead to a desire for co-sleeping.

Common Sleep Problems

Bedtime struggles and resistance are common at this age and are often related to various developmental achievements. With increasing independence, parents often choose to transition their toddler from a crib to a bed. This typically occurs between two and three years of age and is often based on safety concerns such as climbing out of the crib. On the other hand, transitioning to a bed too early can lead to increases in bedtime and nighttime struggles due to a child's newfound freedom. It is, therefore, recommended that parents delay transitioning their toddler into a bed until closer to three years of age. A "crib tent" can be used to prevent a child from climbing or falling out of the crib while helping parents to set limits during an often challenging developmental stage.

Naptime is also often problematic for toddlers. Nap concerns at this age are numerous and include scheduling of naps, as well as number and duration of naps. While it is important for a toddler not to nap too close to his or her bedtime, it is also important not to restrict the length of a child's nap (Mindell, Meltzer, et al., 2009). Sleeping less during daytime naps will not help a child to sleep better at night. At this age, "sleep begets sleep."

Bedtime bottles and night feedings continue to be a problem during toddlerhood. Feeding to sleep may lead to a problematic sleep onset association, which may inhibit the child's ability to self-soothe to sleep. Night feedings are no longer needed nutritionally at this age and are almost always behaviorally based sleep associations, in that children who feed to sleep at bedtime often require feeding to return back to sleep following normal nighttime arousals.

Prevalence of Sleep Problems

Studies indicate that 25–50% of toddlers have sleep problems (Armstrong et al., 1994; Owens et al., 2005), with bedtime resistance and stalling occurring in 25–30% of toddlers. Problematic night wakings are even more common, occurring in up to 50% of toddlers. Nighttime fears and nightmares are also very prevalent in this age group. The most common sleep disorder in this age group is Behavioral Insomnia of Childhood, including Sleep Onset Association, Limit Setting, and Combined Type (Mindell & Owens, 2009; American Academy of Sleep Medicine, 2005). In addition to sleep onset association type discussed above, limit-setting issues often contribute to sleep disturbances in toddlers. In order to meet diagnostic criteria for limit-setting type, a child must: (1) have difficulty initiating or maintaining sleep, (2) stall or refuse to go to bed at an appropriate time or refuse to return to bed following a nighttime awakening, and (3) have insufficient or inappropriate limit setting from the caregiver to establish appropriate sleeping behavior (American Academy of Sleep Medicine, 2005). Combined type refers to children who meet diagnostic criteria for sleep onset association type (defined in the infant section) and limit setting type. In other words, children with combined type have bedtime stalling or refusal, which leads to problematic sleep onset associations (co-sleeping with parents) and night wakings.

Treatment of Toddler Sleep Problems

Parental education continues to be the primary treatment in this age group with a focus on establishing healthy sleep habits. A review by Mindell, Kuhn, Lewin, Meltzer, and Sadeh (2006) showed that parental education was cost effective and efficacious particularly with sleeping through the night. As previously discussed, a short and simple bedtime routine can be a very effective intervention. In fact, bedtime routines have been shown to reduce sleep onset latency and improve nighttime sleep in toddlers (Mindell, Telofski, et al., 2009). Bedtime routines for toddlers should be consistent, in the same order each night, relaxing, and enjoyable. Picture charts may help toddlers to comply with bedtime routines and help to ease bedtime anxieties. Bedtimes, wake times, and nap times should be kept consistent to maximize sleep quantity and quality and to minimize bedtime struggles. Transitional objects may also help to ease toddlers' bedtime fears and increase their ability to be independent during the night. Thumb sucking and pacifier use are commonly employed as transitional objects at this age. These are usually very effective and do not need to be discouraged or discontinued before the age of four.

Behavioral insomnias of childhood including sleep onset association, limit setting, and combined types are very common in toddlers (see previous sections for definitions). These behaviorally based insomnias include bedtime problems and problematic night wakings. Behavior treatments are considered the standard of practice for these sleep problems and produce reliable and durable changes. In fact, a recent review of all behavioral treatment studies showed that 94% of studies indicated that behavioral interventions were efficacious in treating bedtime problems and night wakings and 80% of studies showed durable changes over three to six month follow ups (Mindell et al., 2006).

Most behavioral treatments for bedtime struggles and/or night wakings involve the use of extinction paradigms. In its purist form, extinction (e.g., standard extinction or "cry it out") involves the parent putting the child to bed at a predetermined bedtime and ignoring his/ her behaviors until a set wake time the next morning. During this process, parents are instructed to ignore all "safe" behaviors including tantrums, crying, and calling out. Parents should continue to respond to "unsafe" behaviors such as injury, illness, or any other unsafe conditions. Standard extinction is very effective if followed consistently; however, parental adherence is a substantial issue with this treatment protocol (Mindell et al., 2006). Executing this protocol can be very stressful for parents and it may be difficult for them to do without assistance and support. When executed successfully, behavioral changes are typically seen quite quickly over the first couple of nights. Parents should be warned to anticipate an "extinction burst" (or temporary increase in undesired behaviors) after a week to two weeks of improved sleep. These behaviors will quickly dissipate providing parents continue to follow the extinction protocol.

In order to address concerns about parental adherence to standard extinction protocols, modified treatment protocols have been created.

These modifications are specifically designed to ease parental and child stress throughout the extinction process. Several modifications have now been examined in the literature, primarily graduated extinction (Mindell et al., 2006). In general, these treatments are equally efficacious and durable when compared with standard extinction; however, it generally takes longer to see a full response to treatment. On the other hand, parents tend to be much more accepting of and adherent to modified extinction protocols, making them the treatment of choice for most behavioral sleep specialists.

Extinction with parental presence is a common modification to standard extinction (Hiscock & Wake, 2002; Sadeh, 1994). This is a simple modification, which involves having the parent stay in the child's room (often sleeping on an adjacent bed or mattress) throughout the night, but ignoring the child and their behavior as they would in standard extinction. By staying in the child's room, both parental and child anxiety are decreased while the child learns to self-soothe and sleep more independently.

A second modification is graduated extinction or "sleep training." This term refers to several different modifications to standard extinction, which all have the goal of decreasing parent and child distress and increasing parental compliance and consistency with treatment (Adams & Rickert, 1989; Hiscock & Wake, 2002; Reid et al., 1999; Rickert & Johnson, 1988). Most often, parents are told to ignore their child's behaviors for scheduled periods of time after which, they may briefly (15 seconds to 1 minute) check on their child and comfort him/her with as little interaction as the parents are able to tolerate. The duration or check-in interval is individually tailored to the child and family and can range from seconds to an hour or more. In general, more anxious children and parents, as well as developmentally younger children, will require a shorter check-in interval. After the initial interval is successfully implemented, it may be gradually extended with an ultimate goal of having the child develop self-soothing skills that permit him or her to fall asleep independently. This intervention can be implemented initially at bedtime only. In many cases, once a child learns to fall asleep independently, he or she will naturally begin to return to sleep independently following night wakings (Mindell & Durand, 1993). Focusing on bedtime only in comparison to sleep training at bedtime and throughout the night also allows the parents and child to get more sleep throughout the modified extinction process.

Another variation of graduated extinction that is commonly employed in children with problematic sleep associations (particularly parental presence) is utilizing a more gradual approach. In this modification, parents gradually eliminate one sleep association at a time until the child learns to fall asleep independently. For example, if a child is being bottle fed, while being rocked and held while falling asleep, a parent might first move the bottle to the beginning of the bedtime routine, but continue rocking and holding their child while he or she falls asleep. After a few nights, they can eliminate another association (e.g., rocking), subsequently taking steps until the child is falling asleep in his/her crib. At this point, parents may wish to gradually move themselves out of the room at bedtime. Similar to the check-in procedure, this variation of extinction is often started at bedtime only.

Finally, positive routines with faded bedtimes have also been examined with promising results as possible treatments for behavioral sleep problems in young children (Adams & Rickert, 1989; Ashbaugh & Peck, 1998; Mindell et al., 2006). This treatment involves developing a consistent bedtime routine similar to the bedtime routines discussed above that occurs in the same way each night. In conjunction with the bedtime routine, the child's bedtime is delayed to the time the child naturally falls asleep in order to increase the likelihood of falling asleep quickly. Once the child is able to fall asleep easily at his or her delayed bedtime, bedtime is gradually moved earlier (15–30 minutes every 1–3 nights) until the child is falling asleep at the desired bedtime.

Preschoolers (3 Years to 5 Years)

Normative Sleep Patterns

Preschoolers typically sleep between 9 and 10 hours at night (Iglowstein et al., 2003; Mindel, Meltzer, et al., 2009). As they get older, their daytime naps decrease from one to none with 26% of 4-year-olds napping and just 15% of 5-year-olds. African American children are more likely to continue napping until a later age than Caucasian children, but also sleep less at night than Caucasian children with no net difference in total sleep time (Crosby, LeBourgeois, & Harsh, 2005).

Developmental Considerations

As cognitive and language skills continue to develop, preschool-aged children may engage in more limit-testing behaviors during the day and at night. Conversely, with improving expressive language skills they will be better able to articulate their needs and fears, which may result in decreased frustration and "acting out." Preschoolers have very active imaginations, which make nighttime fears a common sleep problem in this age group (Gordon et al., 2007).

Common Sleep Problems

Co-sleeping or parental presence at the time of sleep onset are both common in preschool-aged children. In fact, nearly 50% of preschoolers have a parent present when they fall asleep at night, which may lead to problems falling and returning to sleep independently (Mindell, Meltzer, et al., 2009).

As previously discussed, nighttime fears are normal in this age group as children develop the cognitive skills to understand that they can be hurt or harmed (Gordon et al., 2007). Fears at this age often involve imaginary creatures such as monsters. They are typically benign, but can become persistent and intense in certain children resulting in consequences for daytime functioning. Nighttime fears can also lead to fears of going to sleep or of the dark and often result in co-sleeping.

As preschool children start school, they may require significant changes in their sleep/wake schedule. These changes often result in temporary disruptions in sleep, but can become persistent and problematic if appropriate modifications are not made. For example, all children experience a normal surge of alertness in the evening (e.g., second wind or "forbidden zone"), but some preschool children may have a more exaggerated surge, which can lead to increased bedtime resistance. Modifications should be made to adjust the child's sleep schedule so that he/she is put to bed before hitting the "forbidden zone."

Prevalence of Sleep Problems

Overall, 15–30% of preschoolers have difficulties falling asleep and/or problematic night wakings (Armstrong et al., 1994; Owens et al., 2005). Studies have shown that if left untreated, sleep problems in this age group can become chronic with 84% of children 15–48 months with sleep problems continuing to have significant sleep disturbances three years later (Kataria et al., 1987; Zuckerman et al., 1987). The most common behavioral sleep disorders in preschoolers are nighttime fears/nightmares, behavioral insomnia of childhood sleep onset association, limit setting, and combined types.

Treatment of Preschool Sleep Problems

A consistent day and nighttime schedule is very important for children in this age group and will help to reduce bedtime struggles. In addition, bedtime routines continue to be beneficial for preschoolers. Behavioral treatments for bedtime problems and night wakings, including behavioral insomnias of childhood, are the same for toddlers and preschoolers. The addition of short-term rewards such as stickers or hand stamps can help preschool children engage in positive nighttime behaviors. Children at this age are developing the capacity to delay gratification, which makes short-term rewards very effective for preschoolers. Parents should be cautioned not to set the standards for a reward too high or their child may become frustrated and disengage with the reward system. In general, rewards should be achievable and provided within a developmentally appropriate period of time.

Nighttime fears are characteristic of this age group (Gordon et al., 2007), and they are typically quite normal and parental reassurance is often sufficient to ease or eliminate nighttime fears (McMenamy & Katz, 1989). When reassuring their child, parents should communicate messages about safety and help their child to develop age-appropriate coping statements such as "mommy and daddy will keep me safe." Security objects such as blankets, stuffed animals, and nightlights may also help to alleviate fears. Parents should also be encouraged to take advantage of their preschooler's active imagination when developing treatments. "Monster spray" or for parents a spray bottle of water is often sufficient to alleviate a preschooler's fear of monsters at bed. Finally it is important for parents to avoid reinforcing "being scared." To do this, parents should set clear limits. For example, a parent may choose to check on their child regularly regardless of the child's behavior so that the child will not feel that he/she only gets attention when scared. Reward systems such as sticker charts can also be used to help children remain in their room throughout the night.

Children who have frequent or problematic nightmares should also receive parental reassurance and communications of safety. It is often most helpful for parents to reassure their child during the night and then help them process (i.e., talk through) it during the daytime if necessary. Children who are prone to nightmares should avoid exposure to frightening or over-stimulating images and reduce exposure to stressors. Security objects and nightlights may be helpful in reducing a child's anxiety following a nightmare. Finally, it is important to ensure that the child is getting adequate sleep, as nightmares are more likely to occur with inadequate sleep.

School-aged Children (6 Years to 12 Years)

Normative Sleep Patterns

School-aged children typically sleep for 9–10 hours per night (Iglowstein et al., 2003; Mindell, Meltzer, et al., 2009). Children in this age group tend to be highly energetic so signs of excessive daytime sleepiness, including frequent napping, should be a red flag and warrant further evaluation.

Developmental Considerations

Increasing cognitive development in school-aged children leads to an understanding of the existence of real dangers (burglars, fires, etc), which may increase nighttime fears. Children at this age can also experience anxieties over social, academic, or other situations leading to nighttime worrying.

As school-aged children become increasingly independent, their parents may have less involvement and knowledge of their child's sleep behaviors (Owens, Spirito, McGuinn, & Nobile, 2000), which may lead to less reinforcement of healthy sleep habits. In addition, school-aged children are often involved in academic and extracurricular activities, which may conflict with healthy sleep schedules. At the same time, increased engagement with peers and use of electronics can interfere with sleep (Owens et al., 1999).

Common Sleep Problems

Insufficient sleep is a common problem for school-aged children resulting in daytime sleepiness and difficulties with attention and learning. There are many reasons why school-aged children do not receive sufficient amounts of sleep. As they get older, children naturally desire a later bedtime, especially on weekends. Unfortunately school-day wake times remain constant or become earlier resulting in less total sleep time and resulting in insufficient sleep. School-aged children often use electronics in bed after their bedtime, often unbeknownst to their parents, which delays bedtime and leads to insufficient sleep. If a child is not getting sufficient sleep, moving their bedtime 30 to 60 minutes earlier on a nightly basis can make a significant difference in their daytime functioning (Fallone, Acebo, Seifer, & Carskadon, 2005; Sadeh, Gruber, & Raviv, 2003). Finally, parental presence at bedtime continues to be quite common in school-aged children with about 30% still requiring a parent to fall asleep (Mindell, Meltzer, et al., 2009).

Prevalence of Sleep Problems

Overall, 37% of school-aged children have a parent-reported sleep problem (Owens et al., 2005), with 15–25% having bedtime resistance, 10% experiencing sleep onset delay and/or anxiety at bedtime, and 10% experiencing daytime sleepiness. Insufficient sleep and inadequate sleep hygiene (practices necessary to have normal, quality nighttime sleep and full daytime alertness) are the most common behavioral sleep disorders in school-aged children.

Treatment of School-aged Sleep Problems

Education about healthy sleep habits is important in this age group. Children especially at the older end of school-age (i.e., 10–12 years of age) may benefit from psychoeducation about the importance and benefits of healthy sleep habits. In particular, parents and children should be educated about the importance of getting enough sleep and encouraged to keep consistent sleep schedules on weekdays and weekends.

Treatments for bedtime problems and night wakings including behavioral insomnias of childhood are the same as those discussed above for younger children. These treatments can be made more developmentally appropriate by building in delayed gratification such as token systems or behavioral charts that lead to a larger end reward. In addition, a "bedtime pass" may be very useful in early school-age children to limit bedtime resistance and shorten sleep onset latency (Freeman, 2006; Moore, Friman, Fruzzetti, & MacAleese, 2007). A "bedtime pass" is a piece of paper such as an index card that may be traded in for one request (another hug, glass of water, etc). If the child does not use their pass, they may trade it in the next morning for a small reward.

Treatments for nighttime fears and/or nightmares for school-age children are very similar to those described for preschoolers. Parents may also want to teach their school-aged child relaxation techniques such as deep breathing or guided imagery. For older school-age children, cognitive restructuring of problematic thoughts may be helpful. This is typically done by examining the reality of a child's fear, for example, a child who is afraid of a burglar may benefit from knowing that there have not been any break-ins in his particular neighborhood in a long time.

Adolescence (13 Years to 18 Years)

Normative Sleep Patterns

Unfortunately, on average, adolescents do not get enough sleep. Most adolescents get between 7 and 7.5 hours of sleep per night, which is far short of the recommended 9 to 9.25 (Wolfson & Carskadon, 1998). In fact, only 20% of adolescents get the recommended amount of sleep. As adolescents get older, their bedtimes get later and their total sleep time decreases, leading to an average two-hour sleep debt per night.

Developmental Considerations

Around the time of puberty onset, adolescents develop a two-hour physiologically based phase delay compared with middle childhood. This shift is thought to be the result of pubertal and hormonal influences on circadian sleep-wake cycles as well as melatonin secretion and its link to Tanner stages rather than chronological age. In addition to physiological drives, delayed sleep may also be related to increasing discrepancies between weekday and weekend sleep and wake times, which are characteristic of adolescence. High school start times only compound the problem, as they tend to be earlier than middle school, reducing sleep opportunity for an already phase-shifted age group (Knutson & Lauderdale, 2009). Adolescents are also highly involved in academic, extracurricular, and social activities in addition to increased electronic use, all of which may interfere with sleep. Furthermore, many adolescents have after-school jobs.

Common Sleep Problems

Insufficient sleep and related daytime sleepiness are the leading sleep problems in this age group (Moore & Meltzer, 2008). Overall, 56% of adolescents report that they get less sleep than they need to feel their best, 51% report they feel too tired or sleepy during the day, 25% report falling asleep at least once a week in school, and 20% report falling asleep while doing homework (Carskadon, Acebo, & Jenni, 2004; Carskadon, Wolfson, Acebo, Tzischinsky, & Seifer, 1998; Laberge et al., 2001). In addition to causing problems with attention and learning, inadequate sleep is associated with increased risk taking behaviors in adolescents (O'Brien & Mindell, 2005).

Caffeine use is common in adolescents with approximately 40% having a daily caffeinated beverage (Pollak & Bright, 2003; Roehrs & Roth, 2008). Daily caffeine use has been associated with less total sleep time (Calamaro, Mason, & Ratcliffe, 2009), as well as daytime sleepiness (Roehrs & Roth, 2008).

Prevalence of Sleep Problems

At least 20% of adolescents have a significant sleep problem (Carskadon et al., 1998; Wolfson & Carskadon, 1998). Adolescents with mood disorders or chronic medical problems may be at increased risk for sleep problems. The most common behavioral sleep disorders in adolescents are insufficient sleep, inadequate sleep hygiene, insomnia, and delayed sleep phase disorder. Studies indicate that 7 to 16% of adolescents have a delayed sleep phase disorder (Crowley, Acebo, & Carskadon, 2007).

Treatment of Adolescent Sleep Problems

Adolescents should be counseled about the importance of sleep and the average sleep needs for children their age. The importance of maintaining a consistent weekday and weekend sleep schedule should be emphasized in addition to the negative impact of caffeine, nicotine, and alcohol use on sleep. Adolescents may also benefit from a discussion and understanding of how pubertal changes impact sleep. It is especially important to discuss the dangers of drowsy driving in this very high-risk group.

More specifically, 9 to 13% of adolescents experience chronic insomnia and 35% experience insomnia several times a month (Crowley et al., 2007; Johnson, Roth, Schultz, & Breslau, 2006; Wolfson et al., 2003). Before a treatment plan can be developed, a comprehensive evaluation of the contributing factors and possible causes of the insomnia must be conducted. Healthy sleep hygiene practices (discussed earlier) including appropriate and consistent sleep/wake times, no napping, avoidance of caffeine, a sleep-conducive environment, electronic avoidance at bedtime, and a relaxing bedtime routine should be evaluated and discussed. Sleep hygiene while helpful is typically not sufficient in the treatment of insomnia. Comprehensive treatment for insomnia involves three main components: stimulus control, sleep restriction, and cognitive restructuring in addition to healthy sleep hygiene practices. Stimulus control, or eliminating activities that are not conducive to sleep (TV, computer, worrying) is often helpful in reducing sleep onset latency in adolescents with insomnia. The basic philosophy is that "the bed is for sleep and sleep is for the bed." Another important aspect of stimulus control is that adolescents should be counseled to only go to bed when they feel sleepy and get out of bed when they are not sleeping.

Sleep restriction is another important aspect of insomnia treatment. For this aspect of treatment, the time in bed should be restricted to a minimum of hours with the ultimate goal of increasing sleep efficiency, consolidating sleep, and helping to disrupt the association of not sleeping in bed. Initially, the time in bed should be set at the estimated total sleep time and gradually increased as sleep efficiency improves.

Cognitive restructuring is particularly helpful for adolescents with insomnia who are prone to worrying (Reid, Huntley, & Lewin, 2009). Basic Cognitive Behavioral Therapy (CBT) approaches are used to identify problematic sleep cognitions. Once identified, cognitions are challenged for validity and replaced with a more appropriate and less anxiety producing thought. In addition to cognitive restructuring, relaxation training may be useful in reducing anxieties and frustrations that are commonly comorbid with insomnia.

Treatment of delayed sleep phase syndrome has two primary goals: shift the sleep/wake schedule earlier and maintain the new schedule (Wyatt, 2004; Campbell, Murphy, van den Heuvel, Roberts, & Stauble, 1999). These goals are achieved through phase advancement or phase delay depending on the severity of the delay. Phase advancement should be used when the difference between the current later sleep onset time and the target sleep onset time is less than three hours. In phase advancement, bedtimes and wake times are shifted earlier by 15 to 30 minutes per day starting at the current sleep onset time. The pace and increment of the advancement should be based on the individual and the chronicity of the problem. While bedtimes are gradually advanced, wake times should be moved to the target wake time immediately, to help build sleep pressure at night.

For adolescents with a three-hour or greater sleep phase delay, a phase delay treatment should be used. In a phase delay treatment, sleep onset time is delayed by two to three hours per night until the desired sleep onset time is achieved. Adolescents often prefer this treatment initially as they are "allowed to stay up later," but treatment becomes increasingly difficult over time. Ideally, this treatment should be scheduled to coincide with a school vacation to avoid missing school.

For both phase advancement and phase delayed treatments, basic sleep hygiene practices should be reviewed. Napping must also be avoided in order to consolidate sleep. Adolescents should be warned of daytime sleepiness during treatment and problem solving techniques should be used to avoid poor adherence.

Phototherapy, or bright light exposure, is another common component of delayed sleep, which may help to shift and maintain sleep/wake schedules (Wyatt, 2004). During phase shifting, it is recommended that adolescents get 60+ minutes of bright light (2,000–10,000 lux) at their scheduled wake time and dim light in the evening. Following treatment, a 30-minute maintenance dose of light at the scheduled wake time is recommended. Melatonin has also been found to be an effective addition to treatment for delayed sleep phase (Lockley, 2005; Mundey, Benloucif, Harsanyi, Dubocovich, & Zee, 2005).

Treatment for delayed sleep phase is complex and involves many components. A printed schedule that includes scheduled sleep, wake, and phototherapy times for each day can help increase patient compliance with the treatment protocol. Following treatment, it is critically important for adolescents to maintain a consistent sleep schedule to avoid "slipping" back.

Family Involvement in Sleep-Related Interventions

Family participation and education is crucial to any successful behavioral sleep intervention. At all ages and developmental stages, it is necessary for parents (and children when appropriate) to come to a consensus on how to handle sleep issues. As with other behaviorally based problems, consistency is key. It is often helpful to engage families in a conversation about how they plan to address problems when they inevitably arise. In addition, it is important to involve children in a developmentally appropriate way in treatment planning. Families may require assistance in allowing an older child to be more independent in their sleep behaviors as they mature, while other families may need encouragement to re-engage in their younger child's routine.

Furthermore, practitioners need to consider the extensive array of family and parent issues that could impact treatment, such as parental depression, marital strife, overall parental competence, and family support. The perfect intervention is one that allows a family to take an achievable step forward toward their ultimate goal within the context of their family, environment, and culture.

Conclusions

Behavioral sleep problems are common in children of all ages and range from developmentally normative nighttime fears to insomnias and chronic sleep deprivation. While these problems are common, they are not benign and if left untreated can persist and have negative consequences for behavior, cognitive functioning, health, and quality of life. Fortunately, effective and durable treatments for behavioral sleep problems of childhood exist. Based primarily in behavioral theory, these treatments are individually tailored and seek to address the child's sleep problem in the context of the child's developmental stage, the family, their environment, and culture. Thoughtful, family-based behavioral treatments can effectively treat most sleep problems of childhood and have positive consequences for the child and family across multiple domains.

REFERENCES

Adachi, Y., Sato, C., Nishino, N., Ohryoji, F., Hayama, J., & Yamagami, T. (2009). A brief parental education for shaping sleep habits in 4-month-old infants. *Clinical Medicine & Research, 7*, 85–92.

Adams, L. A., & Rickert, V. I. (1989). Reducing bedtime tantrums: Comparison between positive routines and graduated extinction. *Pediatrics, 84,* 756–761.

American Academy of Sleep Medicine (2005). *International classification of sleep disorders: Diagnostic and coding manual* (2nd ed.). Westchester, IL: American Academy of Sleep Medicine.

Anders, T. F., & Keener, M. A. (1985). Developmental course of nighttime sleep-wake patterns in full-term and premature infants during the first year of life: I. *Sleep, 8,* 173–192.

Armstrong, K. L., Quinn, R. A., & Dadds, M. R. (1994). The sleep patterns of normal children. *Medical Journal of Australia, 161,* 202–206.

Ashbaugh, R., & Peck, S. M. (1998). Treatment of sleep problems in a toddler: A replication of the faded bedtime with response cost protocol. *Journal of Applied Behavior Analysis, 31,* 127–129.

Burnham, M. M., Goodlin-Jones, B. L., Gaylor, E. E., & Anders, T. F. (2002). Nighttime sleep-wake patterns and self-soothing from birth to one year of age: A longitudinal intervention study. *Journal of Child Psychology and Psychiatry, 43,* 713–725.

Calamaro, C. J., Mason, T. B., & Ratcliffe, S. J. (2009). Adolescents living the 24/7 lifestyle: Effects of caffeine and technology on sleep duration and daytime functioning. *Pediatrics, 123,* e1005–1010.

Campbell, S. S., Murphy, P. J., van den Heuvel, C. J., Roberts, M. L., & Stauble, T. N. (1999). Etiology and treatment of intrinsic circadian rhythm sleep disorders. *Sleep Medicine Reviews, 3,* 179–200.

Carskadon, M. A., Acebo, C., & Jenni, O. G. (2004). Regulation of adolescent sleep: Implications for behavior. *Annals of the New York Academy of Sciences, 1021,* 276–291.

Carskadon, M. A., Wolfson, A. R., Acebo, C., Tzischinsky, O., & Seifer, R. (1998). Adolescent sleep patterns, circadian timing, and sleepiness at a transition to early school days. *Sleep, 21,* 871–881.

Chang, J. J., Pien, G. W., Duntley, S. P., & Macones, G. A. (2009). Sleep deprivation during pregnancy and maternal and fetal outcomes: Is there a relationship? *Sleep Medicine Reviews.* Advance online publication. doi: 10.1016/j.smrv.2009.05.001.

Crosby, B., LeBourgeois, M. K., & Harsh, J. (2005). Racial differences in reported napping and nocturnal sleep in 2- to 8-year-old children. *Pediatrics, 115,* 225–232.

Crowley, S. J., Acebo, C., & Carskadon, M. A. (2007). Sleep, circadian rhythms, and delayed phase in adolescence. *Sleep Medicine, 8,* 602–612.

DeLeon, C. W., & Karraker, K. H. (2007). Intrinsic and extrinsic factors associated with night waking in 9-month-old infants. *Infant Behavior and Development, 30,* 596–605.

Dørheim, S. K., Bondevik, G. T., Eberhard-Gran, M., & Bjorvatn, B. (2009). Sleep and depression in postpartum women: A population-based study. *Sleep, 32,* 847–855.

Fallone, G., Acebo, C., Seifer, R., & Carskadon, M. A. (2005). Experimental restriction of sleep opportunity in children: Effects on teacher ratings. *Sleep, 28,* 1279–1285.

Freeman, K. A. (2006). Treating bedtime resistance with the bedtime pass: A systematic replication and component analysis with 3-year-olds. *Journal of Applied Behavior Analysis, 39,* 423–428.

Gaylor, E. E., Burnham, M. M., Goodlin-Jones, B. L., & Anders, T. F. (2005). A longitudinal follow-up study of young children's sleep patterns using a developmental classification system. *Behavioral Sleep Medicine, 3,* 44–61.

Gaylor, E. E., Goodlin-Jones, B. L., & Anders, T. F. (2001). Classification of young children's sleep problems: A pilot study. *Journal of the American Academy of Child and Adolescent Psychiatry, 40,* 61–67.

Goodlin-Jones, B. L., Burnham, M. M., Gaylor, E. E., & Anders, T. F. (2001). Night waking, sleep-wake organization, and self-soothing in the first year of life. *Journal of Developmental and Behavioral Pediatrics, 22,* 226–233.

Gordon, J., King, N., Gullone, E., Muris, P., & Ollendick, T. H. (2007). Nighttime fears of children and adolescents: Frequency, content, severity, harm expectations, disclosure, and coping behaviours. *Behaviour Research and Therapy, 45,* 2464–2472.

Hiscock, H., & Wake, M. (2002). Randomised controlled trial of behavioural infant sleep intervention to improve infant sleep and maternal mood. *British Medical Journal, 324,* 1062–1065.

Iglowstein, I., Jenni, O. G., Molinari, L., & Largo, R. H. (2003). Sleep duration from infancy to adolescence: Reference values and generational trends. *Pediatrics, 111,* 302–307.

Jenni, O. G., Fuhrer, H. Z., Iglowstein, I., Molinari, L., & Largo, R. H. (2005). A longitudinal study of bed sharing and sleep problems among Swiss children in the first 10 years of life. *Pediatrics, 115,* 233–240.

Jenni, O. G., & O'Connor, B. B. (2005). Children's sleep: An interplay between culture and biology. *Pediatrics, 115,* 204–216.

Johnson, E. O., Roth, T., Schultz, L., & Breslau, N. (2006). Epidemiology of DSM-IV insomnia in adolescence: Lifetime prevalence, chronicity, and an emergent gender difference. *Pediatrics, 117,* e247–e256.

Kataria, S., Swanson, M. S., & Trevathan, G. E. (1987). Persistence of sleep disturbances in preschool children. *Journal of Pediatrics, 110,* 642–646.

Kerr, S., Jowett, S. A., & Smith, L. N. (1996). Preventing sleep problems in infants: A randomized controlled trial. *Journal of Advanced Nursing, 24,* 938–942.

Knutson, K. L., & Lauderdale, D. S. (2009). Sociodemographic and behavioral predictors of bed time and wake time among US adolescents aged 15 to 17 years. *Journal Pediatrics, 154,* 426–430.

Laberge, L., Petit, D., Simard, C., Vitaro, F., Tremblay, R. E., & Montplaisir, J. (2001). Development of sleep patterns in early adolescence. *Journal of Sleep Research, 10,* 59–67.

Lockley, S. W. (2005). Timed melatonin treatment for delayed sleep phase syndrome: The importance of knowing circadian phase. *Sleep, 28,* 1214–1216.

McMenamy, C., & Katz, R. C. (1989). Brief parent-assisted treatment for children's nighttime fears. *Journal of Developmental and Behavioral Pediatrics, 10,* 145–148.

Mindell, J. A., & Durand, V. M. (1993). Treatment of childhood sleep disorders: Generalization across disorders and effects on family members. *Journal of Pediatric Psychology, 18,* 731–750.

Mindell, J. A., Kuhn, B. R., Lewin, D. S., Meltzer, L. J., & Sadeh, A. (2006). Behavioral treatment of bedtime problems and night wakings in infants and young children. *Sleep, 29,* 1263–1276.

Mindell, J. A., Meltzer, L. J., Carskadon, M. A., & Chervin, R. D. (2009). Developmental aspects of sleep hygiene: Findings from the 2004 National Sleep Foundation Sleep in America Poll. *Sleep Medicine, 10,* 771–779.

Mindell, J. A., & Owens, J. A. (2009). *A clinical guide to pediatric sleep: Diagnosis and management of sleep problems* (2nd ed.). Philadelphia: Lippincott Williams & Wilkins.

Mindell, J. A., Owens, J. A., & Carskadon, M. A. (1999). Developmental features of sleep. *Child and Adolescent Psychiatric Clinics of North America, 8*, 695–725.

Mindell, J. A., Telofski, L. S., Wiegand, B., & Kurtz, E. S. (2009). A nightly bedtime routine: Impact on sleep in young children and maternal mood. *Sleep, 32,* 599–606.

Moore, B. A., Friman, P. C., Fruzzetti, A. E., & MacAleese, K. (2007). Brief report: Evaluating the Bedtime Pass Program for child resistance to bedtime—a randomized, controlled trial. *Journal Pediatric Psychology, 32*, 283–287.

Moore, M., & Meltzer, L. J. (2008). The sleepy adolescent: Causes and consequences of sleepiness in teens. *Paediatric Respiratory Reviews, 9*, 114–121.

Morin, C. M., Hauri, P. J., Espie, C. A., Spielman, A. J., Buysse, D. J., & Bootzin, R. R. (1999). Nonpharmacologic treatment of chronic insomnia. An American Academy of Sleep Medicine review. *Sleep, 22*, 1134–1156.

Morgenthaler, T. I., Owens, J., Alessi, C., Boehlecke, B., Brown, T. M., Coleman, J., Jr., . . . Swick, T. J. (2006). Practice parameters for behavioral treatment of bedtime problems and night wakings in infants and young children. *Sleep, 29*, 1277–1281.

Mundey, K., Benloucif, S., Harsanyi, K., Dubocovich, M. L., & Zee, P. C. (2005). Phase-dependent treatment of delayed sleep phase syndrome with melatonin. *Sleep, 28*, 1271–1278.

O'Brien, E. M., & Mindell, J. A. (2005). Sleep and risk-taking behavior in adolescents. *Behavioral Sleep Medicine, 3*, 113–133.

Owens, J., Maxim, R., McGuinn, M., Nobile, C., Msall, M., & Alario, A. (1999). Television-viewing habits and sleep disturbance in school children. *Pediatrics, 104*, e27.

Owens, J. A., Sheldon, S. H., Ferber, R., & Kryger, M. H. (2005). Epidemiology of sleep disorders during childhood. In S. H. Sheldon, R. Ferber, & M. H. Kryger (Eds.), *Principles and practices of pediatric sleep medicine* (pp. 27–33). Philadelphia, PA: Elsevier Saunders.

Owens, J. A., Spirito, A., McGuinn, M., & Nobile, C. (2000). Sleep habits and sleep disturbance in elementary school-aged children. *Journal of Developmental and Behavioral Pediatrics, 21*, 27–34.

Pinilla, T., & Birch, L. L. (1993). Help me make it through the night: Behavioral entrainment of breast-fed infants' sleep patterns. *Pediatrics, 91*, 436–444.

Pollak, C. P., & Bright, D. (2003). Caffeine consumption and weekly sleep patterns in US seventh-, eighth-, and ninth-graders. *Pediatrics, 111*, 42–46.

Quillin, S. I., & Glenn, L. L. (2004). Interaction between feeding method and co-sleeping on maternal-newborn sleep. *Journal of Obstetric, Gynecologic, & Neonatal Nursing, 33*, 580–588.

Reid, G. J., Huntley, E. D., & Lewin, D. S. (2009). Insomnias of childhood and adolescence. *Child and Adolescent Psychiatric Clinics of North America, 18,* 979–1000.

Reid, M. J., Walter, A. L., & O'Leary, S. G. (1999). Treatment of young children's bedtime refusal and nighttime wakings: A comparison of "standard" and graduated ignoring procedures. *Journal of Abnormal Child Psychology, 27,* 5–16.

Rickert, V. I., & Johnson, C. M. (1988). Reducing nocturnal awakening and crying episodes in infants and young children: A comparison between scheduled awakenings and systematic ignoring. *Pediatrics, 81,* 203–212.

Roehrs, T., & Roth, T. (2008). Caffeine: Sleep and daytime sleepiness. *Sleep Medicine Review, 12,* 153–162.

Sadeh, A. (1994). Assessment of intervention for infant night waking: Parental reports and activity-based home monitoring. *Journal of Consulting and Clinical Psychology, 62,* 63–68.

Sadeh, A., & Anders, T. (1993). Infant sleep problems: Origins, assessment, interventions. *Infant Mental Health Journal, 14,* 17–34.

Sadeh, A., Gruber, R., & Raviv, A. (2003). The effects of sleep restriction and extension on school-age children: What a difference an hour makes. *Child Development, 74,* 444–455.

Sadeh, A., Mindell, J. A., Luedtke, K., & Wiegand, B. (2009). Sleep and sleep ecology in the first 3 years: A web-based study. *Journal of Sleep Research, 18,* 60–73.

Scher, A., & Cohen, D. (2005). Locomotion and nightwaking. *Child Care Health and Development, 31,* 685–691.

St. James-Roberts, I., Sleep, J., Morris, S., Owen, C., & Gillham, P. (2001). Use of a behavioural programme in the first 3 months to prevent infant crying and sleeping problems. *Journal of Paediatrics and Child Health, 37,* 289–297.

Task Force on Sudden Infant Death Syndrome. (2005). The changing concept of sudden infant death syndrome: Diagnostic coding shifts, controversies regarding the sleeping environment, and new variables to consider in reducing risk. *Pediatrics, 116,* 1245–1255.

Weissbluth, M. (1995). Naps in children: 6 months–7 years. *Sleep, 18,* 82–87.

Wolfson, A. R., & Carskadon, M. A. (1998). Sleep schedules and daytime functioning in adolescents. *Child Development, 69,* 875–887.

Wolfson, A. R., Carskadon, M. A., Acebo, C., Seifer, R., Fallone, G., Labyak, S. E., Martin, J. L. (2003). Evidence for the validity of a sleep habits survey for adolescents. *Sleep, 26,* 213–216.

Wolfson, A., Lacks, P., & Futterman, A. (1992). Effects of parent training on infant sleeping patterns, parents' stress, and perceived parental competence. *Journal of Consulting and Clinical Psychology, 60,* 41–48.

Wyatt, J. K. (2004). Delayed sleep phase syndrome: Pathophysiology and treatment options. *Sleep, 27,* 1195–1203.

Zuckerman, B., Stevenson, J., & Bailey, V. (1987). Sleep problems in early childhood: Continuities, predictive factors, and behavioral correlates. *Pediatrics, 80,* 664–671.

Index